Henri Ternaux-Compans, Francisco López de Gómara

The Pleasant Historie of the Conquest of the West India

now called New Spaine. atchieued by the most woorthie prince Hernando Cortes

Henri Ternaux-Compans, Francisco López de Gómara

The Pleasant Historie of the Conquest of the West India
now called New Spaine. atchieued by the most woorthie prince Hernando Cortes

ISBN/EAN: 9783337247119

Printed in Europe, USA, Canada, Australia, Japan

Cover: Foto ©ninafisch / pixelio.de

More available books at **www.hansebooks.com**

THE
Pleasant Historie of
the Conquest of the
West India, now called
new *Spaine*.

Atchieued by the most woorthie Prince
Hernando Cortes, Marques of the Valley of
Huaxacac, most delectable to reade.

Translated out of the Spanish tongue, by
T. N. *Anno.* 1578.

LONDON
Printed by Thómas Creede.
1596.

To the right Honourable
Sir Francis Walsingham Knight, principall
Secretary to the Queenes most excellent Maiestie, and one of her highnesse most Honourable priuie Counsell.

Hilest I abode (right Honorable) in the Isle of Palma, in affaires of merchandize for the worshipfull *Thomas Lock* deceased, and his cõ-pany, time then permitted me, to haue conference with auncient gentlemen which had serued in the Conquest of the Weast India, now called new Spaine, vnder the princely Captaine *Hernando Cortes*. By whom as present witnesses at many of the actes herein contained, I was credible infor-med, that this delectable and worthie Historie is a most true and iust report of matter past in effect: wherfore I did the more willingly turne ouer and peruse the same, which is a Mirrour and an excel-lent president, for all such as shall take in hand to gouerne new Discoueries: for here they shall be-hold, how Glory, Renowne, and perfit Felicitie, is

a 2   not

The Epistle.

not gotten but with great paines, trauaile, peril and daunger of life: heere shall they see the wisdome, curtesie, valour and pollicie of worthie Captaines, yea and the faithfull hearts which they ought to beare vnto their Princes seruice: heere also is described, how to vse and correct the stubborn and mutinous persons, and in what order to exalt the good, stout, and vertuous Souldiours, and chiefly how eto preserue and keepe that beautifull Dame *Ladie Victorie*, when she is obtained. And where it was supposed, that the golden mettall had his beginning and place in the East and West *India*, neare vnto the hote Zoan, (as most learned writers held opinion) it is nowe approoued by the venterous trauellour and worthie Captaine *Martin Frobisher*, Esquier, yea and also through the great paines, procurement, and first intention of the worshipfull *Michael Locke* Merchant, that the same golden mettall dooth also lie incorporate in the bowels of the Northwest parties, enuironed with admirable Towers, pillars and pinacles, of rockes, stone, and Ise, possessed of a people both straunge, and rare in shape, attire and liuing, yea such a Countrey and people, as al *Europe* had forsaken and made no account of, except our most gracious Queene and her subiects, whom vndoubtedly God hath appointed, not onely to be supreame Princesse ouer them; but also to be a meane that the name of Christ may bee knowne vnto this heathenish and sauage generation.

Not long since (right Honourable) I happened

to

The Epistle.

to trauell from the famous Citie of *Toledo* in *Spaine*, towarde high *Castile*, and by fortune ouertooke an auncient Gentleman, worshipfully accompanied, vnto whom I was so bolde as to approch, beseeching his worship to aduertise me of his iourney: who (after hee had behelde my white head and beard) answered full gently, that his intent was to trauell vnto the king of *Spaines* Court, and welcomed me vnto his companie. In short space that we had iourneied togither, and communed of each other his Countrey, it pleased him to say as followeth : My good friend, if you knewe my sute vnto the Kings maiestie, you would iudge that I were a mad man, and therfore to shorten our way, I will declare my attempted sute vnto you. You shall vnderstand, that I am a Gentleman of three score and ten yeares of age, and sometimes I serued in the ciuill warres of *Pirru*, where I was wounded in diuerse parts of my bodie, and am now therby lame in one of my legges and shoulder. I haue neither wife nor childe, and at this present (God be praysed) I haue in the Contractation house in the Citie of *Siuill*, in golde and plate, the summe of thirtie thousand Duckets : and I haue also in *Pirru* in good landes and possessions, the yearely rent of twelue thousande Duckets, which rentes and readie money is sufficient to mainteine a poore Gentleman. But al this notwithstanding, I do now sue vnto the kings Maiestie, to haue a licence and authoritie to discouer and conquer a certaine part of *India*, which adioyneth with *Brazile*, and is part

The Epistle.

of the Empire of *Peru*, I pray you nowe declare what you think of my sute. By my troth sir (quoth I) I trust your worship will pardon a rash and suddene iudgement, which you now demaund at my hand: yea truly (quoth he) say what you list. Then (quoth I) my opinion is, that you are not well in your wit, for what would you haue? will not reason suffice you? or els would you now in your old daies be an Emperor, considering that your Sepulchre attendeth for you. Now truly I thanke you (quoth he) for of your iudgement are most men: but I say vnto you, considering that all flesh must finish, I seek for no quiet rest in this transitorie life: yea the wise and Christian doctors doe teach and admonish, that euery true Cristian is born, not for his owne priuate wealth and pleasure, but rather to helpe & succor others his poore brethren. Likewise do I consider the great number of gentlemen yonger brethren, and other valiant persons, who through want of liuing, doe fall into many disorders. Wherefore to accomplish my dutie towarde God and my prince, & to relieue such poore Gentlemen, doe I now attempt this iourney, with the aduenture of my bodie & goods, and for that purpose I haue in readines foure tall ships, well furnished in the port of *S. Lucar de Barrameda*, hoping assuredly, that before the life depart out of my bodie, to heare these valiant yong gentlemen (whom now I mean to haue in my company) say, oh happie day, when olde *Zarate* (for so is my name) brought vs from penurie, yea and from a number

of

The Epiftle.

of perils that we were like to fall into. I hope alfo, that the royall eftate of my Prince fhall bee by my paines, and poore feruice enlarged: beleeue you me, this is the onelie fumptuous tumbe that I pretend to build for my poore carkas. But yet I know there are fome, vnto whō I may compare the Bore that lieth wallowing in the Stie, who will not let to fay, what need we anie other world, honour, or kingdoms? let vs be contented with that we haue: who may eafily be aunfwered, Sir glutton, your panch is full, and little care you for the glorie of God, honour of your Prince, neither the need and necefsitie of your poore neighbours. With this conclufion the Gentleman ended his tale, the iudgement whereof, I leaue to noble Gentlemen his peeres to be determined.

And where our Captaine *Hernando Cortes*, of whofe valiant acts this hiftorie treateth, hath deferued immortal fame, euen fo doubtleffe I hope, that within this happie Realme is nowe liuing a Gentleman, whofe zeale of trauell and valiant beginning doth prognofticate great, maruellous, and happie fucceffe: for perfection of honor and profit is not gotten in one day, nor in one or two voyages, as the true hiftories of the Eaft and Weft conquefts by Spaniardes and Portingals doe teftifie. And calling to remembrance the great zeale and good will which your honor hath alwaies extended to good and profitable attempts, and especially in the proceedings of the new difcouerie, your honor hath not only vfed liberality in your aduentures,

The Epistle.

tures, but also taken great paines in Court to aduaunce and further the voiage, a number I say of Gentlemen, Mariners, and other Artificers, shall haue great cause to pray for your honour. And where I for my part haue tasted of your honours goodnes sundrie waies, I am now most humblie to beseech your honor to accept this poore gift, the which I haue trāslated out of the Spanish tongue, not decked with gallant colours, nor yet filed with pleasant phrase of Rhetorike, for these things are not for poore Merchant trauelers, but are reserued to learned Writers: yet I trust the Author will pardon me, because I haue gone as neare the sense of this historie, as my cunning would reach vnto. I also craue, that it may please your honour, when your great and waighty matters will permit, to behold this worke, and that shalbe for me an encouragement to take in hand the translation of the East *India*, which is now enioyed by the king of Portingale. Thus I end, beseeching the Almightie to preserue your honorable estate.

Your honors most readie at commandement
Thomas Nicholls.

Stephan Gosson in praise of the Translator.

THe Poet which sometimes hath trod awry,
And sung in verse the force of firie loue,
When he beholds his lute with carefull eye,
Thinkes on the dumpes that he was wont to proue.
His groning spright yprickt with tender ruth,
Calles then to minde the follies of his youth.

The hardie minde which all his honor gotte,
In bloudie field by frute of deadly iarre,
When once he heares the noyse of thirled shotte,
And threatning trumpet sound the points of warre.
Remembers how through pikes he lovde to runne,
When he the price of endlesse glory wonne.

The traueller which nere refusde the paine,
To passe the daunger of the streights he found,
But hoysted saile to search the golden vaine,
Which natures craft hath hidden in the ground.
When he perceiues Don Cortez here so peart,
May well be mindfull of his owne desert.

Then yeeld we thankes to Nicholas for his toyle,
VVho strings the Lute that putteth vs in minde,
How doting dayes haue giuen vs all the foyle,
VVhilste learned wits in forreine lands do finde.
That labour beares away the golden fleece,
And is rewarded with the flower of Greece.

Loe here the trumpe of euerlasting fame,
That rendes the aire in sunder with his blast,
And throwes abroad the praises of their name,
VVhich oft in fight haue made their foes agast.
Though they be dead, their glory shall remaine,
To reare aloft the deeds of haughtie Spaine.

Loe here the traueller, whose painfull quill,
So liuely paints the Spanish Indies out,
That English Gentlemen may view at will,
The manly prowesse of that gallant rout.
And when the Spaniard vaunteth of his gold,
Their owne renowne in him they behold.

FINIS.

In Thomæ Nicholai occidentalem Indiam Stephan Gosson.

SOr defcant Crœfi radiantia tecta Pyropo,
    Et iaceat rutili pompa superba Mydæ.
Aurea fœlici voluuntur secula cursu,
    Pactoli assiduè flumina vera tument.
Terra ferax pandit, sua viscera plena metallis
    Prægnans, diuitias parturit illa suas.
India luxuriat, locupleti prole triumphat,
    Pingue solum gemmis, fundere gestit opes.
O ves qui patriæ cupitis fulcire ruinam,
    Et dare mella bonis aurea, mentis apë.
Cortezi hos animo cupidè lustrate labores,
    Postque, reluctanti credite vela Salo.

To the Reader.

Thought it good gentle Reader, to aduertise thée to consider in reading this historye, that Hernando Cortes was not the firste that did discouer the newe Spaine, for after the Ilands of Santo Domingo and Cuba were discouered, conquered, and inhabited by the Spanyardes, Hernando Cortes, was then a dweller in the Iland of Santo Domingo, and at that time was gouernoure in the Iland of Cuba one Iames Velasques, who had vnderstanding (by others) that néere vnto those Ilands stoode a firme land, rich of golde and plate, wherupon the same Velasques prepared certaine Ships, and in them sent for Generall a kinsmã of his, called Iohn de Grijalua, who with one Francisco Hernãdez de Cordoua, discouered the said firm land in trafike of marchandise, and for things of little value, he broughte greate treasure, as shall appeare in an Inuentorie placed in this historie.

 This Grijalua pretended not to conquer, nor yet to inhabite, but onely to fill his hungry bellie with golde and siluer, for if he had pretended honour, then Cortes had not enioyed the perpetuall fame which now is his, although his corpse be clothed in clay.

 In this historye doth appeare the simplicitie of those ignorant Indians in time past, yea and how they wers deluded

b

To the Reader.

lued in worshipping Idolles and wicked Mamon, their bloudie slaughter of men in sacrifice, and now the greate mercie of Jesus Christ extended vpon them in lightning their darknesse, giuing them knowledge of the eternitie, and holy trinitie in vnitie, whereby they are nowe more deuoute vnto heauenly things then we wretches Christians,(who presume of auntient Christianitie)especially in Charitie, humilitie, and liuely workes of faith.

And now(gentle Reader) I do for my part but onely craue, that it may please thee to accept these my paines taken, in good part, for other benefite I seeke not.
Farwell.

(T. N.)

The Conqueſt of the Weſt India.

The byrth and linage of *Hernando Cortez*.

In the yeare of our Sauiour, 1485. beyng kings of Caſtill and Aragon, the Catholike princes Fernando and Iſabel his wife, was borne Hernando Cortez, in a towne called Medellin, ſituated in the prouince of Andulozia: his father was named Martin Cortez de Monroy, and his mother was called Katherin Piſarro Altimirano, they were both of good birth, and procéeded of foure principal houſes, that is to ſay, the houſe of Cortez, the houſe of Monroy, the houſe of Piſarro, & the houſe of Altamirano, which foure houſes are ancient, noble and honourable: yet theſe parents but poore in goods, but rich in vertue and good life, for which cauſe they were much eſtéemed and beloued among their neighbors. His mother was of inclination denout, but ſomewhat hard: his father was charitable and mercifull, who in his youth applied himſelfe to the warres, and was lieutenant to a companie of horſemen. Hernando Cortez in his childhood was very ſickly, ſo that many times he was at the poynt of death. And when he came to xiiij. yeares of age, his parents ſent him to the vniuerſitie of Salamanca, where he remained two yéres, learning Grammer, and then returned to Medellin wearie of his ſtudie, yea poſſible for

B   want

The Conquest of

want of mony: yet his parents were much offended with him for leauing his studie, for their onely desire was to haue had him a student at law, which is a facultie both rich and worshipfull, considering their son to be of a good wit and abilitie: yet he caused much strife in his fathers house, for he was a very vnhappie lad, high minded, and a louer of chiualrie, for which cause he determined with himselfe to wander abroad to seeke aduentures. And at that instant hapned two iourneys fit for his purpose and inclination. The one of them was to Naples with Gonsalo Hernandez of the Citie of Cordoua, who was a worthy man, and named the great captaine. And the other iourney was to the West India, with the Lord Nicholas de Ouando, a knight of the order of Larez, who was then appointed for gouernor of those parties. And musing with himselfe which way to take, determined to passe into India, chiefly because the gouernor was of his acquaintance, and such a one as would haue care of him. And likewise the great desire of gold made him to couet that voyage more then the iourney vnto Naples. Now in the meane while that the flete was preparing for India, it chanced Hernando Cortez pretended to go vnto a certaine house in the night season to talke with a woman, and climing ouer a wall which was of weake foundation, both he and the wall fell togither: so that with the noise of his fall, and ratling of his armour which he ware, came out a man newly maried, and finding him fallen at his doore, would haue slaine him, suspecting somewhat of his new married wife, but that a certaine olde woman (being his mother in lawe) with great perswasions staied him from that fact. Yet with the fal he fel into a grieuous ague, and continued sicke a long season, so that he could not procede vpon his voyage with the gouernour Ouando. And when he had obtained, and fully recouered his health, hee

minded

the West India.

minded to passe into Italie, and so tooke his way towarde Valencia, wandering here and there almost a whole yeere with much necessitie and pouertie, and then returned home againe to Medellyn, with determination to proceede vpon his pretended voyage of India: Whereupon his father and mother weping their sonnes estate, desired God to blesse him, and gaue him money in his purse for his iourney.

The age of Cortez when he passed into India.

Ernando Cortez was of the age of nineteen yeeres, in the yeere of Christ, 1504. & then he went toward India, and agreed for his passage and victual with Alonso Quintezo, who went in companie of other foure ships laden with marchandice, which nauie departed fro S. Lucas de Barramedo, with prosperous nauigation, vntill they ariued at y Iland of Gomera, one of the Cauary ilãds, wher they did prouide theselues of al things necessarie for so long a voyage as they then had in hand.

Alonso Quintezo, being greedie of his voyage, and desirous to come to the Iland of Santo Domingo before his fellowes, hoping to sell his commoditie the better, departed from Gomera in the night season without knowledge giuing vnto his company. But incontinent after he had hoysed vp his sayles, arose vp so great a winde and tempest, that his maine mast brake, whereby he was forced to returne backe againe to the Ilante of Gomera. And he made earnest request to them of the other Shippes to stay for him, vntill he had mended his Maste, who friendly and neighbourly graunted his desire,

The Conquest of

and departed altogether, sayling in sight the one of the other certaine dayes: yet the saide Quintero, seeing the weater stedfast, and harping vpon gaines, flew from his fellowes againe. And where as Frances Ninio de Guelua his pilote was not expert in that nauigation, they knewe not where they were: at length the Mariners gaue sundrie iudgements. The Pilote was in great perplexitie and sadnesse, their passengers lamented, and bewayled their vnfortunate successe: the Maister of the ship layde the fault to the Pilote, and the Pilote likewise charged the Maister, for it did appeare they were fallen out before. In this meane time their victuall waxed scant, and their fresh water wanted, so that they prepared themselues to die. Some cursed their fortune, others asked mercie at Gods hand, loking for death, and to be eaten of the Cariues. And in this time of tribulation came a Doue flying to the ship, being on good Friday at Sunne set, and sate him on the ship toppe: whereat they were all comforted, and toke it for a myracle, and good token, and some wept with ioy, some sayd that God had sent the Doue to comfort them: others saide that land was neare, and all gaue heartie thankes vnto God, directing their course that way that the Doue flew: and when the Doue was out of sight, they sorrowed againe, but yet remained with hope to see shortly land. And on Easter day they discouered the Island of Santo Domingo, which was first discried by Christopher Zorso, who cried, land, land, a chéerfull voice to the saylers. The Pilote loked out, and knew that it was the point, or cape of Semana. and within foure daies after, they arriued in the port of Santo Domingo, which was long wished for, and there they found the other ships of their companie arriued many dayes before.

Comfort of God.

The

the weſt India.

The time that Cortez abode in Santo Domingo.

Done after that the Gouernour Ouando was in his regiment and office, Cortez arriued at Santo Domingo, and the Gouernours Secretarie, called Medina, receyued and lodged him, and also informed him of the eſtate of the Iſland, and aduiſed him what was needefull to doe, wiſhing that hée would be a dweller there, and that he ſhould haue a plot to build vpon, with certaine ground for huſbandrie. But Cortez his thought was cleane contrarie: for he iudged, that as ſoone as he came thither, he ſhould lade with gold, whereby he did little eſtéeme his friend Medina his counſell, ſaying, that he had rather goe to gather gold, then to trauell in huſbandrie. Medina yet perſwaded him, that he ſhould take better aduiſement, for to finde golde, was doubtfull, and veris troubleſome. This talke ended, Cortez went to kiſſe the Gouernors hands, and to declare the cauſe of his comming, with other newes from Eſtremadure the Gouernours countrey. The gouernour friendly welcomed him, and alſo perſwaded him to abide there, the which counſell hée accepted, and ſhortly after went to the warres, whereof was captaine Iaymes Velaſques, in the prouince of Anigua Iaqua, and Guaca Iarima, and other Lordſhips which were not as yet pacified with the late rebellion of Anacoana widow, who was a gentlewoman of great liuing. Ouando gaue vnto Cortez certaine Indians in the Countrey of Daiguao, and alſo the office of publike notarie in Azua, a towne which the Gouernour had builded, and there dwelt Cortez fiue or ſixe yeares, and began to play the good huſband. Now in this meane ſeaſon hée woulde haue gone to Veragua,

B 3   which

The Conquest of

which was reported to bée maruellous riche, with the Captayne Iames de Nicuesa: but because of an empostume that he had vnder his right knée, he went not, and as it happened, he was therein fortunate, for that thereby he escaped great perils and troubles, whiche happened to them that went on that voyage and iourney.

Things that happened to Cortez in the Iland of Cuba.

The Lord Iames Colon being Admiral and chiefe Gouernour of ye new India, sét one Iames Velasques to conquer the Iland of Cuba, in the yeare. 1511. And gaue vnto him men, Armour, and other thinges necessary. And then Hernando Cortez wet to that conquest as a clearke to the Treasorer, called Michaell de Passamontes, for to képe the accompts of the Kings fiftes and reuenewes, being so intreated and required by the same Iames Velasques, because he was holdē for a man both able and diligent. And it folowed, that in the repartition of ye lands conquered, Iames Velasques gaue vnto Cortez the Indians of Manicorao, in coniunct company with his brother in lawe called Iuan Xuarez, whereupon Cortez did inhabite in Saint Iames de Barucoa, which was the first place of habitation in that Ilande, whereas hee bredde and brought vp kine, Shéepe, and Mares, and was the first that hadde there any heard or flocke, and with his Indians he gathered great quantitie of golde, so that in short time he waxed riche, and ioyned in company with one Andres de Duero a Marchaunt, and put in two thousande Castlins for his stocke. He was also highly estéemed with Iames Velasques and put in authoritie to dispatch businesse, and to

giue

the weſt India.

giue o:der fo: edifices. In his time he cauſed a money houſe to be built, & alſo an Hoſpital. At that time one Iuan Xuarez naturall of the Citie of Granada, carried to the Ile of Cuba his mother and three ſiſters, whiche came to the Iland of Santo Domingo, with that vicequéene the Lady Mary of Toledo, in Anno. 1509. hoping to marry them there with rich men, for they were verie poore. And the one of them named Cathelina was woont to ſay, That ſhe ſhoulde be a greate Gentlewoman: it was eyther by dreames and fantaſies, or elſe ſome Aſtronomer hadde made her beléeue ſo, but her mother was reported to bée very cunning. The maydens were beautifull, for which cauſe, and alſo being there but fewe Spanniſhe women, they were muche made of, and often feaſted. But Cortez was woer to the ſaide Cathelina, and at the ende married with hir: Although at the firſt there was ſome ſtrife about the matter, and Cortez put in priſon, becauſe he refuſed hir for his wife, but ſhe demaunted him as hir huſband by faith and troth of hand: wherein Iames Velaſques did ſtande hir friende, by reaſon of another ſiſter of hirs which he had, but of an euill name. It ſo fell out that one Baltazar Bermudez, Iuan Xuares, & the two Anthony Velaſques, with one Villegas accuſed Cortez, that he ought to marrie with Cathelina, yet theſe witneſſes ſpake of euill will many things, as touching y affaires cōmitted to his charge, alleadging y he vſed ſecret dealing with certaine perſons. The which cauſes although they were not true, yet they carried great colour therof: for why many wẽt ſecretly to Cortez his houſe, complayning of Iames Velaſques. Some becauſe they had not iuſt repertitiō of the cōquered Indians, and otherſome not accoording to deſerte. Contrariwiſe Iames Velaſques gaue credit to his talebearers, becauſe Cortez refuſed to marry w Cathelina Xuarez & vſed vncourteous wordes vnto him in y preſece of many

B 4 that

The Conqueſt of

that ſtood by, and alſo commaunded him to warde. And when Cortez ſawe himſelfe in the ſtockes, he feared ſome proces of falſe witneſſe, as manie times doth happen in thoſe parties. At time conuenient he brake the locke of the ſtockes, and laide hand vpon the ſworde and target of the keeper, and brake vp a window, eſcaping thereby into the ſtréete, and tooke the Church for Sanctuarie. But when Iaymes Velaſques had notice therof, he was greatly offended with Chriſtopher Lagos the Jailer, ſaying that for money hée had loſed him: wherefore hée procured by all meanes to pluck him out of the Sanctuary. But Cortez hauing intelligence of his dealing, did reſiſt and withſtand his force. Yet notwithſtanding, one day Cortez walking before the Church dore, and being careleſſe of his buſineſſe, was caught by the backe with a Sergeant called Iohn Eſquier, and others, and then was put aborde a Ship vnder hatches. Cortez was well beloued among his neighbours, who did well conſider the euill will that the gouernour bare vnto him. But now Cortez ſéeing himſelfe vnder hatches, diſpaired of his libertie, and did verely thinke, that he ſhould be ſent priſoner to the Chancerie of Santo Domingo, or elſe to Spaine, who béeing in this extremitie, ſought all meanes to get his foote out of the chaine, and at length hée got it out, and the ſame night he chaunged his apparell with a lad that ſerued him, and by the Pumpe of the Shippe hée got out, not heard of anie his keepers, climbing ſoftly along the Shippe ſide, he entred the Skiffe, and turnt his way therewith, and becauſe they ſhoulde not purſue after him, he loſed the Boat of another ſhip that road by them. The Currant of Macaguanigua, a Riuer of Barucoa, was ſo fierce, that he could not get in with his Skiffe, becauſe he had no helpe to row, and was alſo very wery, fearing to be drowned if he ſhould put himſelfe to the land, where-

Cortez eſcapeth.

the weſt India.

wherefore he ſtripped himſelfe naked, and tied a night-kercheffe about his head, with certaine writings appertaining to his office of Notarie and Clearkſhip to the Treaſurer, and other things that were agaynſt the Gouernour Iames Velaſques, and in this ſort ſwamme to lande, and went home to his owne houſe, and ſpake with Iohn Xuarez his brother in law, and toke Sanctuarie againe with armour. Then the Gouernour Iames Velaſques ſent him worde, that all matter ſhould be forgotten, and that they ſhould remayne friendes as in time paſt they had béene, and to goe with him to the Warres agaynſt certaine Indians that had rebelled. Cortez made him no aunſwere, but incontinent married with miſtreſſe Catalina Xuares, according to his promiſe, and to liue in peace. Iames Valaſques procéeded on his iourney with a great companie agaynſt the Rebels. Then ſaide Cortez to his brother in lawe Iohn Xuares, bring mée (quoth he) my Launce, and my Croſbow to the Townes ende. And ſo in that euening hée went out of Sancturie, and taking his Croſſebowe in hande, hee went with his brother in lawe to a certaine farme, where Iames Valaſques was alone, with his houſholde ſeruants, for his armie was lodged in a village thereby, and came thither ſomewhat late, and at ſuch tyme as the Gouernour was peruſing his Booke of charges, and knocked at his doore which ſtode open, ſaying: Héere is Cortez that would ſpeake with the Gouernour, and ſo went in. When Iames Valaſques ſaw him armed, and at ſuch an houre, hee was marueylouſly afraide, deſiring him to reſt himſelfe, and alſo to accept his Supper: No Sir (quoth he) my onely comming is, but to know the complaints you haue of mée, and to ſatiſfie you therein, and alſo to bee your friend and ſeruitor. They then embraced each other, in token

The gouernor was ſore afraide.

C of

The Conquest of

of friendship. And after long talke, they lay both in one bedde, where Iames de Orrelano found them, who went to carrie newes to the Gouernour, how Cortez had fledde. After this sort came Cortez againe to his former friendship with Iames Velasques, and proceeded with him to the Warres, but afterward at his returne, he was like to haue bin drowned in the sea: for as he came from the Caues of Bani, to visite certaine of his shepheardes and Indians that wrought in the Mines of Barucoa, where his dwelling was, his Canoa or little bote ouerthrew, being night, and halfe a league from land, with tempest, whereby he was put to his shifts, and forced to swim, and happened to espie light that certaine Shepheards had, which were at supper neere the sea side. By such like perils and dangers, run the excellent men their race, vntil that they arriue at the hauen where their good lot is preserued.

The discouerie of new Spaine.

Frances Hernandes de Cordoua, did first discouer Xucatan, going with three ships for Indians, or else to barter. These Shippes were set forth by Christopher Morante, and Lope Ochoa de Saizedo, in Anno 1517. And although hée brought home nothing at that time but stripes, yet he brought perfect relation, how the countrey was riche of gold & siluer, and the people of the country clothed. Then Iames Velasques gouernor of the Iland of Cuba, sent the next yere following his kinsman, called Iohn de Grijalua with two hundred Spaniards in foure ships, thinking to obtaine much gold and siluer for his marchandise at those places, which Frances Hernandes had informed him: So

that

the weſt India.

that Iohn de Grijalua went to Xucatan, and there foughte with the Indians of Campoton, and was hurt. From thence he entred the riuer of Tauaſco, which Grijalua had ſo named, in the whiche place he bartered for things of ſmall value. He had in exchaunge golde, cloth of cotten wooll, and other curious things wrought of feathers. He was alſo at Saint Iohn de Vlhua, and toke poſſeſſion for the King, in the name of Iames Velaſques, and there alſo exchaunged his haberdaſhe wares, for Golde, and Couerlets of cotten, and feathers: and if he had conſidered his good fortune, hee would haue planted habitation in ſo rich a land, as his company did earneſtly requeſt him, and if he had ſo done, then had he bin as Cortez was. But ſuche wealth was not for him which knew it not, although he excuſed himſelfe, ſaying, he went not to inhabite, but to barter onely in traffike of his Marchandiſe, and to diſcouer whether that land of Xucatan were an Ilande, or no. And finding it a maine land, and populous, he left off for very feare. Likewiſe, ſome of his company were deſirous to returne to Cuba, among whom, was one Pedro de Aluado, who was farre in loue with a woman of that countrey. So they determined to returne, with relation to the Gouernoure of ſuche things as hadde happened till that day, and ſayled homewardes along the coaſt to Panuco, and ſo came to Cuba, to the greate griefe of many of his company. Yea ſome of them wept with ſorrowe, that hée would not abide in that rich countrey. He was fiue monethes vpon his voyage homewarde from lande to lande, and eight moneths till his returne to the Citie. But when he came home, the Gouernoure hauing hearte of his proceedings, would not loke vpon him, whiche was his iuſt reward.

Men tangled in fooliſh loue.

C 2 The

The Conquſt of
The Inuentorie of the treaſure that Grijalua brought for his wares.

Ohn de Grijalua, bought of the Indians of Potōchan, Saint Iohn de Vlhua and other places of that coaſt, ſuch things as made his fellowes farre in loue with ẏ conntrey, & loth to depart frō thence. The workmanſhip of many of the things that they bought, was more worth than the thing it ſelfe, as this Inuentorie particularly both ſhew.

The Inuentorie.

A Little Idoll of gold hollow.

A greater of golde, with hornes and haire, with a ſtring of beadſtones about his necke, and a Flyflap in his hand, and a little ſtone for his nauill.

A péece of golde, like a patent of a Chalice, garniſhed with ſtones.

A Skull of gold, with two hornes, and blacke haire.

Two and twentie eare-rings of gold.

Two and twentie péeces of another faſhion.

Foure bracelets of golde very broad.

A paire of beades of golde, the ſtones hollowe, with a Frogge of gold hanging at the ſame.

Another paire with a Lyon of gold.

A great paire of ear-rings of gold.

Two little Eagles of gold hollow.

A little Saltſeller of gold.

Two ear-rings of gold with Turkie ſtones.

A coller to hang about a womans necke, of twelue péeces, with foure and twentie ſtones hanging thereat.

A great coller of gold.

Sixe little collers of gold thin,

Seuen

the vveſt India.

Seuen other collers of gold with ſtones.
Foure ear-rings of golden leafe.
Twentie fiſhing hookes of gold.
Twelue graines of gold, waying fiftie Duckets.
A headlace of gold.
Certaine thin planches of gold.
A Pottage pot of gold.
An Idoll of gold hollow.
Certaine thin brouches of gold.
Nine bead ſtones of gold.
Two paire of gilt beades.
One paire of wooden beads gilt.
A little cuppe of golde, with eight purple ſtones, and twentie thrée ſtones of another colour.
Foure belles of gold.
A little ſawcer of gold.
A little boxe of gold.
Certaine ſmall collers of gold of ſmall value.
A hollow apple of gold.
Fortie hatchets of gold mixed with copper, valued in two thouſand fiue hundred Duckets.
A whole harneſſe or furniture for an armed man of gold, thin beaten.
An other whole armour of wood with leaues of gold, garniſhed with little blacke ſtones.
A certaine péece made like vnto a feather, of an hide and gold ioyntly wrought.
Foure péeces of armour of wood made for the knées, and couered with golden leafe.
Two Targets couered with feathers of many and fine colours.
Diuerſe other targets of gold and feathers.
A tuffe of feathers of ſundrie colours, with a little bird in the middeſt, very liuely.

The Conqueſt of

A wing of gold and feathers.
Two flyflappes of feathers.
Two liatle chamberpottes of Allabaſter, beſet with many trimme ſtones, and ſome fine, & among them there was one eſtéemed at two thouſand Duckets.
Certaine beades of tinne.
Fiue paire of wooden beades rounde and couered with a leafe of gold very thinne.
A hundreth and thirtie hollow bead ſtones of gold.
Many beades of wood gilt.
A paire of Siſſors of wood gilt.
Two gilt viſors.
A viſor of ſtrange ieſture of gold.
Foure viſors of wood gilt.
Foure diſhes of wood couered with golden leafe.
A dogges head of gold beſet with ſtones.
An other beaſts head garniſhed with gold.
Fiue paire of ruſh ſhoes.
Thrée red hides.
Seuen razors of flint ſtone, for to cut vp men that were ſacrifiſed.
Two painted diſhes of wood with an Ewer.
A garment with halfe ſléues of feathers of excéeding fine colours.
A couerlet of feathers.
Many couerlets of cotten very fine.
Many other couerlets of cotten courſe.
Two kercheffes of good cotton.
Many perfumes of ſwéete odour, much of that countrey fruite.
They alſo brought a gentlewoman that was giuē them, and other priſoner Indians. And for one of them was offered his weight in golde, but Grijalua woulde not take it.

They

thevvest India.

They also brought newes that there were Amazons women of warre, in certaine Ilandes, and manie gaue credit, being amazed at the things that they had brought bartered for things of a vile price: as here-vnder appeareth the Marchandice that they gaue for all the aforesaid Iewels.

The Inuentorie of the Spanish Marchandice.

Sixe course shirts,
Three paire of Mariners breeches of linnen.
Fiue paire of womens shoes.
Fiue broad leatherne girdles wrought with coloured thred, with their purses.
Manye purses of shæpes skinne.
Sixe glasses a little gilt.
Foure brouches of glasse.
Two thousand beadstones of glasse græne.
A hundred paire of beads of diuerse colours.
Thentie wooden combes.
Sixe paire of Sissers.
Fiftæne kniues great and small.
A thousand taylers nædles.
Two thousand pinnes of sorts.
Eight paire of corded shoes.
A paire of pinsers, and a hammer.
Seuen red night cappes.
Three coates of colours.
A fræse coate with a cap of the sains.
An old græne veluet coate.
An olde veluet cap.

The

The Conquest of

The determination of Cortez to prepare a Nauie for discouerie.

Ecause Iohn de Grialua was absent a longer season than was Frācisco Hernandez de Cordoua, before his return or giuing aduise of his procéedings, ý gouernor Valasques prepared a Caruel, & therin sent one Christopher de Olid, for to séeke Grijalua with succour if néed were, & gaue Olid great charge, ý he should return with newes frō Grijalua with all spéed. But this messenger taried but a smal while vpon his voiage, and saw but little of Yucatan, & not finding Grijalua, he returned back again to Cuba, which returne hapned not wel for the gouernor, nor yet for Grijalua. For if he had procéeded foorth on his way to S. Iohn de Vlhua, hée had then met with whom he sought for, & likewise caused him to haue inhabited there: but he excused himself, alledging ý he had lost his ankers, & was therfore forced of necessitie to returne.

And as sone as Olid was departed on that voyage, Pedro de Aluarado returned to Cuba, with full relation of the discouerie, & brought many things to him, wrought in gold, with strange coloured feathers, and cotten woll. The gouernor Iames Valasques reioiced much to behold those principles: And all the Spaniardes of Cuba wondered thereat, & likewise to heare the whole relation of the iourney. Yet the gouernour feared the returne of his kinsmen, because some of his companie that came sicke and diseased from those parties, saide that Grijalua meaned not to inhabite there, and that the people and land was great, and also how the same people were warlike: likewise the gouernour feared the wisedome and

courage

the weſt India.

courage of his kinſman. Whereuppon he determined to ſend thither certaine ſhippes, with ſouldiers and armour and other trifling things, thinking chiefly to enrich himſelf by barter, and alſo to inhabite by force. He requeſted one Baltazer Vermudez to take that voyage in hand, who accepted the offer, but he demaunded three thouſand duckets for his furniture and proviſion. Their gouernour hearing this demaund, anſwered, that in ſuche ſorte the charges would be more then the profite: And ſo for that time lefte off that matter, becauſe he was couetous, and loth to ſpend, thinking to prouide an army at other mens coſt, as he had done before, when Grijalua went firſt on that voyage, for at that time one Fraciſco de Montezo did furniſh one ſhippe. And alſo certaine gentlemen called Alaunſo Fernandez, Porto Carero, Alaunſo de Auila, and Iames de Ordas, with many others, went with Grijalua at their proper coſtes and charges. It followed that the gouernour brake the matter to Cortez, and required that the voyage ſhould be ſet forth betwixt them, knowing that Cortez had two thouſande Caſtlins of golde in the power of one Andres de Duero, a merchant, and alſo that Cortez was a man diligent, wiſe, and of ſtoute courage. Cortez being of haughtie ſtomacke, accepted both the voyage and the charges, thinking the coſt would not be much, &c. So that the voyage and agrement was concluded, wherupon they ſent one Iohn de Sanzedo to the kings councell and chauncery, reſident in the Iland of Santo Domingo, (who were then religious perſons) to haue and obtain of them licence, freely to goe and traffike into thoſe parties of newe diſcouery, and alſo to ſeeke for Iohn de Grijalua, for they imagined that without him ſmall trafficke woulde bee hadde, whiche was, to exchaunge trifles of Haberdaſhe for golde and ſiluer.

The chiefe Rulers of gouernement at that tyme

D iſ

The Conqueſt of

in the kings counſell there, were theſe following, Segniour Alounſo de Santo Domingo, Segnior Luys de Figueroa, and Segniour Barnardo de Munſanedo, who graunted the licence, and appointed Hernando Cortez for captaine Generall of the voyage, and ſetter foorth in company of Iames Velaſques. They alſo appointed a Treaſurer, and Surueyour, to procure for the kinges portion or parte, which was according to cuſtome one fifte part. In this meane ſeaſon Cortez prepared himſelfe for the Iourney, and communed with his eſpeciall friends to ſée who wold beare him company: And hée founde thrée hundreth men that agreed to his requeſt. Hée then bought a Caruell and Mergantine, and another Caruell that Pedro de Aluarado brought home. An other Mergantine hée had of Iames Velaſques: he prouided for them armour, artillery, and other Munition: he brought alſo wyne, Oyle, Beanes, Peaſe, and other bittailes neceſſary: hée toke vp alſo vppon his credite, of one Iames Sauzedo muche Haberdaſhe, to the value of ſeuen hundreth Caſtlyns in golde. The Gouernour Velaſques deliuered vnto him a thouſande Caſtlyns whiche hée poſſeſſed of the goods of one Pamfilo de Naruaiz in his abſence, alleaging that he had no other money of his owne proper. And being in this manner agreed, the Articles and Couenaunts were drawne and ſet downe in writing, before a Notary, called Alounſo de Oſcalantes, the thrée and twentie day of October, 1518.

The comming home of Griialua.
In this meane time arriued at Cuba, Iohn de Grijalua, vpon whoſe arriuall, the Gouernour chaunged his purpoſe and pretence, for hée refuſed to diſburſſe any more money, nor yet would conſent that Cortez ſhould furniſh his Nauie. For the onely cauſe was, that he ment to diſpatch backe againe his kinſeman and his army. But to beholde the ſtoute courage of Cortez, his charges, and liberalitie.

the weſt India.

beralitie in expences, it was ſtraunge, and to ſée how hé was deceiued. And alſo to cõſider, the flatterie and deceite of his aduerſarie, yea what complaints were made to the Lord Admiral, ſaying that Cortez was ſubtil, high minded, and a louer of honor, which were tokẽs that he wold rebel, being in place conuenient, and that he woulde reuenge old griefes. Alſo it grieued Vermudez that he had not excepted the voyage, vnto whõ it was once offered, ſeeing the great treaſure that Grijalua had brought, and what a rich land the countrey newly diſcouered was. Alſo he pretended that the gouernor would be chieftain of ỹ fléet, although his kinſman were not fit for ỹ roome. The gouernor alſo thought that he being ſlack, Cortez would alſo be ſlack. But yet he ſéeing Cortez earneſtly procéed, he ſent one Amador de Larez a principal man, to intreat him to leaue off ỹ voyage (conſidering ỹ Grijalua was returned) and ỹ he would pay him al the coſts & charges that he had layd out. Cortez vnderſtãding the gouernors mind, made anſwer vnto Larez, that he would not leaue of the Iorney for very ſhame, nor yet breake the agrément made. And alſo if Velaſques would ſend a Nauie for his own accoũt, he would be contente, for (quoth hée) I haue alreadie my licence and diſpatcht of the fathers & gouernours. And thẽ he conferred with his friendes, to knowe their mindes if that they would fauour and beare him company, at whoſe handes he found both ready healpe and friendſhippe. Yea ſought then for money, and tooke vp vpon his credit foure M. Caſtlins in gold, of his friend Andreas de Duero, & of Pedro de Xerez & others. With ỹ which money he bought two ſhips, 6. horſes, and much apparrel, and begũn to furniſh a houſe, & kéep a good table for cõmers & goers: he wẽt alſo armed like a captaine, and many waiting & attẽding vpon him, wherat diuerſe murmured, ſaying that he was a Lord without rente. In this meane while came

The gouernour an old enemy.

Courage of Cortez.

Grijalua

The Conqueſt of

Grijalua to the Cittie of Sainte Iames de Cuba: but his kinſeman the Gouernour woulde not looke vppon him becauſe hee had left and forſaken ſo riche a lande. Alſo it grieued him inwardly that Cortez proceeded thitherward ſo ſtrong and mightie, and coulde by no meanes diſturbe or let him, and to ſee the great traine that wayted vpon him, with many of them that had bene the other voyage with Grijalua: yea if that hee ſhould diſturbe him, bloodſhead would follow in the Cittie. So that he was forced to diſſemble his ſorrow. Yet (as many affirme) hee commaunded that hee ſhould haue no victualls ſolde vnto him. Now Cortez departed from thence, proclaiming himſelfe for Generall, and that the Gouernour Velaſques had nothing to do with his Nauie, requeſting his ſouldiers to embarque themſelues with ſuch victualls as they had. He alſo bargained with one Fernando Alfonſo, for certaine Hogges and Sheepe that were prepared for the ſhambles, and gaue vnto him a chayne of golde and brouches for payment, and alſo money, to paye the penaltie that the Butcher fell into for not prouiding the Cittie. And ſo he departed from Saint Iames de Barracoa, the eighteenth of Nouember, with about three hundreth Spaniards in ſixe ſhippes.

The Nauie and men that Cortez carried with him to the Conqueſt.

Ortez departed from Saint Iames de Baracoa, with ſmall proviſion of victualls for ſuch a number of men, and alſo for the Nauigation whiche as yet was vncertaine. And bæing out of that parte, hee ſente Pedro Xuarez

the weſt India.   21

Xuarez Gallinato, with a Caruel to Iaymaica for vittails, commaunding him, that theſe thinges which hee ſhould there buy, to goe there with to Cape de Corientes, or to S. Anthonies pointe, whiche is the fartheſt parte of that Iland Weſtward. And he himſelfe went with his companie to Macaca, and bought there great quantitie of bread, and ſome Hogges, of one Taymaio Then he proceeded to the Trinitie Ilande, and there bought an other Shippe of one Alonſo Guillen. And of particular perſons he bought three Horſes, and fiue hundred buſhels of Corne. And being there at road, he had aduice, that Iohn Nonez Sedenio paſſed that way with a Ship laden with vittails, for to make ſale thereof at the Mines. Whereupon he ſent Iames de Ordas, with a Caruell well armed, for to take him, and to bring him vnto S. Anthonies point. Ordas went and tooke him at the Chanel de Iardines, and brought him to the place appointed. Sedenio brought the regiſter of his marchandice, which was great ſtore of bread, Bacon, and Hennes. Cortez gaue him chaines of gold, and other peeces for payment, and a bill for the reſt. In conſideration whereof, Sedenio went with him to the Conqueſt. In the Trinitie Iland Cortez gathered togither two hundred men more, who had bin in Grijalua his companie, and were dwellers in that Iland, and in Matancas, Carenias, and other Uillages, and ſenting his ſhips forward, he went with his men by land to Hauana, which was then inhabited on the South ſide in the mouth of the riuer called Onicaxinall, but there they would ſell him no prouiſion, for feare of the Gauernor Velaſques. But yet one Chriſtopher Galſada, rent gatherer to the Biſhop, and receyuer for the Popes Bulles, ſolde to him great ſtore of Bacon and bread of that Countrey called Maiz, and other prouiſion, whereby his fleete was reaſonably prouided, &c. And then he began to diſtribute his men and

D 3   vittailes

The Conquest of

vittailes aboord ech vessell in good order. Then came Aluarado with his caruell, with his other friends Christopher de Olid, Alonso de Auila, Fracisco de Monteio, & many others of Grijalua his companie, who had bin to talke with the Gouernour Velasques. And among them came one Garnica, so called, with letters for Cortez from Velasques, wherein he wrote, desiring him to abide there, for that he meant to come himselfe, or els to send vnto him, to treate of matters profitable for them both.

Also the said gouernor sent other secret letters to Iames de Ordas, and others, requiring them to apprehend & take prisoner Cortez. Now Ordas did inuite Cortez to a banket aboord his Caruell, thinking by that meanes to catch Cortez in a snare, and so to carry him prisoner to the citie of Saint Iamas de Barocoa. But Cortez vnderstood y matter, and fained himselfe to be very sicke, and also fearing some vprore, he went aboord his ship Admirall, and shot off a peece of Ordinance, giuing warning to his nauie to be in a readinesse to make saile, and to follow him to saint Anthonies point, which was don with expedition, & there in the Towne of Guani Guaniga, he mustred his men, and found fiue hundred and fiftie Spaniards, whereof fiftie were mariners. He diuided them into eleuen companies, and appointed these persons following for captaines, that is to say, Alonso de Auila, Alonso Fernandez Porto Carrero, Iames de Ordas, Francisco de Monteio, Francisco de Morla, Francisco de Salzedo, Iohn de Escalante, Iohn Velasques de Leon, Christopher de Olid, and one Escouar, and he himselfe as Generall tooke one companie. He made these manie Captaines, because his whole fleete was eleuen sayle, and that each of them should senerally be Captaine, both of Shippe and men. He also appointed for chiefe Pilote Anthonio de Alaminies, who had taken charge before with Francisco de Hernandez

A snare layd for Cortez.

the weſt India.

nandez de Cordoua, and Grijalua, &c. He caried alſo 200. Indians, borne in the Jle of Cuba, to ſerue and to cary baggage, & alſo certaine Negros, with ſome Indian wome, and ſixtene horſes and Mares, with great prouiſion of bacon, corne, bisket, hennes, wine, oyle, peaſe, and other fruits, with great ſtore of Haberdaſh, as bels, necklaces, beades of glaſſe, collers, points, pinnes, purſes, nedels, girdels, thred, kniues, ſiſſers, pinſers, hammers, hatchets, ſhirts, Coyfes, headkirchiefs, handkirchiefs, breches, coates, clokes, caps, Marriners breches. All the which marchandiſe he diuided among his nauie. The ſhip admirall was of the burthen of a hundred Tunnes. Other thre ſhips of the burthen of eighty Tunnes the pece. All the reſidue were ſmall without ouerloppe, and bergantines. The deuiſe of this enſigne or auncient, was flames of fire in white and blewe, with a red croſſe in the middeſt, and bordred round with letters, in the Latine and Spaniſh tongs, which ſignified this in effect: friends, let vs follow the Croſſe, and with liuely faith with this ſtandard we ſhall obtaine victorie. The premiſſes (as ye haue heard) was the furniture that Cortes prouided for his iourney, and with ſo ſmall a thing he conquered ſo great and mighty an Empire, and ſtrange countreys vnknowne at that time. There was neuer captaine that did with like army ouercome ſo infinit a people, & bring both them and their country vnder ſubiection. He caried no mony to pay his ſouldiers, but was rather much indebted to others at his departure. And to ſay the truth, there needed any mony to make pay to thoſe ſouldiours that went to the Conqueſt, for if they ſhould haue ſerued for wages, they wold haue gone to other places nere hand. But in India, euery one pretedeth ye ſtate of a noble man, or elſe great riches. Now all the floet being in readineſſe (as ye haue heard,) Cortez began an exhortation to his company as folowe th.

The

The Conqueſt of
The Oration that Cortez made to his Souldiers.

MY louing fellowes, and déere frientes, it is certaine that euerie valiant man of ſtoute courage, doth procure by déedes to make him ſelfe equall with the excellent men of his time, yea, and with thoſe that were before his time. So it is, that I doe now take in hand ſuch an enterprise, as God willing ſhall be hereafter of great fame, for mine heart doth prognoſticate vnto me, that we ſhall win great and rich countries, and manie people, as yet neuer ſéene to any of our Nation, yea, and (I beléeue) greater Kingdomes then thoſe of our Kings. And I aſſure you, that the deſire of glorie doth further extend, then treaſure, the which in ſort, mortall life doth obtaine. I haue nowe prepared Shippes, armour, horſes, and other furniture for the warres, with vittaile ſufficient, and all things that are vſed as neceſſarie in Conqueſts. I haue béene at great coſts and charges, wherein I haue not onely employed mine owne goodes, but alſo the goods of my friends, yet me thinketh that the employment thereof doth encreaſe my treaſure and honour. Wée ought (louing fellowes) to leaue off ſmall things, when great matters doe offer themſelues. And euen as my truſt is in God, euen ſo greater profite ſhall come to our kings, & a nation of this our enterprise, then hath heretofore of any other. I doe not ſpeake how acceptable it will be to God our Sauiour, for whoſe loue I do chiefly and willingly hazard my goods and trauell. I will not new treate of the perils and daunger of life that I haue paſſed ſince I began this voyage. This I ſay, that good men doe rather expect renowne, then treaſure. We doe now attempt and begin warre that is both good and
                                                                iuſt,

the west India. 25

iust, and the almightie God in whose name and holy faith this voyage is begunne, will assuredly graunte vnto vs victory, and the time will shew the end of things well begunne. Therfore we will now haue an other manner in our proceedings, than either Cordoua or Grijalua hadde, whereof I meane not nowe to dispute, for the presente time doth hasten vs away, but at our arriuall, we will do what shall seeme vnto vs conuenient. Heere deere friends do I lay before you great gaynes, but wrapped in greate trauell, yet Vertue is an enimie to idlenesse. &c. Therfore if you will accept hope for Vertue, or Vertue for hope, and also if ye forsake me not, as I will not forsake you, I will with Gods help make you in shorte time the richest men that euer passed this way. I doe see you are but fewe in number, but yet such men of haughtie corage, that no force or strength of Indians can offende. Likewise we haue experience, that Christ our sauiour hath alwayes fauoured our nation in these parties. Therfore my deere friendes, let vs now in Gods name depart ioyfull, expecting good successe, according to our beginning. &c.

The entrance of Cortez into the Iland of Acusamill.

With the aforesaid comunication, Cortez gaue great hope to his copany of waightie matters, yea & great admiration of his person, so that all his copany had an earnest desire to proceede on that iorney. And Cortez likewise reioyced, to see his men so willing: and incontinente, they embarqued them selues, and after their prayers made vnto God, hoysed vp their sailes, and with faire winde departed the eighttenth day of February. Anno 1519. And being at Sea, he willed all his nauie (as the vse is) to haue S. Peter for

their

their patrone, warning them alwaies to follow the Admirall (wherin he went) because he carried a light for the night season to guide them the way, whiche was almost East and West from S. Anthonies point, being the nerest part of Cuba to Cape de Cotoche, which is the first land point of Yucatan, whither they were bound, so that being there, they might run along the coast, betweene the North point and the West. The first night ꝥ Hernando Cortez, began to passe ouer the gulfe betweene Cuba and Yucatan, being little aboue lx. leagues, the winde rose vp at North east with much force, so that all the Fleete were separated without sight ꝥ one of the other: yet by the accompt that their Pilots kept, they arriued all sauing one at the Iland of Acusamil, althogh not at one time, and those that last arriued, were the Admirall, and Captaine Morla his Ship, who had lost his Ruther, but by shoting off a peece, Cortez vnderstoode his necessitie, and came bering to him, and armayned his sailes to succour him, being in ꝥ night season. Yet when the day appeared, it pleased God that the rage of the tempest ceassed, & being cleare day, they found agayne their Ruther, and trimmed the Ship, and mate saple, and sayled that day and the next following, without sighte of land, or any of the Fleete. But the thirt day they arriued at a cape or point of land, called Womens cape. Cortez commanded Morla to follow him, directing his course to seeke the residue of his Fleete, and arriued in this sorte at the Iland of Acusamil, and there found all his nauie excepte one, whereof they heard no newes in many dayes after.

The feare of the Indians of Acusamil.

The people of that Ilande beholding suche a straunge sight, were in great feare and admiration, so that they gathered their stuffe and wente vp into the Mountaines. Cortez caused a certaine number of his men to goe a land to a Towne which was neere the place where they were arriued, and they found the towne wrought with Masons worke, and good building, but they founde no creature therein;

the west India.

therein, yet in some houses they found cloth made of cotten wooll, and certain iewels of gold. Also they entred into a high tower made of stone worke, neare the sea side, and there they founde nothing but Idolls of earth and stone. With this newes they returned to Cortez, and enformed him what they had seene, and also many faire sowen fi. los. of Maiz, and great store of hiues of Bees, and many trees of fruites, and also presented vnto him the gold and other things that they had found. Cortez reioyced with ẏ newes, but yet marueiled that the people were fled, considering that when Grijalua was there, they had not so done, wherby he iudged, that his nauie being greater, caused them to feare and flie, and likewise he feared least a snare were prepared for him. Then he commanded to vnship his horses for three causes: the one to discouer the Countrey, and the other to fight if need were: and also to graze them, hauing there abundance. Also he vnshipped his men of war, and sent them to discouer the land. And in the thickest of the Mountaines, they found foure women, and three children, whom they brought to Cortez, so that not vnderstanding their language, by signes and tokens they imagined, that one of them was the mother to ẏ children, & mistresse to the other women. The poore creatures bewayled their captiuitie. Cortez made much of them, and apparelled the mistresse as wel as he might with Spanish attire: and to his seruants he gaue looking glasses and sissers: and to the litle children others toyes to play withall, vsing no dishonestie towards them. And then he determined to send one of the wenches to call her maister, & to enforme him how well they were intreated. In this meane season came certaine spies lurking a far off, by the commandement of their Lord, who was called Calachuni, to bring newes of his wife, and what else passed. Cortez receiued them gently, & gaue vnto them certaine trifles, & sent others to their Lord, & returned them to embassage on his behalfe & his

How the people were found.

C 2   wiues,

The Conquest of

wiues, to defire him to come vnto him, and to fee thofe folke from whome he had fledde, promifing, that neyther his perfon, nor none of his countrey fhould receyue anye moleftation of him, nor of any of his company. Calachuni vnderftāding this friendfhippe, and alfo with the loue hée bare to his wife and childrē, came the next day following with all the Townfemen, in whofe houfes ye Spanyards were lodged, who woulde not permitte that their guestes fhould giue place. And the Lorde commaunded, that they fhould be wel entertained, and frō that day forward prouided them of bread, fifh, honney, & fruite. Calachuni fpake and faluted Cortez with greate humilitie and ceremonie, and euen fo was hée louingly receyued, & wel entertained. Cortez did then declare vnto him by the commoditie that would enfue vnto him by that nation. And alfo prefented, vnto him & his cōpany many toyes, which were vnto them of fmall baleiue, but muche efteemed among them, yea more then golde. And moreouer Cortez cōmaunded, that

A facte worthy of praife.

all the golde and other things that his men had taken in the Towne, fhoulde be broughte before him, and placed it fo that euery Indian knewe his owne, and was reftored vnto them, whereat they were not a little ioyfull, wondering at the liberalitie of the ftraungers, and departed both merrie and riche with their ftraunge giftes, and went throughout al the Iland, fhewing to their fellowes their prefentes, commaunding them in the name of Calachuni their Lord, to returne euery man to his houfe, with their wiues and children, commending highly the honeft and gentle nature of the ftraungers. With this newes and commaundemente, euery man returned to his houfe and Towne from whence he had fledde. And after this fort their feare was paft, and they prouided the Camp abundantly of honey, bread, waxe, fifhe, and frute, all the time that they abode in that Iland.

The

the weſt India.

The Indians of Acuſamil gaue newes to Cortes of certaine bearded men.

NOw Cortez ſeeing theſe Indians quiet and wel pleaſed, and alſo very ſerulceable, he did determine to take away their Idols, & to giue them a remembrance of Jeſus Chriſt, borne of the virgin Mary, by one Melchior a fiſher man, & very ruſtical, who had bin ther before with Francisco Hernandez de Cordoua, who declared vnto them, that Cortez his lord and captaine would enforme them of a better God, and better lawes, thē thoſe which they maintained. The Indians anſwered, that they were contented therewith, and went with them vnto their temples, and there brake downe their Idols, and celebrated diuine ſeruice, teaching them to adore and worſhip Chriſt crucified, ſo that they were very attentiue to the doctrine, and ceaſed ſacrifice of men which they were wont to vſe. Theſe Indians did wonder much at the ſhips and horſes, yea, and maruelled as much at our colour and beards, ſo that many times they would come and feele them, and ſignified vnto them by ſignes and tokens towardes Yucatan, that there were flue or ſix bearded men. Then Cortez conſidering how profitable it would be to haue an interpreter, to vnderſtand and to bee vnderſtood, he beſought Calachuni that he would appoint a meſſenger to carrie a letter to the bearded men, who were in the power of a great Lord and Tyrant, and Calachuni found none that durſt take that iourney in hand, fearing that they ſhould be ſlaine and eaten. Cortez ſeeing this, entreated with faire wordes, three of the Indians that ſerued him to accept the iourney, and gaue them rewardes for their labour: yet the Indians excuſed them, ſaying that

Newes of bearded men.

they

The Conqueſt of

they ſhould be ſlayne, notwithſtanding with faier promiſes and rewardes, they accepted the voyage, ſo that Cortez wrote with them this letter following.

Worſhipful ſirs, I departed from Cuba with eleuen ſaile in my fléete, furniſhed with fiue hundred and fiftie Spaniardes, & I am here at Acuſamil from whence I write you this letter. The people of this Iland haue certifico me, that there is in that countrey fiue or ſixe bearded men, and in all points like vnto vs: they cannot here enforme me of anye other ſignes or tokens, but hereby I do conjecture, and certainly beléeue, that ye be Spaniardes. Both I and theſe gentlemen of my company do come to diſcouer and inhabite this land, we hartily pray you, that within ſixe dayes after the receit hereof, ye come vnto vs, without any excuſe or delay, and if ye ſo doe, at we of this nauie wil gratiſie your gentleneſſe and good ſeruice that ye ſhall do vnto vs. I do ſend you a Bergantin, wherein you may come, and two ſhippes for your ſafe conduct.   Hernando Cortes.

This letter being written, there was found an inconuenience, which was, they knew not how to carrye the letter ſo ſecretlyy it might not be ſéene, and they taken for eſpies, wher of the ſaide Indians ſtood in greate feare. Then Cortez bethoght him, yt the letter would paſſe wrapped in the haire of the head of one of thé, for ordinarily the Iudians wear lōg haire, & on their ſolemn feaſts & in wars they vſe their haire platted aye bout about their forheads. And ye appointed captaine of the Bergantine wherin the meſſegers wét, Iohn de Eſcalāte. & Iames de O. das for captaine of the other two ſhips, with fiftie men if any nede ſhould happen. So ſhortly after the ſhips arriue at the place appointed, Eſcalante ſet a land his meſſengers, and abode there eight dayes they returne, although he promiſed them to abide there but ſixe dayes. And the ſeing that

they

the vveſt India.

they came not, he ſurmiſed that they were either ſlaine or taken captiues: and ſo returned backe againe to Acuſamil without his meſſengers, wherof al the army were ſorow-ful, & chiefly Cortez, thinking that the Indians had wrong informed him. Now in this mean ſeaſon they trimmed their ſhippes of the hurt receiued by the late tempeſt, and at the returne of the two ſhips and Mergantine, they hoy-ſed vp ſayles and departed.

A miraculous chance how Geronimo de Aguilao came to Cortez.

Alachuni and all his ſubiects were full of heauines (as it ſeemed) with the departure of the Chriſtians, becauſe they were well vſed at their hands. From Acuſamil the fleete ſayled to get the coaſt of Yucatan to the cape called Womens point, with pro-ſperous weather, and ther Cortez came to an anker, deſi-rous to ſee the diſpoſition of the land, and the maner of the people: but it liked him not, ſo that the next day folowing being ſhrouetueſday, he departed, meaning to double the ſaid Cape, and ſo to paſſe to Cotoche, and to biewe it. But before they had doubled the poynt, Peter de Al-uarado ſhotte off a peece, in token that he was in great perill, wherevpon the other Shippes drewe neare, to knowe what had happened: And when Cortez vnder-ſtoode that Aluarados ſhippe was in ſo great a leake that with two pumpes they might not emptie the water, he found no other remedy but to returne backe againe to Acuſamil with al his fleet. The Indians of the Iland came incontinent to the water ſide very ioyfull, and to knowe whether they had left any thing behind them. The Chri-ſtians informed the of their miſhap, and came a ſhore, & in ſhort time found the leake and amended it. The ſaterday following they tooke ſhipping againe, all the army except

Hernando

The Conquest of

Hernando Cortez, and fiftie of his companie, then the wind arose contrarie, and so much, that they could not depart that day: and the furie of the wind endured all that night, but in the morning it waxed calme, so that they might proceede on their voyage. But for as much as that was the Sabboth day, they determined to heare diuine seruice, and after dinner to make saile. When their seruice was ended, and Cortez sitting at his meate, there was newes brought him that a little vessell called a Canoa, came vnder saile towarde the shippes, which seemed to come from Yucatan: with that newes Cortez arose from his meat, to behold whether the Canoa went, and perceiuing that she left the way towarde the shippes, hee sent Andrew de Tapia with certaine others, as secret & closely as might bee deuised, to lye in ambush for their comming a shoare. The Canoa arriued in a calme place, out of the which came foure men all naked, except their priuie members, and the hairy of their heades platted and bounde about their foreheades like vnto women, with bowes and arrowes in their hands: three of them which were Indians, were afraid when they saw the Spaniards with their drawen swordes, and would haue fled againe to their Canoa, but the Christian feared not, and desired his-fellowes in the Indian tongue to abide with him. And then he beganne to speake in the Spanish tongue in this wise: Maisters are ye Christians, yea (quoth they) and of the Spanish nation. Then he reioyced so much, that the teares fell from his eyes, and demaunded of them what day it was, although he had a Primer wherein hee daily praied.

He then besought them earnestly to assist him with their praiers and thanksgiuing vnto God for his deliuery, and kneeling deuoutly downe vpon his knees, holding vp his handes, his eyes toward heauen, and his face bathed
with

the weſt India.

with teares, made his humble prayer vnto God, giuing moſt hartie thankes, that it hadde pleaſed him to deliuer him out of the power of Infidels and infernall creatures, and to place him among Chriſtians and men of his owne nation. Andrew de Tapia holpe him vppe, and toke him in his armes, & ſo did al the others embrace and louingly ſalute him. Then he commaunded the other three Indians to follow him, and went talking with his friendes, where Cortez aboade, who receiued him ioyfully, and gaue vnto him ſuch apparrel as he needed, and with greate pleaſure hauing him in his companye, hée demaunded the eſtate af his misfortune, and what was his name, who aunſwered before them all, ſaying, Sir my name is Geromino de Aguilar, I was borne in the Citie of Eſija in the Andolozia, and by misfortune I was loſt after this ſorte. In the warres of Darien and in the time of the contentions and paſſions of Iames de Nicueſſa, and Vaſco Nonez Balboa, I came with Captaine Valdinia in a little Caruell, toward Santo Domingo, to giue aduice to the Admirall and gouernour, of the troubles which had happened, and my comming was for men and victuals: and likewiſe we brought twentye thouſand Duckettes of the kinges in Anno. 1511. And whē we apported at Iamayca, our Caruel was loſt on the ſhallowes whiche were called the Vipars, and with greate pain we entred (about twenty perſons) into the boate, without ſayle, water or bread, and weake prouiſion of oares: we thus wander thirtéene or fourtéene dayes, and then the currant, which is there very great & runneth alway weaſtward, caſt vs aſhoare in a prouince called Maija, & trauelling on our way, ſeauen of our fellowes died with hunger and famin. And captain Valdinia & other 4. were ſacrificed to the ydols by a cruel and curſed Cacike, that is to ſay, a Lord in whoſe power we fell, &c.

The coming of Aguilar to Cortez.

F.   And

The Conqueſt of

And after the ſacrifice, they were eaten among the Indians for a ſolemne banket: and I, & other ſix were put into a Cage or coupe, to be fatned for an other ſacrifice. And for to eſcape ſuch abhominable death, we brake the priſon and fled through certaine mountaines: ſo that it pleaſed God that we met with another Cazike, who was enemie to him that firſt toke vs, his name was Quinqus, a man of more reaſon and better condition, he was lord of Xamanſana: he accepted vs for his captiues, but ſhortly after he died, and then I aboad with Taxmar his heire. Then deceaſed other fiue of our fellowes, ſo that there remained but onely I, & one Gonſalo Guerrer, a mariner, who now abideth with Nachancan the lord of Chetemal, and he maried with a rich gentlewoman of that countrey, by whom he hath children, and is made a captaine, and well eſtæmed with the Cazike for the victories that he hath had in the wars againſt the other lords. I ſent vnto him your worſhips letter, deſiring him that he would come with me hauing ſo fit a paſſage, but he refuſed my requeſt, I beléue for very ſhame, becauſe he had his noſe ful boared of holes, and his ears iagged, his face and hands painted according to the vſe of the country, or elſe he abode there for the loue he bare to his wife and children. All thoſe which ſtod by and heard his hyſtory, were amazed, to heare Geronimo de Aguilar report how thoſe Indians did ſacrifice and eate mans fleſhe. They alſo lamented the miſerie and death of his fellowes, & highly prayſed God, to ſée him frée frō his bondage, and from ſuch cruell and barbarous people, and to haue likewiſe ſo good an enterpreter with them, for vndoubtedly it ſéemed a miracle, that Aluarados ſhip fel into a leak, for with that extremitie they returned back againe to that Iland, whereas with contrary winde they were conſtrained to abide the comming of Aguilar. And certainly he was the meane and ſpéech of all their

procéé-

the weſt India.

procéedings. And therfore haue I bin ſo prolixious in the rehearſall of this matter, as a notable point of this hiſtorie. Alſo I wil not let to tel how the mother of Geronimo de Aguilar, became mad, &c.

When ſhe heard that her ſon was captiue amõg people that vſed to eat mans fleſh, & euer after when ſhe ſaw any fleſh ſpitted or roaſted, ſhe would make an open outcrie, ſaying, oh I miſerable woman, behold this is the fleſh of my dearely beloued ſon, who was all my comfort.

The Iland of Acuſamil.

The Indians naturall of that countrey doe call their Iland Acuſamil, and corruptly Coſumil. Iohn de Grijalua was the firſt Spaniard that apported ther, and named it the holy Rood; becauſe he fell in ſight thereof on holie Rood day. It containeth ten leagues in length, and thrée leagues in breadth, although ſome ſay more, ſome leſſe: it ſtandeth xx. degrées on this ſide the equator, & fiue leagues from the womens cape: it hath thrée vilages, in the which lineth neré 3000. men. The houſes are of ſtone and brick, and conered with ſtraw & bowes, and ſome w̃ tile. Their teples and towers are made of lime and ſtone very well built: they haue no other freſh water but out of wels & rain water. Calachuni is their chiefe lord: they are browne people, and go naked: and if any weare cloth, it is made of cotten wol only to couer their priuy members: they vſe long haire, platted and bound about their foreheads; they are great fiſhermen, ſo that fiſh is their chiefeſt fod and ſuſtenance, they haue alſo Maiz which is for bread: alſo good fruits and hony, but ſomewhat ſoure: and plots for bées, which containe 1000 hiues. They knew not to what vſe wax ſerues, but when they ſaw our mẽ make cãdels therof, they woored therat

F 2   Their

The Conquest of

Their dogges haue Foxe faces and barke not, these they gelde and fatten to eate. This Iland is ful of high mountaines, and at ye fœte of them, good pastures, many Deare, and wilde Boares, Connyes and Hares, but they are not great. The Spaniardes with their hand guns and crossebowes prouide them of that victual, fresh, salt, and dryed. The people of this Iland are Idolaters, they doe sacrifice children, but not manye. And manye times in stead of children they sacrifice dogges. They are poore people, but very charitable and louing in their false religion and beliefe.

The religion of the people of Acusamil.

He temple is like vnto a square Towre broad at the fœte, and steps round about it, and from ye middest vpward very straight: the top is hollow and couered with straw: it hath foure windowes with frontales and galleries. In the hollow place is their chappel, whereas their Idols do stand. The temple that stode by the sea side was such a one, in the which was a maruellous straunge Idoll, and differet muche from all the rest, although they haue manye and of diuerse fashions. The bodie of this Idol, was greate and hollow, and was fastened in that wall with lime: hee was of earth. And behinde this Idols backe was the Vesterie, where was kept ornaments & other things of seruice for the temple. The priests had a little secret dore hard adioyning to the Idol, by which dore they crept into ye hollow Idol, and answered the people ye came with prayers & petitiōs. And with this deceit ye simple souls beléeued al ye the idol spake, and honored ye god more thē al ye rest, wt many perfumes &

A straunge Idol.

sweete

the vveſt India.

ſwéte ſmelles, and offred bread and fruite, with ſacrifice of Quailes bloud, and other birds, and dogges, and ſometims mans bloud. And through the ſame of this Idoll and Oracle, many Pilgrimes came to Acuſamil from many places. At the fote of this Temple was a plotte like a Churchyard, well walled and garniſhed with proper pinnacles, in the middeſt whereof ſtode a Croſſe of ten fote long, the which they adored for God of the rayne, for at all times when they wanted rayne, they would goe thither on Proceſſion deuoutly, and offered to the Croſſe Quailes ſacrificed, for to appeaſe the wrath that the God ſéemed to haue againſt them: and none was ſo acceptable a ſacrifice, as the bloud of that little birde. They vſed to burne certaine ſwéte gumme, to perfume that god withall, and to beſprinckle it with water, and this done, they beléeued aſſuredly to haue raine. Such is the Religion of thoſe Indians of Acuſamil. They could neuer knowe the original how that goo of Croſſe came amongſt them, for in all thoſe parties of India, there is no memorie of any Preaching of the Goſpell that had bene at any time, as ſhall be ſhewed in another place.

The God of raine.

The Battell and winning of Potonchan.

Ortez procéded with his Fléete very ioyfull, bicauſe he had found one of his ſhips which he thought had bene loſt, and aported at the riuer de Grijalua, which in the Indian tongue is called Tauaſco, & anckred at ye riuers mouth, fearing to enter in with ye bigger veſſels ouer the barre: and incontinent came many Indians to gaze at them & their ſhips, who were armed with feathers,

The Conqueſt of

thers, and ſuch like armor as they vſe, ſéeming a farre off trim fellowes. They wondred not much to ſée our ſhippes and men, becauſe they had ſéene before Iohn de Grijalua in the ſame Riuer. The behauiour of that people, and ſcituation of the Countrey, liked Cortez very well, ſo that leauing ſufficient guarde in his ſhippes, he manned his Vergantines and Boates, and carried with him certaine pieces of Ordinance, and with force of Oares he entered the Riuer againſt the ſtreame, which was very great, and hauing rowen little more then halfe a league, they eſpied a greate Towne walled with Timber, and the houſes made of mudwall, couered with ſtrawe. The Townewall was verye ſtrong, with lope holes to offende withall. And before oure menne came neare the Towne, they mette with manye little Boates, whiche the Indians call Tahucup, full of armed menne, ſhewyng themſelues deſirous of battaile. Cortez procéeded forwardes, and made vnto them ſignes of peace, declaring vnto them by his enterpreter, that his comming thether was not to moleſt or diſquiet them, but onely to take freſhe water, and to buy victualls, as menne that trauelled by Sea, and ſtode in néede thereof, promiſing good paymente for any thing that they ſhoulde take. The Indians bearyng their requeſt, promiſed to ſhewe their meſſage to the Townesmen, and woulde alſo returne with theyr aunſwere and vittayles, and ſo departed. In ſhort ſpace they returned againe, and brought bread and fruite, and eyght Turkie Cockes, and preſented it franckely vnto
Policie them. Cortez gaue them thankes, but (quoth he) the proviſion that ye haue brought, is very little, for y̆ néede that I and ſo many perſōs which I haue within yonder great veſſels locked and ſhutte vp, therefor I pray you to bring me more vittales, or elſe to permitte and ſuffer mée and my folkes to come vnto youre Towne to ſéeke oure remedie.

the weſt India.

remedie.

The Indians demaunded one nyghtes ſpace to doe the one and the other, and departed towarde the towne. Cortez alſo went to a little Ilande that ſtandeth in the riuer, to abide their aunſwere, ſo that eache pretended to deceiue the other, for the Indians demaunded that time, to the intent to carrye that night away their goodes, and to put in ſafetie their wiues and children in the Mountaynes, and likewiſe to gather their men of warre to defende their Towne. Cortez alſo commaunded his Harquabuſhiers and Croſſebowmen to goe a lande vppon the Ilande, and cauſed the Riuer vpwardes to bée ſought for way, to wade ouer, ſo that theſe things were done that nyghte without anye knowledge to the contrarye ſide. And all thoſe whiche aboute abowte the Shippes, came vnto Cortez, and thoſe who wente to ſéeke the paſſage, founde within leſſe then halfe a league vpwardes, a place that was of depth to the girdle of a manne. And likewiſe, founde ſuche couerte of woodées, that they myghte come nére vnto the Towne, and not to bé ſéene.

Diligence of a good Captaine.

Thys newes liked well Cortes, whereuppon he appoynted two Captaines, whoſe names were Alonſo de Auila, and Peter de Aluarado, and to eache of them fiftie menne. The ſame nighte hé ſente certaine Soul-dyers with a ſea compaſſe, to lie in an ambuſhe in the woode whiche ſtode betwéene the riuer and the towne, for two conſiderations. The one, bycauſe the Indians ſhoulde ſée, that there were no moe Spanyardes in the Ilande, then were the daye before. And the other was, that hys menne hearing their watchword, ſhoulde aſſaulte the towne on the land ſide. And as ſoone as the day appeared, came eight boates of Indians armed, wheras once Campe was pitched, who broughte a little

F 4 victuall,

The Conquest of

vittaile, saying they could get no more, because that the inhabitants of the Towne were fledde, with feare of them, and their deformed vessels, desiring them to returne aboord their Shippes, and not to disquiet the people of that Countrey. The interpreter aunswered, that it was against humanitie to suffer them to perish with hunger, yea, and if they would heare the cause of their comming they should shortly see what profite would redound vnto them. The Indians replied, that they would take no counsell of straungers, and men whome they knew not. Likewise, they thought not good to lodge such guests in their houses, for they seemed terrible, and such as would be commaunders. But if they would needs haue water, they might take riuer water, or else make welles on the shore, for so did they at their neede.

Then Cortez seeing that wordes preuailed not, hee signified vnto them that he woulde enter their Towne by force, to see it and their Countrey, for to giue thereof relation to the greatest prince in the worlde, who had sent them thither: requesting them to be therewith contented, considering he ment not to disquiet them: and if they would not permit the same, he woulde commend himselfe to his God, and to the strength and force of his men. The Indians aunswered againe, that they should depart, and not thus bragge in other mens land, for in no wise they would permitte them to enter their Towne. And if with this warning they would not depart, they meant to kill both him, and as many as were with him. Yet Cortez ceased not to vse all humanitie with those barbarous people, according to the commaundement and instructions giuen vnto him by the King of Castill, which was, to require those people oftentimes with peace, before the attempting of warre, or entring perforce into their Townes and Countrey, so that yet againe

the weſt India. 41

gayne he conuited them with peace, promiſing them libertie with good entertainement, aſſuring them of things profitable both for body and ſoule, and that they myghte accompt themſelues happie with the knowledge thereof: but if now they would refuſe his offer, he did then warne them to make them ready for the euening, for before the going downe of the Sunne, he did hope with the help of his God, to reſt and take vp his lodging in the Towne, in deſpite of all the inhabitants thereof, who had refuſed his offer.

The Indians laughed at his talke, and ſkorning at him, they returned to the Towne, to enforme their fellowes of the pride and madneſſe that they thought they had heard. Then the Spanyardes went to dinner, and hauing well refreſhed themſelues, they putte on their Armour, and went aboorde their Boates and Uergantines, looking for ſome aunſwere from the Indians, and ſeeing the Sunne decline apace, and no aunſwer, Cortez aduiſed the Spanyardes that lay in ambuſhe in the woode, to giue aſſault, and he embarqued himſelfe with his rapier and Targette, gyuyng likewiſe aſſaulte with neere two hundred men, who comming neere the Towne walles, diſcharged his Ordinance, and lept into the water to the knees, and began valiantly to aſſault the walles and bulwarkes. The Indians ſeeing their enimies ſo nigh vnto them, beganne to fighte with courage, ſhooting arrowes, throwing of dartes and ſtones, wherewith they hurte aboute twenty Spanyardes: yea, and though the fearefull noyſe of the Ordinance did many times ſo annoy them, being things ſo ſtraunge, and neuer before ſeene of them, yet they fledde not from the walles, but reſiſted the Chriſtians valiantlye, and ſuffered them not to enter the Towne that way, if they had not bin aſſaulted in another place. But when the Company that lay in ambuſh

G   hearde

The Conqueſt of

heard the ſhooting of their fellowes, they began likewiſe their onſet. The Indians knowing nothing what was prepared behinde their backs, and hauing alſo their hands full in defending the entrance by the riuer: and the Chriſtians finding that part of the towne without reſiſtance, entred in with a terrible noyſe, killing as many as they met. Then the townesmen vnderſtood their ouerſight, and would haue remedied it, and fledde from the place where Cortez was giuing combat, whereby Cortez and his company entered the towne at eaſe, without contradiction, ſo that bee and the other company of his Souldiers met together at the Market place, and expulſed all the Indians out of the towne, except thoſe that were taken priſoners, and the carkaſes of the dead. Then the Chriſtians ſought the ſpoyle, and founde nothing but Turkie Hennes, and ſome things wrought of Cotten wooll, but very little Gold.

There was that day aboue foure thouſand Indians in fight and defence of the towne: There was much Indian blood ſhed, becauſe they fought naked, many were wounded, and fewe captiue. Cortez lodged himſelfe with his armie in the chiefeſt Temple of the Idolles, where was roome ſufficient. They kept that night good watch, as in a houſe of enemies, but the poore Indians durſt not once interrupt them. After this ſort was Potonchan taken, being the firſt Cittie that Cortez wanne by force in all his Conqueſt.

The

the weſt India.   41

The Battell of Cintla.

All that night Cortez ſlept not, but rather occupied himſelfe in carrying the wounded men, and o- *Care of a*
ther ſtuffe abord the ſhips, and alſo to diſenbarke *good Cap-*
thirtéene Horſes, and the reſidue of his men that *taine.*
he had left abrod, the which he brought to paſſe before the
Sunne riſing, although the Tauaſcans had notiſe thereof. When the Sunne was riſen, hée had with his company made vnto G D their prayers, and muſtered
his men, where were at that time in Campe neare
fiue hundreth Spanyardes, thirtéene Horſes, and ſixe
péeces of Ordinaunce: Theſe Horſes were the firſt that
euer came into that Countrey, whiche nowe is called
new Spaine. He planted his men and Munition in good
order, and thus marched forwards towarde Cintla. The
Indians ſéeing this preparation, began alſo to make rea-
die, and to place in good order fortie thouſand men in fiue *Fortie thou-*
companies: their méeting was in ploughed land among *ſand Indians.*
many déepe lakes and pondes, very daungerous to paſſe,
ſo that our men by reaſon thereof were brought out of
order. And Hernando Cortez with his horſemen went to
ſéeke a better paſſage, and to encloſe himſelfe among certaine trées on their left hand, for to ſet vpon the enemies
when time ſhould ſerue. The footmen procéeded on, and
paſſed many mariſhe groundes, vntill they came to the
tilled. The Indians were expert in thoſe places where
they beganne the battaile, ſhooting with their bowes
and ſlinges, and throwing of dartes. Although our men
did ſome hurt among them with their Croſſebowes, handgunnes, and ordinance, when they were in place to ſhot,
yet the Indians purſued our men ſo thick, that they could
not put them off, for by pollicie, the Indians of Potonchan
hadde ſought out that place: and it is to bee thought

G 2   that

44 The Conquest of

that they were not barbarous, nor of small vnderstanding in warres, yet notwithstanding with muche payne, our men gatte out of that place, and obtained another somewhat better, and more playner grounde, whereas they might vse their Ordinance, and fighte with their weapons bodye to body. But the Indians beyng so greate a number, draue our men to so narrowe a place, that they were fayne to ioyne backe to backe for their owne defence, yea and for all that were in maruellous great daunger, for they had no roome to vse their Ordinance, nor yet Horsemen to make them waye. They beyng in thys perplexitie, and readie to flye, sudaynely appeared a Horseman with a speckled Horse, whome they iudged to be Captaine Morla, which Horseman sette vppon the Indians, and made them retyre; and hauing more space then before, they sette afreshe vppon the enimies, and slewe some of them. In this meane tyme the Horsemanne baded away, and was not sene, and with his absence the Indians beganne afreshe, and enclosed the Christians in the same daunger that they were in before: then the Horsemanne appeared againe nere onre menne, and made maruellous way among the enimies; whereupon our menne seing this succoure, gaue the onset againe with great courage, and slewe and hurt many Indians, but at the best season, the Horseman bannished away cleane out of sighte, and when the Indians sawe not the Horsemanne, with feare of whome they fledde, thinking that he hadde bin a Centaure, and that the Horse and man was all one incorporate, they returned againe with liuely courage, and vsed our Christians worse than they hadde done before. Then the Horseman returned the chird time, and putte the Indians to flight with great hurte, whom our footeman pursued with great slaughter.

Perill of the Christians.

A miracle.

Þaꝭe

the vveſt India.

Now at this inſtant came Cortez with all his company of horſmen, being wearied with the trauell in paſſing ſuch ſtrange lakes and wilderneſſe, whereof the country is repleniſhed. Our men being ioyfull of his comming, they began to enforme him what wonders they had ſéene a horſeman do, which came to ſuccour them, demaunding of him which of their companie it was. Cortez anſwered and faithfully aſſured them, that it was none of their cōpany, becauſe it was not poſſible for any of them to come any ſooner: Then they all gaue God praiſe, beléeuing that it was a helpe ſent from heauen. Cortez ſaid (my deare fellowes) forwards, for God is with vs. Then the horſmen ſet vpon the Indians, and with force of launce droue them out of the mariſh ground, and brake their maine battell. The Indians incontinent left the field, and fled into the thicke woods, the fotmen followed them, and ſlue aboue thrée hundred Indians, beſides many other that were hurt. There were aboue ſeuentie Spaniards wounded with arrowes and ſtones.

And whether it were with labour of the battel, or with A ſodaine
exceſſiue heate, or with drinking the water of that place, diſeaſe.
there fell ſuch a ſtitch in their loynes, that about a hundred
of them fel flat vpon the ground, not able to go nor ſtand,
their fellowes being forced to carry them on their backs.
But it pleaſed God that the ſame night the paine went
from them, being in the morning wel again. Who ſéeing
themſelues deliuered from ſo manye perils, gaue moſt
humble thankes to the almightie God, that had myraculouſly deliuered them. They all agréed that thrée times
they had ſéene the ſtraunge Horſeman, with the ſpeckled
horſe, fight in their fauour, as is aforeſaid, beléeuing generally it was a myracle, as certainly it did appeare, for
the Chriſtians did not alone ſée this thing, but alſo the
Indians did much note it, for the maruellous fierceneſſe

G 3 where

The Conqueſt of

wherewith hee came vppon them, with ſuch great murther, that they were amazed, and almoſt blinde with his brightneſſe, being ſo trodden vnder his feete. The captiue Indians after the battell declared the circumſtaunce thereof.

The Lord Tauaſco ſubmitteth himſelfe to the Chriſtians.

Ortez releaſed ſome of his Priſoners, and ſent them to their Lorde, ſaying: that it grieued him the hurt done on both parties, but the fault was theirs. And that God was witneſſe of his innocencie, and alſo of his curteſie offered vnto them. But notwithſtanding all that was paſt, he pardoned their errour with ſuch condition, That incontinent or within two dayes, their Lorde woulde come vnto him, to yeelde ſatiſfaction of their malice and ſtubbornneſſe, and to treate of peace and friendſhip, warning and aduiſing them, that if they came not within the time appointed, hee woulde enter into his Countrey, burning and ſpoyling with ſlaughter both great and ſmall, armed and vnarmed: with which meſſage the meſſengers departed, and Cortez returned to the Towne to cure his wounded men. The next day came fiftie auncient Indians to craue pardon for their offence, and alſo licence to bury the dead, with likewiſe ſafeconduct that their rulers and principall perſons might ſafely come vnto the towne. Cortez graunted their requeſt, warning them to make any lyes or yet to conſpire againe: and alſo

The Caxike embaſſadors.

the vvest India.

so if their lordes came not personally, he would not heare any more embassadors: with this rigorous comandement and protestatiō they departed. These Indians feeling their strength woulde not preuaile, thinking the Christians to be inuincible, their Lordes and chiefest persons did determine to goe and visite the christians and their capitaine. And according to the time appointed ye the Lorde of that towne and other foure Lords his neyghbours came vnto Cortez with a good trayne of their vassals and seruitours, and presented vnto him, bread, turkie hennes, and fruites, with other like prouision for his hoste, with foure hundred pieces of gold of the value of 400. double duckets, w other small iewels, and certaine Turkie stones of small value. And twentie women slaues, to serue to make breade and dresse meate for the whole army. He craued and besseched Cortez to pardon his former offence. And to accept and receiue them into his friendshippe. And in token of his obedience, hee and his fellowes did willingly deliuer their bodies, landes and goods into his handes and power. Cortez did louingly receiue them, & gaue vnto them certaine trifles of his warres, which they esteemed much. And those Indians hearing the horses and maresneye, they maruelled at their neying, thinking that the horses could speake, and demaunted of the Christians what they said, (mary quoth they) these horses are sore offended with you because ye fought with them, and would haue you corrected and chastened for your so doing. The simple Indians hearing this, presented roses and Gynea Hens vnto ye horses, desiring them to eate and to pardon them.

Certaine

The Conquest of

Certaine queſtions that *Cortez* deuiſed of the Cacike Tauaſco.

Any things paſſed betwéene our men and the Indians: for where the Indians vnderſtood them not, their behauiour was much to laugh at. And vſing conuerſation with our men, and ſéeing they receyued no hurt of them, they brought to the town their wiues and children, which were no ſmall number. And among many matters that Cortez communed with Tauaſco, by the mouth of Ieronimo de Aguila his interpreter.

The firſt queſtion was: Whether there were mines of gold or ſiluer in that countrey, and from whence they had that ſmall quantitie that they had brought vnto them?

The ſecond queſtion was: Why they denied him their friendſhip, more then the other captaine that had bene there the yeare before?

The third was: Why they being ſo many in number, fled from them being ſo few?

The fourth was: To giue thẽ to vnderſtand the mightie power of the king of Caſtill. And laſt of all to giue them knowledge of the faith of Ieſus Chriſt.

_{The anſwere of Caciks.} As touching ſir (quoth he) the Mines of gold and ſiluer in our countrey, we ſéeke for none, for we ſéeke not after treaſure and richas, but we procure and deſire a quiet life. And that gold which we haue, was found by chance: for we know not what mines doe meane. Yet notwithſtanding further within the land, whereas the Sun doth hide himſelfe, there the people do find much gold, and are giuen to ſéeke the ſame.

And

the west India.

And as touching the Captaine that was here of late, we seeing the men and shippes to be such as we had neuer before seene, spake vnto them and demaunded what they would haue, they said that their comming was, to change their merchandise for gold and nothing else, wherfore we graunted to their request. But now seeing greater vessels and moe in number, we feared least ye came to take our substance. And I knowing my selfe nothing inferiour to any of my neighbours, would not permit any iniury to be offered me, and that he & his subiects did esteem themselues the most valiant of men of warre in all these parties, and that none durst take away their goods, women, and children, to bee sacrificed by force, wherevpon he thought to withstand those fewe Christians, but (quoth he) I found my selfe deceiued, seeing we could not kil any of your company. And likewise the brightnesse of your weapons did blinde vs, and the woundes you made were incurable.

But the noyse and lightning of your ordinaunce did more amaze vs, then either thunder-clappes or tempest: and also the great spoyle that you made among vs therewith: likewise your straunge horses made vs greatly to wonder, to behold their open mouthes, wee feared to be swallowed. And then to consider their swiftnesse in running, we knew no creature could escape them. But the first horse that fought with vs, put vs in maruellous fear, being but one, but when wee espied many, then all our helpe was past, for wee beleued that the horse and man was all one incorporate.

How

The Conqueſt of

How the Indians of Potonchan brake downe their Idols, and worſhipped Chriſt.

WIth the relation of Traualco Cortez ſawe that the countrey was not for Spaniardes, nor yet hee tooke it a thing conuenient to ſettle themſelues where no golde nor ſiluer was, or other riches. And ſo pretended to paſſe forwardes to diſcouer Weſtward the land endewed with golde. But before his departure, hée declared to thoſe newe conquered Indians, that the Lord in whoſe name he and his company had taken that iourney, was king of Spaine and Emperour of Chriſtians, and the greateſt Prince in the worlde, vnto whom many Kinges and Princes did homage and obey. And that his rule and gouernement in iuſtice proceeded from God, being iuſt, holie, peaceable and ſwéete, and alſo the Monarchie of the vniuerſall did appertaine vnto him. And for theſe cauſes he required them to yéeld themſelues as his ſubiectes. And if they would doe ſo, there ſhould enſue vnto them great profite, lawes and pollicie. And as touching their religion, he declared their blindneſſe & great abuſes which they vſed in worſhipping many Gods, and in making ſacrifice vnto them with mans bloud, yea and thinking that thoſe images and Idols, did or coulde doe good or euill vnto them, being dumbe, without life or ſoule, yea and the worke of their owne handes. He certified them of one good maker of heauen and earth, and all creatures whom the chriſtians did worſhip and ſerue, and
that

the west India.

that all creatures ought to doe the same. In conclusion with this doctrine they brake downe their Idols, and re-retued the crosse, Cortez hauing first declared vnto them the great miseries that the son of God suffred on the crosse for mankinde. And in the greatest temple of Potonchan, set vp a Crosse in remembrance of the death of Christ, and celebrated the feast vpon their knees, and the multitude of Indians likewise, and departed to their meate. Cortez desired them within two daies to come againe to their diuine seruice. And that day was Palme Sunday, And so they did, and brought an infinite number of men, women and children of other villages with them which was strange to beholde. And there generally gaue their vassalship to the king of Spaine into the handes of Hernando Cortez, with protestation of perpetuall friendship with the Spanish nation. So that these were the first vassals that the Emperour had in the new Spaine. And this feast and ceremonie ended, our men tooke shipping with the palme boughes in their handes. In this doing Cortez deserued no lesse praise then in his victorie, for he vsed wisedome with manhoode in all his doinges: he left those Indians with a new faith, and the towne free and without hurt, he tooke none for slaues, nor yet any spoile, nor exchanged his merchandize for any thing, although he aboade there twentie daies. The towne is called in the Indian tongue Potonchan, that is to say, a place that stincketh, and our menne named it, the Victorie.

The Lord (as ye haue heard) was called Tauafco, and therefore the first Spaniardes that came thither, named the riuer Tauafco, but Grijalua called it after his owne name, whose name and remembraunce will not so sone be forgotten. And truely all those that doe discouer

H 2. new

The Conqueſt of

newe Countries, ought to make perpetuall their owne names. This town doth containe neare fiue and twentie thouſand houſes (as ſome ſay) but as euery houſe ſtandeth by himſelfe like an Iland, it ſeemeth much bigger then it is indeed. The houſes are great, made of lime, ſtone, and brick: others there are made of mud-wall and rafters, and couered with ſtraw or bordes. Their dwelling is in the vpper parte of the houſe, for the great moyſtneſſe of the riuers and lakes, and for feare of fire, they haue their houſes ſeparated the one from the other. Without the towne they haue more fairer houſes then within, for their recreation and pleaſure. They are browne people, and go almoſt naked, and eat mans fleſh ſacrificed. Their weapons are bowes and arrowes, ſlings, dartes, and lances. The armor wherewith they defend themſelues, are Targets and ſkulles made of wood or barke of trees, and ſome of gold very thinne. They haue alſo a certaine kinde of harneis made of cotten wooll wrapped about their ſtomacke.

The good entertainment that Cortez had in Saint Iohn de Vlhua.

Aptaine Cortez and his company being embarked, ſayled Weſtwards as nigh the ſhoare as they might. And this coaſt hauing no harboures, they found no place where they might anker ſafely with their greater veſſels, vntill they arriued vppon Maundie-Thurſday at Saint Iohn de Vlhua, which ſeemed a good harbor for them. The Indians of this place call this harbor Chalchicoeca, there the firſt came to anker. They were not ſo ſoone at Roade, but incontinent

came

the weſt India.

came two little boates named Acalles, enquiring for the Generall of the Fléete, who when they came to his preſence, did humble reuerence vnto him, and ſayd vnto him, that Teudilli the Gouernour of that Prouince ſent to knowe what people they were, and what they woulde haue, and whether they meant to ſtay there, or proſcéde further. Aguilar did not well vnderſtande that language. Cortez cauſed him to come abourde his Shippe, gyuing them thankes for their paynes, and viſitation. Hé made vnto them a banquet of Wine and Conſerua, and ſayde vnto them, that the next day followyng hé woulde come alande, and talke with the Gouernour, whom hé beſought not to alter him, nor his people with his comming a ſhore, for he meant not to moleſt him, but rather to pleaſure and profite him. So that theſe meſſengers were rewarded with certayne giftes, they eate and dranke, but yet ſuſpected euill, although they liked the Wine well, wherefore they deſired to haue thereof, and alſo of the Conſerua, to preſent vnto their Lord, which was giuen them, and ſo departed.

The next day beeing good Fryday, Cortez came alande with his Boates full of menne, and brought his Horſes and Artillarie aſhore, by little and little, with all his men of warre, and two hundreth Indians of Cuba, which ſerued to toyle and laboure. Hé planted himſelfe in the beſt ſcituation that hé could finde among the ſandie Bankes on the Sea ſide, and there pitched his Campe, and hauing neare that place manie trées, they buylt them Cottages with boughes.

From a little Uillage that was at hand, came manie Indians to gaze at things ſo ſtraunge, and the like neuer ſéen vnto them, and brought with them gold to barter for

ſuch

such toyies as the two little Boates had brought from them before. They brought also bread and meate ready dressed after their vse likewise to sell. Our men chaunged with them Bead-stones of Glasse, looking Glasses, Sissers, kniues, Pinnes, and such other wares, whereof the Indians were not a little glad, returning home to their houses, shewing their neighbours. The ioy and pleasure that these simple soules tooke with these trifles, was so great, that the next day they came againe with other Indians laden with Iewels of gold. Turky hens, bread, meate, and fruit, that suffised for all the Campe, and for the same they receyued needels, and Bead-stones of Glasse, but the poore soules thought themselues therewith so rich, that they knewe not where they were with ioy and pleasure, yea, and they thought that they had deceyued the Straungers. Nowe Cortez seeing the great quantitie of golde brought and bartered so foolishly for trifles of no valewe, proclaymed throughout all his hoste, that no Christian shoulde take anie golde vppon great penaltie, and that they shoulde all shewe, as though they knewe not to what purpose the golde serued, and that they passed not for it, because they shoulde not thinke that the desire thereof had brought them thither, and so they did dissemble that great demonstration of golde, to see what was meant thereby, and whether the Indians hadde brought that Golde, to proue whether their comming was for that or no. On Easter day in the morning, came Teudilli the Gouernor to the Campe, from Cotosta his dwelling place, which was eight leagues from thence. He brought attending vppon his person foure thousande men without weapon, and the most part well cloathed, some of them with garments of Cotton, rich after their manner. And others naked, laden with victuals in great abundance, which was

Wisedome.

The comming of the gouernour.

the weſt India. 55

was ſtraunge to ſée. Teudilli accoɀding to their vſance, did his reuerence to the Captaine, burning frankinſcnſe, and little ſtrawes touched in the blood of his owne bodie, he pɀeſented vnto him the victuals, and certaine Iewels of golde verie rich and well wɀought, and other things made of feathers verie curious, ſtraunge and artificiall. Cortes embɀaced him in his armes, and receyued him ioyfully, ſaluting all his companie. He gaue to Teudilli a coate of ſilke, a bɀoch, and a coller of glaſſe, with manie other péeces of haberdaſh wares, whichɀ was highly eſtéemed of him. *A ſtrange ſalutation.*

The talke of Cortez with Teudilli.

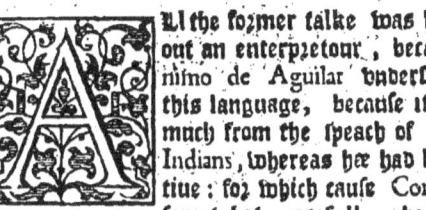

All the former talke was had without an enterpɀetour, becauſe Ieronimo de Aguilar vnderſtode not this language, becauſe it differed much from the ſpeach of the other Indians, whereas hée had béene captiue: foɀ which cauſe Cortez was ſomewhat carefull, becauſe hée would largely haue diſcourſed with Teudilli. It chaunced that among thoſe twentie women giuen him in Potonchan, one of them ſtode talking with a ſeruaunt of Teudilli, becauſe ſhée vnderſtode them as men of her owne language. Cortez eſpying this, called her aſyde, and pɀomiſed her moɀe then libertie, ſo that ſhée woulde bée a truſtie and faithfull interpɀeter betwixt him and thoſe Indians, and that he would eſtéeme her as his Secretarie. And further demaunded of her of what linage ſhée was, then ſhée aunſwered, that ſhée was naturall of the Countrey that boɀdereth vpon Xalixco, and of a towne *A maruellous hap.*
called

The Conqueſt of

called Viluta, daughter vnto riche parentes, and of the kinred of the Lorde of that lande. And béeing a little girle, certaine Merchantes did ſteale her away in tyme of warre, and brought her to be ſolde at the fayre of Xicalanco, which is a greate Towne nere Coaſaqualco, not farre diſtant from Tauaſco: and after this ſorte ſhe came to the power of the Lord of Potonchan. This woman was Chriſtened Marina. She and her fellowes were the firſte Chriſtians baptiſed in all the newe Spayne, and ſhe onely with Aguilar, were Interpreters betwixt the Indias and our men.

Nowe Cortez béeing aſſured of his true Interpreters, hée celebrated his accuſtomed diuine ſeruice, and Teudilli with him, and after they hadde dyned in Cortez hys Tente in preſence of many Spanyardes and Indians, Cortez enformed Teudilli howe that hée was vaſſall to the Lord Charles of Auſtria, Emperour of the Chriſtians, and King of Spayne, and Lorde ouer a greate parte of the worlde, whome great Kinges and princes did ſerue and obey: and that all Princes were glad to bée his friendes for his Vertue and mighte. And hée hauing aduertiſemente of that Countrey and Lorde thereof, hadde ſente him thyther to viſite him on his behalfe, and to informe him of certaine ſecrete matters, the effecte whereof he hadde in wryting. Sir (quoth Teudilli,) I am very glad to heare the Maieſtie and Vertue of the Emperoure youre maiſter, but you ſhall vnderſtande, that my Lorde the Emperoure Melzuma is as greate and as good a Prince as hé. And I doe muche marnell, that there ſhoulde bée anye ſo greate a Prince in the whole worlde, but yet accordyng to youre requeſt, I will certifye hym, and knowe hys pleaſure, for I truſt (quoth hée) in the clemencie of my Prince, that youre newes and meſſage ſhall bée acceptable vnto him,

The aunſwere of Tendilli.

and

the weſt India.

and you well recompenſed for your paines. Cortez then commanded al his men to ſet themſelues in order of battayle with phife and drumme, and to ſkirmiſh before Teudilli. And that the Horſemen ſhould runne, and the ordinaunce ſhotte off, to the entent that Mutezuma ſhoulde be aduertiſed thereof. The Indians did muche behold the geſture, apparell and beardes of our men, they wondered to ſee the horſes runne, they feared the brightneſſe of the ſwordes, and at the noyſe of the ordinaunce they fell flatte to the ground, thinking that the heauens did fall. And the ſhippes, they held opinion was the God of the ayre called Quezalcoualt, which came with the temples on his backe, for they dayly loked for him. Teudilli diſpatched the poſte to Mexico, to Mutezuma, aduiſing him of all that he had ſeene, and demaunded golde of him for to giue vnto the Captaine of that newe people. Becauſe Cortez had inquired of him, whether Mutezuma had gold or no, he aunſwered (yes) mary quoth Cortez, I and my fellowes haue a certayne diſeaſe of the harte, and golde helpeth vs. This meſſage wente from the campe to Mexico in one day and a night, which is 210. mile, and the poſte carried paynted, the horſes and horſemen vpon them, the maner of their armour, & howe many peeces of ordinaunce they had, and what number of bearded men there were: and as for the ſhippes, he had giue aduiſe as ſoone as they arriued, ſhewing the greatneſſe and quantitie of them. All theſe things aforeſayd, Teudilli cauſed to be paynted in cloth of Cotton very liuely, that Mutezuma mought ſee it. The cauſe that this meſſage wente ſo farre in ſo ſhorte a ſpace, was, they had certaine places that poſtes attended, as we may ſay horſepoſtes, which gaue alwaies from hand to hande the paynted cloth: they doe runne on foote faſter in this ſorte, then by horſepoſt, and is more of antiquitie than horſepoſt: Alſo Teudilli ſent to Mutezuma the garments & many

The diſeaſe of the Spaniards.

I   other

The Conqueſt of

other things which Cortez had giuen him, which things
were afterwards found in the treaſorie of Mutezuma.

The preſent and anſwere that Mutezuma
ſent vnto Cortez.

After the meſſage ſent, and the anſwer
promiſed, Teudilli tooke his leaue, and
within two flight ſhote of Cortez his
campe, he cauſed a thouſand cottages
of boughes to be made, and left there
two principall men as Captaines o-
uer two thouſand perſons, men & women, and then departed for Cotoſta his
dwelling place. The two Captaines had charge to prouide ye Chriſtians of all things neceſſary, and the women
ſerued to grinde their corne and make bread of Maiz,
and to dreſſe their fiſh and fleſh and other vittails, and the
men ſerued to carry the dreſſed meate to the Chriſtians
campe, and wood, water, and graſſe for the horſes, and all
other neceſſaries, and this they paſſed eight daies. In this
meane ſeaſon returned the poſte with a riche and gentle
preſent, which was many couerlets and clothes of cotten,
white, and of other colours wrought, many tuffes of feathers very faire, and ſome things wrought with gold and
feathers, quantitie of Iewels & peeces of gold and ſiluer,
two thinne wheeles, the one of ſiluer which wayed 25.
markes with the ſigne of the Moone, and the other wheele
of gold which wayde a hondreth markes, made like vnto
the Sunne, with many leaues and beaſts, a very curious
peece of worke, theſe two things they helde for Gods in
that countrey, & giueth them the colours of the mettal that
is like it them, euery wheele was two yards & a half broad,
and ſo proportionally in compaſſe rounde about, this preſent was eſteemed at 20000. Ducats. This preſent ſhould
haue

the weſt India.

haue bene giuen to Grijalua, if he had not ſo ſoone departed as the Indians reported. He alſo gaue vnto Cortes this anſwere, that Mutezumas his Lorde was verye gladde to know, & to be friend to ſuche a mightye Prince as the King of Spayne was, and that in his time ſhould arriue in his coūtrey ſuch new people, & the like neuer ſeene before, and that he was readie to ſhew them al pleaſure & honour, requeſting him to ſee what things he ſtoode in neede of for the time that he meant to abide there, as well for himſelfe as for his ſhips, armye and deceaſſe, and it ſhould be prouided abundantly: yea and alſo if he could finde any thing in that countrey to his contentment, to preſent to the Emperour of Chriſtians, he would willingly prouide it. And as touching the deſire that Cortez had to come to biſite & to haue comunication with him, he thought it vnpoſſible, becauſe that he was ſickly and coulde not come vnto the ſea coaſt, and likewiſe for Cortez to come where he did abide, it was harde, troubleſome and difficill, as well for the many and cragged mountains, as alſe the countrey, wild, deſart, and without habitation, and ſhoulde be conſtrayned to ſuffer hunger, thirſt, and other neceſſitie: and moreouer the enhabitaunts of much part of the way that he ſhoulde paſſe, were his enemies, both cruel & curſed people, and knowing the̅ to be his friendes, they ſhould not eſcape with life.

All theſe excuſes did Mutezuma by the mouth of Teudilli declare vnto Cortes, thinking to driue him fro̅ his purpoſe & pretēded iourney, alleaging the foreſaid difficulties and perils, the Indians did alſo hope that with ſome cōtrary weather they ſhould be forced to leaue that coſt and coūtrey. Notwithſtāding this re_,_ ction, ſo much the more deſire had Cortes to biſite Mureʒuma, who was ſo great a prince in that parties, & throughly to diſcouer the treaſure which he imagined to be ther. And hauing receiued y̅ preſent, & alſo y̅ anſwer, he gaue vnto Teudilli a garmēt of his

The excuſe of Mutezuma.

I 2 owne

The Conqueft of

owne wearing, and many other trifles of his Haberta{{h}}, to be fente vnto Mutezuma, faying that if it were for no other purpofe but onely to ſée ſo mightie and vertuous a Prince, it ſhould be requiſite and iuſte to trauayle vnto his Court, how much the more, he was of duetie conſtrayned to doe the Embaſſage which the Emperour of Chriſtians had willed and commaunded him to doé, for otherwyſe hée ſhoulde incurre the diſpleaſure of the King his mayſter, wherefore he beſought Teudilli yet once againe to aduertiſe Mutezuma of his conſtant determinatiõ, becauſe he ſhoulde vnderſtande that hée would not leaue off his pretended purpoſe for any inconuenience that was obiected vnto him. Alleagyng moreouer, that he who had cõmen 2000. leagues by ſea, mought well goe 70. leagues by lande, and conſidering that he had many at his charge with ſmall prouiſion, and likewiſe his ſhippes in daunger, he required that with all expedition the meſſengers ſhould be diſpatched. Teudilli deſired him to recreate himſelf, & not to take any griefe, for as much as he himſelfe did dayly aduertiſe Mutezuma of his proceedinges, euen ſo with all expedition the full reſolution ſhoulde come from Mexico, although it were ſomewhat farre off. And as for his victuals, he ſhoulde take no care, for abundantly he ſhould he prouided. And alſo deſired him for ſo much as he was not well placed among thoſe ſandy bankes, that it might pleaſe him, to goe with him to certaine townes aboute fire or ſeuen leagues frõ thence. Cortez refuſed that offer, wherevpõ Teudilli departed, and he aboue there ten dayes loking for anſwere from Mutezuma.

How

thevvest India.

How Cortez knew of difcord and diffention to be in the Countrey

IN this meane feafon, certain Indians were efpied, that went lurking a far off among the fandy hilles. And thofe came not neare the Indians that ſerued the Spaniard, Cortez demaunded what people they were, and for what caufe they went lurking fo far off, and came not nérer vnto them.

The two captaines anſwered, that they were hufbandmen, that went about their hufbandry. Cortez lyked not their anſwer, but fufpected that they had told him a lie: for it ſéemed vnto him that thofe people defired to come among the Chriſtians, and that they durſt not for feare of the Indians of Teudilli, and fo it was in very déede. For all that coaſt and maine land within as farre as Mexico, was full of the newes and ſtraunge things that our men had done in Potonchan. Wherefore they all defired to ſée them, and to talke with them, but they durſt not for feare of the Indians of Culhua, who are ſubiects vnto Mutezuma, whereupon Cortez ſent fiue Spaniards to cal them with fignes and tokens of peace. This company of Indians were in number twentie, and were glad to beholde thofe fiue men comming towardes them, and were defirous to ſée ſuch ſtrange people and ſhips, wherefore they came willingly altogither vnto Cortez his Tent.

Theſe Indians did differ much from all the other Indians yet ſéene, for they were bigger of perſon, and had the griſtles of their noſes ſlitte, hanging ouer their mouthes, and rings of Iette and Amber hanging thereat. They had alſo their nether lippes bored, and in the holes rings of gold, and Turky ſtones, which weyed ſo much, *The Indian attire.*

I 3   that

The Conquest of

that their lips hanged downe ouer their chinnes, and their teeth remained bare: The which custome although they vsed for a brauerie, it seemed a foule and vgly sight in the Spaniards eyes, and very loathsome.

The other Indians of Mutezuma, had their lippes and eares bored, with rounde stones hanging at the iagges thereof, yet they had not such foule giftes in their noses, but they had such bored holes that a man might put any finger of his hand through them, with rings of golde and stone hanging thereat, the euill fauoured sight of their faces made our men to muse.

Cortez communed with them by his interpreter Marina, to knowe from whence they were, they aunswered, that they were dwellers in Zempoallan, a Citie distant from thence one dayes iourney, situated vpon a riuer side, and bordered vpon the Countrey of Mutezumazia, and that their Cazike or Lord had sent them, to see what Gods were come in those Teucallis, that is to say, temples, saying, also that they durst not come soner, not knowing what people they were.

Cortez made much of them, and shewed a cheresull countenannce vnto them, for they seemed very bestiall, he declard vnto them that hee was glaude of their comming, and to knowe the good will that their Lorde bare vnto him, and gaue them haberdash toyes, and shewed them the horses and armoor, a strannge sight to them. And so they went through the armie looking and gazing here and there as men amazed. And in all the time they abode there, they vsed no conuersation with the other Indians. Cortez enquired of Marina the cause thereof, and she said, that those men did not only speak an other language, but also did appertaine to another Lord, who was not vassall to Mutezuma, but by force and extortion.

Cortez was verie glad of that newes, for hee coniectures

thevvest India.

lectured by the talke of Teudilli, that Mutezuma had warres and enemies, wherevpon hee toke aside three of those Indians which semed most wysest, and demaunded of them by Marina, what Lordes there were in that Countrey: they aunswered that Mutezuma was Lorde ouer all, although in euerie Citie and Prouince was a Lorde, yet neuerthelesse all in generall did pay tribute and serue him as vassals, nay rather like slaues. But yet many of them of late dayes did reknowledge him by force of armes, and payde vnto him such tolls and tribute that they were not accustomed to pay, of which number their Lorde of Zempoallan was one of them, and other his neighbours, who many times helde him warre, to be fre from his tyrannie and bondage, but yet sayd they, it preuayled not, for his host was great and his warriours valiant.

Cortez receyued great pleasure to finde in that Countrey dissention and discord among some noble men, and diuision among themselues, thinking thereby the better to bring his purpose to passe. He gaue thankes vnto those Indians for their aduise, offering vnto them his fauour, helpe and friendship, praying them to come often to his campe: and so toke his leaue of them with his commendations to their Lorde, and sent his certaine presents with aduertisement, that shortly he would come and se him, yea, and also serue him, &c.

How

The Conqueſt of

How Cortez went to ſuruey the countrey with foure hundred men.

AT the end of tenne dayes came Teudilli backe againe, and brought certaine cloth of Cotton, and other things made of feathers, well wrought, for recompence of the thing ſent vnto Mexico. And warned Cortez to depart, for at that time there was no remedy to ſée Mutezuma, and to looke what was neceſſarie for his proniſion and furniture, and it ſhould be prouided, offering the ſame ſeruice at any time that hée ſhould happen to come that way. Cortez would not accept the offer, ſaying: That he would not depart from that Countrey, vntill he had both ſéene and talked with Mutezuma. The gouernour Teudilli yet againe replied, that he ſhould not contend therein, and with thoſe wordes departed from him. The next night following he with all thoſe Indians, as well men as women which attended to ſerue and prouide the Spaniſh campe, went from thence: ſo that in the morning all the cottages were emptie, where thoſe ſeruitors had béene.

Cortez ſuſpecting this alteration, prouided himſelfe with preparation for battel, and finding the matter contrary to his expectation, he deliberated to ſéeke a ſure road or harbor for his nauy, and alſo a good plot or ſituation to build vpon, for then he fully ment to obtaine perpetuitie, and to conquer the land, conſidering that he had found ſuch great tokens of gold, plate, & other riches, and there about within a whole league compaſſe, was ſo fit place for the purpoſe: for why? all was ſandy ground, & ſuch as toſſed to & fro with the wint, with other moriſh ground not méete for habitation. In conſideration whereof he ſent Franciſco de Mōteio, with two bergantines, and fiftie men, to runne along the coaſt,

the weſt India.

coaſt, vntill they ſhould finde ſome reaſonable poart and good ſcituation to build vpon.

Monteio proceeded on his voyage, and ſayled in ſight of lande, vntill he came to Panuco, without finding any port or harbour, ſauing the ſhadowe of a Rocke, which ſtoode ſomewhat diſtant from the lande a ſea-boord, ſo that at three weekes ende hee returned backe againe with the foreſayd newes. Hauing runne ſo little a way, he fell into ſuch terrible currants, that although hee made waye with oares and ſayles, yet the ſaide Currant forced him backe againe. Alſo he brought newes, that the Indians of that coaſt did let themſelues bloud, offering the ſame vnto them vppon little ſtrawes, in token of friendſhip or amitie.

The relation of Monteio contented not Cortez, yet notwithſtanding hee pretended to goe to the ſhade or ſuccoure of the Rocke, becauſe hee was enformed, that neare that place, was two faire Riuers, with ſtore of woodes, neceſſary for Timber and fire wodde, great quantitie of ſtones to builde with, faire paſtures, and grounde for tillage, although the harbour was not ſufficient for his Nauie and contratation, becauſe that roade was without defence, and open vppon the North, which is the winde that moſte ruleth with greateſt hurt vpon that coaſt.

And alſo conſidering that Teudilli and his menne were departed, fearing alſo the want of victualls, and likewiſe, that his Shippes mighte periſhe vppon the ſhore, hee commaunded to lade abourde all their ſtuffe, and hee with foure hundreth menne, and all his Horſes, followed on the hyghe waye that the Indians haue gone.

After hee had iourneyed three leagues, hee came to a faire vadeable Riuer, and paſſing ouer the Riuer, hee founde

founde a towne not inhabited, for the inhabitantes there
of were fledde with feare: he entered into a great houſe,
which ſeemed the place of the Lorde of the Towne, built
with timber and earthen walles, the foundation whereof
was raiſed with handie worke, about a fadome high: the
roofe was couered with ſtrawe, but of a faire and ſtraunge
workemanſhippe inwardes, with many great partiti-
ons, ſome full of pottes of honey, and Maiz, with other
graine which they keep in ſtore all the year: other roomes
had cloth of Cotten wooll, wrought with feathers, golde
and ſiluer.

 Cortez commaunded Proclamation to be made, that
none of his company ſhoulde take any thing away, vpon payne of death (onely victualls excepted) to the en-
tente to obtaine the good will and friendſhip among the
Indians.

 There was in that Village a Temple, which had
a little Tower with a Chappell on the toppe, and twentie ſteppes to come vnto the Chappell, where they found
ſome Idolles, and many bloodie papers, and much mans
blood of thoſe which hadde bene ſacrificed, as Marina did
certifie.

 They founde alſo the blocke whereupon they vſed to
cutte open the men ſacrificed, and the raȝours made of
Flint, wherewith they opened their breaſtes, and plucked out their hearts being aliue, throwing them vp toward Heauen as an offering, and after this done, they
annoynted their Idolles, and the papers they offered, and
then burned them.

 This ſight put a great compaſſion, yea and a feare a-
mong our Spanyards, who did beholde theſe things. From
this Village they went to other three or foure, and founde
none about two hundred houſes, and all without people,
yet well prouided with victuall, as the firſt towne was.

Cortez

the weſt India.

Cortez returned from thence to diſcharge his ſhips, and to take order to ſend for moe men: and with deſire to beginne habitation, in theſe affaires hee occupied himſelfe tenne dayes.

How Cortez rendred vp his charge and office with pollicie.

When Cortez was come where his ſhippes were, and the reſidue of his company, he began this talke, ſaying: Now my louing friendes and fellowes, ye doe ſee what great mercie God hath ſhewed vnto vs, in bringing vs ſafe and in health to ſo good and riche a Countrey, as by manifeſt ſignes and tokens we haue alreadie ſéene, yea and how plentifull of meats, inhabited of people, better cloathed, and of more iudgement & reaſon, then the others, which ye haue ſéene, ſince your firſt comming: alſo better buildings, fieldes of grain & corne: yea and it is to be thought, that the things not yet ſéene, do ſurmount all that hitherunto ye haue plainly ſéene. Wherefore we ought to giue moſt hartie thankes vnto God, and to begin our habitation here, whereas we ſhall enioy the grace and mercy of God. And to bring this matter to paſſe, me think beſt that we abide here, vntil we may finde a better port or ſcituation, Alſo that we make a wall or Caſtell for our defence, if néede ſhould happen, for the people of this land hath little ioy of our comming and abiding here.

It was then conſidered that from that place they might the ſooner haue friendſhippe and contraction with the Indians and Townes nexte adioyning, as Zempoallan, and others whiche were enemies to Mutezuma, and béeing in this order once placed, they mighte

K 2   diſcharge

The Conqueſt of

diſcharge their ſhippes, and ſende them incontinent to Cuba, Santo Domingo, Iamayca, Borriquen, and other Iſlandes, or elſe to Spayne for more men, armour and Horſes, and for clothing and victuals.

Pollicie.

Moreouer, it was thought iuſt and mǽte, to ſende relation of all their procǽdings to the Emperoure their king and maiſter, with the demonſtration of golde, ſyluer, and other riches, which they had in their power.

And becauſe all theſe things ſhould be done in good order, Cortez determined as captaine generall, to appoint a Councell, Aldermen, and Iudges.

And alſo ordeyne all other offices that ſhould be neceſſary and nǽdefull to rule & gouerne a Citie, which he then pretended to edifie and erecte, the whiche Magiſtrates ſhoulde fully commaund, vntill ſuch time that the Emperour ſhuld otherwiſe prouide in matters conuenient for his ſeruice.

After this diligence put in vre, he ſolemnely toke poſſeſſion of all the land, in ye name of the Emperour Charles King of Caſtill, with all the actes and ceremonies, as to ſuch a matter apperteyned. And demaunded of Franciſco Fernandez notarie appointed, that he ſhoulde giue vnto him by teſtimonie in writing, all the actes done therein.

A good ſubiecte.

All his company aunſwered, that they did very well allowe hys procǽdings and prayſed, and alſo approoned his determination, beſeeching him to procǽde accordingly, ſithence they were come to ſerue and obey hym. Then Cortez named Iudges, Aldermen, Attorney, Serieant, Notary, and Towne clarke, and all other officers apperteyning to the good gouernement of a Citie, in the name and behalfe of the Emperoure his naturall Lorde, and deliuered incontinent to the Iudges white robes to beare in their handes in token of Iuſtice, and named the name Citie to be builte, The riche Towne

De la

the weſt India.

De la vera Crux, becauſe that on gœdfriday they had entred into that land. After theſe things finiſhed, Cortez began before the ſaid Notary, another act in preſence of the iudges, who were Alounſo Fernandez Portocarero, and Franciſco de Mōreio, in whoſe hands he made ceſſion, and did deſiſt from all rule and offices whiche heretofore hee had receiued, which was his gouernerſhip, captainſhip, and generall diſcouerer, receiued in the Chauncerie of Santo Domingo, at the handes of the Preſidentes, who were there chiefe of the kings counſell, and Preſidents, likewiſe he proteſted not to vſe the power and authoritie of the gouernour of Cuba, Admirall of India, for ſo much that now none of them had any rule or gouernment in that Countrey which he and his fellowes had newly diſcouered, and begun to inhabite in the name of the king of Caſtill, as his naturall ſubiects. The which authoritie he likewiſe required to be ſet downe in record, and to haue a copie of the ſame.

How the Souldiers choſe Cortez for Captaine Generall, and chiefeſt ruler in Iuſtice.

Ll the new Officers toke poſſeſſion and charge of their Offices, and entered into the Towne-houſe to counſell, according to the vſe and cuſtome of Caſtill. In the which congregation or counſel then holden, many matters were had in queſtion as touching the good gouernemente of the Commonweale. And among many other things, they all agreed to elect Hernando Cortez for Captaine generall and chiefe Iuſtice, and to giue vnto him full power and authoritie

K 3 for

The Conquest of

for all matters appertaining to the warres and conquest, vntill such time as the Emperour should otherwise prouide: with this determination the next day following all the Aldermen, Judges, and Counsellers, went vnto Cortez, and said vnto him: Sir, we haue great neede of a guide and captaine for the warres, to proceede vppon the conquest of this coûtrey, wherfore vntill such time as the Emperour shall prouide therein, they all besought him to accept that office and charge, approuing him a man most fit for the same, both to rule & gouerne, for the great experience that they had seene of his courage, wisedome, and policie, and by vertue of their offices, did commaund him to accept the same, saying, that in so doing, God and the king should be faythfully serued. And they woulde thankfully gratifie the same, knowing that at his handes they should be ruled with iustice, vsed with humilitie, and bee preserued with diligence and strength. And for that purpose, they had chosen him for that office, giuing vnto him their full & whole authority, submitting theselues vnder his hats, iurisdiction & defence. Cortez accepted the charge at smal entreating, for he desired nothing so much.

And being in this sort elected general, the councell said vnto him. Sir you do wel vnderstand, that vntil such time as we shall be better planted in this countrey, we haue not wherwith to maintaine our selues but only with such things as are abord our ships. Therefore it may please you to commaund it to be brought a shore, and that you take therof what shall seeme good vnto you, for your houshold and familie, and the residue may be taxed at a reasonable price, & so to be diuided among them: and for payment they would al bind themselues, or else ŷ presently it should be deducted out of the stocke, after that the kings fift part were subtracted. Likewise they desired him to value his ships and artillerie, because they would make

like

the weſt India.

like payment for the ſame, and that from thence forwards the ſhippes ſhould ſerue in common, for to paſſe to the Ilands for bread, wine, clothes, weapons, horſes, and other things which ſhould be needful for the new towne and army, for thereby they mought bee better cheape prouided then if merchaunts ſhould prouide them, conſidering alway they ſeeke for exceſſiue gaine, ſaying that if it would pleaſe him to accept this offer and requeſt, they woulde thankfully requite the ſame. Cortez anſwered, that at the time he made his preparation and furniture in Cuba, hee ment not to ſell his prouiſſion as others vſed to do, but he woulde and did franckely giue it vnto them, although hee had ſpent his goods and indebted himſelfe therin. And incontinent hee commaunded the maiſters of the ſhips and purſers, to bring a land al their victual to the town houſe, requiring the Aldermen to diuide it equally, to euerie man his part, without making any difference of him or of any other, for (quoth he) in time of neede of victualls the yongeſt hath as much allowaunce as the eldeſt. And although I am indebted and do owe more then ſeuen M. Duckets, I giue this victuall all franckly vnto you. And as concerning the ſhips, I wil do that which ſhall be moſt conuenient for you all. And (quoth he) I will determine nothing to be done with them, but will firſt giue you aduertiſement of the ſame.

All this did Cortez for to get their loue and fauour, becauſe there were many that loued him not, although in very truth he was of his owne nature liberall and large in experience with all his ſouldiers in the warres.

The

The Conqueſt of

The receyuing of Cortez into Zempoallan.

Oɀ as much as the ſituation there was not conuenient to place the newe woɀke, they determined to goe from thence, to Aguiahuiztlan, which ſtandeth neare the ſhadowe of the rocke that Monteio had infourmed them of, whereupon Cortez commaunded the Shippes to depart foɀ that place. And hée with his foure hundɀed men and hoɀſes would goe by land, and there méete them, which may be about ten leagues iourney. In this oɀder the fléet departed, and likewiſe Cortez with his company toward Zempoallan, which ſtode directly weſtward, and after he had iourneyed thɀée leagues, he came to the riuer which diuided the Loɀdſhip of Mutezuma and Zempoallan, and could finde no paſſage, wherefoɀe hee was foɀced to returne to the ſea ſide, where with much a toe they paſſed ouer, and ſo trauelled on that ſide of the riuer, and found cottages of fiſhermen, and other poɀe houſes, and ſome ſowne ground, and pɀocéeding on their iourney, at length they came into very faire valleys, where was great ſtoɀe of deare, and ſtill they went along the riuer ſide, hoping to finde ſome good towne, and in ſhoɀt ſpace, they eſpied neare twentie perſons vppon the top of an hill. Cortez commaunded foure of his hoɀſemen to fetch them vnto him, willing them to make ſigns of peace vnto them, but if they flie (quoth he) then follow them, vntill you ouertake them, foɀ they ſhall ſtand vs in ſtead, as well to leed vs the way, as to ſerue vs foɀ enterpɀeters.

The

the weſt India.

The horſemen tooke on their way, and when they came to the hill toppe, they made ſignes of peace vnto them, but the poore and fearefull Indians fledde with ſpeede, yea being amaſed and in great feare to beholde ſuche a monſtrous thing as a horſeman, beleeuyng aſſuredly, that horſe and man was one thing incorporate, but in theyr flight they were ſone ouertaken, and they yeelded themſelues, and ſo were all brought vnto Cortez. *Simplicitie.*

Theſe men had in their eares and noſes bored holes, with ringes of golde hangyng thereat, for ſo was the vſe of Zempoallan: they enformed Cortez that the Citie was neare at hande. Cortez demaunded the cauſe of their commyng thither, they anſwered, to behold and ſee ſo ſtraunge a ſight, but why fledde you then (quoth he?) for feare only ſir ſayde they, of people which he knew not. Then Cortez willed them to put all feare aſide, and tolde them that he with his ſmall company woulde goe vnto their Citie to viſite their Lorde, and to be acquainted with him: the Indians ſayde, that the day was farre ſpent, and that it was late to goe that night to Zempoallan, but if it pleaſed him they would conduct him to a village whiche ſtode on the otherſide of the Riuer and within ſight, and although it were but a ſmall village, yet there was reaſonable lodging with meate ſufficiente for his armie: their counſell ſeemed well, ſo they wente to that village, and when they were comen thether, the Indians craued licence to goe to aduertiſe their Lorde how the ſtraungers abode in that place, promiſing to returne the nexte day with anſwere. Some of the Indians had licence to do the meſſage, the others abode there, attendyng and prouiding for the newe geſtes, & in this order they were al lodged and their ſupper abundantly prouided. That night Cortez fortified himſelfe as ſtrong as mought be, and the nexte morning came a hundreth men laden with Hennes, ſaying that

L they

The Conqueſt of

their Lord much reioyced at their comming, and becauſe he was ſo groſſe and vnwealdie, hee came not perſonally vnto him, but yet notwithſtanding he aboade in the cittie expecting his comming. Cortez friendly welcomed them, and with that preſent, hee and his company brake their faſte, and then proceeded with his guides in good order, with two fauconets in readineſſe, if néede ſhould happen: and from that paſſage of the Riuer they had a faire way vntill they came to another Riuer, which being likewiſe waded ouer, they diſcried Zempoallan, which ſtood a myle diſtant from them, all beſet with faire Orchards & Gardens, very pleaſant to behold: they vſed alwaies to water them with ſluſes when they pleaſed.

There proceded out of the Towne many perſons, to behold and receiue ſo ſtraunge a people vnto them. They came with ſmiling countenãce, and preſented vnto them diuers kindes of Floures, and ſundry fruites, which none of our men had heretofore ſéene. Theſe people came without feare among ye Ordinance, with this pompe, triumph and ioy, they were receiued into the Citie, which ſéemed a beautifull Garden: for the trées were ſo gréene and high, that ſcarcely the houſes appeared.

At the Citie gate ſtode many graue perſons of noble litie, as Magiſtrates of the Citie, who ſolemnely welcomed the ſtraungers. Sixe Horſemen, which haude gone before the army to diſcouer, returned backe as Cortez was entring into the Cittie, ſaying, that they had ſéene a great houſe and Court, and that the walles were garniſhed with ſiluer. Cortes commaunded them to procéede on, willing them not to ſhewe any token of wonder of any thing that they ſhould ſée. All the ſtréetes were repleniſhed with people, which ſtode gaping and wondering at the horſes and ſtrangers. And paſſing through a great market place, they ſaw on their right hand, a great walled

Men's folly with a great lie.

the weſt India. 75

ted houſe made of lyme and ſtone, with loupe holes and towers, whited with plaiſter that ſhined like ſiluer, being ſo well burniſhed and the ſunne gliſtering vpon it. And that was the thing that the Spaniards thought had bene walles of ſiluer. I doe beleeue that with the imagination and great deſire which they had of golde and ſiluer, al that ſhined they déemed to be the ſame mettall.

Within this great houſe was a long rew of lodgings, and on the other ſide ſix or ſeuen Towers one higher than another. They procéeded on, diſſimulyng the errour of the ſiluer walles, and followed their guide vntill ſuche time as they came to the Lordes lodging, who came forth accompanied with many auncient perſons, & better attired then the other Citizens were, with two Gentlemen that ledde him by the armes. They ſaluted eche other according to the vſe of their coūtreys, and then entred into the pallaice, where certaine principall men conducted Cortez and all his traine to their lodgyng, & Captaine Cortez was lodged in ye houſe which had the glittering walles, ſituated in the markette place, whiche houſe was ſufficient for him and all his companye. And when they were placed, and behelde the walles, they were aſhamed of their owne folly: for where they thought thoſe walles had bene adorned with ſiluer, they found them cleane contrary. Cortez deuided his men, cauſed his horſes to be trimmed, & planted his ordinance at his doze, making himſelf as ſtrong as though he had bene in campe and nere his enimies. And commaunded, that none of his men ſhoulde goe out of the houſe without his expreſſe licence vpō paine of death. The officers of the Lord prepared a plenteous ſupper for them, and bedding according to their vſe.

A vigilant Captaine.

L.2   The

The Conqueſt of

The talke that the Lord of Zempoallan had with Cortez.

He next day in the morning came the Lorde, to viſite Cortez with an honorable company, and preſented vnto him many garments wrought of Cotten woll, according to their faſhion, with a knot on y͗ ſhoulder like vnto the Egiptian garments, and certaine iewels of golde that might be worth two thouſand Ducates, beſéechyng both him and his company to recreate themſelues and take their reſte, and at that preſent he meante not to trouble him with any matters: And ſo toke his leaue for that time as he had done the day before, willing him to demaund and call for any thing that he ſhould néede. Cortez gaue him hartie thankes and ſo departed.

Then came moe Indians in number then there were Spaniardes, with their courſes & ſernice of meate ready dreſſed, and many boughes of daintie fruits. In this ſorte they were feaſted & banketed fiftéene daies moſt plétiouſly. The next day following, Cortez ſent vnto the Spaniards certaine olde garments of the Spaniſhe faſhion, and many other trifles, beſéeching him to appoynt a day of conference at his owne pallayce: word was ſent agayne that he was ready and very well contented. Whereupon Cortez toke with him fiftie of his men all armed, and left the reſidue at his lodging in a good readineſſe, and appoynted an vnder Captaine to gouerne them. The Lorde hearing of his comming, came out of his Courte into the ſtréete to receiue him. And hande in hand they entred togither into a lowe hall, whiche they vſe for the extremitie of heate in that countrey, the plotte that they buyld vpon, is raiſed a fatome from the grounde, ſo that they aſcende

vpon

the vveſt India.

vpon ſteppes, and the walles plaiſtred with verie white lime, their tile is either of ſtraw, or leaues of trées, very beautifull and ſtraungely wrought, and a good defence againſt the raine. The Lord and Cortez ſate them downe vpon thrée footed ſtooles, made all of one péece, the Lorde commaunded his ſeruitours to ſtande aſide, and by their interpreters they began to commune of their affayres a great ſpace, in demaunds and anſweres, becauſe Cortez deſired to bee well inſtructed of the affayres of that countrey, and likewiſe of that mightie king of Mutezuma.

This Cacike or lord, although he were huge and laden with fleſh, yet in his demaundes and queſtions ſeemed verie wiſe. The ſumme of all Cortez his talke, was to ſhewe the cauſe of his comming thither, and who had ſent him, euen as he had done in Tauaſco to Teudilli, and others.

This Cacike after he had heard Cortez attentiuely, he began a long communication, making his complaint, and opening his griefe in this ſort.

Mightie Sir, my Anceſtors liued a long time in great peace, libertie and quietnes, but of late yéeres my countrey and Citie was deſtroyed by tyrannie, becauſe the Lords of Mexico Tenuchtitlan with their men of Culhua, did not only vſurpe my citie, but alſo my lands by force of armes, in ſuch ſort that my power coulde not reſiſt them. And in the beginning thoſe Princes began their vſurpation by way and colour of religion and holineſſe, and afterwards with force of armes, and with this title became Lords ouer vs. *The Indians complaint.* *Vnder colour of holineſſe.*

And nowe we ſéeing our errour, haue thought it too late to preuaile agaynſt them, to take away our yoke of ſeruitude and bondage, although wée haue attempted it. And as often as wee haue ſo done, ſtill the victorie was theyrs, and the ouerthrow ours. Nowe all ſuch as doe

L 3 ſubmit

The Conquest of

submit themselues vnto them, are taxed with certaine tributes, and reknowledging them for Lordes, are defended by them, and esteemed as friends. But if after such submission made, any chaunce to speake agaynst them, or rebell, then they are terribly corrected, yea murthered, and after Sacrifice made to the Goddes of warre, called Tezcatlipuca and Vitzilopuchtli of their carkasses, then is their flesh eaten in banquet, & those who remaine aliue, doe serue for slaues, yea, and the Fathers, Mothers and children, are compelled to labour and toile from the Sunne rising, to the Sunne setting, with confiscation of all their goods and landes. And besides all this crueltie and vituperie, they send their officers and Sergeants, to execute the premisses, who without eyther pitie or mercie, many times suffereth them to sterue with hunger. And beeing thus cruelly punished of Mutezuma, who now raigneth in Mexico, who would not suffer to bee Vassall willingly to so good a Prince as you enformed me of the Emperour, although it were but onely to bee free from such vexation and robberie, which such a mightie King coulde doe. And with these wordes the teares gushed out of his eyes, and pawsing a while, he began to extoll the strength, magnificense and situation of Mexico, planted in a great lake of water; also he exalted the riches, Court, Maiestie, and mightie power of Mutezuma. Hee sayde also howe Tlaxcallan, Huexocinco, and other Prouinces thereabout, as also the people called Totonaquez of the Montaines, were of contrarie opinion to the Mexicans, yea enemies vnto them, who had intelligence what had happened in Tauasco. Yea, sir (quoth he) if it please you, I will treate such a compact with this people, that Mutezuma with all his power shal not preuaile against vs.

Cortez reioyced in heart to heare this newes, and

the vvest India.   79

ſaid vnto him. It grieueth me to heare of the euill vſage of Mutezuma toward his Countrey and ſubiects. But I aſſure you with Gods helpe I will deliuer you, yea, and reuenge all your iniuries, for my comming hither is to take away all euill cuſtomes, and to helpe the oppreſſed, to fauour the priſoner, and comfort the afflicted, and chiefly to aboliſh tyrannie. And for the good entertainment that I haue receyued at your hands, I remaine yours to doe you any pleaſure, and to defend you againſt your enemies, and the like will I doe for your friends, wherefore I pray you aduertiſe them thereof, as many as are of our confederacie.

Cortez then tooke his leaue, ſaying that he had bene many dayes there, and that hee had great neede to goe viſite his ſhippes, and men, who much deſired his returne, and aboue in Aquiahuiztlan, where hee meant to ſoiourne for a certaine ſeaſon, and from thence dayly they might conferre of their affayres. The Lords of Zempoallan ſayde, that if it pleaſed him to abyde with him, hee would gladly accept it, and if his buſineſſe were ſuch that he might not, that then he beſought him to remember him.

Then the Lord commaunded eight maydens to be called, who were very well apparelled after their maner, their attire was much like the Moriſca faſhion, (the one of them was more coſtly apparelled then the others) and ſaid vnto Cortes, all theſe maydens which you here ſee are gentlewomen, noble and rich, and this maiden which is beſt attyred, is a Ladie of Maſſa's, and my brothers daughter, I doe preſent her vnto you (meaning that Cortez ſhould marry her.) And the others you may beſtowe vpon the Gentlemen in your companie, in a token of perpetuall loue and friendſhip.

Cortez receiued the preſent with thankes, becauſe hee
                                                    would

The Conquest of

would not offend the giuer thereof. And so departed with their women riding behind them, with many Indian women to wait vpon them, and many Indian men to beare them companie, and to purney all things necessarie.

Things that happened to Cortez in Chiauiztlan.

The same day that they departed frō Zempoallan, they came to Chiauiztlan, and yet the ships were not arriued. Cortez marvelled at their long tarrying in so short a iourney. There was a village within shot of a hargabush, from the rocke called Chiauiztlan, standing vpon a hill. Cortez hauing little to do, went thither with his men, and the Indians of Zempoallan, who certified Cortez that the village was apperteyning to a Lord oppressed by Mutezuma. They came to the foote of the hill, without sight of any man of the towne, except two, that Marina vnderstoode not, and going vp the hill, the horsmen to fauour their horses would alight, because the ascending was cragged and euill way. Cortez commaunded that they should not alight, because the Indians should thinke that there was no place high nor lowe, but that these horses shoulde and coulde come vnto it. So by little and little they came into the towne, and finding no creature there, they feared some deceyte, yet approching further, they met with twelue auncient men, which brought with them an interpreter, who vnderstoode the language of Culhua and the speach of that place, which is the language of the Totonaquez, or inhabitauntes of the Mountaines. These auncient menne declared that the cause of their going out of the

the west India.

the towne, was because that they had neuer séene anye such men as the Spaniardes were, nor yet heard that any such had passed that way, wherefore with feare they had fledde from thence. But (quoth they) when the Lord of Zempoallan aduertised vs, how you did hurt no bodye, but rather being a people good and peaceable, then wée were well assured who ye were, when we saw you come toward vs. And wée are nowe comen vnto you on the behalfe of the Lord, to bring you to your lodging.

Cortez gaue them thankes, and went with them to a certaine place where the Lorde was abyding their comming well accompanyed: he shewed vnto the Christians great good wil, and maruelled to sée those straungers with their long beardes.

The Lord tooke a little chafingdishe in his hande, and cast into it a certaine gum which sauoured in swéete smell much like vnto frākinsence. And with a sencer he mocked Cortez, with the ceremony they vse their salutations to theyr gods and nobilitie. *A straunge salutation.*

This done they set them down, and Cortez enformed him of the cause of their comming into that country, as he had done in all other places where he had bin. *A straunge hap.*

The Cacike certified Cortez euē as the Lord of Zempoallan had done, but he stood in great feare lest Mutezuma shoulde be offended for receyuing and lodging him within that towne, without his commaundement, and being in this communication, sodeinly appeared twentie men entring where they sate, w certain wands like cudgels in their hāds, which did signifie ȳ they were rent gatherers, and in ech other hand, a fly flap of fethers, the Cacike & his company were sore afraide. Cortez demaunded wherefore he so altered himself, he answered, bicause these twēty Indians were collecters of Mutezuma, and that he feared that they would complayne of him, hauing founde those

Christians

The Conquest of

Christians there, hee feared likewise cruell punishment for the same. Cortes comforted him, saying that Mutezuma was his friend, and that he would so vse the matter that he should receiue no blame at all, but rather that Mutezuma should giue him thanks for that which he had done: And if Mutezuma did not, or would not so accept it, that then he wold defend both him and his subiects, for (quoth he) euery one of my mē is sufficient for a thousand Mexicans, as Mutezuma himselfe was well enformed by the late warres at Potonchan.

Yet for and notwithstanding all this talke, the Lorde and all his folke were in great feare, and meant to arise and to lodge the receiuers. Cortes would not suffer him, and because (quoth he) thou shalt see what I and my men can do, command thy seruaunts to apprehend and take prisoners these receiuers of Mexico, and I wil abide here with thee, in such sort that Mutezuma with all his power shall not offend thee.

With the courage that hee receiued at these words, he commaunded to laie hand vpon the Mexicans, and because they defended themselues, they were sore beaten, *The receiuers* and laide euery one in a seuerall prison, and bounde them *put in prison.* to a great poste, whereat they were tied by the throate, feete and handes, and being in this sorte imprisoned, they asked of Cortes whether they should kill them. Cortes requested that they should not be slaine, but that they might remaine as they were, with good watch, that they might not escape. Then they were brought into a hall in the Spaniards lodging, and were placed rounde about a good fire, but yet bound hand and foote with garde of watchmen. Cortes also appointed certaine of his men to watche the hall doore, and then went to his lodging to supper, where he and his company was wel prouided at the Cazikes furniture.

The

the weſt India.

The meſſages ſent by Cortez vnto Mutezuma.

The night being far ſpent, and the Indians that kept ye watch being aſleepe, Cortez ſent vnto the Spanyards that watched at the hall roze where ye priſoners were, and commanded them to let go two of the priſoners as ſecretly as they might, and to bring them vnto him. The Spaniards handled ye matter ſo well, that they fulfilled his deſire, and brought two of them to Cortes his chamber, who looked vpon them as though he had not knowen them, and willed Aguilar and Marina to demand who they were, and what they would haue, and why they had bin in priſon. They anſwered, that they were vaſſals of Mutezuma, and yt they had the charge to receiue certaine tributes, that thoſe of that towne and prouince paide vnto their Lord. And alſo (quoth they) we know not for what cauſe wee are now impriſoned and ſo cruelly vſed. We rather wonder to ſee this new cuſtom and malneſſe, for in time paſt theſe men were wont to meete vs & receiue vs with great honour & curteſie, ſhewing all ſeruice and pleaſure. Therfore we thinke that the cauſe of this alteratiō is through the fauour of you & your company, who beare ye name of immortality. We alſo feare leaſt our felowes which are in priſon ſhalbe ſlaine, before Mutezuma haue knowledge thereof. Alſo ſaid they, theſe barbarous people dwelling in the Mountains, wold be glad to rebell if they found any ſuccor or aide, only to put their Prince to coſt and charges, as heretofore they haue done. Therefore they made humbly beſought Cortes that hee ſhould not permit them and their fellowes to bee ſlaine,

Pollicie.

The Conquest of

nor yet to abide in the hands of their enemies wherein he should do singular pleasure to Mutesuma their Lord, and otherwise if they should perish, their Lord would be very sorrowfull that his olde, faithfull, and trustie seruaunts, should haue such a reward for their good seruice.

A wise man.

Cortez answered that it grieued him much, that Mutezuma his friend should bee misused where hee was, no nor yet his seruaunts euill entreated, and that he would haue as much care ouer them as of his owne, willing them to praise the God of heauen, and to be thankfull vnto him that had commaunded them to be set at libertie, in the grace and friendship of Mutezuma, he certified that in all haste they should bee dispatched for Mexico with certaine businesse, therfore (quoth he) get you to meate, and make you strong to take in hand that iourney, trusting to your féete, least ye should be taken againe to your great perill and daunger, Iwis their meate was soone eaten with the great haste they had to be gone.

Cortez brought them out of the towne and gaue them victuall to carry with them. And charged for the libertie and curtesie shewed vnto them, that they should signifie to Mutesuma their Lord, how that hee was his assured friend, and that after he had vnderstanding of his fame, goodnes and mightie power, he much desired to serue him, yea and that he helde himselfe happie, to finde himselfe of such a time and season to lose those his seruants, and to shew therein his good will, likewise he would do all that lay in him to preserue the honor and authoritie of so great a Prince as hee was, and also to defende his subiects, and to looke to his affaires as his owne proper, although his highnesse did little estéeme his friendshippe, as appeared by Teudilli, who departed from him without bidding him farewell, and likewise absenting all the people of the sea coaste, yet this notwithstanding hee would not

let

the weſt India.   85

let to doo him ſeruice at all times when occaſion ſhoulde ſerue, and to procure by all meanes poſſible his grace, fauour, and friendſhip, and that hee was fully perſwaded, that his highneſſe woulde not refuſe his good will and friendſhip, conſidering that with his acquaintance, God had done much for him, to meete with a ſeruaunt of the Emperours, for thereby he might know great ſecrets of holy things, and alſo receiue great benefites, if then hee wold refuſe the ſame, the fault ſhould be his: but yet notwithſtanding hee truſted in his wiſedome, that conſidering the thing well, he would be glad both to ſee him, and talke with him, and alſo to be friend and brother with the King of Spaine, in whoſe happie name, both he & his company were come thither. And as touching his ſeruaunts that remained in priſon, he would ſo vſe the matter, that they ſhould eſcape all perill, promiſing alſo to ſet them at libertie to pleaſure him, and that incontinent hee would haue done it, but onely becauſe hee would not offende the Lord of the Towne, who had friendly entertained him with great curteſie, for which cauſe hee woulde not preſume to controll him in his owne houſe, nor yet to ſhewe himſelfe vnthankfull. The meſſengers departed with this meſſage very glad and ioyfull, promiſing to accompliſh faithfully the charge committed vnto him.

The confederatie and rebellion done by the induſtrie of Cortez.

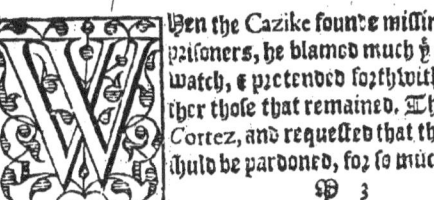

Hen the Cazike founde miſſing ye two priſoners, he blamed much ye guard or watch, & pretended forthwith to murther thoſe that remained. Then came Cortez, and requeſted that their death ſhuld be pardoned, for ſo much as they were

were but officers obedient to their lord and maister, and according to iustice they had committed no offence, nor yet deserued any correction in the fact, which was seruice to their King: but for so much as they shall not fare as the other two haue done, deliuer them vnto me, and I will take them to my custodie and charge.

Upon this request the eighteene prisoners were deliuered vnto Cortez, who sent them abord his Shippes, and there commaunded them to bee put in yrons. The Lorde and his counsellors fearing what might followe, entred into councell what was best to doe, considering that they certainely beleeued that the two prisoners which were escaped, would certifie in Mexico the shame and cruell entertainment done vnto them. Some replyed that it was iust and requisite to sende vnto Mutezuma his tribute, with other presents, to mittigate his anger, and to excuse them, and accuse the Christians, who were the causes of the apprehension of his officers, and to craue pardon of their errour and ouersight which they had committed as madde men, in dishonour of the maiestie of Mexico. Others answered againe, that it were much better to cast off that yoke of bondage and slauerie, and to giue no longer obedience to the Mexicans, who were both cruel and wicked tyrants, and also considering that now they had on their side those false Gods, and inuincible horsemen, saying likewise that they should not want many others their neighbors and borderers to help and succour them.

Diuers opinions in coūsell.

In this sort they resolued themselues fully to rebell, and not to lose so good an occasion, whereuppon they besought Hernando Cortez to be their defender and Captaine, considering that for his sake they had begun that enterprise, and whether Mutezuma should prepare his armie agaynst them or no, yet they on their part were
fully

the weſt India.

fully pretended to hold him warre, and to defiſt from ſervitude.

God knoweth how glad Cortez was to heare this matter, for he well weyed that it was the high way to his iourneys ende: yet diſſembling the cauſe, he anſwered that they would well looke to the thing which they meant to take in hand, becauſe (quoth he) I vnderſtande that Mutezuma is a mightie Prince, but if ye will valiantly proceede, I will bee your Captaine, and ſafely defende you, for I doe more eſteeme your friendſhip, then the good will of Mutezuma, which I nothing care for: therefore let mee knowe what number of men of warre yee are able to make. Sir (quoth they) among all our friends wee are able to make a hundreth thouſande menne of warre. I like that well (quoth Cortez) wherefore incontinent ſende your poſtes, with aduice vnto all your frientes in league agaynſt Mutezuma, and certifie them of this agreement and ſuccour of the Chriſtians, not (quoth he) that I ſtand in neede of your helpe, for I alone with my companie, are able to ſtande agaynſt thoſe of Culhua, although there were as many more, but reaſon required that they ſhoulde be warned of your pretence, and to be in readineſſe for the ſame, fearing leaſt Mutezuma might ſend his armie vpon a ſudden, and find you vnprouided.

With this aduice and encouragement of Cortes, and alſo they themſelues béeing a people heauie, and of ſmall conſideration, they diſpatched incontinent their meſſengers to al the townes and villages of neighbours and friends, aduertiſing them what they had determined, exalting the ſtraungers aboue the cloudes.

And by this meanes rebelled many Cacikes, and towns, and al the whole mountains, ſo that there was not left any collector or other officer in Mexico in al thoſe borders,

with

The Conquest of

with open proclamation of warres against Mutezuma, and all his adherents.

Cortez his intent was on the other side, to stir vp these Indians, to get both their goods, willes, and landes, for otherwise, he could not well bring his matter to passe: he only caused the officers of Mutezuma to bee taken prisoners, and to be losed againe, he fained a great loue to Mutezuma, and stirred his subiects against him, he offered to be their defendour, and left them rebelled, to the intent that they should stand in néede of him.

The foundation of the riche Towne called Vera Crux.

AT this instant the Fléete was arriued at the port, then went Cortez to visite them, and carried with him many Indians of the Rebels, both of ỹ towne, and also of Zempoallan, who did good seruice to cut downe timber, and to carry stones to the place appointed, for the building of the Citie, named the rich Towne of Vera Crux, according to the determination, when the officers were appointed for the same, and chosen in S. Iohn de Vlhua, and in good order made repertition to the inhabitants of the ground, and plottes to build vpon.

They appointed also a place for the high Churche, a Market place, a Towne house, a Gayle, store houses, a Kay or Wharfe, to lade or vnlade, a butcher row, & other places necessary to the good gouernement and pollicie of a Towne. They also drew out a plot to build the Castle or Fort on, neare the roade in a place conuenient, and in this sort began their worke, and their houses made with mudwall, for the earth there is good for that purpose.

And euery man being thus occupied in this new worke,

came

the West India.

came from Mixico two kinsmen of Mutezuma, with other foure graue learned menne for Councellours, and many seruing men that attended vppon them, as Ambas- *Embassadors.* sadors from Mutezuma, they presented vnto Cortez certayne cloth of Cotten well wouen, and feathers curiously and finely wroughte, other peeces of golde and siluer wrought, and a Casket of graines of golde, as they were founde in the Mynes not molten, which wayed altogether two thousand & ninetie Castlins, and said ȳ Mutezuma hadde sente him the golde in the Casket, to cure theyr disease, and woulde gladly knowe how they fared, giuing also vnto him most hartie thankes, for loosing his two housholde seruauntes, and preseruing the others from slaughter, beseeching him to make accompte, that he woulde doe the like in anye affayres of his, desiring him also to procure the libertie of the other eyghtéene Prisoners: and because those Indians hadde entertayned him well in their houses, he did parton theyr vproze, yet notwithstanding he knewe very well that they were suche a kinde of people, that in shorte space they woulde committe some other offences, whereby they might bée chastened for all together euen as a Dogge deserueth stripes. And as concerning the rest of his request, theyr Lorde was not well at ease, and also occupied in matters of warre of great importaunce, whereby at that presente, there was no remedie to visit eache other, but in processe of time his desire shoulde be accomplished.

Cortez welcommed them friendly and ioyfully, and also lodged them in Cottages néere vnto the water side, and sent forthwith for the Lorde of Chiautzclan, that had rebelled, who came at his commandement. Cortez sayd vnto him, lo sée what troth I haue vsed with thée, for Mutezuma dareth not to send any army, no nor yet displease anye

person

The Conquest of

person where I am. Therefore from this daye forwarde you and all youre lignage and frientes maye accompte your selues frée and exempt from the seruitude of Mexico, without rendering the tributes accustomed. He requested to set at libertie the prisoners, and to restore them to the Ambassadors of Mutezuma. This Cazike willed Cortes, to doe what pleased him, for saide he, euen as wée haue chosen you for oure Captaine, we will not excéede one iote of youre commaundemente: whereuppon hée returned home to his towne, and the Ambassadors toward Mexico, all pleased and content.

Nowe fame flew abroade, blazing that Mutezuma feared the Christians, whereupon all the Tetonaques prepared themselues for the warres, taking cleane awaie from Mexico, their tribute and obedience.

The Ambassadors departed form Cortes with theyr prisoners, and manye other thinges that were giuen them, of linnen, wollen, skinnes, glasse, and yron, being greatly amazed at the things which they had séene.

How Cortez tooke by force of armes Tizapansinca.

Ot long after ȳ these things had happened, the Indians of Zempoallan sent vnto Cortez, to desire him of succor against ȳ garisō of Culhua, which Mutezuma maintained in Tizapansinca, who did greatly anoy thē, in spoyling, burning, and destroying their corne in the fieldes, and flew their husbandmen, and toke many prisoners. The Towne of Tizapansinca, both confine with the Totonaquez and with ȳ grounde of Zempoallan, and is a good strong Towne, scituated
neere

the weſt India.

neere the Riuer, and hath a fort ſtanding vpon a high rocke. And becauſe this towne was ſtrong, and planted among them who were alwayes ſeditions and Rebelles, Mutezuma placed there his garriſon, who ſeeing the officers of receyuers and auditours come flying thither for helpe, being perſecuted of the rebels, they went out to paciſie the rebellion, and for to chaſten them, they burned and deſtroied whatſoeuer they found, and alſo had taken many priſoners.

Cortes hearing this newes, departed toward Zempoallan, and from thence in two dayes iourney with a great army of Indians Tizapanſinca, which ſtod eight leagues and more from that citie.

The garriſon of Culhua came into the field, thinking to haue had battell onely with thoſe of Zempoallan, but when they ſawe the horſemen, and the bearded men, they loſt their courage, and beganne to flie as faſt as they might poſſible: their ſuccour being neere, they were ſone in holte: they would haue entred into their Caſtell, but for the ſwiftneſſe of the horſes which ſtopped their way. *The valiant courage of Cortez.*

And when the horſes could not aſcend vp vnto the fort, Cortez alighted with other foure of his men, and among the preaſſe of the towneſmen got into the fort: and being within, they kept the doore till their companie came with many friends, vnto whom he deliuered the fort & towne, deſiring to doe no hurt to the inhabitants, but to ſuffer them to depart freely without weapon and ſtandard. It was a new world to thoſe Indians, who did fulfill Cortez his commaundement in all poynts. This done, Cortez returned againe to the ſea coaſt, by the ſame way which he had come.

This was the firſt victorie that Cortes had among the ſubiects of Mutezuma, whereby all the Mountaynes

M 2 remained

The Conqueſt of

remained free from the vexations of the Mexicans, and all our men with great fame and reputation, as well among their friendes, as among their enimies, in so much that afterwardes when any néede did happen among the Indians, they wold immediatly send vnto Cortez for one of his men, saying, that one man alone of the Chryſtians, was ſufficient to be their Captaine and ſecuritie.

This was a good beginning for the pretence of Cortez. Nowe when hee came to Vera Crux with his company triumphantly, he founde there Francisco de Salzeda, who was come with his caruell whiche he had boughte of Alóſo Caúallero, a dweller in Saint Iames de Cuba, and was left there to be grounded and dreſſed at his departure from thence. He brought with him .70. Spanyardes, and nine Horſes and Mares, wherewith they all marueilouſly reioyced.

The preſents that Cortez ſent to the Emperour for his fifte.

Cortez made great haſt in building vp the new town and the Caſtle, becauſe the Citizés and ſouldiers might haue ſuccoure againſte winde and rayne, and commoditie of houſhold, and likewiſe to be aſſured of defence againſte enemies if néedes ſhould happen, pretending likewiſe withall expedition, to enter within the land toward Mexico, to viſit Mutezuma, and to leaue in that new worke all thing in good order, he finiſhed many things, touching as well the peace as the warre.

He

the vvest India.

Hee commaunded to bee brought a lande out of his ships all the armour and other furniture for the warres, with the Merchandise, victuall, and other prouision, and to deliuer it to the rulers of the newe Cittie, accoding to his promise. He also signified vnto all his company that it was méete and conuenient, to sende relation to the King of all their proceedings and dealings in that countrey, with demonstration of Golde and Siluer there founde.

And (quoth he) to deale vprightly in this case, it is necessary to diuide equally our treasure to euery man his portion, accoding to the vse of the warres, the diuision being made, then first and principally lette vs deduct the Kings fift part. And for the better performance thereof, I do name and appoynt Alounfa de Auila Treasurer for the King, and also I do elect Gonſalo Mexia Treaſurer of the armie.

All the new Magistrates ratified his sayings, and allowed his discretion and wisedome, praising the election of the new officers as men most méete for such an office, and besought them to accept their charge.

This diligence done, he commaunded to bring forth into the market place all the goods and treasure whiche they had gotten, as well cloath of Cotten, Feathers, Golde, and Plate, which mought amount vnto in value the summe of 27000. Ducates: The same he caused to be deliuered vnto the newe elected Treasurers by account, requesting the whole counsel of the Cittie that they should make diuision thereof. The counsellours and communaltie replied, saying: Sir, here is nothing to diuide, for deducting the fift part which appertaineth to the King, all the rest shall be to make payment for the furniture which you prepared for this voyage, and you being satisfied, then the ships, munition and furniture, shall serue in common

The Conqueſt of

for vs all, beſeeching him with one aſſent to take all the treaſure, and to ſende vnto the Kings Maieſtie his portion or fifte part, euen as ſhould ſeeme moſt conuenient vnto him.

Liberalitie of Cortez.

Cortez replied and ſaide, that time hereafter ſhould ſerue to pay him according to their gentle offer: But for this preſent time my louing fellowes (quoth he) I will receiue no more then the ſhare or portion that apperteineth vnto my office of generall Captaine, and all the reſidue ſhall be for the Gentlemen of my company, wherewith ye may begin to make payment of your debts, which ye ought when ye made your prouiſion to come with me on this voyage.

And where I haue appointed certain things to ſend to the King, of more value then his fift part, it might pleaſe them, for as much as they were ſuch things as could not be well diuided, and likewiſe the firſt fruits of that Conqueſt, freely to giue him libertie to vſe his diſcretion in that onely poynt. They all in generall graunted to his requeſt, whereupon he tooke out of the Cocke, theſe things following.

Inuentarie.

Firſt the two wheeles of golde and ſiluer, which Heudilli preſented vnto him on the behalfe of Muteſuma.

A coller of gold of eight peeces, whereat hanged a hundreth and foureſcore and three little Emeraldes, and two and thirtie little redde Stones, like vnto Rubies,

the west India.

bies of small value: there hanged at the same coller se∣uen and twentie litle belles of gold, and certain heads of pearle.

Another coller of foure doubled twiste, with a hundreth and two Rubies, and a hundreth and seuentie and two Emeraldes, and tenne good pearles well sette, and for border, or fringe sixe and twentie belles of golde: both those collers were beautifull to beholde, and had many other fine things wrought in them, then is here decla∣red.

Many graynes of golde of the bignesse of a pease, euen as they were founde.

A Casket of graynes of golde of the same sorte.

A Helmet of woode champed with golde, and besette with stones, and the beuer fiue and twentie belles of golde, and vpon the toppe a grene birde, with his eyes, beake, and fete of golde.

A sallet of planches of golde, and belles rounde aboute it, decked with stone.

A bracelet of golde of small weight.

A rodde like vnto a roiall Scepter, with two rings of golde hanging thereat, garnished with pearle.

Foure forkes with three shephookes at ech, couered with feathers of sundry colours.

Many payres of shoes made of Deere skinnes, sowed with golde threede, and in the soales, were sette certains stones of colour white and blewe, which shined faire.

Sixe paire of Letherne shoes of diuers colours, garnished with gold, siluer, and pearle.

A Target of wood couered with leather, besett rounde a∣bout with belles of Latten, and the bosse in the midst was

The Conquest of

was planched with gold, and there was engrauen vpon the same Vitſilopuchthli, God of the warres, and also
foure heads set crossewise, which heades were of a Lion, a Tigre, an Eagle, and an Owle, very liuely made
with feathers.

Many skinnes of beast and foule, curried and dressed in
their feathers and in haire.

Foure and twentie targets of gold feathers, and set with
pearle, both curious and gallant to behold.

Fiue targets of feathers and siluer.

Foure fishes of gold well wrought.

Two birds called Auaues, and other birds of gold.

Certaine Hatches and a rod of latten.

Diuers loking glasses garnished with gold.

Many Myters and Crownes of gold & feathers, wrought
of many colours, beset with pearle and stone.

Many faire feathers of sundry colours.

Many tuffes of feathers adorned with siluer and gold.

A garment like a coape of cotten, wouen of sundrie colours, and in the middest a blacke wheele made of feathers.

Many surplices, vestments, palles, frontals and ornaments of Idols, Altars and Temples.

Many couerlets of cotten, of diuerse colours, which shewed like vnto vnshorne veluet.

Many shirtes, Jackettes, headclothes, and other naperie.

Many Carpets and hangings of cotten.

Al these things were more beautiful then rich, althogh
the wheeles were very rich, the workemanship of all the
rest, was more worth then the thing it selfe. The colours
of the cloth of cotten twol was exceeding fine, and the feathers naturall.

    The pounced worke in gold and siluer did exceede our
gold-

the weſt India.

goldſmiths, of which things we will write in an other place. They ioyned with this preſent certaine Indian bookes of figures which ſerue to their vſe for letters: theſe bookes are folden like vnto clothes, and written on both ſides. Some of theſe bookes were made of cotton & glew, and others were made of leaues of a certaine trée called Melt, which ſerue for their paper, a thing ſtraunge to behold. *Strange paper*

At that time the Indians of Zempoallan had many priſoners to ſacrifice: Cortez demanded them to ſend vnto the Emperour, but the Indians deſired him to pardon them, for if we ſo do (quoth they) we ſhall offend our gods, who will take away our corne, and children from vs, yea, and alſo our lines in ſo doing.

Yet notwithſtanding, Cortez tooke foure of them, and two women which were all yong and luſtie.

But it was verie ſtrange to ſée thoſe that ſhould be ſacrificed, how they wer trimmed and deckt with feathers, and went daunſing through the Citie, aſking almes for their ſacrifice & death. It was alſo ſtrange to ſée the offerings that were giuen them. They had at their ears hanging, rings of gold beſet with Turky ſtone, and likewiſe other rings at their lips, which ſhewed their téeth bare, a grieſely ſight to ſée, but yet eſtéemed among them a thing beautifull.

Letters from the armie and Magiſtrates of the new towne, directed to the Emperour.

Hen this preſent and fift part was layde aſide for the king, Cortez required ye magiſtrates to name and appoint two atturnyes, to carry the Emperors portion vnto Spaine. And that he for his part would giue

The Conquest of

giue vnto them his full power, and letter of attourney, with also one of the best Shippes for that voyage.

The Councell of the newe Towne chose Alonso Fernandez Portocarero, and Francisco de Monteio for that iourney: whereof Cortes was verie glad, and gaue them Antonio de Alominos for their pilot, with gold and plate sufficient for turne and returne of the voyage. Cortez gaue them instructions what they shoulde doe particularly for him in the Court of Spaine, as also in Ciuill, and the towne where he was borne. He sent to his Father and Mother certaine money, with newes of his prosperitie: hee sent also with them the ordinaunces and actes instituted, and wrote by them a large Letter to the Emperour, in the which hee gaue full aduertisement of all things, which hadde passed from the tyme of his departure from the Ilande of Cuba, vntill that day, and of the discorde betwéene him and Iames Velasques, and of their great trauaile and paines, with the great good will which they all bare vnto his royall seruice: hée certified likewise of the riches of that Countrey, with the Maiestie and power of Mutezuma.

Hee offered to bring in subiection vnto his royall Crowne and state of Castill, all that Empire, and to winne also the great Citie of Mexico, and to bring that mightie king Mutezuma to his handes quicke or dead. Beséeching the Emperours Maiestie to haue him in remembraunce when offices and prouisions shoulde bée sent vnto that newe Spaine latelye discouered at his great costes, and in recompence of his paines and trauell.

The Councell and Magistrates of Vera Crux wrote also

the weſt India.

alſo two Letters to the Emperour, the one was touching the ſucceſſe of their proceedings in his royall ſeruice. In that Letter, went onely the Aldermens firmes, and Iudges.

The other Letter was firmed by the generalitie and chiefeſt of the armie, the contents whereof was in ſubſtaunce, that they ſhould holde and kéepe that towne and Countrey wonne, in his royall name, or end their lines in the quarrell, if his Maieſtie did not otherwiſe determine. <small>A good proteſtation.</small>

They alſo moſt humblie beſought him, that the gouernement thereof, and of all that hereafter ſhould bée conquered, might bée giuen to Hernando Cortez their guide, generall Captaine, and chiefe Iuſtice by them elect and choſen, ſaying, that wel he had deſerued the ſame, for that he alone ſpent more then the whole armie vppon that iourney. And that it might pleaſe his maieſty to confirme that, which they generally of frée will had done for their owne ſafegard and ſecuritie, in the name of his royall Maieſtie.

And if by chaunce his Maieſtie had alreadie giuen the ſayde office of gouernement to any other perſon, that it might pleaſe him to reuoke it.

For ſo ſhould it be expedient for his ſeruice, and quietneſſe of the countrey. And thereby might bec excuſed, rumours, ſlaunders, perils, and ſlaughters, that might enſue, if any other ſhoulde gouerne and rule as Captaine generall.

And moreouer, they beſought his Maieſtie to graunt them aunſwere with breuitie, and good diſpatch of their Attourneys, who departed from the port of Aguihuiſtlan in a reaſonable ſhip, the twentie ſixe of Iulie. Anno. 1519.

D 2   They

The Conquest of

They touched by the way at Marien a port of Cuba, declaring that they went to Hauana: they passed through the chanell of Bahama without disturbance, and sayled with a prosperous winde, till they arriued in Spaine.

The cause why the generaltie had written these letters was, suspecting Iames Velasques, who had friends and great fauour in the Court and councel of Indians, and also some secret friends in Cortes his campe. For Francisco Salzeda brought newes that Iames Velasques had alreadie obtained a grant of the Emperour for the gouernment of that land, by the meanes of one Bonito Martinez going into Spaine. And although they knew not the certaintie thereof, yet it was most true, as shall appeare in another place.

An vprore among the sonldiers agaynst Cortes, and the punishment for the same.

There were some in the host that murmured against the election of Cortes, for therby was excluded Iames Velasques, vnto whom they bare good will.

Some were Velasques friends, and other some his kinsfolks, who letted not to say openly that Cortez by flatterie, subtiltie and gifts, had gotten and obtayned his purpose.

And that the dissimulation in making him selfe to bee entreated and prayed to accept that charge and office, was a thing craftily feigned, whereby such election coulde not bee of any value, and chieflye without any such authoritie of the Ierome Friers dame,

who

the vvest India.

who ruled and gouerned the Indians as chief presidentes: how muche more they hadde newes that Iames Velasques had already obtained the gouernement of that land, and Yucatan. Then Cortez began to vnderstand in those matters, and made information who had raysed vp this murmuration, and being knowne, he apprehended the chiefest, and sent them prisoners aboorde his Ship: and to mollifie their wrath, he shortly releassed them againe, the which afterwardes was cause of more mischiefe, for these his enimies woulde haue fledde with a Brigantine and killed the maister, pretending to flye vnto the Ilande of Cuba, for to aduertise Iames Velasques of the great present sent vnto the Emperour, to the intent it shoulde be taken from their Attorners passing neare the port of Hauana, with all the letters and relations of their businesse, because the Emperour shoulde not see it, to conceiue well of their proceedings. Then Cortez began to be agreued in earnest, and apprehended diuers of them, whose confessions being taken, the matter was manifestly knowen to be true, and thereuppon according to the processe, hée condemned those that were most culpable, and caused forthwith two of them to be hanged, who were Iohn Escudero, and Iames Cermenio pilot, and condemned Gonsalo de Vmbria, and Alonso Penate to be whipped, & incontinent execution was done, all the rest being pardoned.

    With this correction Cortez was more feared, and also estéemed, than before he was, for certainely if he hadde vsed gentlenesse, he shoulde neuer haue tamed them, yea and if he had not loked to them in time, he had béene spoyled: for their pretence was, to haue aduertised Iames Velasques, who woulde haue preuented them of their Shipps and present, and yet afterwarde he sente a Caruell after the said Ship, although it were too late.

Mischiefe.

Two hanged, and two whipped.

The Conqueſt of

Cortez cauſed all his ſhippes to be ſunke, and broken vpon the ſhore, a moſt worthy fact.

Cortez purpoſed to go vnto Mexico, and would not giue his Souldiers to vnderſtand it, becauſe they ſhould not refuſe the iourney, through the talke of Teudilli, eſpecially hearing that citie of Mexico was ſituated vpon water, which they imagined to be excéeding ſtrong, as in effect it was: to the intent that they ſhould all followe him, although againſt their willes, he determined to ſpoile all his ſhips, which was a ſtrange caſe, perillous, and a great loſſe. His intent thoroughly weyed, he little eſtéemed the loſſe of his ſhips to withſtand his men from diſturbance of his enterprize, for doubtleſſe they would haue ſtaied him, yea and rebelled, if they had knowen his mind and pretended purpoſe. He did ſecretly accord with one of the maiſters of his fléete, in the night ſeaſon to bore holes in them, that thereby they might ſinke, without any remedie to recouer them againe.

A famous fact.

Alſo he requeſted the other Maiſters and Pylotes to publiſh among the army, that the ſhips were ſo rotten and wormeaten, that they were not fit to go to ſea againe, and and that they ſhould, when they chanced to eſpie him and many of his Souldiers togither, come and certifie him openly of the eſtate and force of the ſaid Ships, becauſe that afterwardes they ſhould not lay any fault to his charge.

According to this inſtruction, the Pylotes and maiſters did accompliſhe his commandement: for ſhortly after, they eſpied him among a flocke of his companie, and then came they vnto him, ſaying: Sir, your nauie is

not

the vveſt India. 103

not to make anie moe voyages, by reaſon that they are all leake, and ſpoiled, rotten, and wormeaten, wherefore according to our duetie, we do certifie you thereof, to prouide therein as you ſhall ſee cauſe. All the Souldiers gaue credite to their tale, becauſe the ſhips had béen there more than thrée monethes. And after long talke about the matter, Cortes commaunded that they ſhoulde profite themſelues by them the beſt that they might, and as for Hulles, let them ſinke or runne aſhore, faining great ſorrowe for ſo great a loſſe, and want of ſuch prouiſion. And in this manner they let runne aſhore fiue of the beſt Shippes, ſauing their Ordinance, Uittailes, Sailes, Cables, Ankers, Ropes, and all other tackle: and ſhortly after they ſpoiled other foure veſſels, but that was done with ſome difficultie, becauſe they beganne to ſurmiſe the intent of Cortes, and beganne openly to ſay, Cortes meant to carrie them to the ſlaughter houſe. He then pacified them with gentle wordes, ſaying, what is hee that will refuſe the warres in ſo riche a Countrey? if there bee any of you that will leaue my companie, he or they may (if it pleaſe them) returne to Cuba in a Shippe that yet remaineth. And this he ſpake, to knowe how many were the cowardes, meaning in time of néede to haue no truſt or confidence in them. Then diuers ſhameleſſe perſons demaunded licence to returne to Cuba, but they were ſuche as tened no warres. There wer alſo others that ſaid nothing, who woulde gladly haue retourned, ſéeing the greateneſſe of the Countrey, and the multitude of the people, but yet they were aſhamed to ſhewe cowardiſe openlye.

Cortes knowing his ſouldiers mindes, commanded the other Ship to be ſunke, ſo that then they were all without hope to go out of that Countrey at that time, crafting
                                                                and

and praising the noble minde of Cortez shewed in that worthie fact. Certainly it was a déede necessary for the present time, and done by the iudgement of a stout Captaine, although hee lost much by his shippes, and abode without succour of the sea. There are fewe of these examples, which are not of valiant personages, as was Omiez Barbaroza with the cut arme, who a few yeares past brake seuen Galleys and Foysts, to winne therby Bugia, as largely I do write thereof in battailes of the sea in our dayes.

How the inhabitants of Zempoallan brake downe their Idolles.

Euery day seemed long to Cortez, with the desire to see Mutezuma. Hée now beganne to publish openly his iourney and departure, and chose out of the bodie of his hoste a hundreth and fiftie men, which hée thought sufficient to leaue for safegarde of the newe towne and fort, which was almost finished, and appointed Pedro de Hircio their Captaine, leauing with them two horses, and two small péeces of Ordinance, with many Indians to serue them, and fiftie Townes rounde about them in faithfull frientship and league, out of the which Townes they might alwayes haue at their néede fiftie thousande men of warre: and he departed with the residue of his Spanyardes towarde Zempoallan, which might bee foure leagues from thence, and was scarcely come to the Towne, when newes was brought him that foure Shippes of Francisco Garray sayled along his coast, and were in sight of Vera Crux. With this newes he returned incontinent with a hundreth of his men, suspecting euill of those shippes. At his comming to Vera Crux,

Newes for Cortez.

the weſt India.

Crux, his Captaine there enformed him both he had gone himſelfe to know what they were, and from whence they came, and what they would, but coulde ſpeake with none of them. Cortez being informed how they roade at anker, toke Captaine Hircio and certaine of his company to expect their comming aſhore, ſuſpecting them muche, becauſe they roade ſo farre off, being by ſignes and tokens willed to come into the Harbor. Cortez hauing wandered neare three miles, mette with three Spaiardes whiche came from the ſhippes, the one of them ſaide that he was a Notary, and the other two were to ſerue for witneſſes in their affaires, which was, to aſcite and notifie certaine writings, whiche they ſhewed not: and alſo to require Cortez by vertue of the ſame, to come and make repartitiō of that countrey with Captaine Garay their generall, for their ſaid Captaine pretented that conqueſt (as firſt diſcouerer of the ſame,) certifying moreouer that hee was determined to inhabite twentie leagues diſtāt from that place Weſtwarde, neare vnto Nahuclan, whiche now is called Armeria. Cortez anſwered, that they ſhould return vnto their ſhippes, and to will their Captaine to come to Vera Crux with his nauie, and there they would commune togither aboute his comming, and if he ſtode in néede of any thing it ſhoulde be prouided. And if it were (as they reported) that he was comen on the Kings affaires, he woulde gladly fauour his procéedings, conſidering that he and all his were there in ſeruice of his highneſſe, beſo muche more being all of one nation.

They anſwered, that in no wiſe their captaine nor none of his army would come aſhore, nor yet come where as Cortes was. With this anſwere Cortes vnderſtod þ matter, and layde holde of them, and went and placed himſelfe in ambuſhe behinde a little hill of ſande, whiche ſtode right ouer againſt the ſhippes, being néere ſunne ſet, and

P ſlepte

The Conqueſt of

ſtept there that night till day approched, and the morning farre ſpent, hoping that Garay his Pilote or ſome of his company would come aſhore, meaning likewiſe to apprehend them, for to be certified what courſe they had made, and what hurt they had done, and finding them guiltie, to ſend them priſoners into Spaine, likewiſe he deſired to know whether they had ſpoken with any vaſſals of Mutezuma, and ſeeing they came not a land his ſuſpition was the greater.

A wiſe practiſe.   Cortez commaunded three of his men to chaunge apparrell with the three meſſengers that came from Garay, and this done, cauſed them to goe to the ſea ſide, wauing with clokes, and calling for the ſhippe boate, now thoſe of the ſhippes thought by their apparel that they were their owne men, and came with a dozen perſons in the ſkiffe, with Croſſebowes and Handgunnes. Then Cortez his men which were cloathed in other mens garments, hid themſelues among buſhes, as who would ſay, they were gone into the ſhadowe, for to flée from the great heate of the Sun, being at that time high noone, and becauſe they ſhould not be knowne.

The Mariners of the Skiffe ſet a lande two men with Hargabuſhes, and other two men with Croſſebowes, and an Indian who went ſtraightway to the buſhes, thinking to find their fellowes. Then ſtept forth Cortes and caught them before they could gette abord the Skiffe, although they meant to haue defenſed themſelues, ſo that one of them who was a Pilote, hauing his Hargabuſhe readie charged, é wold haue ſhot at captain Hircio, and aſſuredly if his match and pouder had bene good he had ſlaine him. When the generall abord the ſhips perceiued this deceit, wold abide no longer, é commanded to make ſaile, not tarying for his ſkiffe. By theſe ſeuen men taken at two times Cortes was ſatiſfied, é alſo certified how captain Garay had

ſayled

the weſt India. 107

ſayled along the coaſt ſéeking Florida, and arriued in a riuer, the King of that prouince was called Panuco, where they founde little golde, bartering aboord their ſhippes, all their golde paſſed not thrée thouſande Caſtelins, but in exchaunge of things of ſmall value, nothing contented Garay on that voyage, becauſe the quantitie of golde was ſmall and not fine.

With this newes Cortez returned to Zempoallan with his men which he brought in his company: and there concluded and fully agreed with thoſe Indians, to pull downe their Idols & Sepulchres of their Cazike, which they did reuerence as Gods, perſwading them to worſhip the God of heauen. And after this doctrine their league of friendſhip was effectually eſtabliſhed, and with other townes adioyning againſt Mutezuma. Thoſe Indians gaue vnto him gages to bee alwaies faithfull of word and promiſe, and offered vnto him as many men fit for warre and ſeruice as he wold require. Cortez receiued the gages which were of the principalleſt perſons of the townes, as Mamexi Teuch, & Tamalli, he tooke alſo a thouſand Tamemes, that is to ſay, men that are carriers, who ordinarily taketh his burden vpon his backe which is halfe a hundreth waight, and thoſe fellowes followe the campe with their bag and bagage: Theſe men ſerued for horſes to draw the ordinance, and to carry other munition and victualls.

How Olintlec exalted the mightie power of Mutezuma.

Cortez departed from Zempoallan, leauing ye towne named Suillia, toward Mexico, the ſirtéene day of Auguſt of the ſame yeare, with 400. Spaniards and 15. horſes, & 6. péeces of ordinance, & 1300. Indians with the carriers & men of Cuba. And whē Cortez departed frō

Zempoallan,

The Conqueſt of

Zenipoallan, he had not one vaſſall of Mutezuma in his campe, to lead them the way toward Mexico, for al were fleode, ſeeing the new league, or elſe by commaundement of their Lord, & the Indians of Zempoallan knew not well the way.

The firſt three daies iourney the army paſſed through countrey of their friendes, and were louingly receiued and lodged, eſpecially in Xalapan. The fourth day they came to Sicuchimatl, which is a ſtrong place ſituated on a hill ſide very craggy, and the way to paſſe thereunto is made with force of mans hande as a ſtayre. And if the inhabitants thereof would haue reſiſted the entraunce, with great difficultie both footemen & horſemen mought haue entred the towne, but as afterwarde appeared, they were commaunded by Mutezuma to lodge them and alſo to honour them. The rulers of that towne ſaide to Cortez, that for as muche as he wente to viſite their Prince Mutezuma, he ſhould aſſure himſelfe that they were and would be his frendes. This towne hath many villages and farmes beneath in the playne, for Mutezuma was alwaies prouided there of 5000. men of warre.

Cortez gaue great thankes to the Lord for his curteſie and good entertainement, muche eſteeming the good will of his Lorde Mutezuma, and ſo departed from thence, and wente to paſſe ouer a mountaine very high, the paſſage wherof he named Nombre de dios, becauſe it was the firſt that he had paſſed, being ſo aſperous and highe, that there is none ſuche in all *Spaine*, for it conteined directly vpright three leagues, and hath in many places grapes and trees with honie. And diſcending downe on the other ſide of that hill, they came to a towne called Theuhixuacan, which is a forte and friende to Mutezuma, where our army was receiued and entertained as in the other towne behinde.

And

the west India.

And from thence he trauelled three dayes in a countrey inhabitable, and passed some necessitie of hunger, & much more of thirst, because all the water that they founde was saltish, and many of his men for want of other, dranke thereof, whereof they fell into sicknesse: and suddenly fell a maruellous haile, with great colde, which increased their grief, yea, and the Indians of their company thought there to end their liues, & some of the Indians of Cuba died there through nakednesse, not being accustomed to so cold a countrey. After the fourth iourney of euill way, they ascended vp an other hill, and vpon the top thereof, (to their iudgement) they found a thousande Cart loade of wood readie cut, neare to a little tower of idolles: they named that place the port of wood: and hauing passed two leagues from the port of wood, they found the Countrey barren, and poore, but soone after the armie came to a place which they named white Castell, because the Lords house was of stone verie white and newe, and the best that they had seene in all that countrey, and so curiously wrought, that they maruelled thereat: that towne in their language is called Zacloran, and the valley neere vnto it is named Zacatami, and the Lords name is Olintlec, who receiued Cortez honorably, and prouided for him and his company abundantly, being so commanded by Mutezuma, as he reported afterward.

And in token that he had receiued that commission from his Lord, he commaunded fiftie men to be sacrificed for ioy, whose blood they saw new and fresh. The Townes men of that towne caried the Spaniards on their shoulders, on such beares as we carry dead men to Church. Cortez enformed them (by his interpreters) of the cause of his comming into that countrey, as he had vsed in other places, and demaunded whether the Lord of this towne were tributry to Mutezuma. This Cazike being amazed

A strange ioy.

at

The Conquest of

at his question, answered, saying: VVhat is he that is not eyther slaue or vassall to the great Mutezuma. Then Cortez certified him, who and what the Emperour king of Spaine was, willing him to be his friend and seruitour, and further enquired if he had any golde to send him some. This Cazike answered that he would do nothing without the commaundement of his Lord, nor yet sende his king any golde although he had inough. Cortez, dissimuled the matter, and helde his peace, yet by and by he desired to knowe the Maiestie and mightie power of Mutezuma, the Cazik, aunswered, that Mutezuma was Lorde of the whole worlde, and that he had thirtie Vassals who were able to make a. 100000. men of warre: eche one of them he also certified that he sacrificed. 20000. men yerely to his Goddes: And also his dwelling was in the most beautifullest and strongest citie of all that euer was enhabited, likewise (quoth he) his house and courte is most greate, noble, and replenished with Gentlemen, his riches incredible, and his charges excessiue. And truely therein he saide the very troth, excepte in the sacrifice wherein he something enlarged, although the slaughter of men for sacrifice in euery temple was very great, yea and some holo opinion, that some yeres were sacrificed aboue. 50000. men. Being in this conuersation, came two Gentilmen of that valley to see the Spaniardes, and eche of them presented vnto Cortes foure women slaues, & certaine collers of golde of small price. Olentlec although he was vassall to Mutezuma, was a greate Lord, and had. 20000. vassals, and thirtie wiues altogither in his house, beside a hundred other women that attended vpon them. And had for his gard a houshold. 2000. persons, his towne was great, & had 13.temples in it, & eche temple many idolls of stone of diuers fashions, before whom they sacrificed men, doues, quailes, & other things w perfumes & great veneration.

the weſt India.

ration. In this place and territorie, Mutezuma had 5000 ſouldiers in garriſon, and ordinarie poſtes from thence to Mexico. Untill this time, Cortes had not ſo amplie vnderſtode the might and power of Mutezuma, yea and though many inconueniences, difficulties, feare, and ſuch like, did repreſent it ſelfe vnto him in his iourny to Mexico, which perhaps would haue amaʒed ſome valiant perſons, yet hee ſhewed not one iote of cowardiſe, hauing heard ſuch a report of that mightie Prince, but rather his deſire was ſo much the more to ſee him.

Conſidering now that he ſhould paſſe through Taxcallon, to go to Mexico, Taxcallon being a great & ſtrong Citie, and warlike people, he diſpatched foure Zeampoallanezes to the Lords and Captaines of that Citie, on the behalfe of Zempoallan and his owne, offering vnto them his friendſhip and fauour, giuing them to vnderſtande, that thoſe fewe Chriſtians would come vnto their Citie to ſerue them, deſiring thē to accept the ſame, thinking aſſuredly that thoſe of Tlaxcallon would haue done with him as the Zempoallanezes had don, which were both good and faithfull, who had alwaies vſed truth with him, euen ſo he thought that now he mought credit thē, for they had enformed him, that the Tlaxcaltecas were their friends, and ſo would be his, conſidering that they were vtter enemies to Mutezuma, and willingly would goe with him to the ſiege of Mexico, with deſire of libertie, and to reuenge olde iniuries and griefes, which they had ſuffered many yeares before of the people of Culhua. Cortez refreſhed himſelfe in Zaclotan fiue daies, where is a freſh riuer, and quiet folke, pulling downe the Idols, and placed a remembrance of Chriſt crucified, as hee had done in all the townes that he had paſſed.

He tooke his leaue of Olintlic, leauing him wel pleaſed, & went to a towne 2. leagues frō thence along the riuer ſide,

where-

The Conqueſt of

whereof was lord Iztacmixtlitan, one of the Gentlemen
who had giuen him the ſlaues and collers of gold.

This towne ſtandeth in a plain ground of two leagues
compaſſe, which is repleniſhed with ſo many houſes as
doth ſéeme to touch one another, in that way that our ar‐
my paſſed: and the towne it ſelfe doth containe fiue thou‐
ſand houſholdes, ſtanding on an hill, and on the one ſide
thereof is the Lordes houſe with a ſtrong fort, béeing the
beſt yet ſéene in thoſe parties, walled with good ſtone
with burbucan and déepe ditch. There Cortez reſted
himſelfe thrée dayes, abiding the foure meſſengers which
he ſent from Zacloton, to knowe the anſwere that ſhould
be brought.

The firſt encounter that Cortez had with the men of Tlaxcallan.

A ſtrange wall.

Cortez ſéing the long tarying of the meſ‐
ſengers, he departed frō Zacloton without
any intelligence frō Tlaxcallan. Our camp
had not marched much after their depar‐
ture from that place, but they came to a
great circuite of ſtone made without lime
or morter, being a fadom and a halfe high, & twentie foote
brode, with lope holes, to ſhote at: that wall croſſed ouer
all the vally, from one mountaine to another, and but one
onely entrance or gate, in the which the one wall dou‐
bled, againſt the other, and the way there was fourtie
paces brode, in ſuch ſort, that it was an euill and perillous
paſſage, if they had béen there to defend it. Cortez deman‐
ded the cauſe of their circuite, and who had built it;
Iztacmixtlitan that went to beare him companie, tolde
him that it was: but a diuiſſon from their countrey and
Tlaxcallan, and that their anteceſſors had made the ſame

to

the weſt India.

to diſturbe the entraunce of the Claxcaltecas in time of warre, who came to robbe and murther them, becauſe of the friendſhip betwixte them and Mutezuma, whoſe vaſſals they were:

That ſtrange and coſtly wall, ſéemed a thing of greate maieſtie to our Spaniardes, and moꝛe ſuperfluous then pꝛofitable, yet they ſuſpected that the Traxcaltecas were valiant warriers, who had ſuche defence made againſt them. And as Cortez and his army ſtoode beholding this woꝛke, Iztacmixtlitan thought he had bin afraide to pꝛocéede foꝛward, and pꝛayed him (foꝛ ſo much as he was his Loꝛdes friende) not to paſſe that way, noꝛ yet thꝛough the Countrey of Tlaxcallan, foꝛ ſo much as he wente to viſit his maiſter, foꝛ (quoth he) if they knowe you to be my Loꝛdes friende, they will ſéeke youre diſpleaſure, as they haue done to others, and I will pꝛouide you of guides to leade you continually thꝛough the dominion of Mutezuma, where you ſhall be well receiued and pꝛouided, vntil you come to Mexico.

But Mamexi and the others of Zempoallan willed him to refuſe that offer and counſell in any wiſe, alleadging that it was an onely pꝛetence to ſeparate them from the friendſhip of that pꝛouince, whoſe people were good, honoꝛable, and valiant, and that Iztacmixtlitans perſwaſion was, to pꝛohibite theyꝛ helpe and ſuccoure againſt Mutezuma, willing him earneſtly to giue no credite vnto his ſayings, foꝛ he and his allyes are falſe Traytoꝛs, and meante to bꝛing him into ſome ſnare, where they mighte kill both him and his company, and féede vppon their fleſhe.

Cortez foꝛ a ſpace was amazed at the talke of ÿ one and the other, but in concluſion he accepted the counſell of Mamexi, foꝛ that he hadde conceiued a better opinion of the Zeampoallanezes his allyed friendes, than of the others.

thers. And setting all feare aside, hee toke the way to Tlaxcallon, bidding Iztacmixtlitan farwell, & with thrée hundred souldiers on a ranke, he entered the way in the wall, and procéded in good order all the way forwardes, carrying the Ordinance readie charged, and hee himselfe the leader of all his army, yea and sometimes he would be halfe a league before them, to discouer and make the way plaine.

And hauing gone the space of thrée leagues from that circuite, he commaunded his fotemen to make baste, because it was somewhat late, and hee with his Horsemen went to descrie the way forwardes, who ascending vp a hill, two of the foremost horsemen mette with fiftéene Indians armed with Swordes and Targets and tuffes of feathers, which they vse to weare in the warres. These fiftéene were spies, and when they sawe the Horsemen, they beganne to flie with feare, or else to giue aduice.

Then approached Cortes with other thrée horsmen, calling to them to stay, but by no meanes they woulde abide: then fixe horsemen ranne after them, and ouertoke them, and ioyned all togither, with determination rather to die then to yéelde, shewing them signes to stand still, yet the horsemen comming to late handes on them, they prepared themselues to battayle, and fought, defending themselues for a while. In this fight the Indians slewe two of theyr horses, and as the Spanyards doe witnesse, at two blowes they cutte off a horse head, bridle and all. Then came the rest of the horsemenne, and the Armie approached, for there were in sighte neare fiue thousande Indians in good order, to succorre their fiftéene fighting menne, but they came to late for that purpose, for they were all slaine with the anger that was taken for the killing of the two

horses,

the weſt India.

horſes, and woulde not render themſelues in time: yet notwithſtanding their fellowes fought, vntill they eſpyed oure Armie comming and the Ordinance, then they returned, leauyng the fielde to oure menne, but our horſemenne followed them, and ſlewe about three ſcore and tenne perſons of them, without receiuing any hurt.

This done, the Indians ſente vnto Cortez two of the foure meſſengers which hadde bene ſent thither before with other Indians, ſaying, that the Tlaxcaltecas knewe nothing of the thinges that were happened, certifying likewiſe that thoſe with whome hee had foughte were of other communities, and not of their iuriſdiction, beeing ſorrowfull for that whiche hadde paſſed: and for ſo muche as it happened in theyr Countrey, they woulde willingly paie for the two Horſes whiche were ſlaine, praying them to come in good time to theyr Towne, who woulde gladly receiue them, and enter into their league of friendſhippe, becauſe they ſeemed to bee valiaunt menne: but all was a fayned and a falſe meſſage. *A ſubtil meſſage.*

Yet Cortez beleeued them, and gaue them thankes for their curteſie and good will, and that accoording to their requeſt hee woulde goe vnto theyr Towne, and accept their friendſhippe. And touching the death of his horſes, he required nothing, for within ſhort ſpace hee expected many moe: but yet God knoweth how ſorrowfull he was for the want of them, and not only ſo much for them, as that the Indians ſhoulde thinke that horſes could die, or be ſlaine.

Cortez proceded forwardes aboute twoo leagues where the horſes were killed, although it was almoſt ſunneſet, and his men wearied, hauing trauelled farre that day.

His will was, to haue pitched his Campe in a strong place of water: wherefore he planted his army by a Riuer side, whereas they remained all that night with good watche both of footemen and horsemen, fearing some assault: but there was no attempt giuen that night, whereby they might haue taken better rest, then they were aware of.

How there ioyned a hundred and fiftie thousand men against Cortes.

The next morning at Sun rising, Cortes departed with his army in good order, and in the midst of them went the farbage and artillerie, and as soone as they were come to a litle vilage there néere at hand, they met with the other two messēgers of Zempoallan, who departed frō them at Zaclotan: they came with pitiful chéer, exclaiming of the Captains of y power of Tlaxcallan, who had bounde them, and deteyning them from returning: but with good fortune, that night they hadde broken loose, and escaped, for otherwise in the morning following, they had bin sacrificed to the God of Victory, and after the sacrifice, to be eaten, for a good beginning of their warres, protesting the like to be done with the bearded men, and with as many as came with them.

They had no sooner tolde their tale, when there appeared behinde a littel hill about a thousande Indians, verye well appointed after their fashion, and came with suche a maruellous noyse and crie, as though theyr voyces shoulde haue pearced the Heauens, hurling at oure menne stones, dartes, and shotte with bowes and arrowes,

Cortes

the vveſt India. 117

Cortes made many tokens of peace vnto them, and by his interpreters deſired them to leaue the battell. But ſo much the more as he entreated for peace, the more haſtie and earneſt were they, thinking either to haue ouercome them, or elſe to holde them play, to the intent that the Spaniards ſhould haue followed them to a certaine ambuſh that was prepared for them, of more then 80000. men, which they had planted in a creeke of a riuer which abutted vpon the high way. Then our men began to ceaſe from wordes, and to lay hande vpon their weapons, for that companie of a thouſand, were as many, as on our ſide were fighting men, they were well practiſed in the warres, very valiant, and alſo pitched in a better place for fight. This battell endured certaine houres, and at the ende the Indians being either wearied, or elſe meaning to take our men in the ſnare appointed, began to flie toward their maine battell, not as ouercome, but to toyne with their owne folke. And our men being hote in the fight, and ſlaughter which was not little, followed them with all their carbage, and vnwares fell into the ambuſh among an infinite number of Indians armed, they ſtayed not becauſe they would not put themſelues out of order, and paſſed through their campe with great haſte & feare. The enemies began to ſet vpon the horſemen, thinking to haue taken their lances from them, their courage was ſo ſtoute: many of the Spaniards had their periſhed, had it not bin for the Indian friends. Likewiſe the courage of Cortes did much animate them, for although he ledde his armie making way, yet diuerſe times, he turned him backe to place his men in order, and to comfort them, and at length came out of that daungerous way into the plaine field, where the horſes mought helpe, and the ordinance ſtande in ſteede, which two things did greatly anoy the enemie to their great wonder and maruell, and

Firſt battell.

80000. men.

Second battel

Q 3   at

The Conquest of

at the fight thereof began to flie.

In both encounters remained many Indians flaine, and wounded, and of the Spaniards some were hurt, but none killed, giuing most heartie thankes vnto God for their deliuerie from so great a multitude of Indians their enemies, with much ioy and pleasure of the victorie. Then they went to pitch their campe in a Village called Teoacazinco, where was a little tower and a temple, and there fortified themselues, and buylt Cottages of bowes and straw. The Indians of Zempoallan, and those of Iztacmixtlitan, did play the valiant men that day, wherfore Cortes honoured them with hearty thankes.

This day was the first of September. The night following, our men slept not quietly with feare of inuasion of their enemies, but they came not, for they neuer vse to fight in the night season. And as sone as it was day Cortes sent to the Captaines of Tlaxcallan, to require them of peace and friendship, willing them quietly to suffer the passage through their Countrey to Mexico, for that they meant them no hurt but rather good will. This done, he left two hundred Spaniards, and the Carreis in the Campe. And toke with him other two hundred, with seuen hundred Indians, and went with them abroade to skirmish in the face of their enemies, and at that time burned fiue or sixe villages, and returned with foure hundred prisoners, without receiuing any hurt, although they followed him to his campe. At his returne he found the aunswere of the Captaines his enemies, which was, that the next day they would come and talke with him, and declare their mindes.

Cortez was well preuented that night, for the answer liked him not, but rather seemed braue, and a matter determined to bee bone as they had saide: likewise those which were taken prisoners, certified that his enemies were

The care of good soldiers.

the vveſt India.

were ioined togither to the nūber of 150000. men to giue 150000. men.
him battell the next day following, & to ſwallow thē aliue
whom ſo moꝛtally they did hate, thinking thē to be frieds
to Mutezuma, vnto whom they wiſhed all euil & miſchief.
It was moſt true that the Tlaxcaltecas had gathered
all their whole power to appꝛehend the bearded men, and
to make of them a moꝛe ſolemne ſacriſice vnto their gods,
then at any time heretofoꝛe they had done, with a generall banquet of their fleſh, which they called Celeſtiall.
The Captaines of Tlaxcallan deuided their ſouldiers into foure battels, ye one to Tepectipac, another to Ocutelul-
co, the third to Tizatlan, and the fourth to Quiahuiztlan,
that is to ſay, the men of the Mountaines, the men of the
Limepittes, the men of the Pinetrées, and the water
men, euery of theſe had their Lordes and Captaines,
whom they ſhould repaire vnto and obey, and all theſe
foure ſoꝛtes of men doth make the bodie of the common
weale and Citie, and alſo commaunde both in time of
warre and peace. So that euery of theſe Captaines had
his iuſt poꝛtion oꝛ number of warriors, but the general of
all ye whole army was called Xicotencatl, who was of the
Limepits: and he had the ſtandart of the Citie, which is a
Crane of gold, with his wings ſpꝛed, adoꝛned with Emeralds & ſiluerwoꝛke, which ſtandart is accoꝛding to their
vſe, either caried befoꝛe the whole hoſt, oꝛ elſe behinde the
all. The ſecond Captaine oꝛ Lieutenant was Maxixca-
zin, & the number of the whole army was 150000. men.
Such a great number they had ready againſt 400. Spaniards, and yet at length ouercome, neuertheles after all
this bꝛoile, they were moſt greateſt friends. Theſe foure
captains came wt their cōpany, that the fields where they
were, ſéemed a foꝛeſt. They were trim fellowes, and well
armed accoꝛding to their vſe, although they were painted
ſo, that their faces ſhewed like diuels, with great tuffes of
feathers,

The Conqueſt of

Indian armor. feathers and triumphed gallantly. They had alſo ſlings, ſtaues, ſpeares, ſwordes, bowes and arrowes, ſbulles, ſplents, gantlets all of Wood, gilt or elſe couered with feathers or leather, their Corſlets were made of Cotten wooll, their targets and bucklers gallant and ſtrong, made of woodes couered with leather, and trimmed with latton and feathers, their ſwordes were ſtaues with an edge of flint ſtone cunningly ioyned into the ſtaffe, which would cut very well, and make a ſore wound.

The hoſt (as is declared) was diuided into foure parts, their inſtruments of warre were hunters hornes, and drummes called attabals, made like a caldron, and couered with vellam. So that the Spaniards in all the diſcouery of India did neuer ſee a better army togither, nor better ordered.

The threatning of the Indian campe againſt the Spaniards.

Theſe Indians were great braggers, and ſaide among themſelues, what madde people are theſe that threatneth vs, and yet knoweth vs not. But if they will bee ſo bolde to inuade our Countrey without our licence, let vs not ſet vpon them ſo ſoone: it is méete they haue a little leſt, for we haue time inough to take and binde them, let vs alſo lend them meat, for they are comen with emptie ſtomacks: And againe *A preſent.* they ſhall not ſay that we doe apprehend them with wearineſſe and hunger. Whereupon they ſent vnto the Chriſtians thrée hundred Ginnea cockes, and two hundred baſkets of bread called Centli. The which preſent was a great ſuccour for the néede that they ſtoode in. And ſome after (quoth they) nowe let vs goe and ſet vpon them, for

by

the weſt India.

by this time they haue eaten their meate, and nowe wée will eate them, and ſo ſhall they pay vs the victuals that we ſent: likewiſe we wil know if Mutezuma commaunded them to come into our countrey, oꝛ who elſe. And if he ſente them, then let him come and deliuer them: and if it be their owne enterpꝛiſe, they ſhall receiue theyꝛ reward accoꝛdingly. Theſe and ſuch like bꝛagges they vſed, ſeing ſo fewe Spaniardes befoꝛe them, and not knowing their ſtrength. Then the foure Captaines ſente two thouſand of their valianteſt men of warre and olde Souldiers, to take the Spaniardes quietly, with commaundement that if they did reſiſt, either to binde them oꝛ elſe to kill them, meaning not to ſette their whole armie vpon them, ſaying that they ſhoulde gette but ſmall honour foꝛ ſo great a multitude, to fight againſt ſo fewe. The two thouſande Souldiers paſſed the trench that was betwixt the two Campes, and came boldely to the Tower where the Chꝛiſtians were. Then came foꝛth the Hoꝛſemen, and after them the footemen, and at the firſt encounter they made the Indians féele how the yꝛon ſwoꝛdes woulde cutte: and at the ſeconde, they ſhewed of what foꝛce thoſe fewe in number were, of whome a little befoꝛe they had ſo ieſted: But at the thirde bꝛunte they made thoſe luſty Souldiers fly, who were come to appꝛehende them, foꝛ none of them eſcaped, but onely ſuche as knewe the paſſage of the trenches oꝛ ditche.

Then the maine battell and whole army ſette foꝛth with a terrible and maruellous noiſe, and came ſo fierce vppon our menne, till they entred into our campe without any reſiſtaunce, and there were at hardye ſtrokes and wꝛaſtling with the Spaniardes, and in a good ſpace coulde not gette them out, killing many of them which were ſo bolde to enter: and in this ſoꝛte they fought foure howꝛes, befoꝛe they coulde make way among

A reckning made before the hoſte.

Battaile.

K their

The Conquest of

their enemies. And then the Indians began to faint, séeing so many dead on their side, and the greate woundes they had, and that they coulde kill none of the Christians: yet the battaile ceased not till it drewe nére night and then they retired. Whereof Cortes and his Souldiers were exceding gladde, for they were fully weried with killing of Indians, so that all that night our men triumphed with more ioy, then feare, considering that the Indians fought not by night, they slepte and toke their rest at pleasure, which they had not done till that time, but alwaies kept both watche and warde.

The Indians finding many of their hoste missing, yet they would not yélde themselues as ouercome, as after did appeare. They coulde not well tell howe many were slaine, nor yet our men had leasure to count them.

Cortez was a painfull man. The next daye in the morning Cortez wente forth to runne the fieldes as he had done before, leauing halfe his menne to képe the campe, and because he shoulte not be espied he departed before day, & burned aboute.x. townes, and sacked one towne, which was of thrée thousande houses, in the whiche were founde but fewe folke of fight, because the most of them were gone to their campe: After the spoyle, he set fire on the towne and came his way to his campe with a greate pray by none time. The enimies pursued thinking to take away their pray, and followed them into the camp, where they fought fiue houres and could not kill one Spaniarde, although many of their side were slaine: for euen as they were many and stood on a throng togither, the ordinaunce made a wonderfull spoyle among them, so that they left off fighting, and the victory remained for our men. The Indians thought that the Spaniardes were inchaunted because their arrowes coulde not hurte them.

The next day following, the foure Captaines sente

thrée

the west India.

thꝛée feuerall things in pꝛesent to Cortes, and the messengers that bꝛought them said: Sir behold here fiue slaues, *A straunge*
and if thou be that rigoꝛous God that eateſt mans fleſhe *preſente.*
and bloud, eate theſe which we bꝛing vnto thée, and we
will bꝛing thée moe. And if thou be the gentle and méeke
God, beholde here Franckinſence and Feathers. And if
thou be a moꝛtal man, take here foule, bꝛead, & Cherries.
 Cortez anſwered, that both he and his were moꝛtal mē
euen as they were. And becauſe that alwaies he had vſed
to tell them trouth, wherefoꝛe did they vſe to tel him lies,
and likewiſe to flatter him, foꝛ he deſired to bée their
friende, aduiſing them to be madde and ſtubboꝛne in
their opinion, foꝛ if they ſo did, aſſuredly they ſhoulde receiue great hurte and dammage. Likewiſe (quoth he) it
is apparant vnto you how many of your ſide are ſlaine
without the loſſe of one of mine, and with this anſincere
ſent them away. Notwithſtanding the anſwere ſent, thers
came aboute. 30000. of them euen to Cortez his campe to
pꝛoue their Coꝛſelettes, as they had done the day befoꝛe,
but they returned with bꝛoken pates. Here is to be noted,
that although the firſt day the whole hoſt of Indians came
to combt with our men, and finally all they came to fight,
yet the next day they did not ſo, but euery ſeueral captaine
by himſelfe, foꝛ to diuide the better the trauail and paines
equally amōg them: & becauſe that one ſhould not diſturbe
another thꝛough ẏ multitude, conſidering that they ſhould
fight but with a few, & in a narrow place, & foꝛ this conſideration, the ir battails were moꝛe freſher & ſtronger, foꝛ
eche captaine did contende who ſhould do moſt valiantly,
foꝛ to get honour, and eſpecially in killing one Spaniard,
foꝛ they thought that all their hurtes ſhoulde be ſatisfied
with the death of one Spaniarde, oꝛ taking one pꝛiſoner.
 Likewiſe is to bée conſidered, the ſtrangeneſſe of
their battaile, foꝛ not withſtanding their controuerſie

R 2   all

The Conqueſt of

Indian policie. all thoſe fiftéene daies that they were there, whether they fought or no. The Indians ſente vnto the Spaniardes cakes of breade, Ginnea cockes and Cherries. But this pollicie was not to giue them that meate for good will, but onely to ſpie and ſée what hurt was done amongſt them, and alſo to ſée what feare or ſtomacke they had to procéede: but the Spaniardes fell not into that reckening, for the eſpies of Tlaxcallan ſaide, that none had fought with them, but certaine outlawes and knaues called Otomies, who liued as vagaboundes without a Lorde or other ruler: And that they were théues, who had they abiding behinde a hill, which they pointed vnto with their hande.

How Cortez cut off the handes of fiftie Indian eſpies.

The next day after theſe preſentes were ſet vnto them as Goddes, which was the ſyxte of September, there came to the Campe fiftie Indians of Tlaxcallan, which ſéemed after their ſorte honeſt men, and gaue vnto Cortez bread, cherries, & Ginnea cocks, as they ordinarily vſed to do, enquiring how all his Spaniardes did and what they meant to doe, and whether they ſtood in neceſſitie of any thing. And after this communication they went vp and downe the camp, gaſing and beholding the horſes, armour and artillery, and ſéemed amaſed to ſée ſuch things. But the effect of their comming was the office of eſpies.

Teuche of Zempoallan marking theſe things, who being of a childe brought vp in wars, by reaſon wherof he was expert & wiſe, came vnto Cortez, ſaying, Sir it ſéemeth not well, that theſe Tlaxcaltecas wander vp & downe your campe

behol-

the weſt India.

beholding the entrance and going out of the ſame, to behold likewiſe the fortitude and weakeneſſe of your power, I like it not: It may pleaſe you to make enquirie whether they be eſpies or no. Cortez hauing heard his tale, gaue him heartie thankes for his good aduice, yea and maruelled, that neyther he himſelfe, nor none of his Spanyardes had noted the thing, the Indians hauing ſo many dayes come vnto them after this ſort, yea and that only Indian of Zempoallan had conſidered it. *The good aduice of a friend.*

Now the originall cauſe was not becauſe Teuch was more wiſe then the Chriſtians, but by reaſon that he had ſeene and heard thoſe Indians commune with the ſubiects of Iztacmixtlitan to ſéele their mindes, and with craft and ſubtiltie to obteine their deſire: whereby Cortez vnderſtood that thoſe fellowes came not to any good purpoſe: he apprehended that Indian which ſtoode next vnto him, and hauing him alone from his fellowes, by his Enterpreters examined him effectually, who incontinent confeſſed that he was a ſpie, and that his comming thither was to view the way how to enter their Campe for to ſpoyle and burne their Tentes: and for ſo much as they had proued fortune all the houres of the day, and all happened contrary to their deſire, againſt their auncient fame and glory which they had obteined by noble exployts in wars, they now meant to proue their ſucceſſe by night, hoping of better fortune: and alſo becauſe their ſouldiers ſhould not feare the horſes, with the darkeneſſe of the night, nor the blowes or ſtripes of the bright ſwordes, nor yet the fire and terrible noyſe of the Ordinaunce: and that Captaine Xicoteucatl was alreadie appointed for that enterprize, with proviſſo of many thouſand ſouldiers which lay in ambuſh in a vale behinde certain hilles, right ouer againſt their Campe. *Confeſſion.*

After this confeſſion taken, Cortez full prudently commaunded

The Conquest of

maunded to take also the seuerall confessions of other foure or fiue, who likewise confessed that they were all espies, vppon whose confessions they were all fiftie taken prisoners, and iudgement giuen, that their one hand should be cut off, which was forthwith executed, and then were returned to their Camp, signifying vnto them that the like iustice should bee executed vppon as many espies as they might take. And also they were charged to shewe vnto their Generall who had sent them, that both day and night he would be readie for them.

A good correction.

When the Tlaxcaltecas sawe their espies come in this pickle, they were in a maruellous feare, and it séemed a newe world vnto them, they also beléeued that our men had some familiar spirites that did instruct them of their thoughts, and with feare of cutting off hands, there went no moe espies with victualls.

An Embassage that Mutezuma sent to Hernando Cortez.

WHen these espies were gone, our men espied out of our Camp a great multitude of men goe crossing ouer a hill, and it séemed that they were those that the Captaine Xicotencatl had in ambush, and although it was neare night, Cortes determined to followe them, and not to abide their comming, fearing at the first brunt they might set fire among his cottages, as was pretended among them, which pretence hauing taken effect, might haue bene the destruction of all his men, either by the fire or otherwise, wherefore he put all his men in good order, and commaunded the horsemen to tecke the breast plates of his horses with belles, and then procéeded toward their enemies,

A carefull Captaine.

the weſt India.

enemies, who durſt not abide their comming, hauing intelligence of the cutting of their eſpies hands, and likewiſe hearing the new noyſe of belles, yet our men followed them till two houres within night, through many fowen fieldes of ſentli, and flew many of them, and then returned with victorie to the Campe.

At that ſeaſon were come ſixe noble men from Mexico, who brought two hundred ſeruing men to wait vpon them. They brought vnto Cortez a preſent, which was a hundred garmentes of cotten, and ſome of feathers, and a thouſand peeces of gold. [Ambaſſage from Muteʒuma.]

Theſe embaſſadors on the behalfe of Muteʒuma, declared, that their Lord woulde be friend with the Emperour, and alſo with him, and his company, requeſting to know what tribute he would yearely demaund, in golde, plate, pearles, ſlaues, or garmentes, or of any other thing that was within his kingdome, and the ſame tribute hee would well and truely pay without delay, with ſuch condition, that neither hee nor his company ſhoulde come vnto Mexico. And this requeſt (quoth they) is not only becauſe you ſhoulde be diſturbed to come into his countrey, but chiefly becauſe the way is euill, barren, and full of rockes, which let doth grieue Muteʒuma, that ſuche valiaunt men as yee be ſhoulde ſuffer in his Countrey, lying in his power not to remedie it. [Excuſes.]

Cortez did thankefully receiue the preſent and gentle offer for the Emperour King of Caſtile: but (quoth he) my earneſt deſire is, that you depart not till ye ſee the end of theſe warres which I haue nowe in hand, becauſe ye ſhall carrie newes thereof to Mexico what I pretend to doe againſt theſe mortall enemies of Muteʒuma.

Then Cortez fell into an ague, for which cauſe he went not

The Conquest of

not out to skirmish as he was wont to do, but only prouided to make his Camp strong against certaine flockes of Indians, which came daily to skirmish, for that was as ordinary, as the meat that was wont to be brought to them: but yet these skirmishes nor furie of the Indians were not like to their fierce beginning.

Cortez now meaneth to take a purgation for his ague: and toke certaine pilles which hee brought with him from Cuba, at such houre of the night as is vsed for purgations.

It happened that the next day following, before his purge had wrought, came three great companies of Indians to besiege his Campe. It should seeme that those Indians had some intelligence of his sicknesse, or else thinking with feare that he durst not come abroad as he was wont to do.

A valiant captaine. Cortez being aduertised of this newes, without any more respect to his purgation taken, toke his horse, and with his menne came to the encounter, and foughte with his enemies all day till it was night, and draue them a good way off, to their great hurt, and then returned to his Camp, and the next day following, he purged as fresh, as though it had bene newly taken. I do not rehearse this for a miracle, but to declare what he passed: for Hernando Cortes was a greate sufferer of trauell and paynes, and one of the first that alway was at any assay or brunt of enemies, and hee was not onely a good man of his hands, but also graue in counsell. And hauing thus purged himselfe, and taken rest those dayes, hee watched euery night that fell to his lotte, as well as any other souldier, and so continually he vsed to do. He was not for this the lesse esteemed, but rather muche the more beloued among his men.

How

the West India.

How Cortez wanne a great Citie called Zimpanzinco.

I
N an euening Cortez went vp to the toppe of his Tower, and looking round about him, he espied about foure leages distant in the Mountaines amongst rockes, and proceding out of a wood diuers smokes, whereby he imagined people to be there: hee opened not his minde to any man, but commaunded two hundred of his men to follow him, and some Indians his friends, and within three or foure houres of the night he toke his iourney toward the Mountaines, being very darke. He had not fully gone a league, when sodainly appeared the likenesse of a greate Bull whiche ouerthrewe them that they could not stirre. The first horseman being fallen, they aduised Cortez therof, who answered, that he should returne with his horse to the Campe: and incontinent fell another, Cortes commaunded him the like: and when three or foure were fallen, his company retired, saying: it was an euill token, desiring him to returne and abide the morning, that they might see whither they went. He answered, saying, ye ought to giue no credit to witchcraftes or fantasies, for God, whose cause we take in hand, is aboue all nature: wherefore I will not leaue my pretended iourney, for I do imagine that of this nights trauell shall come great ease and pleasure, saying, that the Diuell hath in this forme of a Bull appeared, to disturbe vs. He had no soner ended his talke, when his horse fell likewise: then counsell was taken what was best to bee done.

It was determined that the horses which were fallen, should

An euill spirit appeared.

A couragious Captaine.

should be returned to the Campe, and that of the residue, eache Horseman should leave his horse by the bridle, and so proceede on their way, and shortly after their horses were well againe, but they neuer knew of what motion they had fallen: with the darkenesse of the night they lost their way to the Mountaines, and chaunced into a cragged rock way, that they thought neuer to haue come out thereof.

And after a while that they hadde gone this euill way, with their haire standing with very feare, they espied a a little light, and tooke the way thither, where they founde a little house, wherein were two women, and those women, with other two women that afterwardes they mette, conducting them to the Wildernesse, where they had espied the smoke, and before day they sette vpon certaine Villages, and slewe manie, yet they burned not those Villages, because they shoulde not be perceiued through the light thereof. They receiued their aduise, that neere at hand were great populations, and soone after he came to Zimpanzinco, a towne of twentie thousand houses, as after did appeare by the visitation of *Cortes*. These inhabitantes being vnaduised of this suddaine hap, were taken in their beddes, and came out all naked through the streetes, to know what the great mourning and lamentation meant: at the first entrance many were slaine, but because they made no resistance, *Cortez* commaunded to cease from killing, nor yet to take any of their goodes, or women.

The feare of these poore inhabitantes was so great, that they fled without respect of the father to the childe, or husbande to the wife, or yet either of house or goodes.

Cortez commaunded signes of peace to bee made vnto them, and with that they staied, and before the Sunne risings

A famous *Cortes*.

the west India.

rising, the Towne was pacified.

Cortez went vp into a Tower to descry the Countrey, and there espied a most great population: hee then demaunded what it was: aunswere was made that it was called Tlaxcallan, and the Towne thereto appertaining. Then he called his Spaniardes, and saide vnto them: beholde, what would it haue preuailed vs to kill these poore soules, hauing yonder so manie enemies? and without doing anye more hurte in that Towne, hee went to a faire Fountaine there at hande, and thither came the Rulers of that Towne, and other foure hundred menne without weapon, and brought with them muche victuall, most humbly they besought Cortez to doe them no more hurte, giuing him likewise great thankes, that hee hadde so fauourably vsed them, offering both to serue and obey him, and from that day forwarde they woulde not onely keepe his friendship, but also trauell with the Lordes of Tlaxcallan and others, that they should doe the same. Cortes replied, that sure he was, howe they hadde fought against him before that time, although that now they brought him meate, yet notwithstanding he pardoned them, and also receiued them into his seruice and friendship, to the vse of the Emperour.

With this communication hee departed from them, and returned to the Campe very ioyfull with so good successe, hauing suche a dangerous beginning, with the sodaine fall of their horses, wherein the prouerbe is fulfilled, which saith, Speake not euill of the day, till it bee at an ende.

They hadde also a great hope, that those newe friendes woulde bee a meane, to cause the Tlaxcaltecas to leaue from warre, and to become their friendes.

The Conqueſt of

From that day forward, he commaunded that none of his Campe ſhould doe any hurt to any Indian, and certified his men that the ſame day his warres were at an end with that prouince.

The deſire that ſome of the Spaniards had to leaue the warres.

WHen Cortez was returned ſo ioyfully to his camp, he found ſome of his men diſcouraged with the ſodaine miſhap of the horſes, fearing that likewiſe ſom misfortune had hapned to Cortes, but when they ſawe him come well, and with victory, their ioy was great, although true it is, that many of his men were not well pleaſed, but deſired much to leaue the warres, and to returne to the coaſt, as they had often requeſted, but now chiefly ſeeing ſuch a great countrey, and full of people, who would not permit there abiding there, and they being ſo few in nũber in the midſt among them without hope of ſuccour, certainly things to be feared.

Murmuration With this murmuratiõ they thought it good to talk with Cortes, and alſo to require him to proceede no further, but returne backe againe to Vera Crux, from wheuce by little and little they might haue intelligence with the Indians, and therevpon proceed according to time, and that hee might prouide more horſes and men, which was the chiefeſt prouiſion of the warre.

And although ſome ſecretly enformed Cortes of this matter, yet hee gaue no eare to their talke, but on a night as hee came out of his Tower to ouerlooke the watch, hee heard a loude talke out of one of the Cottages, and beganne to hearken what their communication was,

the vveſt India. 133

was, and the matter was, that certaine ſouldiers ſayde
theſe wordes: If our Captaine be made, and goe where
he may be ſlaine, let him go alone, what néede we to follow him. Cortez hearing this talke, called two of his
friends for witneſſe, willing them to hearken his ſouldiers talke, for he that durſt ſpeake ſuch wordes would be
readie to doe it. Alſo he heard others ſay, what ſhall our
iourney be as Pedro Carbonerotes was? who went into
Barbaria to take Moores, and he and all his were there
ſlaine, wherfore ſaid they, let vs not follow him, but turne
in time. It grieued Cortes much to heare this talke, who
woulde faine haue corrected them, but it was not then
time, wherefore he determined to lead them with ſuffe-
rance, and ſpake vnto them as followeth.

The Oration made by Cortex to his Souldiours.

Aſters and louing friends, I did chooſe
you for my fellowes, and ye choſe mée
for your Captaine, and all was for
the ſeruice of God, and the augmen-
ting of his holy faith, and alſo the ſeruice of our ſoueraigne Lord the king,
now Emperor: and next for our owne
commoditie, I (as ye haue ſéene) haue
not failed, nor yet diſpleaſed yée, nor ye likewiſe haue o-
therwiſe done to me vnto this day. But now I doe féele
faintneſſe in ſome, yea and an euill will to goe forward
in the warres which we haue in hand: but (God be prayſed) it is now finiſhed, at the leaſt the ende is vnderſtoode,
what it may be, and alſo the wealth that may follow, as
partly you haue ſéene, but much without compariſon of
that you haue not ſéene, which is a thing that doth excéede

S 3 the

The Conquest of

the greatnesse of our wordes or thoughts.

Feare not (my louing fellowes) to goe and abide with mée. God forbidde that I should thinke, yea or that any shoulde report, that feare bereth my companie, or else disobedience to their Captaine, which is a perpetuall infamie, if wee shoulde leaue this lande, this warre, this way alreadie made, and returne as some doe desire, shall wée then liue at rest, loytering as idle and lost folke: God forbidde, that euer our Nation shoulde haue such a name, hauing warres of honour. And whither (I pray) shall the Oxe goe where hée shall not helpe to plough the ground? Doe ye thinke peraduenture that yée shall finde lesse people, worse armed, and not farre from the sea? I doe assure you, that in so thinking yée séeke after fiue féete for a Catte, yea, and you shall trauell no way, but that you shall méete some euill passage (as the Prouerbe sayth) yea and farre worser than this that wée haue in hande. For why (God be thanked) since wee came into this Countrey, wée neuer wanted meate, friendes, neither money nor honour. For nowe yée sée that yée are estéemed moze than menne, yea as persons immortall, and Gods, if it might bee spoken, for these Indians being so many, and without number, and so armed, as ye your selues affirme, yet can they not kill one of vs; and as touching their weapons, you sée that they are not poysoned, as the Indians of Carthagena, Veragna, and the Caribez doe vse, which haue killed many of our Nation therewith, dying as madde menne raging.

And if there were no other cause then this onely, you shoulde not séeke others, with whome to warre: I doe confesse that the Sea is somewhat farre from vs, and neuer Spaniarde trauelled so farre into the maine lande of India, as we haue done: for why? nowe we leaue the

Sea

the vvest India.

Sea a hundreth and fiftie miles behinde vs, nor yet euer any hath come to neare Mexico where Mutezuma both reside, from whome such messages and Treasure wee haue receiued. It is nowe but three score miles thither, and the worst is past, as you doe see, if wee come thither, as I trust in Iesus wee shall, then shall we not onely gette and winne for the Emperoure our naturall Lorde, a riche lande, great Kingdomes, infinite Vassalles, but likewise for our selues much riches, as Golde, Siluer, Precious stones, Pearles, and other commoditie: and besides this, the greatest honour that euer any nation did obtaine. For looke how great a king this is, howe large his Countrey is, and what great multitude of people hee hath, so much the more is our glorie.

Besides all this, wee are bound as Christians, to exalt and enlarge our Catholike faith, as we haue begunne, abolishing Idolatrie and blasphemie against our Sauiour Christ, taking away the bloudie Sacrifice and eating of mans flesh, so horrible and agaynst nature, and many other grieuous sinnes so much here vsed, for the foulenesse whereof I name them not. And therefore (I say) feare you, nor yet doubt you the victorie, considering that the worst is past. Of late we ouercame the Indians of Tabasco, and also an hundred and fiftie thousand this other day of the Tlaxtaltecas, who haue the only name of breakers of Lions lawes: so with Gods helpe you shall be conquerours of the rest, if ye faint not, and follow me.

All his companie was pleased and content with this comfortable exhortation, and those that were faint hearted recouered strength. And his valiant Souldiours recouered double strength, & those who hated him, began to honour him: and in conclusion he departed from thence

exceeding

The Conquest of

excéeding wel beloued of all his company. But al his former talke was very néedfull as time then required: for why? some of his (as you haue heard) were desirous to returne: likewise vpon diffention, rebellion mought haue growne, and he forced to returne to the sea coast, where all his toyle and trauell taken had béene lost.

How Xicotencatl came for Embassadour to Cortez his campe.

Cortes had not so soone made an ende of his talke, when Xicotencatl came entering into the campe, who was chiefe and generall captaine in Tlaxcallan, and of all the wars: he brought in his companie fiftie persons of authoritie to kéepe him companie. They approched néere where Cortez was, and saluted ech other accoording to the vse of their countrey. Their salutations ended, and the parties setten downe, Xecotencatl began the talke, saying: Sir, I am come on mine own behalf, and also of my fellow captaine, and lieutenant Maxixca, and in the name of many other noble personages, and finally in the name of the whole state & common weale of Tlaxcallan, to beséech and pray you to admit vs into your friendship, and to yéeld our selues and countrey vnto your King, crauing also at your hand pardon for our attempt in taking armes against you, wee not knowing what you were, nor what you sought for in our Countrey. And where we presumed to resist and defende your entrance, wee did it against the straungers whom wée knewe not, and such menne as wee had neuer heretofore séene: and fearing also that you had béene friends to Mutezuma, who is, and alwayes hath béene our mortall enemie. And these things we suspected, séeing Mutezuma his seruants

in

the weſt India.

in your company, or elſe wee imagined that you were comen to vſurpe our libertie, the which oft times without memorie weé haue poſſeſſed, as our forefathers did with the ſhedding of their bloud. And of our owne naturall prouiſion weé want Cotten wooll to cloath vs, wherefore in time paſt weé went as naked as weé were borne, but ſome of vs vſed other cloth to couer our nakedneſſe, made of the leaues of the treé called Melt: and Salt alſo we wanted, which two things ſo neceſſarie to humaine life, Mutezuma had great ſtore, and other our enemies, of whome wee are round about enuironed. And likewiſe where wee haue no golde ſtones of value, or any rich thing to barter with them, of verie pure neceſſitie many times weé are forced to ſell our owne bodyes to buy theſe wantes. And this extremitie (ſaide he) weé néeded not, if that wee would bée ſubiectes and vaſſals to Mutezuma. But yet had wee rather all in generall to ende our liues, then wee woulde putte our ſelues in ſuch ſubiection, for we thinke our ſelues as valiaunt menne in courage as our forefathers were, who alwayes had reſiſted agaynſt him, and his grandfather, who was as mightie as nowe is he : we woulde alſo haue withſtande you and your force, but wee coulde not, although we proued all our poſſibilitie by night and day, and found your ſtrength inuincible, and we no lucke agaynſt you. Therefore ſithence our fate is ſuch, wee had rather bee ſubiect vnto you then vnto any others. For we haue knowne and heard by the Zempoallanezes, that you doe no euill, nor came not to vexe any, but were moſt valiaunt and happie, as they had ſéene in the warres, being in your companie. For which conſideration, wee truſt that our libertie ſhall not be diminiſhed, but rather our owne perſons, wiues, and familie, better preſerued, and our houſes and huſbandrie not

T   deſtroyed.

The Conqueſt of

deſtroyed. And in ſome of all his talke, the teares trickling downe his cheekes, he beſought Cortes to ſay that Tlaxcallan did neuer at any time reknowledge any ſuperiour King or Lorde, nor at any time, had commen any perſon among them to commaunde, but onely he, whome they did voluntarily elect and choſe as their ſuperior and ruler.

It can not be tolde, how much Cortez reioyced with this Embaſſage, and to ſee ſuch a mighty Captaine come vnto his campe to ſubmitte himſelfe : and alſo it was a matter of great waight to haue that Citie in ſubiection, for the enterprice which he had in hande, whereby he fully made an account that the warres were at an ende, to the great contentation of him and his company, and with great fame and reputation among the Indians.

Cortez with a mery and louing countenaunce anſwered, laying to their charge the hurte and damage whiche he had receiued in their countrey, becauſe they refuſed at the firſt to hearken vnto him, and quietly to ſuffer him to enter into their countrey, euen as he had required and deſired by his meſſengers of Zempoallan ſente vnto them frō Zaclotan. Yet al this not withſtāding he did both pardon the killing of his two horſes, the aſſaulting of him in the highe way, and the greate lies, which they had moſte craftily vſed with him, (for where as they themſelues fought againſt him, yet they laide the faulte to others) likewiſe their pretence to murder him in the ambuſh prepared for him, (enticing him to come to their Citie,) without making firſt defiance, according to the law of armes.

Theſe cauſes notwithſtanding, he did louingly receiue their offer made in ſubiection to the Emperour, and in this ſorte departed, ſaying, that ſhortely he woulde be with him in Tlaxcallan, and preſently he coulde not goe with

the west India.

with him for the dispatch of the Ambassadours of Mutezuma.

The receiuing and entertainment of Cortez in Tlaxcallan.

It grieued much the Embassadours of Mutezuma, to see Xicotencates in the Spanish Camp, and the offer made vnto Cortez in the behalfe of his king, of their persons, Citie and goods, aduising Cortes to giue credit vnto them, for all their saying (quoth they) is treason and lies, and to the entent to locke you vp in their Citie.

Cortes answered, that although their aduice were true, yet he did determine to go thither, for that he feared them lesse in the Towne then in the fielde. They hearing this answere and determination, besought him to giue vnto one of them licence to returne vnto Mexico, to aduertise Mutezuma of all that was past, with an answere to their Ambassage, promising within sixe dayes to haue newes from Mexico, and till then prayed him not to depart with his Campe.

Cortes graunted their request, and abode there the time appointed, expecting the answere. In this meane season came many of Tlaxcallan to the camp, some brought Ginnea cockes, other brought bread and cherries, and gaue it for nothing in comparison, with merry countenance, desiring them to goe home with them vnto their houses.

The sixth day the Mexican came, according to promise, and brought vnto Cortes tenne Iewelles of Golde, both rich and well wrought, and a fifteene thousand garments of Cotten exceeding gallant, and most earnestly besought *A rich present.*

T 2 him

him on the behalfe of Mutezuma, that he shoulde not daunger himselfe in trusting to the wordes of the Tlaxcaltecas, who were so poore that with necessitie woulde robbe him of the things whiche his maister had sente him, yea and likewise murder him, knowing of the friendshippe betwéene his maister and him: likewise all the chiefest Lordes of Tlaxcallan came to intreate him to goe with them to Tlaxcallan where he shoulde be cherished, lodged, and well prouided. For it was a greate dishonour and shame for them to permitte suche personages to abide in such vile cottages as they were in.

And if (quoth they) you truste vs not, that then wée are ready to giue you for your securitie whatsoeuer gages you shall demaunte: notwithstanding they did bothe sweare and faithfully promise, that they might safely goe with them, saying also that the Othe and faith of their common weale should neuer be broken for all the goods in the worlde.

Wherevpon Cortez séing the good will of so many Gentlemen his newe friendes, and likewise the Indians of Zempoallan, of whome he had good credite, did so importune him and assure him of his going, he commaunded his fardage to be laden and also his ordinaunce, and departed towarde Tlaxcallan, whiche was fyue leagues from that place, with as good order as it had bene to a battaile: And at the Tower where he had pitched his campe, he left certaine Crosses for a memorie, with a greate heape of stones, and entred into Tlaxcallan the eightenth of September. There came out such a multitude of people to sée him and to méete him in the way, that it was a wonder to sée.

Entrance into Tlaxcallan.

He was lodged in the greatest temple, which had many greate and faire lodgings, sufficient for him and all his companie, except the Indians his friendes which were

lodged

the weſt India.   141

lodged in other Temples. He ſet certaine limittes, out of the which he commaunded ſtraightely that none of his company ſhould paſſe, vpon paine of death, and alſo commaunded that they ſhoulde take nothing, but what ſhould be giuen them. His commaundement was well obſerued, for none preſumed to goe a ſtoanes caſt without his licence. The Indian Gentlemen ſhewed great pleaſure and curteſie to the ſtrangers, and prouided them of all things neceſſarie, and manye of them gaue their daughters vnto them, in token of true friendſhippe, and likewiſe to haue fruite of their bodies, to be brought vp for the warres, being ſuch valiant men.

This Countrey liked well our men, and the greate loue of the people. They abode there at their pleaſure twentie daies, in which time they did procure to knowe particularlye the eſtate of the common weale and ſecretes, and alſo were ſufficiently inſtructed of the eſtate of Mutezuma.

The deſcription of Tlaxcallan.

TLaxcallan is properly in the Indian tong as much to ſay, as bread well baked, for there is more graine called Centli gathered, than is in all ỹ prouince round about. In times paſt ỹ Citie was called Texcallan, that is to ſay, a valley betwixt two hilles. It is a greate Citie, and planted by a riuer ſide, whiche ſpringeth out of Atlancatepec, and watreth the moſt parte of that prouince, and from thence iſſueth out into the South ſea, by Zacatullan. This Citie hath foure goodly ſtrætes, which are called Tepeticpac, Ocorelulco, Tizatlan, Quiahuiztlan. The firſt ſtræte ſtandeth on high vpon a hill, farre from the riuer, which maye be aboute

T 3   halfe

halfe a league, and because it standeth on a hill, it is called Tepeticpac, that is to say, a hill, and was the first population wyich was founded there on high, because of the warres.

An other streete was situate on the hill side towarde the Riuer, because at the building thereof, there were many Pine trées: they named it Ocotelulco, which is to say, a pine apple plot. This stret was beautifull, and first inhabited of all the Citie, and there was the chiefest Market place, where all the buying and selling was vsed, and that place they called Tianquiztli: in that stréete was the dwelling house of Maxixca. Along the Riuer side in the plaine, standeth another stréet called Tizatlan, because there is much lime and chalke. In this stréete dwelled Xicotencatl, Captaine generall of the common weale. There is another stréete named by reason of the brackish water, Quiahuiztlan, but since the Spaniardes came thither, all those buildings are almost altered, after a better fashion, and built with stone. In the plaine by the riuer side, standeth the Towne house, and other offices, as in the Citie of Veuice. This Tlaxcallan was gouerned by noble and rich men: they vse not that one alone should rule, but rather flie from that order, as from tyrannie.

In their warres (as I haue sayde before) they haue foure Captaines, which gouerneth each one stréete, of the which foure, they do elect a Captaine generall. Also there are other Gentlemen that are vndercaptaines, but a small number. In the warres they vse their standarde to be carried behinde the armie, but when the battaile is to be fought, they place the standarde where all the hoste may sée it, and hee that commeth not incontinent to his auncient, payeth a penaltie. Theyr standard hath two Crossebowe arrowes set thereon, which they esteeme as

the

the weſt India.

the reliques of their auncetors. This ſtandard two old ſoldiers, and valiant men, being of the chiefeſt Captaines, haue the charge to carrie, in the which ſtandard an abuſing of ſoothſaying, either of loſſe or victorie is noted. In this order they ſhoote one of theſe arrowes agaynſt the firſt enemies that they meete, and if with that arrow they doe either kill or hurt, it is a token that they ſhall haue the victorie: and if it neither kill nor hurt, then they aſſuredly beleeue that they ſhall loſe the field.

This Prouince or Lordſhip of Tlaxcallan, hath 28. villages and townes, wherein is contained 150000. houſeholdes. They are men well made, and good warriors, the like are not among the Indians. They are very poore, and haue no other riches, but onely the graine or corne called Centli, and with the graine and profite thereof, they doe both cloath themſelues, and pay their tributes, and prouide all other neceſſaries. They haue many Market places, but the greateſt and moſt vſed dayly, ſtandeth in the ſtreete of Ocotelulca, which is ſo famous, that 30000. per A ſtrange ſons come thither in one day to buy and ſell, which is to contradiction. ſay, changing one thing for another, for they knowe not what money meaneth.

They ſell ſuch things in that market, as here we vſe, and all thing vnto them needful to eat, and cloth for themſelues, and neceſſaries for building.

They haue all kinde of good policie in the Citie: there are Goldſmiths, Featherdreſſers, Barbers, Hotehouſes, and potters, who make as good earthen veſſell, as is made in Spaine. The earth is fat and fruitfull for corne, fruite, and paſture, for among the Pine trees groweth ſo much graſſe, that our men feede their cattell there, which in Spaine they cannot doe.

Within two leagues of that Citie ſtandeth a rounde hill of ſixe miles of heyght, and fiue and fortie miles in compaſſe,

The Conquest of

compasse, and is now called Saint Bartholmewes hill, where the snow freeseth. In times past they called that hill Matealcucie, who was their God for water. They had also a God for wine, who was named Ometochtli, for the great drunkennesse which they vsed. Their chiefest God was called Camaxtlo, and by another name Mixcouatl, whose Temple stoode in the streete of Ocotelulco, in the which temple there was sacrificed some yeares aboue eight hundred persons. In Tlaxcallan they spake three languages, that is to saye, Nahualh, which is the courtly spæch, and chiefest in all the land of Mexico: another is called Otomir, which is most commonly vsed in the Villages: There is one onely streete that spake Pinomer, which is the grosest spæche. There was also in that Citie a common Jayle, where fellons lye in prisons, and all things which they held for sinne, was there corrected.

Correction. It chanced at that time a Townesman to steale from a Spaniard a little golde, whereof Cortez complained to Maxixca, who incontinent made enquirie, that the offender was found in Chololla, which is another Citie fiue leagues from thence, they brought the prisoner with the golde, and deliuered him to Cortez, to doe with him his pleasure: Cortez woulde not except him, but gaue him thankes for his diligence, then was he carried with a Cryer before him, manifesting his offence, and in the Market place vppon a skaffolde they brake his ioyntes with a cudgell; our men maruelled to see suche straunge Justice.

The

the weſt India.

The anſwere of the Tlaxcaltecas touching the leauing of their Idolles.

VVHen Cortez ſawe that theſe people executed Iuſtice, and liued in Religion after their manner, although abhominable and diuelliſh: and alwayes when he deſired them to leaue off from their Idolatrie and that cruell vanitie, in killing and eating men ſacrifiſed, conſidering that none among them how holy ſoeuer he were, would willingly be ſlaine and eaten, required them to beléeue in the moſte true God of the Chriſtians, who was the maker of heauen and earth, the giuer of raine, and Creator of all things that the earth produceth only for the vſe and profit of mortall man.

Some of them anſwered, that they would gladly do it, onely to pleaſure him, but they feared that the Commons would ariſe and ſtone them. Others ſaid, that it was an hard matter to vnbeléeue that which their forefathers had ſo long beléued, and that it ſhould be a cauſe to condemne their forefathers and themſelues.

Others ſaid, that it might be in time they would conuert, ſéeing the order of the Chriſtian Religion, and vnderſtanding the reaſons and cauſes to turne Chriſtians, and likewiſe perceiuing throughly the maner and life of the Chriſtians, with their lawes and cuſtomes: and as for warlike feates, they were ſatiſfied, and had ſéene ſuch trial, that they held them for men inuincible in that point, and that their God did helpe them.

Cortez promiſed them, that ſhortly hee woulde bring them ſuche men, as ſhould inſtruct and teache them, and then they ſhould ſée which way was beſt, with the great ioy and fruite that they ſhoulde féele. They accepting that counſell which hee like a friend had giuen them, and

T for

The Conquest of

for as much as presently it coulde not be brought to passe by reason of his iourney to Mexico, he desired them, that the Temple wherein he was lodged, shoulde be made a church for him and his company, and if it pleased them, they might also come to see and heare their diuine seruice.

The Indians graunted his request, and dayly came among them all the time of their abode there, and some came and dwelte with the Spanyardes, but the chiefest friende was Captaine Maxixca, who neuer went from Cortez.

The discord betweene the Mexicans and Tlaxcalteca.

Cortez being throughly satisfied of theyr hartie good willes, he demaunded of them the estate and riches of Mutezuma. They exalted him greatly, as men that had proued his force. And as they affirmed, it was neere a hundred yeares that they maintained warre with him and his father Axaiaca, and others his Unckels and Grandfathers. And saide also, that the golde and treasure of Mutezuma, was without number, and his power and dominion ouer all the lande, and his people innumerable: for (quoth they) he ioyneth sometime two hundreth thousand men, yea and three hundred thousande for one battaile. And if it pleased him, he woulde make as manye men double, and thereof they were good witnesse, because they had many times fought with the.

Maxixca desired y Cortez should not aduenture himselfe into the power of the men of Culhua, whereat some of the Spaniards feared and suspected euill of the matter.

Cortes

the weſt India.

Cortes tolde him, that notwithſtanding al thoſe things which they had tolde him, he was fully minded to goe to Mexico, to viſit Mutezuma, wiſhing him to aduiſe him what he mought do, or bring to paſſe for them with Mutezuma, for he ſhould willingly do it, for the curteſie ſhewed vnto him, and that he beléeued Mutezuma would graunt him any lawfull requeſt.

Then they beſought him to procure for them a licence to haue cotten wooll and ſalte out of his Countrey, for (ſaid they) in time of the warres we ſtode in great néede thereof, and that they had none but ſuche as they boughte by ſtealthe of the Comercans very déere, in change of golde: for Mutezuma had made a ſtrait lawe, whereby all ſuche as carried anye of thoſe commodities to them ſhoulde be ſlaine. Then Cortez enquired the cauſes of their diſorder and euill neighborhood. They aunſwered, that their griefes were olde, and cauſe of libertie: but as the Ambaſſadors did affirme, and Mutezuma afterward declare, it was not ſo, but for other matter farre differente. So that eache partie alleadging their cauſes, their reaſons were, that the yong menne of Mexico and Culhua did exerciſe and bring them vppe in warlike feates néere vnto them, and vnder theyr noſes, to theyr greate annoyance, whereas they mought haue gone to Panuco and Teocantepec, his frontiers a farrre off.

Likewiſe their pretence was, to haue warre with them béeing theyr neighbours, onely to haue of them to ſacrifice to their Gods: ſo that when they would make any ſolemne feaſt, then would they ſend to Tlaxcallan for men to ſacrifice, with ſuch a great army, that they might take as many as they néeded for that yeare: for it is moſt certaine if Mutezma woulde, in one daye he moughte haue broughte them in ſubiection, and ſlayne them all.

all, ioyning his whole power in effect: but his purpose was, to keepe them for a pray to hunt withall, for men to be sacrificed to his Goddes, and to eate, so that he would neuer sende but a small Armie against them: whereby it did chance that sometimes those of Tlaxcallan did ouercome.

Cortez receiued great pleasure to heare these discords betwixt his new friendes & Mutezuma, which was a thing fit for his purpose, for by that meanes hee hopes to bring them all under subiection, and therefore he used the one and the other secretly, to build his pretence vppon a good foundation.

At all this communication there stood by certaine Indians of Verozinco, which had bene against our men in the late warres, the which Towne is a Citie as Tlaxcallan, and ioyned with them in league of friendship against Mutezuma, who oppressed them in like effect of slaughter for their Temples of Mexico, and they also yeelded themselues to Cortez for vassals to the Emperour.

The solemne receiuing of the Spaniards into Chololla.

THe Ambassadors of Cortez seeing the determination of Cortes to proceede on his iourney toward Mexico, they besought him to goe by Chololla, whiche stood fiue leagues from thence, certifying that Chololla was a citie in their friendship, and y there he might at his pleasure abide y resolutiō of their Lord Mutezuma, whether it were his pleasure y he should enter into Mexico or no. This request was only to haue him from thence, for truly it greeued much Mutezuma of their new friendship and league,

fearing

the vveſt India. 149

fearing that thereof would ſome great diſpleaſure happen towards him, and therefore procured all that was poſſible to haue him from thence, ſending him alwayes preſents to allure him to come frō thence the ſooner. But when the Tlaxcaltecas ſaw that he would go to Chololla, it grieued them much, ſaying vnto Cortes, that Mutezuma was a lier and fraudulent perſon, & that Chololla was a Citie his friend but not conſtant, and it might happen that they would diſpleaſe him, hauing him within their Citie, wiſhing him to loke wel to himſelfe. And if nœdes he would go thither, yet they would prouide 20000. men to képe him company. A gentle offer.

The women that were giuen to the Spaniards at their firſt entraunce, had vnderſtanding of a ſnare that was layd to murther them at their comming to Chololla, by meanes of one of the foure Captaines, who had a ſiſter which diſcouered the thing to Pedro de Aluarado who kept her. Cortes incontinent called that captaine out of his houſe, and cauſed him to be choked, and ſo was the matter kept cloſe, that his death was neuer knowne, whereby the ſnare was vndone without any rumour. It was a wonder that al Tlaxcallan had not made an vprore ſéeing one of their greateſt Captaines dead. There was inquirie made of that ſnare, and the truth being knowne, it was approued, that Mutezuma had prepared, 30000. Souldiers who were in campe for that purpoſe within two leagues of the Citie, and that the ſtrétes of Chololla were ſtopped vp with timber and railes, and the toppes of their houſes prouided with ſtones, which houſes are made with plaine roofes, or ſotties, and the high way ſtopped vp, and other falſe byways made, with déep holes pitched full of ſtakes very ſharpe, to ſpoile and lame both horſe and man: theſe engines were finely couered with ſande, and could not be eſpied, although the ſcoute had Correction of treaſon.

M 3   gone

The Conqueſt of

gone before on foote to diſcouer. The matter alſo was verie ſuſpicious, for theſe Citizens of Chololla had not at any time come to viſite him, or ſent any preſent vnto him as others had done.

Whereupon Cortes conſulted with the Tlaxtaltecas, to ſend certaine meſſengers to Cholollo, to requeſt their captaines and rulers to come vnto him, who did their meſſage accordingly, and the Cholollans would not come, but yet they ſent three or foure perſons to excuſe them, ſaying that they were not well at caſe, praying him to ſignifie vnto thẽ what he would haue: the Tlaxcaltecas enformed Cortez, that thoſe meſſengers were men of ſmall credite, and of low degrée, wiſhing him not to depart till theyr Captaine came. In this ſort Cortes returned their meſſengers backe againe, with commaundement written, declaring that if they came not within thrée dayes, hée would proclaime them rebels, and his vtter enemies, and as ſuch would he chaſten them with all rigour.

When this commandement came vnto them, the next day following came many Lords and Captaines to make their excuſe, ſaying, that the Tlaxcaltecas were their enemies, and that through them they could not liue in ſafety: likewiſe they knewe of the euill report which they had made agaynſt them : wherefore they beſought him to giue no credite vnto them, for why, they were both falſe and cruell men : beſéeching him alſo to goe with them to their Citie, and then he ſhould ſée that all was but a mockerie that had béene tolde them, and they his good and faithfull friends : and laſt of all they offered to ſerue him as tributary ſubiects.

Cortes commaunded that all this talke ſhould bée ſet downe in writing before the Notarie, and his interpreters, and ſo tooke his leaue of the Citizens of Tlaxcallan. Maxixca wept at his departure, but there went in his com-

the vvest India.

companie, a hundred thousand men of warre: there were amõg them many Marchants that went to barter for salt and mantels.

Cortez commanded that those hundred thousand men should go alwaies by themselues: that day he reached not to Chololo, but abode by a brooke side, and thither came many of the citie, to desire him that ye Tlaxtaltecas should not doe any hurt in their Countrey: whereupon Cortez commanded them to returne backe again, all sauing 5000 or there about, much against their willes. But they still required him to take good heede of those euill folke, who be not (quoth they) men of warre, but pedlers, and men of double heart: and they of their parts would bee very loth to leaue him in any perill or danger, hauing giuen themselues to be his true and faithfull friends.

The next day in the morning the Spaniards came to Chololla, and there came out néere 10000 Indians to receiue him with their Captaines in good order: many of them presented vnto him bread, foule, & roses, and euery Captaine as hée approached welcomed Cortez, and then stoode aside, that the rest in order might come vnto him. And when he came entring into the Citie, all the other Citizés receiued him, maruelling to see such men & horses.

After all this, came out all the religious menne, as Priests and Ministers, to the idols (who were many and straunge to beholde,) and all were clothed in white like vnto surplesses, and hemmed with Cotten thréede: some brought instruments of musicke like vnto Cornettes, other brought instrumëts made of bones, other an instrumët like a kettel couered with skin, some brought chafing dishes of coales with perfumes, others brought idols couered, and finally they al came singing in their language, which was a terrible noise, and drew néer Cortes and his company senting them with swéet smels in their senses.

With

The Conqueſt of

With this pompe and ſolemnitie (which trulie was great) they brought him into the Citie, and lodged him in a houſe where was roume inough for him and his, and gaue vnto each of them a Ginnea cocke, and his Indians of Tlaxcallan, Zempoallan and Iztacmizelitan, were prouided by themſelues.

The conſpiracie of the Cholollans to kill Cortes and his men.

All that night folowing Cortes was vigilant with al his company, for both in the way & in the towne they had founde ſome of the things whereof they had been aduiſed before in Tlaxcallan, and although their firſt preſent was a Ginnea cock to each mans alowance, other three dayes following they gaue them nothing almoſt to eate, and very ſeldome the captaines came to viſite them, whereof Cortes had great ſuſpition.

And in this meane while the Embaſſadours of Mutezuma entreated him to leaue off his iourney to Mexico, alledging that their great King would die in beholding their beards and ieſture: other times they ſayd that there was no paſſage, other times they would ſay that they wanted wherewith to ſuſtaine them. And ſeeing them fully, and in euery reſpect annſwered to all theſe points, they cauſed the Townes men to enfourme them, that where Mutezuma his abiding was, were monſtrous Liſards, Tigers, Lions, and many other fierce beaſts, the which when Mutezuma commaunded to be loſed, were ſufficient to plucke in péeces, and to deſtroy thoſe fewe ſtraungers: and ſæing that all theſe pollicies auailed not, they conſulted with the Captaines and chiefe Citizens to murther

the weſt India.

murder the Chriſtians. And becauſe they ſhoulde ſo bring it to paſſe, the Embaſſadours promiſed the Citizens great rewardes on the behalfe of Mutezuma, and preſented to their generall a drumme of Golde, and promiſed to bring the thirtie thouſand Souldiers which lay aboute two leagues from thence: the Chololláns promiſed to deliuer them bounde hande and fœte. But yet they would not conſent that thoſe Souldiers of Culhua ſhoulde come into their Citie, fearing that they (vnder colour of friendſhippe) woulde remaine with the Towne, for why the Mexicans had vſed the like ſleyght. And in this ſorte they with one bolte meante to kill two birdes at a ſhœte, for they thought to take the Spaniardes ſlæping, and then to remaine with the Towne of Chololla. Alſo it was determined, that if all theſe pretences coulde not be brought to paſſe, that then they ſhould be conducted a contrary way to Mexico vpon the left hande, in the which were many daungerous places, becauſe the way was all ſandy, with many ſluces, diches, and holes, of three fadom dæpe, meaning there to mæte them, and to carry them bound to Mutezuma: this matter being fully agrǽd, they beganne to take away their houſeholde ſtuffe, and to carry it with their wiues and children vp into the mountaines. *Many perils*

And our men being alſo ready to departe from thence for their ſmall chǽre with euill countenaunce, it happened, an Indian woman (being wife to one of the principalleſt Cittizens,) hauing ſome affection to the bearded men, ſaide vnto Marina, that ſhæ ſhoulde abide there with hir, for that ſhe loued hir well, and that it woulde griefe her that ſhe ſhould be ſlaine with hir maiſter. Marina diſſimuling the matter, procured to knowe what they were that had conſpired the thing, and hauing knowledge thereof, ſhe ranne to ſǽke Aguillar hir fellow interpreter, and *Helpe from God.*

both

The Conquest of

both togither enformed Cortes of the whole matter.

Cortes hearing this newes, slept not, but incontinent examined two of the Cittizens, who confessed the thing euen as it passed, and as the Gentlewoman had declared: whereupon Cortes stayed his iourney two dayes, to mollifie the matter and to disappoint them of that euill pretended purpose, and also to correct their offences, he commaunded their rulers to be called, saying that he had to talke with them, and when they were comen, he required them neyther to vse lies nor deceits with him, but rather like men to defie him to the field and battaile, for (quoth he) honest men vse rather to fight then to lie. They all answered that they were his friends and seruitours, and no liars, and that it might please him to shewe them when he would depart, for they would goe armed to kéep him company. He answered that he wold depart the next day following, and that he required but only some of their slaues to carry his farbage, because his owne Tamemez or Carriers were wearied: likewise hee required some prouision of victuall.

At this last request they smiled, saying among themselues, to what purpose will these men haue victuals, for shortly themselues shalbe boyled and eaten with the sause called Axi, yea, and if Mutezuma had not pretended their bodies for his owne dish, they had bene eaten here before this time.

The

the West India.

The punishment that Cortez executed for conspiracie.

THe next day in the morning the Cholollans thinking that they had their determinate purpose in good readinesse, they came & brought many to carry their carbage, and othersom to carry the Spaniardes vpō their backes, hoping to apprehend them in the same order. Ther came alſo many armed men of the moſt valianteſt, to kill him that ſhould diſorder himſelfe. Likewiſe that day their Prieſts ſacrificed tenne children of three yéeres of age to their God Quezalcouatl, fiue of theſe children were men, and the other fiue wemen, whiche was their cuſtome when they began their warres: the Captaines placed themſelues at the foure dores of Cortez his houſe with some armed men. Cortez earely in the morning had ſecretly in a readines the Indians of Zempoallan and Tlaxcallan, and other friends: he commaunded his horſemen to take their horſes, giuing them this watchword, that whē they heard the noiſe of the ſhotte of a handgun, that then they ſhould play the men, for it imported all their liues. And he ſéeing the townſmen approch néere his lodging, commaunded the captaines and chiefeſt of them to come vnto him, ſaying, that he woulde take his leaue of them: there came many, but he would not ſuffer aboue thirtie perſons to come in, who were the principalleſt, and declared vnto them, that alwaies he had dealte truly with them, and they with him nothing but treaſon and lies. Likewiſe they had vnder colour requeſted that his fréds the Tlaxcaltecas ſhoulde not come vnto their towne, and that he fulfilled therin their deſire, and alſo commaunded his owne men in no wiſe to be hurtfull vnto them, yea and although they had not prouided him of victuals

O worthie Cortes.

X 2 as

The Conquest of

as reason did require, yet he would not permit any of his men to take the value of one henne from them, so that in recompence of all his gentle dealings and good will, they had moste wickedly procured the death of him and all his companie. And because they coulde not performe it in their owne towne, they had prepared the slaughter in the high way, at those daungerous places whiche they had determined to leade them vnto, pretending also the help of thirtie thousand men, Souldiers of Mutezuma, which army stoode not fully two leagues from thence. And for this horrible and detestable wickednesse ye shall all die, and in memorie of traytors I will destroy this citie, and turne the foundations vpwardes, so that there shall remaine no remembraunce of you.

Their offence being manifest, coulde not be denied, and looking one vpon an other, their colours waxed pale and wanne, saying, this man is like vnto our Goddes, who knoweth all things, therefore lette not vs denie the truth, and openly before the Embassadours of Mutezuma confesse their errour and euill facte.

Then said Cortes to the Embassadours, you do see that we should haue bene slain by the Cholollons, and through the procuremēt of Mutezuma, but yet I beleue it not, considering that he is my friende and a mightie Prince, saying also that Noble men vsed neither treason nor lyes, wherefore feare not you, but these dissembling Traytors shal be punished, for you are persons inuiolable, and messengers of a Prince, whome he meante to serue and not offend, because he had an assured opinion in Mutezuma, to be a vertuous Prince, and one that woulde not committe villanie.

All these wordes he spake, because he woulde not fall out with Mutezuma, vntill he sawe himselfe within the Citie of Mexico.

Inconti-

the weſt India.

Incontinent he commaunded ſome of thoſe Captaines to be ſlaine, and kept the reſidue bounde. Then he ſhot off his handgunne, which was the watch vnto his armie, who forthwith ſet vpon the Towneſmen, and within two houres ſlew ſixe thouſand perſons and moꝛe.

Cortez commaunded that they ſhould kill neither woman noꝛ childe, they fought welueare fiue houres: they ſit fire on all the houſes & Towers that made reſiſtance, and dꝛaue all the inhabitants out of the Towne. The dead carkaſſes laie ſo thicke, that of foꝛce they muſt tread vpon them.

There were twentie Gentlemen, and many Pꝛieſts, who aſcended vp to the high tower of the temple, which hath a hundꝛeth and twentie ſteppes, from whence with arrowes and ſtones they did much hurt, and would not yelde, wherevpon our men ſet fire to the Tower, and burned them all. Then they exclaimed on their Goddes, who would neither helpe them noꝛ their Citie and holie ſanctuary.

The Citie being ſacked, our men tooke the ſpoyle of golde, plate, and feathers, and the Indians their friendes tooke cloathes and ſalt, which was the treaſure that they deſired.

Cortez commaunded to ceaſe the ſpoyle. The other Captaines that laie bounde, hearing of ſuch a great deſtruction and puniſhment, moſt pittifully beſought Cortez to loſe ſome of them, foꝛ to ſee what was become of their Gods and common people. Likewiſe they humbly beſought him to pardon them, who had not ſo much fault as Mutezuma, who perſwaded and entiſed them to that pꝛetended treaſon.

Vpon their lamentable requeſt, he loſed two of them, and the next day following the Citie was as ful of people againe, that there ſeemed not one to be wanting. At

X 3

The Conquest of

At the sute of the Tlaxcaltecas who were put for mediators, Cortez pardoned them all, and set his prisoners at libertie, assuring them that the like correction he would do vppon all them that should dissemble or shewe an euill countenaunce, or make lies, or finally vse anye kinde of treason toward him: whereupon they all abode in greate feare. He made the knot of friendship betwéene them and the Tlaxcaltecas, which in time past had ben betwixt the, for Mutezuma and his auncestors made them enemies, with faire promises, words, and also feare.

The Citizens hauing their generall slaine, chose an other with licence of Cortez.

The Sanctuary or holy place among the
Indians, was Chololla.

Hololla is a citie as Tlaxcallan, and hath but one perso who is gouernour and general Captaine, chosen by the consent of al the Citizens. It is a Citie of twentie thousande householdes within the walles, and in the suburbes as much more. It sheweth outwardes very beautifull, and full of towers, for there are as many temples as dayes in the yeare, and euery temple hath his tower. Our men counted foure hundred towers. The men and women are of good disposition, wel fauoured, and very wittie.

The women are Goldsmithes and also Caruers, the men are warriers, and light fellowes, and good maisters for any purpose: they goe better apparelled then any other Indians yet séene. They weare for their vtter garment, clokes like vnto Morifcos, but after another sort. All the Countrey round about them is fruitfull and earable

the weſt India.

able ground, well watered, and so full of people, that there is no waſt ground, in respect whereof, there are some poore which begge from doore to doore. The Spaniardes had not seene any beggers in that Countrey before they came thither.

Chololla is a citie of moſt deuotion and religion in all India, it is called the Sanctuarie or holy place among the Indians, and thither they trauelled from many places far diſtant in pilgrimage, and for this cause there were so many temples.

Their Cathedrall Temple was the beſt and higheſt of all the new Spaine, with a hundred and twentie ſteps vp vnto it.

The greateſt Idoll of all their Gods was called Quezalcouately, God of the aire, who was (say they) the founder of their Citie, béeing a Virgin of holy life, and great penance. He inſtituted faſting, and drawing of blood out of their eares and tongues, and left a precept, that they ſhould ſacrifice but onely Quailes, Doues, and other foule.

Hee neuer ware but one garment of Cotten, which was white, narrow, and long, and vpon that a mantle beſet with certaine red croſſes.

They haue certaine gréene ſtones which were his, and those they keepe for relickes. One of them is like an Apes head. Here they abode twentie dayes, and in this meane while there came ſo many to buy and ſell, that it was a wonder to ſée. And one of the things that was to be ſéene in thoſe faires, was the earthen veſſel, which was exceeding curious and fine.

The

The Conquest of

The hill called Popocatepec.

Here is a hill eight leagues fr$\bar{o}$ Chololla, called Popocatepec, which is to say, a hill of smoke, for many times it casteth out smoke and fire. Cortes sent thither ten Spaniards, with many Indians, to carry their victuall, and to guide th$\bar{e}$ in the way. The ascending up was very troublesome, and full of craggie rockes. They approched so nigh the top, that they heard such a terrible noise which proceeded from thence, that they durst not go unto it, for the ground did tremble and shake, and great quantitie of ashes which disturbed the way: but yet two of them who seemed to be most hardie, and desirous to see strange things, went up to the top, because they would not returne with a shamelesse answer, and that they might not be accounted cowards, leauing their followes behinde them, proceeding forwards. The Indians said, what mean these men? for as yet neuer mortall man tooke such a iourney in hand.

These two valiant fellowes passed through the desart of Ashes, and at length came under a great smoke verie thicke, and standing there a while, the darknesse vanished partly away, and then appeared the vulcan and concauitie, which was about halfe a league in compasse, out of the which the ayre came abounding, with a great noise, verie shrill, and whistling, in such sort that the whole hill did tremble. It was to be compared unto an ouen where glasse is made. The smoke and heate was so great, that they could not abide it, and of force were constrained to returne by the way that they had ascended: but they were not gone farre, when the vulcan began to lash out flames

of

the weſt India.

of fire, aſhes, and imbers, yea and at the laſt ſtones of burning fire: and if they had not chaunced to finde a rocke, wherevnder they ſhadowed themſelues, vndoubtedly they had there bene burned.

When with good tokens they were returned where they left their fellows, the other Indians kiſſed their garments as an honor due vnto gods. They preſented vnto them ſuch things as they had, and wondred much at their fact.

Theſe ſimple Indians thought, that, that place was an infernall place, where all ſuch as gouerned not well, or vſed tyrannie in their offices, were puniſhed when they died, and alſo beléued, that after their purgation, they paſſed into glorie. *Purgatorȳ.*

This Uulcan is like vnto the Uulcan of Cicilia, it is high and round, and neuer wanteth Snowe about it, and is ſéene a farre off in the night, it laſheth out flames of fire.

There is néere about this hil many cities, and Huexecinco is one of the higheſt.

In tenne yeares ſpace this ſtraunge hill of working did expell no vapoure or ſmoke: but in the yeare 1540. it beganne againe to burne, and with the horrible noyſe thereof, the neighbours that dwelt foure leagues from thence were terrified, for the eſpeciall ſtraunge ſmokes that then were ſéene, the like to their predeceſſors had not bene ſéene.

The aſhes that procéeded from thence came to Huexozinco, Quelaxcopan, Tepiacac, Quauhquecholla, Chololla, and Tlaxcallan, which ſtandeth tenne leagues from thence, yea ſome ſay, it extended fifténe leagues diſtant, and burned their hearbes in their gardens, their fields of corne, trées, and cloathes that lay a drying.

The

The Conqueſt of

The conſultation that Mutezuma had, concerning the comming of Cortez into Mexico.

Cortez pretended not to fall out with Mutezuma, before his comming to Mexico, and yet hee vnderſtood all Mutezuma his pretence, wherevpon he complaineth to the Ambaſſadours, ſaying, that hee much maruelled that ſuch a mighty Prince, who by ſo many Gentlemen had aſſured his friendſhip vnto him, ſhould now procure his totall deſtruction, in not keeping his promiſe and fidelitie. In conſideration whereof, where he meant to viſite him as a friend, that now hee would goe to his Court as an enemie. The Ambaſſadors excuſed their maiſters cauſe, beſéeching him to withdraw his furie, and to giue licence to one of them to go to Mexico, who woulde bring anſwere from thence with all ſpéede.

Cortez graunted vnto the requeſt, the one of them went, and returned againe within ſix dayes, in company of another meſſenger that had gone thither before, who broughte tenne platters of golde, and a thouſande fiue hundred mantels of cotten, with much victuall, and Cacao, which is a kinde of fruit that ſerueth for currant money among them. Likewiſe they brought a certaine kind of wine or licoure made of Cacao and Centli. They enformed Cortes, that Mutezuma was innocent of the conſuration in Chololla, nor by any meanes priuie to their dealings, affirming moreouer, that the garriſon of ſouldiers did apperteine to Acazinco, and Acazan, who were neighbors to Chololla, who by inducement of ſom naughtie perſons, had procured that thing, ſaying that he ſhould both ſée and vnderſtand him to be his faithfull and louing

friend,

the West India.

friend, praying him to come forward on his iourney, for he would abide his comming in Mexico.

This ambassage pleased well Cortes, but Mutezuma feared, when hee heard of the slaughter, and burning of Chololla, and said to his friends, these are the people that our Gods said should come and inherite this land. *Prophecie of the Diuel*

Mutezuma went incontinent to his Oratorie, and shut in himselfe alone, where he abode in fasting and prayer eight dayes, with sacrifice of many men, to aslake the fury of his Idols, who seemed to be offended.

The voyce of the Diuell spake vnto him, bidding him not to feare the Christians, saying they were but fewe, and when they were come, he should do what he listed with them, willing him in no wise to ceasse from the bloudie sacrifice, least some mischance might happen vnto him. And assured him that he should haue the Goddes Vitzpucheli, and Tescatlipuca, to preserue and keep him. And because Quezalcouatle was agréeued for wante of bloudie sacrifice, hee permitted the straungers to punish them of Chololla. And Mutezuma hearing this diuellish Oracle, and likewise Cortes hauing warned him that he would visite him as an enemie, he was by this perswasion of Sathan, the better willing to receiue him into Mexico.

Likewise Cortes whē he came to Chololla, was strong, and had at commaundement a mightie power, and there made himselfe stronger, the fame whereof, was blowne abroad, throughout all the dominions of Mutezuma. And wheras the poore Indians had but only maruelled at their persons and furniture, now they beganne to tremble and to feare at his doings, so that wheresoeuer he came, they opened him the gates with pure feare, more then for any loue.

Mutezuma at the beginning pretended to feare Cortes

Y 2 with

with the fearfull passages and other perils and daunger, as the fortitude of Mexico, with his great multitude of subiects, and the great number of Princes that did both serue and obey him: and seeing that all these things profited not, hee thought to haue ouercome him with giftes and treasure, knowing that he hadde required gold: yet he sawe that nothing woulde preuaile, for that Cortez woulde needes come to see him, wherevpon, hee tooke counsell of the Diuell what he should do in that case, vpon which counsell hee was satisfied by his Priests and Captaines, that he ought not to warre against so fewe Straungers, for if he so did, the dishonour would be his, and chiefly, because Cortez certified that he was an Ambassadour, and vsing him otherwise, it might so fall out, that his own subiects would rebel against him their Lord and Prince, saying likewise, that it was manifest that the Otompica and Tlaxcaltecas would fauour his side, and also many others, for to destroy and spoyle Mexico, vpon which consultation it was openly proclaimed, that his wil was that the straungers should enter into Mexico freely, thinking that if at any time they should displease him, to make a a breakefast of them the next day.

An euil counsellour.

Things that happened to Cortez in his iourney to Mexico.

Cortez hauing so good an answere of the Ambassadors, he gaue licence to as many of the Indians his friends, as listed to depart home to their houses, and he likewise departed from Chololla, with some borderers that would needs follow him.

the vveſt India.

He left the way that the Mexicans had perſwaded him to come, for it was both euill and daungerous, as the Spaniard which went to the vulcan had ſeene, he went another plainer way, and more nearer. That day he trauelled but foure leagues, becauſe he ment to lodge in the villages of Huexozinco, wher he was friendly receiued, and they preſented vnto him ſlaues, garments, and golde, although but little, for they are poore, by reaſon that Mutezuma hath enuironed them about, becauſe they were of the parcialitie of Tlaxcallan. The next day in the morning he aſcended vp a hill couered with ſnow, which was ſixe miles of height, where if the 30000. ſouldiers had waited for them, they might eaſily haue taken them, by reaſon of the great cold: and from the top of that hill, they diſcouered the land of Mexico, and the great lake, with his villages round about, which is an exceeding goodly ſight. But when Cortes ſaw that beautifull thing, his ioy was without compariſon, and he toke not ſo much pleaſure, but ſome of his men feared as much, and there was a murmuration among them to returne backe againe, yea and like to haue bene a mutinie among them. But Cortes with his wiſedome and diſſimulation did pacifie the matter, with courage, hope, and gentle wordes, and they ſeeing that their Captaine at all aſſayes was the firſt him ſelfe, they feared the leſſe the things that they imagined. And diſcending downe into the plaine, they found a great large houſe, ſufficient for him and all his companie, with ſixe thouſand Indians of Tlaxcallan, Huexozinco, & Chololla. And ye ſeruants of Mutezuma made cotages of ſtraw for the Tamemez or carriers, who were lade with the farbage, and vittailes: there was a good ſupper prepared for them, and great fires to warme them, and all things neceſſary. Whither came many principal perſons from Mexico, to viſite him, among whom was a kinſman of Mu-

Oh wiſe Cortez.

P 3 tezuma,

The Conquest of

tezuma, who presented vnto Cortes the value of thrée thousand ducats in gold, and besought him to returne backe againe, and to haue consideration of the pouertie, hunger, and euill way, yea and to passe in little boats in danger of drowning. And as for tribute to be giuen to the Emperor, a greater summe should be appointed, then though he went personally to Mexico, yea and that it should be paid at what place he would appoint. Cortes welcomed them, as reason did require, and presented vnto them haberdasheries, which they esteemed in much, & chiefly he did louingly entertaine Mutezuma his kinsman, vnto whome hée made this answer, saying, I would gladly serue and pleasure such a mightie prince as your soueraigne Mutezuma is if it lay in my handes without offence of the King my master: and concerning my going to Mexico, Mutezuma shall receiue both pleasure and honour, rather than otherwise, & after I haue talked with him, I wil soone returne, likewise hunger I feare not, neither yet doubt that I nor none of mine shall want, and for my passage on the water, I say it is nothing in comparison of two thousande leagues, which I haue sailed onely to come and visit him.

But yet for all this talke, if they had found him careless, they would haue pinched him as some doth say, for he gaue them to vnderstand, that he nor his men slept not by night, nor yet vnarmed themselues, yea, and also if it chanced thē to finde in the night season any that were not of their company, they slue them out of hand, desiring him to aduise his men therof, least any of them should happen to fall into that daunger, which would much grieue him, and with this talke they went all to take their rest.

The next day in the morning he proceded forward and came to Amaquemecan which is 2. leagues from thence, and standeth in the prouince of Chalco, a town ȳ containeth 20000. housholders. The Lord of that towne presented

to

to Cortez fortie women slaues, and 3000. ducats in gold, with meat abundantly for two daies, & secretly made complaint vnto him of Mutezuma. And from thence he went to another towne foure leagues from thence, the halfe thereof was built vpon the lake, and the other halfe vpon the land at the foot of a ragged hill. There went in his companie many subiects of Mutezuma for purueyors, but yet both they and the townesmen would faine haue laid hands vpon the Spaniards, and euery night would send their spies to see what the Christians did, but the watch flue about twentie of them, whereupon the matter staied, and their pretence toke no effect: sure it is a thing to laugh at, for at euery fancie they would proue to kill thē, and yet they were not for the purpose. The next day in the morning came twelue Lords from Mexico, among whom was Cacama, neuew to Mutezuma, who was Lord of Tezcuco, a yong man of xxv. yeares of age, whom the Indians did much honour: he was carried vpon their shoulders, and when they set him downe, one went before with a brome to sweepe the dust out of his way. These Gentlemen came to accompanie Cortes, excusing Mutezuma, saying that he was not well at ease, and therfore he came not personally to receiue him. And yet they intreated Cortes to returne back againe, and not to come vnto Mexico, giuing him to vnderstand by signs, that they would there displease him, and so defend the passage and entrance, a thing easie to be done, but they were either blinded, or else they durst not breake the cawsey. Cortes entertained thē like noble men and gaue vnto them of his haberdash, and departed fro the towne w^t many graue personages, who carried with them a great traine, which filled vp the way well nigh as they should passe, wondring at their beards, harnesse, apparell, horses and extinece, saying to themselues, these be Gods. Cortes gaue them warning not to come among the horses

The Conquest of

nor among his men, for feare they would kill them. This he made them beleeue because he would not haue his way stopped, for that the number of them was so great. They then came to a towne built vppon the water, of two thousand houses, and before they came thither, they had gone more then halfe a league vpon a faire Cawsey, which was twentie foote broad: the towne had faire houses and many towers: the Lord of the towne did receiue them worshipfully, and prouided all things plentifully, desiring him to abide there that night, and secretly made complaintes against Mutezuma, of many wrongs and exactions done by him, and certified him, that from thence the way was very faire to Mexico, & all the like cawsey as he had passed. With this newes Cortes was very glad, for he meant to haue stayed there for to haue built Barkes and Foysts, and yet he feared least they would breake y cawsey, wherfore he had alwayes a care ouer Cacama, who with the other Lordes desired him not to abide there, but to procéede forward to Iztacpalapan, which was but two leagues off, and that the Lord thereof was another Nenew to Mutezuma. To admit their request he wét with them to that towne, and from thence to Mexico was but two leagues, the which the next day he might go at pleasure, and come timely into the citie, & in this order came to Iztacpalapan.

Euery two houres came messengers betwixte Cortes and Mutezuma: then came Cuetlauac Lord of that towne, with the Lorde Culhuacan his kinsman to receiue him, who presented vnto him slaues, garments, and feathers, and to the balew of foure thousande Ducates in Golde. Cuetlauac receiued al the Spaniards into his own house, which hath verie faire lodgings all of stone, and Carpenters worke, excéeding well wrought, with high & low rowmes, with all kind of seruice: The chambers were hanged with cloth of Cotten very rich, after their maner.

There

the weſt India.

There were faire gardens repleniſhed with many ſwéet floures, and ſwéete trées garniſhed with networke, made of Canes, and couered with roſes and other fine hearbes, with ſundrie pondes of ſwéete water. There was another garden very beautifull of all ſortes of fruites and hearbes, with a great ponde walled with lime and ſtone, and was foure hundreth paces ſquare, made with faire ſteppes to diſcende vnto the bottome in many places, and was full of diuers kindes of fiſhes, and many kinde of water birdes, which ſomtimes couered the pond, as Gulles, Mewes, and ſuch like. Iztapalapan is a towne of 10000. houſholds, & is planted in a lake of ſalt water, the one halfe of the towne built on the water, and the other on the land.

The Solemne pompe wherewith Cortes was receiued into Mexico.

From Iztacpalapan to Mexico is two leagues all vpon a faire Calſey, vpon the which eight horſemen may paſſe on ranke, and ſo directly ſtraight as though it had bene made by line. And who ſoeuer hath good eieſight might diſcerne the gates of Mexico frō thence. Coyoacan is a towne of ſixe thouſand dwellers, Vizilopucheli is of fiue thouſād. Theſe townes are planted in the lake, and are adorned with many temples, whiche haue many faire towers, that doe beautifie exceedingly the lake. There is great contractatiō of Salte, which is made there, and from thence is carried abroad to faires and markets, which thing was a greate rente to Mutezuma. Vpon this Calſey are many drawne bridges built vpon faire arches, that the water paſſeth through.

Cortes paſſed this calſey with 400. Spaniardes, & 6000. Indians his friends: they paſſage was with much ado, by

Z reaſon

The Conquest of

reason of the great multitude of Indians which came to see him, & comming néer the citie, there adioyned another cal sey with a broder passage, where standeth a strong bul warke of stone of the heigth of 2. fatom, with two towers on each side, and two gates very strong. Here at this fort came thrée thousande Courtiers and Citizens to re ceiue him, and euery of them touched the ground with his right hand and kissed it, and passed forwards in the order as they came. These salutatiōs endured an houre & more. From the bulwark the calsey lieth directly, and before the entraunce into the stréete there is an other drawe bridge made of timber ten paces broad, vnder the which the wa ter passeth to and fro. At this bridge came Mutezuma to receiue Cortez vnder a Canapie of gréene feathers & gold, with much argentery hanging thereat, which Canapie foure noble men did carry. And the two princes Cuetlauac and Cacama his neuews, did leade him by each arme: all thrée were rich apparelled & all of one fashion, except Mu tezuma, which had a paire of shoes of gold beset with pre cious stones, and the soles were tied to the vpper parts with latchets, as is painted of the Antikes. His gentle men went by two and two, laying downe and taking vp mantels and couerlets vpon the ground, because his féete should not touch the same: then followed him as in pro cession, 200. noble men barefooted, with garments of a ri cher liuery then the first thrée thousand. Mutezuma came in the middest of the stréete, and the others came behinds him as nigh the wal as they mought, their faces towards the grounde, for it was a great offence to looke him in the face. Cortez alighted from his horse, and acrording to our vse went to embrace him, but the Princes who led him by the armes would not suffer him to come so nigh, for they held it for sin to touch him, but yet saluted each one ye other.

Cortez put about Mutezuma his necke a coller of Mar
garites,

the weſt India.

garites, Diamonds, & other ſtones all of glaſſe. Mutezuma receiued it thankfully, and went before with one of the princes his neuewes, and commaunded the other to leade Cortes by the hand, next after him in the midſt of ye ſtreet: and proceeding forward in this order, then came the Gentlemen in the richeſt liuery to welcome him, one by one, touching the ground with their hands, and after returned to their ſtanding. And if the Citizens had come as they requeſted, all that day would not haue ſerued for ſalutations. The coller of glaſſe pleaſed well Mutezuma, and becauſe he would not take without giuing a better thing, as a great prince, he commaunded to be brought two collers of redde prawnes, which are there much eſteemed, and at euery one of them hanged eight ſhrimpes of gold, of excellent workemanſhip, and of a finger length euery one, he put theſe collers with his owne handes about Cortes his necke, the which was eſteemed a moſt great fauour, yea and the Indians maruelled at it. At this time they were come to the ſtreete ende, which was almoſt a mile long, broad, ſtraight, and very faire, and full of houſes on eache ſide, in whoſe dores, windowes and tops, was ſuch a multitude of Indians to behold the ſtraungers, that I know not who wondered moſt, our men to ſee ſuch a number of them, or elſe they to ſee our men, their ordinance & horſes, a thing ſo ſtraunge vnto them. They were brought vnto a great court or houſe of idols, which was the lodging Axalaca, at the dore whereof, Mutezuma tooke Cortes by the hand, and brought him into a faire hall, and placed him vpon a rich carpet, ſaying vnto him, Sir now are you in your owne houſe, eate and take your reſt and pleaſure, for I will ſhortly come and viſite you againe. Such (as you heare) was the receiuing of Hernando Cortez by Mutezuma a moſt mightie King, into his great and famous Citie of Mexico, the eight day of Nouember, 1519.

Z 2   The

The Conqueſt of

The Oration of Mutezuma to the Spaniardes.

THe houſe where the Spaniardes were lodged was great and large, with many faire chambers ſufficient for them all: it was nete, cleane matted, and hanged with cloth of Cotten, and feathers of many colours, pleaſant to behold. When Mutezuma was departed from Cortez, he began to ſette his houſe in order, and placed the ordinaunce at his dore, & hauing all his things in good ſort, he went to a ſumptuous dinner that was prepared for him. As ſoone as Mutezuma had made an end of his dinner, hearing that the ſtraungers were riſen from the table, and repoſed a while, then came he to Cortez, ſaluting him, and ſatte downe by him. He gaue vnto him diuers iewels of gold plate, feathers, and many garmēts of Cotten, both riche, wel wouen, and wrought of ſtrange colours, a thing comely, that did manifeſt his greatneſſe, and alſo confirme their imagination. This gifte was deliuered honorablie, and then began his talke as foloweth: Lorde and Gentlemen, I doe much reioyce to haue in my houſe ſuch valient men as ye are, for to vſe you with curteſſe, and intreate you with honour, according to your deſerte and my eſtate. And where heretofore I deſired that you ſhoulde not come hither, the onely cauſe was, my people had a greate feare to ſée you, for your ieſture and grimme beardes did terrifie them, yea, they reported that ye had ſuch beaſts as ſwallowed men, and that your comming was frō heauen, bringing with you lightning, thunder, & thunderbolts, wherwith you made the earth to trēble and to ſhake, and that ye ſlew therwith whom ye pleaſed. But now I do ſée & know that you are mortal mē, and that ye are quiet & hurt no man: alſo I haue ſéne your boxes,

which

the weſt India.

which are but poor ſeruants, and your Gunnes like vnto ſhooting Trunkes. I doe now holde all for fables and
lyes which haue bin reported of you, and I doe alſo accept
you for my meere kinſman. My father tolde mee that hee
had heard his forefathers ſay, of whome I doe diſcende,
that they helde opinion howe they were not naturals of
this land, but come hither by chaunce, in companie of a
mightie Lorde, who after a while that he hadde aboue A ſtraunge
here, they returned to their naturall ſoile: After manie opinion.
yeares expyred, they came againe for thoſe whom they
had left heere behinde them, but they would not goe with
them, becauſe they had here inhabited, and hadde wiues
and children, and great gouernment in the land. Nowe
theſe mightie Lordes ſeing that they were ſo ſtubborne,
and woulde not returne with them, departed from them
ſore diſpleaſed, ſaying, that hee woulde ſend his children
that ſhould both rule and gouerne them, in iuſtice, peace,
and auncient Religion. And for this conſideration, wee
haue alwayes ſuſpected and beleeued, that ſuch a people
ſhould come to rule and gouerne vs, and conſidering from
whence you come, I doe thinke that you are they whome
we loked for, and the notice which the great Emperour
Charles had of vs, who hath now ſent you hither. Therefore Lorde and Captaine, be well aſſured, that wee will
obey you, if their be no feyned or deceitfull matter in
your dealings, and will alſo diuide with you and yours
all that wee haue. And although this which I haue ſayde
were not onely for your vertue, fame, and deedes of valiant Gentlemen, I would yet do it for your worthineſſe
in the battels of Tauaſco, Teocazinco, and Chololla, beeing ſo few, to ouercome ſo many.

Now againe, if ye imagine that I am a God, and the
walles and roofes of my houſes, and all my veſſell of ſeruice, to be of pure golde, as the men of Zempoallan, Tlaxcallan,

Z 3

The Conquest of

Callan, and Huexozinco, hath enformed you, it is not so, and I iudge you to be so wise, that you giue no credite to such fables. You shall also note, that though your cōming hither, many of my subiects haue rebelled, and are become my mortall enemies, but yet I purpose to breake their wings. Come feele you my bodie, I am of flesh and bone, a mortall man as others are, and no God, although as a king I doe esteeme my selfe of a greater dignitie and preheminence then others. My houses you doe also see, which are of timber and earth, and the principallest of Masons worke, therefore now you doe both knowe and see what odious liers those talebearers were. But troth it is, that gold plate, feathers, armour, iewels, and other riches, I haue in the treasurie of my forefathers a long time preserued, as the vse of kings is, all the which you and yours shall enioy at al times. And now it may please you to take your rest, for I know that you are wearie of your iourney. Cortes with ioyfull countenance humbled himself, seeing some teares fall from Mutezuma his eies, saying vnto him, vpon the trust I haue had in your clemencie, I insisted to come both to see, and talke with your highnesse, and nowe I know that all are lies which hath beene tolde me. The like your highnesse hath heard reported of vs, assure your selfe, that the Emperour King of Spaine is your naturall Lord, whom ye haue expected for, he is the onely heire from whence your linage both proceede, and as touching the offer of your highnesse treasure, I do most heartily thanke you.

After all this communication, Mutezuma demaunded whether the bearded men which came with him, were either his vassals, or his slaues, because he would entersaine each one accorᵭing to his estate. Cortez aunswered, that they were all his brethren, friends, and fellowes, except some that were his seruants.

A louing answere.

Then

the weſt India. 175

Then he departed,and went home to his Pallace,and there informed himſelfe particularly who were Gentlemen, and who were not,and accoꝛding therevnto, ſent euery one particular gift oꝛ pꝛeſent. To the Gentlemen he ſent his reward by his Controller, and to the ſpartiners and other ſeruitoꝛs,by a Page of his houſhold.

The Maieſty and order,wherewith Mutezuma was ſerued.

Vtezuma was a man of a ſmall ſtature,and lean,his colour tawny as all the Indians are. He had long haire on his head,ſix little haires vpon him,as though they had béene put in with a bodkin. His thin beard was black. He was a man of a faire condition, and a doer of iuſtice, well ſpoken, graue and wiſe,beloued and feared among his ſubiects. Mutezuma doth ſignifie ſadneſſe.

To the pꝛoper names of Kings and Loꝛds,they do adde this ſillible C. which is foꝛ curteſie and dignity,as we vſe Loꝛd. The Turk vſeth Zultan. The Mooꝛe oꝛ Barbarian calleth his Loꝛd Mulley, and ſo the Indians ſay Mutezumazin. His people had him in ſuch reuerence, that he permitted none to ſit in his ſight, noꝛ yet in his pꝛeſence to weare ſhoes, noꝛ looke him in the face, except verie fewe pꝛinces. He was glad of ẏ conuerſation of the Spaniards, and would not ſuffer them to ſtand on foote, foꝛ the great eſtimatiõ he had of thẽ, ẽ if he liked any of the Spaniards garments,he would exchange his apparell foꝛ theirs,

He chaunged his owne apparel foure times euery day, and hee neuer cloathed himſelfe againe with the garments which hee had once woꝛne, but all ſuch were kept

The Conquest of

kept in his Guardrobe, for to giue in presents to his seruants and Ambassadours, and vnto valiant Souldiours which had taken any enemie prisoner, and that was esteemed a great reward, and a title of priuiledge.

The costly mantels whereof had béene diuerse sent to Cortes, were of the same Guardrobe.

Mutezuma went alwaies very neate and fine in his attire. Hée bathed him in his hotehouse foure times euerie day. He went seldome out of his Chamber, but when hée went to his meate. He eate alwayes alone, but solemnelie, and with great abundance. His table was a pillow, or else a couple of coloured skinnes. His Chaire was a foure footed stoole made of one péece, and hollowe in the middest, well wrought and painted. His table clothes, napkins, and towels, were made of Cotten wooll, verie white and newe; for he was neuer serued but once with that naperie. Foure hundred Pages brought in his meate, all sonnes of great Lordes, and placed it vppon a table in his great Hall. The meate beeing brought in, then came Mutezuma to behold the dishes, and appoynted those dishes that liked him best, and chafing dishes were prepared to kéepe that meate warme, and seldome would eate of any other dish, except the Lord Steward or Controller should highly commend any other dish.

Before he sate downe, came twentie of his wiues of the fayrest and best esteemed, or else those that serued wéekely by turne, brought in the Bason and Ewer, with great humblenesse. This done, he sate him downe, and then came the Lord Steward, and drew a wooden nette before him, because none shoulde come nigh his Table. And this noble man alone placed the dishes, and also took them away, for the Pages who brought in the meate, came not neare the Table, nor yet spake any worde, nor no man else.

While

the weſt India.

While the Lord Mutezuma was at his meate, except ſome Ieſter, they all ſerued him barefooted. There aſſiſted alwayes ſomewhat a farre off, ſire auncient and Noble men, vnto whome he vſed to giue of the diſh that beſt lyked him, who receiued the ſame at his hand with great reuerence, and eate it incontinent, without looking in his face, which was the greateſt humilitie that they coulde vſe before him. He had muſicke of Fidle, Flute, and of a Snayle ſhell, and a Cauldron couered with a ſkinne, and ſuch other ſtraunge inſtruments. They had very euill voyces to ſing. Alwayes at dinner time he had Dwarfes, crookebackes, and other deformed counterfeits, all for maieſtie and to laugh at, who had their meate in the Hall among the Ieſters and Idiots, which were fed with part of the meate that came from Mutezuma his table, all the reſt of the meat was giuen to three thouſand of the guard, who attended ordinarily in the yard or court, and therfore they ſay that there was brought for his table three thouſand diſhes, and as many pottes of wine, ſuch as they vſe, and that continually the Buttrey and Pantrey ſtood open, which was a wonder to ſee what was in them. The platters, diſhes, and cuppes, were all of earth, wherof the king was ſerued but once, and ſo from meale to meale new. He had likewiſe his ſeruice of gold and plate very rich, but he vſed not to be ſerued with it, (they ſay) becauſe he would not be ſerued twice therwith, the which he thought a baſe thing.

Some affirme, that yong children were ſlaine and dreſſed in diuers kinde of diſhes for Mutezuma his table, but it was not ſo, onely of mans fleſh ſacrificed hee feede now and then. The table being taken vp, then came againe the Gentlewomen to bring water for his hands, with the like reuerence as they vſed at the firſt, and then went they to dinner with the other wiues, ſo that then the Gentle-

A a   men

men and pages waited as their course fell.

The footeplayers that plaied before Mutezuma.

When his table was taken vp, and his seruitors gone to meate, Mutezuma sate still: then came in the suiters that hadde any affaires to deale with him, barefooted, for all the persons did vse that reuerence, excepte some Princes his kinsmen, as the Lords of Tescuco, and Tlacopan, and a fewe others: and being cold weather, they vsed to weare old ragged clothes vppon their rich garments. All suiters vsed to make three or four curtesies, not loking toward his face, and speaking vnto him their heads downewardes, and in that order retired backe againe. Mutezuma aunswered his suiters very grauely, with lowe voice, and in few words, and not to al suters, for others his secretaries or coūsellers that stood by, answered for him, and hauing their answer, they returned backewardes, not turning their tailes to the prince. After these businesses done, he vsed som recreatiō, hearing Iesters or songs, wherin he delighted much, or else to loke vpon the plaiers, who play with their feete, as we do with our handes. These haue a cudgel like vnto a pastlers rowler, which they tosse high & low as it wer a bal in the aire, straunge to behold. They vse other plaies to passe y time, in such an order, y it seemed maruellous to the lookers on. Cortez broughte into Spaine some of these players. Also they vse Marachines, in suche sorte they do play, that there stande eache vppon other shoulders, and he that standeth highest, sheweth many feates. Sometime Nutezuma did beholde the players, who played at a game called Pacoliztli,

the weſt India.

toliztli, which is muche like oure Tables, and they play with beanes, ſquared like dice, which they cal Patolli, and throw them out of both their hands vpon a matte, or elſe vpon the ground, where are made certaine ſtrikes, vpon which they ſette downe the chance that is throwne: and at this game they play all that they haue, and many times they bale to their owne bodies, and playe that into captiuitie, and to remaine a ſlaue, I meane ſuch as are common gameſters of ſmall eſtate.

The Tennis play in Mexico.

Sometimes Mutezuma went to the Tennis Courte. Their ball is called Villamaliztli, and is made of the gum which commeth frō a trée called Vlli. This trée groweth in a hote Countrey. The gumme being kneded together, and ſo made round, is as blacke as pitch, and ſomewhat heauie, and very harde for the hande, but yet good and light to rebound, and better than our windballes. They play not at chaſes, but at bandie, or at check, that is, if the ball touch the wall it loſeth. They may ſtrike the ball with any part of their bodie, but there is alwaies a penaltie if they only ſtrike not with the buttoke or ſide, which is the fineſt play: whereof they vſe a ſkinne vpon each buttocke. They play ſo many to ſo many for a packe of mantels, or according to the abilitie of the players. Alſo they play for golde and feathers, and ſometime for their owne bodyes, as they vſe at Patolli, which is there permitted & lawfull. The Tennis Court is called Tlachco, and is a Wall long and narrow, but wider vpwards, then downewardes, and higher on the ſides then at the ends, which is an induſtrie for their play. The houſe is alwaies white and ſmooth in the ſide walles: they haue certain ſtones like vnto milſtones, w a little hole in

Aa 2 the

The Conquest of

the middeſt that paſſeth through the ſtone, the hole is ſo ſmall, that ſcarcely the ball may pay paſſe through, but he that chanceth to ſtrike the ball into the hole, which ſildome happeneth, winneth the game, and by an auncient lawe and cuſtome among Tennis players, he ought to haue the cloakes of all thoſe that ſtand and behold the play, on that ſide that the ball went in, and in ſome Tennis Courtes, the halfe of the garments of them that ſtand looking on. The winner is then bounde to make certaine ſacrifice to the God of the Tennis play, and to the ſtone where the ball entred. The beholders of the play would ſay, that ſuch a winner ſhould bee a théefe and an adulterer, or elſe that he ſhould die quickly.

They vſed in the Temple of the Tennis play, two Images of the God of the ball, which ſtood vpon the two lower walles. The Sacrifice was celebrated at midnight, with many Ceremonies and Witchcrafts, and ſonges for that purpoſe. Then came a Prieſt from the Cathedrall Church, with other Religious perſons to bleſſe the Sacrifice, ſaying certaine diuelliſh praiers, and throwing the ball foure times in the Tennis Court. In this order was the Tennis play conſecrated, and after this conſecration it was lawfull to play, or elſe not, for this diligence was firſt to bee done when any Tennis Court or play was newly built.

The owner of the Tennis Court alſo woulde neuer ſuffer any to play, vntill he had firſt offered ſomething to the Idoll, their ſuperſtition was ſo great.

Mutezuma brought the Spaniards to behold this paſtime, and gaue them to vnderſtand, that hee delighted much in this game, and alſo to ſée our men play at Cardes and Dice.

The

the vvest India.

The number of wiues that Mutezuma had in his houfe.

Vtezuma had many houses as well in Mexico as without, for his recreation and pleasure, as also for his ordinarie dwelling. To write of all it should be tedious, but where his continuall abiding was, he named Tepac, that is to say, palace. And that pallace had twentie doores or gates whiche had their outcomming into the common streetes.

It hath three courtes, and in the one standeth a fayre fountaine, many halles, and a hundred chambers of twentie three, and thirtie foote long, an hundred bathes and hothouses: and although the building was without nailes yet very good workmanship.

The walles were made of masons worke, and wrought of Marble, Jaspe, and other blacke stone, with vaines of redde, like vnto rubies and other stones, which glittered very faire: the Rooffes were wrought of Timber, and curiously carued: the Timber was Cedre, Cipers, & Pinetre: the chambers were painted and hung with cloth of cotten, and cloth made of Conneis haire and feathers. The beddes were poore and of no balewe, for they were nothing but Mantels laide vpon mattes, or vpon Hay, or else mattes alone: fewe men lay within those houses.

There were a thousande women, and some affirme that there were three thousand, accounting gentlewomen, seruaunts and slaues: the most were noble mens daughters, Mutezuma toke of them for his selfe, those that liked him best, and the others he gaue in marriage to Gentlemen his seruaunts.

Aa 3 The

The Conquest of

The saying was, that he had at one time a hundreth and fiftie women his wiues with childe, who through the perswasion of the diuel, tooke medicines to cast their creatures, because they knew that they should not inherit the state: these his wiues, had many olde women for their Guard, for no man was permitted to looke vpon them.

The shield of armes that is set in his Pallace, and likewise carried to the warres, is an Eagle soring vpon a Tiger his talents, bent as taking pray. Some thinke it is a Gryphon and not an Eagle. The Gryphons in time past, say they, did cause the vale of Auacatlan to be dispeopled, for they were great deuourers of men, and that their abiding was in ye Mountains of Teoacan: they approue that these Mountaines were called Cuitlachtepelt, of Cuitlachtli, which is a Gryphon, bigger then a Lion: but the Spaniards did neuer see any of them.

The Indians by their old Pictures do paint those Gryphons to haue a kinde of haire and no feathers, and also affirme, that with their talandes and teethe they breake mens bones. They haue the courage of a Lion, and the countenaunce of an Eagle: they painte him with foure féte, and téeth, with a kind of downe, more like wooll then feathers, with his beake, talandes, and wings.

And in all those things the picture agreeth with our painting and writing, in such sort that a Gryphon is no approued naturall Foule, nor yet beast. Plinie iudgeth this tale of Gryphons to bee lies. There are also other Lords that giue the Gryphon in their armes, flying with a heart in his talandes.

A house

the vveſt India. 183

A houſe of Foule, which were onely preſerued for their feathers.

Vtezuma had another houſe, with very good lodgings and faire gallaries, built vpon pillers of Iaſpe, which extendeth toward a goodly garden, in the which there are tenne pondes or moe, ſome of ſalt water for ſea foule, & other ſome of freſh water for riuer foule and lake foule, which pondes are deuiſed with ſluces to emptie and to fill at their pleaſure, for the cleanneſſe of the feathers. There is ſuch a number of foule that ſcarcely the pondes may hold them, and of ſuch diuers kindes both in feathers and making, as ſure it was an admiration for the Spaniards to behold, for the moſt of them they knew not, nor yet had at any time ſéene the like. And to euery kinde of foule they gaue ſuch bayte as they were wont to féede of in the fields or Riuers. There did belong to that houſe thrée hundreth perſons of ſeruice: ſome were to cleanſe the pondes: other ſome did fiſh for bayte: other ſome ſerued them with meate: other did looſe them and trimme their feathers: others had care to looke to their egges: others to ſet them abroad: others cured them when they were ſicke; and the principalleſt office was to plucke the feathers; for of them was made rich Mantels, Tapiſſary, Targats, tuffes of Feathers, and many other things wrought with Gold and Siluer: a moſt perfite worke.

A houſe

The Conqueſt of
A houſe of foule for hawking and other ſtraunge things.

Her is another houſe with large quarters and lodgings, which is called a houſe foꝛ foule, not becauſe there are moꝛe then in the other, but becauſe they be bigger and to hauke withall, and are foule of rapine, wherfoꝛe they are eſtœmed as moꝛe nobler then all the others.

There are in this houſe many high halles, in the which are kept menne, women and Childꝛen: in ſome of them are kept ſuche as are boꝛne white of colour whiche doth very ſeldome happen: in other ſome are dwarfes, crokedbackes, burſtenmen, counterfaites, and monſtrous perſons, in greate number: they ſay that they vſed to deformme them when they were Childꝛen, to ſette foꝛth the kings greatneſſe: every of theſe perſons were in ſeuerall Halles by themſelues.

In the lower Halles were greate Cages made of Timber: in ſome of them were Lions, in other Tigers, in other Ounꝛes, in others Wolues: in concluſion, there was no foure ſoted beaſte that wanted there, onely to the effect that the mightie Mutezuma might ſay that he had ſuch things in his houſe.

They were fed with their oꝛdinarie, as Ginea cockes, Deare, Dogges, and ſuch like.

There was alſo in other Halles great earthen veſſels, ſome with earth, and ſome with water, wherin were ſnakes, as groſſe as a mans thigh, Uipers, Crocodzilles, which they call Caymanes, oꝛ Lizarts of twenty foote long, with ſuch Scales and head as a Dꝛagon hath: Alſo other little Liꝛartes, and other venemous beaſtes and
Serpents

the weſt India.

Serpentes as well of the water as of the lande, a terrible ſight for the lokers on.

There were alſo other Cages for foule of rapine of all ſortes, as Hawkes, Kightes, Boyters, and at the leaſt nine or ten kind of Haukes. This houſe of foule had of dayly allowance fiue hundred Gynea cockes, and thrée hundred men of ſeruice, beſides the Falconers and Hunters, which are infinite. There were many other ſortes of Foules that our men knewe not, which ſemed by theyr beake and talents good to Hauke withall.

To the Snakes and other venemous beaſtes they gaue the bloude of men ſacrificed, to féede them, and ſome ſay they gaue vnto them mannes fleſhe, whiche the great Liſarts doe eate very well. The Spaniardes ſawe the floure couered with blood like a iealy in a ſlaughter houſe, it ſtunke horribly.

It was ſtraunge to ſée the officers in this houſe howe euery one was occupied. Our men toke greate pleaſure in beholding ſuche ſtraunge things, but they coulde not awaye with the roaring of the Lyons, the fearefull hiſſing of the Snakes and Aders, the dole full howling and barking of the Wolues, the ſorrow full yelling of the Ounzes and Tigres when they would haue meate.

Moſte certaine, in the nighte ſeaſon it ſéemed a Dungeon of Hells, and a dwelling place of the Deuill, and euen ſo it was in déede, for neare at hande was a Hall of a hundred and fiftie foote long, & thirtie foote broade, where was a Chappel with the Roofe of ſiluer and golde in leafe, Wainſcotted, and decked with great ſtarre of pearle and ſtone, as Agattes, Cornerinos, Emeralues, Rubies, and diuers other ſortes, and this was the Oratory where Muetzuma prayed in the nighte ſeaſon,

The Conqueſt of

and in that chappell the diuell did appeare vnto him, and gaue him anſwere accoꝛding to his pꝛaiers.

He had other houſes like vnto Barnes, onely foꝛ the feathers of foules, and foꝛ mantels which pꝛocéeded of his rentes and tributes, a thing much to bee ſéene: vppon the dooꝛes was ſet his armes, which was a Connie.

Here dwelted the chiefe officers of his houſe, as Treaſurer, Controller, Receiuers and other officers apperteining to the Kings reuenewes. Mutezuma had no houſe wherein was not an Oꝛatoꝛy foꝛ the diuel, whome they woꝛſhipped foꝛ the Iewels there. And therfoꝛe thoſe houſes were great and large.

The Armory of Mutezuma.

Vtezuma had ſome houſes of Armoꝛ, vpon the dooꝛes whereof ſtoo a bowe and arrowes. In theſe houſes was great ſtoꝛe of all kinde of Munition whiche they vſe in their warres: as Bowes, Arrowes, Slings, Launces, Darts, Clubbes, Swoꝛds and Buckelers, and gallant Targettes moꝛe trimme with ſtones, Skulles and Splintes, but not many, and all made of wood, gilt oꝛ couered with leather. The wood whereof they make their Armour and Targettes, is very hard and ſtrong, foꝛ they vſe to toaſt it at the fire, and at their arrowe endes they encloſe a little péece of ſharp ſtone, oꝛ a péece of a fiſh bone called Libiſa, and that is venemous, foꝛ if any bee hurt therewith and the head remaine in the wounde, it is ſoſore that it is almoſt incurable.

Their

the west India.

Theyr swordes are of woode, and the edge thereof is flint stone, encloſed or ioyned into a ſtaffe, with a certaine kinde of glewe which is made of a roote called Zacolt, and Teuxalli, which is a kinde of ſtrong ſande, whereof they make a mixture, and after kneade it with blood of Battes or Bearemice, and other foule, which doth glewe marueilous ſtrong, and lightly neuer uncleaueth: of this ſtuffe, they make naples, pearcers, and augers, wherewith they bore timber and ſtone: with their ſwordes they cut ſpeares, yea and a horſe necke at a blowe, and make dents into iron, which ſeemeth a thing unpoſſible and incredible.

In the Citie no man may weare weapon, but onely in warres, hunting, and among the Kings Guard.

The Gardens of Mutezuma.

Eſides the foreſaide houſes, hee had many others for his onely recreation and paſtime, with excellent faire Gardens of medicinal hearbes, ſweete floures, and trées of delectable ſauour, whiche were many, and a thing to giue praiſe to God the maker & Creator of all.

In that Garden were a thouſand perſonages, made and wrought artificially of leaues and flowers. Mutezuma woulde not permitte that in this Gardeine ſhoulde be any kinde of potte Hearbes, or things to bee ſolde ſaying, that it did not appertaine to Kings to haue thinges of profite, among their delightes and pleaſures,

The Conquest of

for suche thinges (saide hée) did appertaine to Merchants.

Yet notwithstanding he had Orchards with many and sundry fruites, but they stode farre from the Cittie, and whither sildome times hee went: hee had likewise out of Mexico pleasaunt houses in woddes and forrestes, of great compasse, enuironed with water, in the which he had fountaines, riuers, pondes with fishe, warrandes of Connies, rockes and couert where were Harts, Bucks, Hares, Foxes, Wolues, and such like, with wildernesse for euery sort.

To these places the Lords of Mexico vsed to goe and sport themselues, such and so many were the houses of Mutezuma, wherein fewe Kings were equall with him.

The Court and Guarde of Mutezuma.

HE had daily attending vppon him in his priuie Guarde, fixe hundreth Noble men and Gentlemen, and each of them thrée or foure seruants, and some had twentie seruaunts or moe, according to his estate: and in this maner he had thrée thousande men attendant in his Court, and some affirme moe, all the which were fedde in his house of the meate that came from his table.

The seruing men alwayes abode belowe in the Court all the day, and went not from thence till after Supper.

It

the west India.

It is to bee thought that his Guard was the greater, because the Straungers were there, although in effect of truth it is most certaine, that all the Lordes that are vnder the Mexicall Empire (as they say) are thirtie persons of high estate, who are able to make each of them a hundred thousand men. There are three thousand Lordes of Townes, who haue many vassals.

These noble men did abide in Mexico certaine times of the yeare, in the Court of Mutezuma, and could not depart from thence without especiall licence of the Emperour, leauing each of them a son or brother behind them for securitie of rebellion, and for this cause they had generally houses in the Citie: such and so great was the Court of Mutezuma,

The great subiection of the Indians to their king.

Here is not in all the dominions of Mutezuma any subiect that paieth not tribute vnto him. The noble men pay their tribute in personal seruice. The husbandmen called Macevaltin, with body and goods. In this sort they are either tenants, or else heires to their possessions. Those which are heires, doe pay one third part of all their fruite and commoditie that they doe reape or bring vp, as dogs, hennes, foule, conies, golde, siluer, stones, salt, waxe, honie, mantels, feathers, cotten, and a certaine fruit called Cacao, that serueth for money, and also to eate. Also all kinde of graine, and garden hearbes, and fruites, whereof they doe maintaine themselues.

The Tenants doe pay monethly, or yearely, as they
can

The Conquest of

can agrée, and because their tribute is great, they are called slaues, for when they may haue licence to eate egges, they thinke it a great fauour. It was reported that they were taxed what they should eate, and all the residue was taken from them. They went verie poorely cloathed, yea and the moſt of their treaſure was an earthen potte, wherein they boiled their hearbes, a couple of Millstones to grinde their Corne, and a matte to lie vppon. They did not onely pay this rent, and tribute, but also ſerued with their bodies at all times when the great King ſhould commaund. They were in ſuch great ſubiection to their prince, that they durſt not ſpeake one word although their daughters ſhould bee taken from them to be vſed at their pleaſure. It was reported that of euerie thrée ſons, they deliuered one to be ſacrificed, but that report was falſe, for if it had béene true, the townes had not bin ſo repleniſhed with people as they were: and also the noble men did not eate mans fleſh, but onely of thoſe which were ſacrificed, and they were ſlaues or priſoners taken in the warres. Aſſuredly they were cruell butchers, and ſlue yearely for that bloody ſacrifice many men, and ſome children, but not ſo many as was reported. All the aforeſaide rentes they brought to Mexico vpon their backes, and in boates, I meane ſo much as was neceſſarie for the prouiſion of the houſe and Court of Mutezuma, all the reſidue was ſpent among Souldiers, and bartred for golde, plate, precious ſtones, and other rich Iewels, eſteemed of Princes, all the which was brought to the treaſurie. In Mexico was large and great barnes and houſes to receiue and kéepe the corne for prouiſion of the Citie, with officers, and vnderofficers, who did receiue the ſame, and kept account thereof in bookes of painted figures.

Alſo in euerie Towne was a receiuer, who bare in
his

his hand a rodde or abush of feathers, and those gaue vp their accounts in Mexico. If any such had béene taken with deceite and falshode, death was his reward, yea and his kinred punished with penalties, as of a lignage of a traitor to his Prince. The Husbandmen, if they paid not well their tribute, were apprehended for the same, and if they were found to bee poore through sicknesse and infirmitie, then they were borne withall, but if they were found to be lasie and slouthfull, they should be vsed accordingly: but in conclusion, if they paied it not at a day appointed, then they should bee solde for slaues to pay their debt, or else be sacrificed.

There were many other prouinces, which paid a certaine portion, and reknosoledged seruice, but this tribute was more of honour then profite. In this sort Mutezuma had more then sufficient to prouide his house and warres, and to heape vp great store in his treasurie. Moreouer, he spent nothing in the buildings of his houses, for of long time he had certaine townes that payd no other tribute, but onely to worke and repaire continually his houses at their owne proper cost, and paide all kinde of workemen carrying vpon their backes, or drawing in sleddes, stone, lime, timber, water, and all other necessaries for the worke. Likewise they were bound to prouide al the firewood that should be spent in the court, which was a great thing, and did amount to 230. hundred weight a day, which was fiue hundred mens burthens, and some dayes in the winter much more. And for the Kings Chimneys they brought the barke of Oke trées, which was best esteemed for the light thereof, for they were great forcerers. Mutezuma had 100. cities with their prouinces, of whom he receiued rentes, tributes, and vassalage, where he maintained garrison of souldiers, and had treasurers in each of them.

His

The Conqueſt of

His dominion did extend from the North ſea to the South ſea, and 600. miles in longitude within the main land, although in very deed there were ſome townes, as Tlaxcallon, Mechuacan, Panuco, and Teocātepec, which were his enemies, and payde him neither tribute nor ſeruice: but yet the raunſome was much, when any of them was taken.

Alſo there were other kings and noble men, as of Texcuto & Tlacopan, which were not in ſubiection vnto him, but onely in homage and obedience, for they were of his own linage, vnto whō Mutezuma maried his daughters.

Thk ſituation of Mexico.

Mexico at the time when Cortes entred, was a city of 60. thouſand houſes. The Kings houſe, & other Noble mens houſes were great, large, and beautifull, the others were ſmall and royniſh, without eyther doores or windowes: and although they were ſmall, yet there dwelled in ſome of them, two, three, yea, and ten perſons, by reaſon whereof, the Citie was wonderfully repleniſhed with people.

This Citie is built vpon the water, euen in the ſame order as Venice is. All the bodie of the Citie ſtandeth in a great large lake of water. There is three ſortes of ſtreetes verie broade and faire, the one ſort are onelie of water, with many briges: an other ſort of onely earth: and the third of earth and water: that is to ſay, the one halfe earth to walke vpon, and the other halfe for Boates to bring prouiſion of all ſortes. Theſe ſtreetes are kept alwayes cleane, and the moſt part of the houſes haue two doores, the one towarde the cawſey, and the other towarde the water, at the which they take Boate to goe

where

the weſt India.

where they liſt. And although this Citie is founded vpon water, yet the same water is not good to drinke, whereof there is broughte by conduit water from a place called Capultepec, three miles diſtant frõ the Citie, which ſpringeth out of a little hill, at the foote whereof ſtandeth two Statues or couered Images wrought in ſtone, with their Targettes and Launces, the one is of Mutezuma, and the other of Axaiaca his father.

The water is brought from thence in two pipes or Canalls in great quantitie, and when the one is foule, then all the water is conueied into the other, till the firſt be made cleane. From this fountaine all the whole Citie is prouided, ſo that they goe ſelling the ſame water from ſtreete to ſtreete in little boates, and doe paye a certaine tribute for the ſame.

This Citie is deuided into two ſtreetes, the one was called Tlatelulco, that is to ſay, a litle Iland, and the other Mexico, where Mutezuma his dwelling and courte was, and is to be interpreted a ſpring. This ſtreete is the faireſt and moſt principall, and becauſe of the Kings Pallace there, the Citie was named Mexico, although the old and firſt name of the Citie was Tenuchtitlan, which doth ſignifie fruite out of ſtone, for the name is compounded of Tetl, which is ſtone, and Nuchtli, which is fruite, called Cuba, Tunas. The tree that beareth this fruite, is named Nopal, and is nothing almoſt but leaues of a foote broade and round, and three ynches thicke, ſome more, and ſome leſſe, accoding to the growth, full of thornes which are venemous: the leafe is greene, and the thorne or pricke ruſſet. After that is planted, it encreaſeth, growing leafe vnto leafe, and the foote thereof commeth to be as the bodie of a tree, and one leafe dothe onely produce another at the pointe, but at the ſides of the ſame leaues proceedeth other leaues: And becauſe heere in Spaine is

The Conquest of

of the same trées and fruite, it néedeth no further description.

In some prouinces where water is scante, they vse to drinke the iuice of these leaues. The fruite thereof called Nucheli, is like vnto figges, and euen so hathe his little kernels or graines within, but they are somewhat larger, and crowned like vnto a Medler. There are of them of sundrye coloures, some are gréene without, and Carnationlike within, which haue a good taste. Others are yellowe, and others white, and some speckled: the best sort are the white: it is a fruite that will last long.

Some of them tasteth of peares, and other some of Grapes: it is a colde and a fresh fruite, and best estéemed in the heate of Sommer. The Spaniardes doe more estéeme them then the Indians. The more the grounde is laboured where they growe, the fruite is so muche the better.

There is yet another kinde of this fruite redde, and that is nothing estéemed, although his tast is not euill, but because it dothe coloure and dye the eaters mouth, lippes, and apparell, yea and maketh his vrine looke like pure bloud. Many Spaniardes at their first cõming into India, and eating this fruite, were in a maze, and at their wittes ende, thinking that all the bloud in their bodies came out in vrine: yea and manye Phisitions at theyr first comming were of the same beliefe: for it hath happened, when they haue bin sent for vnto such as haue eaten this fruite, they not knowing the cause, and beholding the vryne, by and by they ministred medecine to staunch bloud: surely a thing to laugh at, to sée the Phisitions so deceiued. Of this fruite Nucheli and Tetl, which is a stone, is compounded Tenuchelitan. When this Citie was begunne to bée founded, it was placed néere vnto a greate stone that stoode in the middest of the lake, at the foote.

the West India.

foote whereof grewe one of these Nopal trées, and therefore Mexico giueth for armes and deuise the foote of a
Nopal trée springing from a stone, according to the Cities name.

Others doe affirme, that this Cittie hath the name
of his first founder, called Tenuch, being the seconde sonne
of Iztacmixcoatl, whose sonnes and descendentes did first
inhabite this lande of Ananac, called nowe newe
Spaine.

Howsoeuer the opinions are, certaine it is that the
scituation is called Tenuchtitan, and the dwellers there
Tenuchca Mexico.

Mexico is as much to say, as a spring or fountaine, according to the propertie of the vowell and spéech.

Others doe affirme, that Mexico hath his name of a
more auncient time, whose first founders were called
Mexiti, for vnto this day ÿ Indian dwellers in one stréete
of this city are called of Mexica. The Mexiti tooke name
of their principallest Idoll called Mexicli, who was in as
greate veneration as Vitzilopuchtli, God of the warre.

Mexico is enuironed with swéete water, and hathe
thrée waies to come vnto it by calsey, the one is from
the West, and that calsey is a mile and a halfe long.
Another from the North, and conteineth thrée miles
in length. Eastwarde the Cittie hathe no entrye. But
Southwarde the Calsey is sixe miles long, which was the
way that Cortez entred into the Citie.

The lake that Mexico is planted in, although it sée-
meth one, yet it is two, for the one is of water saltishe,
bitter, and pestiferous, and no kinde of fishe liueth in it.

And the other water is wholesome, good and swéet, and
bringeth forth small fishe.

The salte water ebbeth and floweth, according

Cc 2   to

to the winde that bloweth. The sweete water standeth higher, so that the good water falleth into the euill, and reuerteth not backward, as some hold opinion. The salt lake conteineth fiftéene miles in breadth, and fiftéene in length, and more then fiue and fortie in circuite, and the lake of sweete water conteineth euen as much, in such sort, that the whole lake conteineth more then thirtie leagues, and hath about fiftie townes scituated round about it, many of which Townes doe conteine fiue thousand housholdes, and some tenne thousande, yea and one Towne called Tezcuco, is as bigge as Mexico. All this lake of water springeth out of a mountaine that standeth within sight of Mexico. The cause that the one part of the lake is brackish or saltish, is, that the bottome or ground is all salt, and of that water great quantite of salt is daily made.

In this great lake are aboue two hundreth thousande little boates, which the Indians call Acalles, and the Spaniards call them Canoas, according to the speech of Cuba and Santo Domingo, wrought like a kneeting trough: som are bigger then other some, according to the greatnesse of the bodie of the trée whereof they are made. And where I number two hundred thousand of these boates, I speake of the least, for Mexico alone hath aboue fiftie thousande ordinarily to carry and bring vnto the Citie victuall, prouision, and passengers, so that on the market day all the stréetes of water are full of them.

The Market place of Mexico.

The Market is called in the Indian tongue Tianquiztli: euery parish hath his Market place to buy and sell in: but Mexico, and Tlatelulco onely, which are the chiefest Citties, haue great faires and

the vveſt India.

and places fit for the ſame, and eſpecially Mexico hath one place where moſt dayes in the yeare is buying and ſelling, but euery fourth day is the great Market ordinarily: and the like cuſtome is vſed throughout the dominions of Mutezuma.

This place is wide and large, compaſſed round about with dores, and is ſo great, that a hundred thouſand perſons come thither to choppe and change, as a Citie moſt principall in all that region. Wherfore the reſort is from farre parties vnto that place. Euery occupation and kind of marchandiſe hath his proper place appointed, which no other may by any means occupy or diſturbe. Likewiſe peſterous wares haue their place accordingly, (that is to ſay) ſtone, timber, lime, bricke, and all kinde of ſtuffe vnwrought, being neceſſarie to build withall. Alſo mattes both fine and courſe of ſundrie workemanſhip, alſo coles, woode, and all ſortes of earthen veſſell, glazed and painted very curiouſly: Deare ſkinnes both raw and tanned in haire and without haire, of manie colours, for ſhoomiakers, Bucklers, Targets, Jerkins, and lining of wooden Corſelets: alſo ſkinnes of other beaſtes and foule in feathers readie dreſſed of all ſortes, the colours and ſtraungeneſſe thereof was a thing to beholde. The richeſt marchandiſe was Salt, and mantels of Cotten wooll of diuerſe colours, both great and ſmall, ſome for beddes, others for garments and clothing, other for Tapiſſarie to hang houſes, other Cotten cloth for linning breeches, ſhirtes, table clothes, towels, napkins, and ſuch like things.

There were alſo mantels made of the leaues of the trée called Metl, and of Palme trée, and Cony haire, which are wel eſtéemed, being very warm, but ỹ couerlets made of feathers are the beſt: they ſell thréede made of Conie haire, péeces of linnen cloath made of Cotten wooll, alſo

Cc 3   ſkaines

The Conquest of

skaines of thrǽde of all colours: also it is straunge to sée the great store of poultrie that is brought to that market. And although they eate the flesh of the foule, yet the feathers serue for cloathing, miring one sort with another. There are of these foule so many sortes and seuerall colours that I cannot number them: some wilde, some tame, some water foule, and other some of rapine. All the brauerie of the market, is the place where golde and feathers ioyntly wrought is solde, for any thing that is in request is there liuely wrought in gold and feathers, and gallant colours. The Indians are so expert and perfect in this science, that they will worke or make a Butterflie, any wilde beast, trǽs, roses, flowers, hearbes, rotes, or any other thing, so liuely, that it is a thing maruellous to behold. It hapneth many times that one of these workemen in a whole day will eate nothing, onely to place one feather in his dew perfection, turning and tossing the feather to the light of the Sunne, into the shade or darke place, to sée where is his most naturall perfection, and till his worke be finished he will neither eate nor drinke. There are few nations of so much steame or sufferaunce. The Art or science of Goldsmiths, among them is the most curious, and verie good workemanship engrauen with toles made of flint, or in moulde. They will cast a platter in moulde with eight corners, and euery corner of seuerall mettall, that is to say, the one of golde, and the other of siluer, without any kinde of sowder: they will also found or cast a little cawdron with lose handles hanging thereat, as wǽ vse to cast a Bell: they will also cast in mould a fish of mettal with one scale of siluer on his back, and another of gold: they will make a Parret or Popin-Jay of mettall, that his tongue shall shake, and his heade moue, & his wings flutter: they wil cast an Ape in mould, that both hands and féet shall stir, and hold a spindle in his
hand

the vvest India.

hand séeming to spinne, yea and an apple in his hand, as though he would eat it. Our Spaniards were not a little amazed at the sight of these things. For our Goldsmiths are not to be compared vnto them. They haue skill also of Amell worke, and to set any precious stone. But nowe as touching the markette, there is to sell, Golde, Siluer, Copper, Leade, Latton, and Tinne, although there is but little of the three last mettels mentioned. There are Pearles, Precious stones, diuerse and sundrie sortes of Shelles, and Bones, Spunges and other pedlers ware, which certainly are many and straunge sortes, yea, and a thing to laugh at their Haberdash toyes & trifles. There are also many kind of hearbes, rootes, and seeds, as well to be eaten, as for medicine, for both men, women, and children, haue great knowledge in hearbes, for through pouertie and necessitie, they seeke them for their sustenance and helpe of their infirmities and diseases. They spend little among Phisitions, although there are some of that Arte, and manie Poticaries, who doe bring into the market, oyntments, sirops, waters, and other drugges, fit for sicke persons: they cure all diseases almost, with hearbs, yea, as much as for to kill lice, they haue a proper hearbe for the purpose.

The seuerall kindes of meates to be solde, is without number, as Snakes without head and taile, little Dogs gelt, Moules, Rattes, long wormes, Lice, yea, and a kinde of earth, for at one season in the yeare they haue Nettes of maile, with the which they rake vp a certaine dust that is bredde vpon the water of the lake of Mexico, and that is kneaded togither like vnto oas of the sea: they gather much of this vittaile, & kéep it in heaps, and make therof cakes like vnto brickbats: they sell not onely this ware in ye market, but also send it abroad to other faires & markets a far of: they eat this meat w as good stomacks

as

The Conquest of

as wee eate chéese, yea and they holde opinion that this skum or fatnesse of the water, is the cause that such great number of foule commeth to the lake, which in the winter season is infinite.

They sel in this market benison by quarters or whole, as Does, Hares, Conies, and Dogges, and many other beastes, which they bring vp for the purpose, and take in hunting. There are a great number of shoppes that sell all kinde of offall and tripes. It is a wonder to sée how so much meate readie dressed could be spent. There is also flesh and fish rosted, boyled, and baked, Pies and Custards made of diuerse sorts of egges: the great quantitie of bread is without number. Also corne of all sortes threshed, and vnthreshed. The great store of sundrie kindes of fruites is maruellous, which are there solde, both gréene and ripe: there is one sort as bigge as Almondes called *Cacao*, which is both meate and currant money. There are diuerse kinde of colours to bee solde, which they make of roses, floures, fruits, barkes of trées, and other things verie excellent: they sell their Honie of sundrie kinds, oile of *Chian*, made of a séede like vnto mustarde séede, and oynting any painted cloath therewith, the water can not hurt it, they also dresse therewith their meate, although they haue both butter and larde. Their sundry sortes of wines shalbe declared in another place: it would bee a prolixious thing to rehearse all the thinges that are to bee solde in that market. There are in this faire many artificers, as Packers, Barbers, Cutlers, and many others, although it was thought that among these Indians were none such. All the things recited, and many others which I speake not of, are solde in euery market of Mexico, all the sellers pay a certaine summe for their shops or standings to the king, as a custom, and they to be preserued and defended from théeues: and for that cause

there

the weſt India. 201

there goe certaine Sergeants or officers vp & towne the market to espie out malefactours. In the middeſt of the market ſtandeth a houſe whiche may be ſeene throughout the ſayre, & there ſitteth twelue anncient men for iudges to diſpatch lawe matters: their buying and ſelling is to chaunge one ware for another, as thus, one giueth a hen for a bundell of Maiz, other giue mantels for ſalte, or money whiche is Cacao, and this is their order to choppe and chaunge: they haue meaſure and ſtrike for all kinde of corne, and other earthen meaſures for Hony and Wine, and if any meaſure be falſified, they puniſh the offenders, and breake their meaſures.

The great Temple of Mexico.

He Temple is called Teucalli, that is to ſay, Gods houſe, Teutl, ſignifieth God, and Calli is a houſe, a vowel very fitte, if that houſe had bene of the true God. The Spaniards that vnderſtand not ye language, do pronoúce and call thoſe Temples Cues, and the God Vitzilopuchtli, Vchilobos. Ther are in Mexico many pariſh churches, with towres, wherin are Chappels and Altars where the images and idols do ſtand, and thoſe chappels to ſerue for buriall places of their ſouders, that ye Pariſhiners are buried in the churchyard. All their temples are of one faſhion, therfore it ſhall be now ſufficient to ſpeake of the cathedral church. And euen as thoſe temples are all in generall of one making in that citie. I doe beleéue that the like was neuer ſeene nor heard off. This temple is ſquare, and doth containe euery way as much ground as a croſſebow can reach leuell: it is made of ſtone, with foure doores that abutteth vpō the thrée calſeys, and vpon another parte of the citie, ye hath no cal-

Dd   ſey

The Conquest of

sey but a faire stréet. In the midst of this Quadern standeth a mount of earth and stone, square likewise, and fiftie
fadome long euery way, built vpward like vnto a pyramide of Egypt, sauing the top is not sharpe, but plain and
flat, and ten fatom square: vpon the west side, were steps
vp to the toppe, in number an hundreth and fourtéene,
which béeing so many, high, and made of good stone, did
séeme a beautifull thing. It was a straunge sight to beholde the Priestes, some going vp, and some downe with
ceremonies, or with men to be sacrificed. Upon the toppe
of this Temple are two great Altars, a good space distant
the one from the other, and so nigh the edge or brimme of
the wall, that scarcely a man mought go behinde them at
pleasure. The one Altar standeth on the right hand, & the
other on the left, they were but of fiue foote high, each of
them had the backe part made of stone, painted with monstrous and foule figures, the Chappell was faire and wel
wrought of Masons work and timber, euery chappel had
thrée lofts, one aboue another, sustained vpon pillers, and
with the height thereof it shewed like vnto a faire tower,
and beautified the Citie a farre off: from thence a man
mought sée all the Citie and townes rounde aboute the
lake, which was vndoubtedly a goodly prospect. And because Cortes & his company should sée the beautie thereof,
Mutezuma brought him thither, and shewed him all the
order of the Temple, euen from the foote to the toppe.
There was a certaine plot or space for the idoll priests to
celebrate their seruice without disturbance of any. Their
generall prayers were made toward the rising of the sun.
Upon each altar standeth a great idoll. Beside this tower
that standeth vpon the pyramide, there are fourtie towers
great & small belonging to other little temples which stand
in the same circuite, the which although they were of the
same making, yet their prospect was not westward, but
other-

the weſt India.

otherwayes, becauſe there ſhould be a difference betwixt the great temple and them. Some of theſe temples were bigger then others, and euery one of a ſeuerall God, among the which there was one round Temple dedicated to the God of the ayre, called Quecalcouatl, for euen as the aire goeth round about the heauens, euen ſo that conſideration they made his temple round. The entrance of that Temple had a doore, made like vnto the mouth of a Serpent, and was painted with foule and Diuelliſh geſtures, with great teeth and gums wrought, which was a thing to feare thoſe that ſhould enter in therat, and eſpecially the Chriſtians vnto whom it repreſented very wel with that ougly face and monſterous teeth. *A ſtrange doore.*

There were other Teucalles in the citie, that had the aſcending vp by ſteps in three places: all theſe temples had houſes by themſelues with all ſeruice, and prieſts and particular Gods. At euery doore of the great temple ſtandeth a large Hall & goodly lodgings, both high and lowe round about, which houſes were common armories for the citie, for the force and ſtrength of euery towne is the temple, and therefore they haue there placed their ſtorehouſe of munition. They had other darke houſes ful of idols, great and ſmall, wrought of ſundry mettals, they are all bathed and waſhed with blood, and do ſhew very blacke through their dayly ſprinkling & annointing them with the ſame, when any man is ſacrificed: yea, and the wals are an inch thicke with blood, and the ground is a foote thicke of blood, ſo that there is a diuelliſh ſtinch. The prieſts or miniſters go dayly into thoſe Oratories, and ſuffer none others but great perſonages to enter in. Yea, and when any ſuch goeth in, they are bound to offer ſome man to be ſacrificed, that thoſe bloody hangmen and miniſters of the diuel may waſh their handes in blood of thoſe ſo ſacrificed, and to ſprinckle their houſe therewith.

Dd 2   For

For their seruice in the kitchin they haue a ponde of water that is filled once a yeere, which is brought by conduct from the principal fountaine. All the residue of the foresaide circuite serueth for places to breede foule, with gardens of hearbes and sweete trees, with Roses and floures for the Altars. Such, so great and strange was this temple of Mexico, for the seruice of the Diuel who had deceiued those simple Indians. There doth reside in the same temple continually fiue thousand persons, and all they are lodged & haue their liuing there, for that temple is maruellous riche, & hath diuers townes onely for their maintenaunce and reparation, and are bounde to sustaine the same alwaies on foote. They doe sowe corne, and maintaine all those fiue thousande persons with bread, fruite, flesh, fish, and firewoode, as much as they n[ee]de, for they spende more firewoode then is spent in the kings court: these persons doe liue at their hearts ease, as seruants and vassals vnto the Goddes. Mutezuma brough Cortez to this temple, because his men should see the same, and to enforme them of his religion and holinesse, whereof I wil speake in an other place, being the most straunge and cruellest that euer was heard off.

The Idols of Mexico.

He gods of Mexico, were two thousand in number, as the Indians reported, the chiefest were Vitcilopuchtli & Tezcatlipuca, whose images stoode highest in the Temple vppon the Altars: they were made of stone in full proportion as bigge as a Giant. They were couered with a lawne called Nacar. These images were beset with pearles, precious stones, & peeces of gold, wrought like birds, beasts, fishes, and

the weſt India.   205

and floures, adorned with Emeralds, Turquies, Calce⸗
dons, and other little fine ſtones, ſo that when the lawne
Naker was taken away, the Images ſeemed very beauti⸗
full to beholde.

  The Image had for a girdle great ſnakes of gold, and   *A wicked*
for collors or chaines about their neckes, ten hearts of *attire.*
men, made of golde, and each of thoſe Idolles had a coun⸗
terfaite viſor with eies of glaſſe, and in their necks death
painted: eache of theſe things hadde their conſiderations
and meanings. Theſe two Goddes were brethren, for
Tezcatlipuca was the God of Prouidence, and Vitcilo-
puchtli God of the warres, who was worſhipped and
feared more then all the reſt.

  There was another God, who hadde a greate Image
placed vppon the toppe of the Chappell of Idolls, and hée
was eſteemed for a ſpeciall and ſingular God aboue all
the reſt. This God was made of all kinde of ſeedes that
groweth in that Countrey, and being ground, they made
a certaine paſt, tempered with childrens blood, and Uir⸗
gins ſacrificed, who were opened with their razures in
the breaſtes, and their heartes taken out, to offer as firſt
fruites vnto the Idoll. The Prieſts and Miniſters doe
conſecrate this Idoll with greate pomp and many Cere⸗
monies. All the Comarcans and Citizens are preſent at
the conſecration, with great triumph and incredible de⸗
uotion. After the conſecration, many deuoute perſons   *A madde*
came and ſticked in the powy Image precious ſtones,   *offering.*
wedges of golde, and other Jewels. After all this pomp
ended, no ſecular man mought touche that holye Image,
no nor yet come into his Chappell, nay ſcarcely religious
perſons, except they were Tlamacazeli, who are Prieſts
of order. They doe renue this Image many times with
new dough, taking away the olde, but then bleſſed is he
that can get one péece of the olde ragges for relikes, and
                       Dd 3   chiefly

chiefly for souldiers, who thought themselues sure therewith in the warres. Also at the confecration of this Idoll,
a certaine veſſell of water was bleſſed with many words
and ceremonies, and that water was preferued very religiouſly at the foote of the altar, for to confecrate the King
when he ſhould bee crowned, and alſo to bleſſe any Captaine generall, when he ſhould be elected for the warres,
with only giuing him a draught of that water.

  The Charnell houſe, or place of dead mens
   ſculles, for remembrance of death.

VVIthout the Temple, and ouer againſt the
principall doore therof, a ſtones caſt diſtant,
ſtandeth the Charnell houſe onely of dead
mens heads, priſoners in warres, and ſacrifiſed with the knife.

 This Monument was made lyke vnto a Theater,
more larger then broade, wrought of lyme and ſtone,
with aſcending ſteppes, in the walles whereof was graſ
ſed betwixt ſtone and ſtone a ſcull, with the teeth outwards.

 At the foote and head of this Theater, were two Towers, made only of lyme and ſculles, the teethe outward,
and this wall hauing no other ſtuffe, ſeemed a ſtraunge
ſight. At and vppon the toppe of the Theater, were 70.
polles, ſtanding the one from the other foure or fiue foote
diſtant, and cache of them was full of ſtaues from the
foote to the toppe. Cache of theſe ſtaues had others made
faſt vnto them, ſo that euery of them had fiue ſculles broched through the temples. Andrewe de Tapia did certifie me, that he and Gonſalo de Vmbria dit recken them
in one day, and found a hundred thirtie and ſixe thouſand
ſculles on the poles, ſtaues, and ſteppes. The other To
              wers

the weſt India.

wers were repleniſhed out of number, a moſt cruell cuſtome, being only mens heads ſlaine in ſacrifice, although
it hath a ſhewe of humanitie for the remembrance there
placed of death. There are alſo men appointed, that
when one ſkul falleth, to ſet vp another in his place, ſo that
the number may neuer want.

How Cortez tooke Mutezuma Priſoner.

HErnando Cortez and his company, were ſixe daies
in beholding and peruſing the ſcituation of the Citie and ſecrets of the ſame, with ÿ notable thinges
before rehearſed: they were often viſited by Mutezuma, and the Gentlemen of his Court, and abundantly
prouided of things neceſſary for his vſe, and the Indians of
his company.

Likewiſe his Horſes were cheriſhed and ſerued with
gréene barley and graſſe, whereof there is plentie all the
yeare: likewiſe of corne, meale, roſes, and of all thinges
that their owners would requeſt, in ſo much that beddes *A ſweete
of floures were made for them in place of litter. But yet beade.
notwithſtanding, although they were in this ſorte cheriſhed, and alſo lodged in ſo riche a Countrey, where they
mighte fill their purſes, they were not yet all contente
and merrie, but rather with great feare and care, eſpecially Cortez, who hadde the onely care as head and chiefe
Captaine for the defence of his fellowes, hée (I ſay)
was penſiue, noting the ſcituation of the Citie, the
infinite number of people, the ſtate and maieſtie of
Mexico, yea and ſome diſquietneſſe of his owne companye, who woulde come and laye vnto his charge
the ſnare and nette that they were in, in thinking it
a thing vnpoſſible that anye of them coulde eſcape,

if

208   The Conquest of

if Mutezuma, were therevnto determined, or else with the least muteny in the worlde, that mought be raised in the Citie, although that euery inhabitant shoulde throw but one stone at them, or else to breake vp the drawbridges, or withdrawing their victuals, things very easie to bee done. With this greate care that he had of the preseruation of his fellowes, and to remedie the perill and daunger that he stoode in, he determined to apprehend Mutezuma, and to builde foure Foystes to haue the lake in subiection, which he had de tofore imagined, and without the apprehension of the King, he coulde not come by the Kingdome: he would very gladly haue built the Foystes out of hand, but he left off that pretence, only because hee would not delay the imprisonment of Mutezuma, wherein consisted the effect of all his businesse, so that forthwith he minded to put in execution his intent, without giuing any of his company to vnderstand therof.

Determination of Cortez.

The quarrell wherewith he had armed himselfe for that purpose, was, that the Lord Qualpopoca hadde slaine nine Spaniardes: likewise encouraged him the great presumption of his letters written to the Emperour Charles his king, wherein he wrote that he would take Mutezuma prisoner, and dispossesse him of his Empyre. These causes considered, he tooke the letters of Pedro Hircio, wherin was written, howe Qualpopoca was the cause of the death of nine Spaniardes, & put those letters into his pocket, and walking vp and downe his lodging, tossing to and fro these imaginations in his brayne, full of care of the greate enterprise that he had in hande, yea he himselfe iudging the matter doubtfull, and his head being in this sort occupied, he chanced to espie one wall more whiter then the rest, and beholding the same, he sawe that it was a dore lately dammed vp, and calling vnto him two of his seruaunts (for all the residue were a sleepe) because

the weſt India.

cauſe it was late in the nighte, he opened that doze, and went in, and there found ſundzy halles, ſome with Jools, ſome with gallant feathers, Jewels, pzecious ſtones, plate, yea and ſuch an infinite quantitie of golde, that the ſight thereof amazed him, and other gallant things that made him to maruell. He ſhutte this doze againe as well as he moughte, without touching any part of that treaſure, becauſe he woulde not make any vpzoze thereaboute, noz yet to delaye the impzſonment of Mutezuma, foz that treaſure was alwaies there to be had.

Treaſory of Mutezuma.

The next daye in the moznig came certaine Spaniards vnto him, and manye Indians of Tlaxcallon, ſaying that the Citizens did goe about to conſpire their deathe, and to bzeake downe the bzidges of the calſeyes, to bzing their purpoſe the better to paſſe. So that with this newes, being true oz falſe, Cortes left the one halfe of his men to defende and kepe his looging, and at euery croſſe ſtrete he planted me, and the reſidue he ſent to the Court by two and two, and thze and thze, and he himſelfe came to the pallaice, ſaying that he muſt talke with Mutezuma of matters that did empozt their liues. Cortez was ſecretly armed. Mutezuma hearing howe Cortes attended foz him, came fozth and receiued him, taking him by the hande, and placed him in his ſeate thirtie Spaniards waited vpon Cortes, and the reſidue abode without at the dze.

Cortes ſaluted Mutezuma accozting to his accuſtomed manner, and began to ieſt and talke merily as he was woont to doe. Mutezuma being careleſſe of the thing that Fortune hadde pzepared againſte him, was alſo very merrie, and pleaſed with that conuerſation. he gaue vnto Cortez Jewels of golde, and one of his daughters, and other noble mens daughters to others of his company. Cortez receiued the gift, foz otherwiſe it had béene

Ee i.frent

The Conqueſt of

a frent vnto Mutezuma. But yet he enformed him, that he was a married man, and that he coulde not marrie with his daughter, for the Chriſtian law did not permitte the same, nor yet that any Chriſtian mought haue more then one wife, vppon paine of infamy, and to be marked in the forehead.

After all this talke ended, Cortes tooke the letters of Pedro Hircio, and caused them to be interpreted vnto Mutezuma, making his grieuous complainte againſte Qualpopoca, who hadde flaine so many Spaniardes through his commaundement, yea and that his ſubiects had publiſhed, that they would kill the Spaniardes, and breake downe the bridges.

Mutezuma excuſed himſelfe earneſtly, as well of the one as of the other, ſaying, the report giuen out againſte his ſubiectes was falſe and vntrue, and as for Qualpopoca who had ſlaine the Spaniardes, he was innocent thereof: and becauſe that he ſhoulde ſee the troth, he called incontinent certaine of his ſeruauntes, commaunding them to goe for Qualpopoca, and gaue vnto them his ſeale, which was a ſtone that he ware at his wreſt, engraued with the figure of the God Vitzilopuchtli, and the meſſengers departed there with incontinent.

Cortez replied and ſaid, My Lord, your highneſſe muſt goe with me to my lodging, and there abide, vntill your meſſengers returne with Qualpopoca, and the certaintie of the deathe of my men: In my lodging youre highneſſe ſhall rule and commaund as you doe heere in Court, your perſon ſhall be well vſed, wherefore take you no care, for I will haue reſpecte vnto youre honor, as to mine owne proper, or the honor of my King, beſeeching you to pardon me in this my requeſt, for if I ſhould do otherwiſe, and diſſemble with you, mine own company would be offended with mee, ſaying that I doe not defende them

accor-

the weſt India.

according to dutie. Wherefore commaund your houſeholde ſeruantes to repoſe themſelues without alteration, for be you aſſured that if any hurt come vnto mee, or vnto anye of mine, youre perſon ſhall pay the ſame with life, conſidering that it lieth in youre hande to goe quietly with me.

Mutezuma was ſore amazed, ſaying, Sir, my perſon is not fitte to be a priſoner, yea, and though I woulde permitte the ſame, my ſubiectes would not ſuffer.

They abode arguing the matter nere foure houres, and at length Mutezuma was content to goe, hauing promiſe that he ſhoulde rule and gouerne as he was wont to do. Cortez commaunded a place in his lodging to be trimmed for him, and he went forthwith thither with Cortes. There came many noble men barefooted, weeping and lamenting the caſe, carrying their beſt garments vnder their armes, and brought a rich ſeate, wheron Mutezuma was placed, & they carried him vppon their ſhoulders.

When it was blowen abroade in the Citie that Mutezuma was carried priſoner to the Spaniardes lodging, all the Citie was on an vprore: but yet Mutezuma did comfort the Gentlemen that carried and followed him weeping, praying them to ceaſe their lamentation, ſaying that he was not priſoner, nor yet went with the Chriſtians againſte his will, but for his onely pleaſure. Cortes appointed a Spaniſh garde for him, with a Captaine, the which he daylye chãged, and had Spaniards alwaies in his cõpany to make him paſtime. Alſo poore Mutezuma was cõtented with their conuerſation, & gaue them ſtil rewards. He was ſerued with his owne ſeruãts Indians, as at home in his pallace. Cortes, alwaies intreated him to put of ſadneſ, & to be merrie, permitting him to diſpatch ſuters, & to deale in all affaires of his eſtate, and to comune and talke openly or ſecretly with his noble men as he was wont to

A ſorrowfull paſtime.

Ee 2　　　　do,

The Conqueſt of

do, and that was but onely a baite to bring them to the hooke. There was neuer Græke nor Romaine, nor any other nation ſince the name of Kings was ordeined, did giue ý like interpriſe, as Hernando Cortez did, in taking Mutezuma priſoner in his owne houſe, béeing a moſt mightie King, & in a moſt ſtrong fort among infinite people, he hauing but only 450. companions.

The creation of Hunting, which Mutezuma vſed

Vtezuma had not only all the libertie that he deſired in the Citie, béeing priſoner among the Spaniards, but alſo Cortes permitted him to hunt and hauke, or to go to the temple, for he was very deuoute, and a great hunter.

When he went a hunting, he was carried vpon mens ſhoulders with eight or ten Spaniardes in his guard, and thrée thouſand Mexicans, who were Gentlemen, his ſeruants, and hunters, of whom he hadde a great number, ſome to ſéeke the game, others to beate the couertes, and others to marke. Some of thoſe Hunters were only for hares and connies, other for all ſorts of Déere, Wolues, foxes, and ſuch like. They were very perfite with their bowes, and good markemen, for he that miſſed his marke at foureſcore paſes diſtant was puniſhed. It was ſtrange to ſée the number of people that wente with him on hunting, and to ſée the ſlaughter of beaſts killed, with handes, ſtaues, nettes, and bowes, ſome of thoſe beaſts were tame, and other braue and fearfull, as Lyons, Tigers, and Ounces. It is a harde thing to take a fierce Lion in hunting as they do, being in manner a naked people, and the beaſt couragious and ſtrong, but yet the Prouerbe ſaith, ſlight and cunning is better then ſtrength.

It

the vvest India.

It is a moje strange thing to take any foule that flieth in the aire, as their Falconers do, for after they haue once marked and set eie vpon any foule, the Falconers of Mutezuma will vndertake to catch him, although the foule be neuer so swift of wing, being at the least so commanded by the King. It happened one day that Mutezuma stode in his Gallerie with his guarde of Spaniards, who had espied a faire Hauke soaring in the ayre, oh quoth they what a faire Hauke flieth yonder, Mutezuma hearing their talke, called vnto him certaine of his Falconers, commaunding them to followe that Hauke, and to bring him vnto him. The Falconers went to fulfil his request, and followed that foule with such diligence, that in short space they brought the hauke vnto him, who presented the same vnto the Spaniards, a thing truly almost incredible, but yet certified by worde and writings of the present witnesses. Their chiefest and most pleasant pastime of hawking was, of Kightes, Rauens, Crowes, Pies, and rothebirds of hartie stomacke, & slow in flight, great and small of all sortes, for the which they had Eagles, Buzters, and other foule of rapine, maruellous swift of wing, and such as would mount verie high in the ayre, with the which they murthered Hares, Wolues, and (as some say) Hartes.

He had other foulers, that vsed Nettes, Snares, and sundry engens, Mutezuma vsed much to shot in a trunke, and with his bow killed many wilde beasts. His houses of pleasure, as I haue before declared, stode fiue myles from the Citie in pleasant woodes: and alwayes when he went a hunting after the time that hee was prisoner, the same day he would returne againe to Cortez his lodging, although he banketted & feasted with the Spaniards at his places of sporting and pastime, and would alwayes at his returne to his lodging giue some present vnto the,

Cc 3   that

that had accompanied him that day.

Cortez séeing the liberalitie of Mutezuma, saide vnto him: sir, my companie are vnruly fellowes, and as I vnderstand, they haue found out some of your treasure, and haue made spoile thereof: wherfore I would know your pleasure what shall be done with the. And in effect it was the treasure that Cortez himselfe had founde out. Mutezuma answered, saying, sir that treasure which they haue founde, did appertaine vnto the Gods: But yet notwithstanding, let them leaue the feathers, and all such things as are neither golde nor siluer, and all the residue take for you and them, and if you will haue more, I will prouide it for you.

How Cortez began to plucke downe the Idols of Mexico.

When Mutezuma went into the temple, he went leaning vpon a noble mans arme, or else was led betwéene two, and a noble personage went alwayes before him with thrée smal wands in his hand, signifying thereby, that the king in person was there at hand, and in token also of iustice and correction. If he had béene carried vpon mens shoulders then at his alighting downe, he toke one of those rods into his owne hand. He was a Prince full of ceremonies in all his doings, but the substance of his estate is alreadie declared, from the time that Cortez entred into Mexico, vntill this present. Those first dayes that the Spaniards came to the Citie, and as oft as Mutezuma went to the Temple, Indian men were slaine in sacrifice. And to prohibit such abominable crueltie and sin, committed in the presence of

the

the vveſt India.

the Chriſtians who went in cõpany of Mutezuma, Cortes required Mutezuma, to commaunde that no mans fleſh ſhould be any more ſpoyled, or bloud ſhed in ſacrifice, and in not fulfilling his requeſt, he would deſtroy both the temple and Citie. Alſo he ſignified vnto him, that he himſelfe would throw downe the idols, before his preſence, and all the Citizens.

Mutezuma replied to his demaũd, ſaying: It may pleaſe you to leaue off your determination, leaſt that in ſo doing all the Citie fall into an vprore and rebellion to defende their good Gods, and auncient religion, the which Gods had alwayes prouided them of water, bread, health, light, and all other things needfull. This notwithſtanding, the firſt time that Mutezuma went to the Temple after his impriſonment, Cortez and his companie went with him, and euery of them laid hands vpon the idols, and threwe them downe headlong from their ſeates, and Altars, and other Chappels. Mutezuma with this ſight was in great agonie, yea and his ſubiects readie to take weapon to ſlay them there preſent, but yet Mutezuma commaunded his ſubiects to ſtay from their pretence: beſæching Cortez to ſtay from his proceedings, at whoſe requeſt Cortes ceaſed, for he thought, as yet time ſerued not for the purpoſe and pretence: but he declared vnto them by his interpreters, as followeth.

The exhortation that Cortes made to Mutezuma, and to the Citizens of Mexico, concerning their Idols.

Al creatures in the world (mightie prince, and ye gentlemen and religious perſons, whether it be ye here or we in Spaine, or whatſoeuer other Nation that it may be) haue I ſay, all one beginning and ending,

The Conquest of

ending of mortall life, which is had from God: we are all formed and made of one mettall, and haue all soules and senses, euen so doubtlesse as we are like in proportion of bodie and soule, yea and kinsfolke in bloud, although that by the prouidence of the same our God, some are borne faire and beautifull, and other some foule and disfigured: some of one colour, and some of another: some prudent and wise, and other some fonde and foolish, without either iudgement or vertue: in the which his maruelous workes God sheweth himselfe iust, holy and almightie, giuing those seuerall giftes, to the intent that the wise and learned mought teach the rude and ignorant, and so guide the blinde into the right way of saluation, by the steppes of true and vnfeigned religion.

Therefore I and my fellowes as your guests and kinsmen, according to equitie doe procure and wish the same vnto you. A man and his life consisteth in three things, as ye shall vnderstande, that is, bodie, soule and goodes: as for your goodes and riches, which is the least that wee desire, for ye know well that we haue taken nothing forcible from you, but onely those things which yee haue freely and liberally giuen vs. Likewise we haue not hurt, misused or molested your persons, wiues or children, nor yet do meane any such thing, your soules health onely is the thing we seeke, for your saluation, and that wee nowe pretende to shewe, and to giue vnto you perfite notice of the true and euerlasting God. There is none of naturall iudgement can denie, but that there is one God, but yet through ignoraunce and deceite of the Diuell, will also thinke that their are many Goddes, and not accrte vnto the true God. But I toe say and most assuredly certifie you, that there is no other true God, but onely he whom we Christians doe serue, adore and worship, the which is one eternall, without beginning, and without ende,

the

the west India.

the onely creator and gouernour of things created: he alone made the Heauens, the Sunne, the Moone, and Starres, the which his creatures you doe worship: he (I say) founded and made the Sea, and the sundry and maruellous fishes therein: he planted and made the lande, with all the monstrous beastes therein, foules likewise in the ayre, Plantes, Hearbes, Stones and suche like. All the which creatures, ye as blinde and ignorant do holde for Goddes.
 Our almightie God after he had finished and made all the former workes with his own blessed handes, made one man and one woman, and being so formed and wrought, he put a soule and breath into each body, and the deliuered the worlde vnto them, shewing them Paradise and glory. So that of that manne and woman, we all mortall menne proceded in generation, and in this sorte are the handy worke of God, kinsmen and brethren. Nowe if we will come vnto God our father, it is needefull and necessary that we be good, vertuous, pitifull, innocent and vnder obedience, the whiche ye can not be if you worshippe statues, images, idols, and vse bloudy sacrifice of mans flesh. Is there any of you that woulde willingly be slaine? no truely: why then doe you flea other so cruelly? and where you can put no soules, why doe you take them from thence? there is none of you, nor your false Gods, that can make soules, nor can forge mens bodies of flesh and bone, for if ye coulde, there is none of you woulde be without children, according to your owne appetite and desire, in fashion, beautie and workemanship. But where our God of heauen doth make all creatures, he vseth therin his owne descretion, and giueth children to whome he pleaseth: and therefore is he GOD alone, and for these causes shoulde ye haue, esteeme, and worshippe him for suche a mightie God, desiring of him by prayers to giue raine and temperature, that the earth

Ff   may

The Conqueſt of

may bring foorth Corne, Fruite, Hearbes, Fleſh, Foule, and all other neceſſaries for the ſuſtentation of life. All theſe things the harde ſtones giueth not vnto you, no nor yet your dry wooden images and cold mettall, neither yet the ſmall ſeedes wherewith your ſeruants and ſlaues, with their filthie handes doe make theſe images and foule ſtatues, the whiche ye doe worſhippe. O what *It was maruel that Cortez was not taken for an here- tike.* fonde people and madde religious perſons, who worſhip their owne workmanſhippe, doe ye thinke that they are Gods that rotte and moldre away, and haue no life, and can neither helpe nor kill? Therefore I ſay vnto you, that nowe and hereafter there is no cauſe that ye ſhoulde haue anye moe idolles, nor yet any moe ſlaugh- ters for ſacrifice, no nor yet to make any moe prayers or ſupplications vnto them, being bothe Blinde, Deafe, and Dumme.

Will ye knowe who is God, and where he is? lifte vp youre eyes vnto Heauen, and then ſhall you vnder- ſtande that aboue is a Godhead or Deitie that moueth the Heauens, and gouerneth the courſe of the Sunne, ru- leth the Land, and repleniſheth the Sea, who prouideth for Man and Beaſt bothe Corne and Water. This God whome ye nowe imagine in your hartes, him (I ſay) ſerue and worſhippe, not with death of menne or bloud- dy ſacrifice abhominable, but with deuotion and humble prayer as we Chriſtians doe. And conſider well, that to teach and inſtruct you theſe things, was the cauſe of our comming hither.

With this exhortation, Cortez aplaked the yre of the Prieſtes and Citizens: their idols being throwen downe, Mutezuma tooke order that no moe ſhoulde be ſette vp, commaunding to ſwepe and make cleane the Chappels of the ſtinking bloud that was in them, forbidding ſacrifice of mans fleſh. Mutezuma and his officers made a ſolemne

bothe

the vvest India.

vow and promise to permit no more slaughter of men, and to set vp a Crosse for remembrance of the death and passion of Iesu Christ borne of the virgin Marie. The which their promise was well fulfilled, for after that day the Spaniardes could neuer heare nor finde of any moe sacrifice: But yet there abode in their hearts a mortall rancor, the which could not long be dissimuled.

Truly in this worthie fact Cortez got more honor then though he had ouercome them in battaile.

The burning of the Lord Qualpopoca and other Gentlemen.

After twentie dayes that Mutezuma had bene prisoner, returned the messengers who had gone with the seale for Qualpopoca, and brought him, his sonne, and other fiftene principall persons, with them, the which by enquirie made, were culpable and partakers in the counsell and death of the nine Spaniardes. Qualpopoca entred into Mexio, accompanied like a great Lord as he was, being borne vpon his seruants shoulders in rich furniture. Assone as he had saluted Mutezuma, he and his sonne were deliuered vnto Cortez, with the other fifteen Gentlemen. Cortez placed them asunder, and commaunded them to be put in irons, and their examinations taken, they confessed that they had slaine those Spaniards in battaile.

Cortez demaunded of Qualpopoca if he were subiect to Mutezuma, why (quoth he) is there any other Prince to whom I might be in subiection? giuing almost to vnderstand that he was a Lord absolute. Cortes answered, that a farre greater Prince was the King of Spaine, whose subiects vnder colour of friendship and safe conduct, he had

The Conquest of

had slaine. But (quoth he) now shalt thou make payment thereof. And being again more straighter examined, they confessed that they had slaine two Spaniards by the aduise and inducement of the great Prince Mutezuma, and the residue were slaine in the warres, and had assaulted their houses, and entred their countrey, wherefore they holde it lawfull to kill them.

Through the confession pronounced by their owne mouthes, sentence was giuen against them, and they condemned to be burned, which sentence was openly executed in the market place in sight of all the people, without any mutinie or slander, and with great silence, terror and feare of the new manner of iustice which they sawe there executed vpon so noble a man, in the chiefe seate and kingdome of Mutezuma, being guests and straungers.

The cause of the burning of Qualpopoca.

AT the time that Cortez departed from Vera Crux, he left in commission to Pedro Hircio, to procure to inhabite in that place which is called Almeria, and not to permit Francisco de Garray to soiourne there, for so much as once he was driuen from that coast. Now Hircio to fulfill his commission, sent to require those Indians with peace and friendship, and to yeeld themselues for vassals of the Emperor. Qualpopoca Lord of Nahutlan, which is now called as aforesaid Almeria, sent to aduertise Pedro Hircio, that he could not come to yeeld his obedience, for the enemies that were in the way: but if it woulde please him to send some of his men, for the securitie of the way, he would willingly come vnto him.
Hircio hearing this answer, sent foure of his men, giuing
credit

the weſt India.

credite to his meſſage, and for the deſire he had to inhabit there.

When the foure Spaniards came into the prouince of Nahuclan, there met with them many armed men, who ſlue two of them, and made thereof a great triumph: the other two eſcaped ſore wounded, and returned with that newes to the town of Vera Crux. Pedro Hircio beléeuing that Qualpopoca had done that iniury, armed out againſt him fiftie Spaniards, and ten thouſand Indians of Zempoallan, with two horſes, and two péeces of Ordinance.

Qualpopoca hearing this newes, came with a mightie power to driue them out of his Countrey, and in that encounter ſeuen Spaniards were ſlaine, and many Zempoallanezes, but at the end he was ouercome, his Countrey ſpoiled, and Towne ſacked, and many of his armie ſlaine and taken captiues. The priſoners declared, that by the commaundement of the great Lord Mutezuma, all this vproze was attempted by Qualpopoca: it might well be, for at the houre of death they confeſſed the ſame, But ſome affirme they ſaid ſo, but to excuſe themſelues, and to lay the fault to the Mexicans. Hircio wrote theſe newes to Cortez being in Chololla, and through theſe letters Cortes apprehended Mutezuma (as is aforze declared.)

How Cortez put a paire of Giues on Mutezuma his legs.

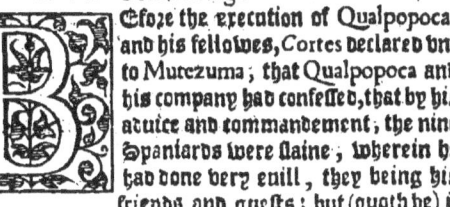

Efore the execution of Qualpopoca, and his fellowes, Cortes declared vnto Mutezuma; that Qualpopoca and his company had confeſſed, that by his aduice and commandement, the nine Spaniards were ſlaine; wherein he had done very euill, they being his friends and gueſts: but (quoth he) if it it were not in respect of the loue I beare vnto you; this matter should not in this sort be shut vp, and then knocked a paire of Giues on his legges, saying, he that killeth ought to be killed, accoding to the lawes of God. These things did Cortez, because he should occupie himselfe in his owne griefe and sorrow, and to let other mens passe.

Mutezuma waxed pale with countenance of death, through the great feare that he was in, seing himselfe in irons, a new and strange thing for such a great king, excusing himselfe that he was innocent of the fact. And as soone as the execution of burning was done, Cortes commaunded to put away the irons that Mutezuma ware, offering him libertie, and willing him to go vnto his own pallace, who reioyced much to see himselfe out of the irons, and gaue Cortes most heartie thanks, and refused to go home to his owne pallace, surmising the offer was but words, or else fearing least his subiects would kill him, seing him out of the Spaniards power, for permitting himselfe to be taken prisoner, and so to be kept. He said also, that if he went from them, his subiects would rebell, and compel him to kill the Spaniards.

Truly the poore simple soule was of small heart and courage, to suffer himselfe to be taken prisoner, and after his imprisonment would neuer procure libertie, Cortes offering it vnto him, and many of his noble men desiring him. And remaining in that order, there was none in Mexico durst offend any Spaniarde for feare of displeasing him, for Qualpopoca came 70. leagues with onely warning him that the great Lord had sent for him, shewing him the figure of his seale: yea and all the peeres of his realme that dwelt farthest off, were ready to obey his commaundements.

How

the weſt India.

How Cortes ſent to ſeeke for Mines of golde into diuerſe places.

Cortes had a great deſire to know how far the Empire of Mutezuma did extend, and what friendſhip was betwixt him and other kings and Princes Comarcans, and alſo to gather togither a good ſum of gold to ſend to Spaine to the Emperor, for his cuſtome or fift part, with full relation of the Countrey people, and things happened vntill that day. Wherefore he prayed Mutezuma to ſhewe him where the mines were, from whence he and his ſubiects had the gold and plate. Mutezuma granted to his requeſt, and incontinent appointed eight Indians, of the which foure were Goldſmiths, who had knowledge and vnderſtanding of Mines, and the other foure were guides for the iourney. He commaunded them that by two and two they ſhould goe into foure Prouinces, that is ſay, Zucolla, Malinaltepec, Tenich, and Tutepec, with other eight Spaniards, which Cortes appointed, to haue knowledge of the riuers and mines of gold, and to bring a moſter of the ſame. The eight Spaniards departed on their iourney, with the other 8. Indians, with tokens frō Mutezuma. Zucolla is 80. leagues from Mexico, and the Lord therof is ſubiect to Mutezuma, who ſhewed vnto the Spaniards three riuers of gold, & gaue of each riuer a moſter thereof, although it were but little, for with want of knowledge they knew not well the maner how to get it out of the riuer. Theſe meſſengers in their iourney to and fro, paſſed through three prouinces full of people and habitation, with good buildings & fruitfull ground, and the people of the one of them called Tlamacolapan, are of good reaſon and iudgement, and better apparelled then the Mexicans.

Malinal-

The Conqueſt of

Malinaltepec is 70. leagues frō Mexico, from whence alſo they brought moſters of golde, the which is had out of a great riuer, by the naturals of that Countrey.

Tenich ſtandeth vp toward the head of the ſame riuer of Malinaltepec, who are people of another language, and would not permit our men to haue relation of the thing that they ſought. The Lord of that place is called Coatelicamatl, who is not ſubiect to Mutezuma, nor yet is his friend, thinking that his men had béene eſpies: but when he was enformed who they were, he gaue the Spaniards licence to be reſolued of their affaires, but ſtraitly commaunded, that the Indians of Mexico ſhould not preſume to come into his dominion. When the Mexicans heard theſe newes, they required the Spaniards not to credite that Cazike, ſaying, that he was an euil and a cruell man, and would ſurely kill them. Our men were ſomewhat amazed, fearing to talke Coatelicamatl, although they had his licence, ſéeing the people of the Countrey armed with Launces of fiue and twentie foote long: but yet at length leauing cowardice aſide, they procéeded forwards. Coatelicamatl receiued them curteouſly, and ſhewed them ſire or ſeuen riuers with golde, out of the which graines of golde were taken in his preſence, who gaue the ſame moſter vnto them, and ſent alſo his Embaſſadors to Cortez, offering his land and perſon vnto him, with certaine mantels and Iewels of golde.

Cortez more reioyced of the Embaſſage, then of the gold and preſents, knowing thereby that Mutezuma his enemies deſired his friendſhip: but Mutezuma and his councell liked not the matter, for although Coalitecamatl is no great Lord, yet his people are good ſouldiers, and his Countrey full of wilderneſſe, of Rockes and Mountaines. The other that went to Tutepec, which ſtandeth néere the ſea coaſt, and twelue leagues frō Malinaltepec,

returned

the weſt India.

returned likewiſe with moſſe of golde of two Riuers, and brought newes that the Countrey was fit to build vppon, with hope to reape much golde, finding once an arte to get it out of the riuer.

Cortez hearing this newes, prayed Mutezuma to build a houſe there in the name of the Emperoure Charles, who incontinente ſente thither workemen and labourers, whiche within two monethes hadde built a greate houſe, and other three little houſes round aboute it, with a ponde of water full of fiſhe, and fiue hundred Duckes, and a thouſand fiue hundred Turkie cockes and hennes, and muche houſholde ſtuffe, ſo that the gifte was worth twentie thouſand Caſtlins of golde. He gaue vnto him alſo twentie buſhels of the graine called Centli, readye ſowen, and two thouſand ſtockes of trees called Cacauatl, whiche bringeth forthe the fruite Cacao, that ſerueth for money and meate. Cortez began this huſbandrye, but yet made not any ende thereof, with the comming of Pamfilo de Naruaiz, and the vprore in Mexico, which ſhortly followed. He alſo beſoughte Mutezuma to certifie him if there were any ſure porte or harbour on the Sea coaſt, where the Spaniſh nauie mought ride in ſafetie: he aunſwered that he knew of none, but that he woulde ſende to make enquirie thereof. And forthwith he commaunded all that coaſt to be painted in a cloath made of cotten wooll, with all the riuers, bayes, crickes and capes that were within his dominion. In all the ſame portrature did not appeare anye porte, ſkale, or ſure roade, ſauing a gulfe that falleth out of the Mountaines, which place is now called the harbor of Saint *Martine*, and Saint Anthonie in ÿ prouince of *Coazacoalco*. The Spaniards thought the ſame to be a ſtraight or paſſage into the South ſea, to paſſe vnto the *Maluccos* and ſpicerie, but they were deceiued although they beléued the thing that they deſired.

Gg   Cortes

The Conqueſt of

Cortes for this purpoſe ſent tenne Spaniardes, all good marriners and Pylots, in companye of the Indians that Mutezuma ſent one that voyage at his owne coſt.

They departed, and came to Chalohicocca, where firſt they came alande, the which place is now called S. Iohn de Vlhua.

They wente 70. leagues along the coaſt, without finding any Riuer, although they mette with many brookes of ſhallowe water, not fitte for a roade for Shippes.

They aported at Coazacoalco, the Lorde whereof was enimie to Mutezuma, his name was Tuchnitlec, who friendly receiued the Spaniardes, for he hadde intelligence of them, at their lying at Potonchan. He gaue vnto them boates, to ſounde and ſeeke the Riuer, where they founde ſixe fadome in depth, and wente vppe that Riuer twelue leagues, where they deſcryed many great townes, and it ſeemed a fruitefull ſoyle. This Cazicke Tuchnitlec, ſente vnto Cortes with the Spaniardes certain gold, precious ſtones, and cloth of cotten, with apparrell made of ſkinnes, and tygers, requeſting his friendſhip, and to admitte him tributarie to the Emperour, paying yearely a certaine proportion of his riches, with ſuch condition, that the Indians of Culhua ſhould not enter into his iuriſdictiō.

Cortes muche reioyced with theſe meſſages, and was glad of the finding of the faire riuer, for the Marriners hadde enformed him, that from the riuer of Grijalua vnto Panuco, was no riuer to be found, but I beleue they were deceiued. Cortes returned backe againe ſome of thoſe meſſengers, with a preſent of Spaniſh ware for Tuchnitlec, and to be better informed of all his meaning, with a ſpeciall charge to know the commoditie of that port and Countrey, who went, and in ſhorte time returned well ſatiſfied of their demaund: whereupon, Cortez ſent thither Iohn Velasques de Leon, for Captain of a hūdred and fifty Spaniards.

the weſt India.

Spaniards, with commiſſion to build a fort.

The impriſonment of Cacama, King of Tezcuco.

He weake courage and ſtomacke of Mutezuma, cauſed his ſubiects not onely to murmure, but alſo to ſéeke meanes of rebellion, eſpecially his nephew Cacamazin, Lorde of Tezcuco, who was a ſtout yong man and an honorable, and one that receiued great griefe of his Uncles impriſonment: and ſéeing that the matter ſéemed long, he beſought his Uncle to procure his libertie, and to ſhewe himſelfe a Lord, and not a ſlaue: but ſéeing at length that hée could not accept and follow his counſell, he began to ſtirre in the matter, threatning the death and deſtruction of the Spaniardes. Som ſaid, that Cacama did begin that matter, to reuenge the iniurie and diſhonour done vnto his vncle. Others ſaide, that his meaning was to make himſelfe King of Mexico. Others held opinion, that his pretence was only to make an end of the Spaniards. But let it be for what ſoeuer purpoſe. Once he gathered a great army, which he could not want, although Mutezuma was priſoner, eſpecially againſt the Spaniards. He publiſhed that he would redéeme his vncle out of captiuitie, and expulſe the ſtraungers, or elſe kill and eate them.

This was a terrible newes for the Chriſtians, but yet for all thoſe bragges Cortez diſmaide not, rather he determined forthwith to prepare himſelfe for the warres, and to beſiege him in his owne houſe and Towne, ſauing that Mutezuma diſturbed him, ſaying that Tezcuco was a place very ſtrong, and ſcituated in water, and that Cacama was a man of bolde and ſtoute courage,

Gg 2 and

The Conqueſt of

and had at commaundement the Indians of Culhua, and was alſo Lorde of Culhuacan and Otumpa, which were fortes of great ſtrength, thinking to bring the matter to a better paſſe another way: ſo that Cortes ruled himſelfe by the counſell of Mutezuma, and ſent vnto Cacama, praying him to haue in remembraunce the friendſhippe that had bene betwixt them two, from the time that he came and brought him into Mexico, and that alwayes peace was better then warre, and eſpecially for a noble man of vaſſals, for the beginning of warres was pleaſaunt to him that knewe not what warres meante: and in ſo doing, he ſhould do both pleaſure and ſernice to the King of Spaine.

Cacama anſwered, that he had no friendſhip with him that would take away his honour and kingdome, and that the warres which hee pretended, was profitable for his vaſſals, and in defence of their Country and Religion, yea and before he determined peace, he meant to reuenge his Vncles wrongs and his goodes.

Cacama was wife.

Alſo (quoth hee) what haue I to doe with the King of Spaine, who is a man that I know not, nor yet wold gladly heare of him.

Cortez turned againe to admoniſhe and require him diuers times to leaue off his determination, and willed Mutezuma to commaunde him to accepte his offer.

Whereupon Mutezuma ſent vnto him, deſiring him to come vnto Mexico, to take ſome order in thoſe controuerſies and diſcordes betwixte him and the Spaniardes.

Cacama anſwered very ſharpely vnto his Vncles requeſt, ſaying, If you had bloud in your eye, or the heart of a Prince, you would not permitte your ſelfe to be priſoner, and Captiue of foure poore ſtraungers, who
with

the vveſt India.

with their faire ſpeach, and flattering talke haue bewitched you, and vſurped your kingdome, no nor yet ſuffer the Goddes of Culhua to be throwne downe and ſpoyled, yea and the Mexican religion and holy places violated, and troden with theeues feete and deceiuers: likewiſe the honour, glorie, and fame of your predeceſſours blotted and abaſed, through your faint ſtomacke and cowardiſe. But notwithſtanding, accoꝛting to your requeſt, and to repair our religion, to reſtoꝛe the Goddes to their Temples, to pꝛeſerue the kingdome, and to pꝛocure libertie foꝛ you and the Citie, I will obey your commaundement: But how? not with my hands in my boſome, but like a warriour, to kill thoſe Spaniards who haue ſo affrented the nation of Culhua. Our men ſtoode in great perill, as well of the loſing of Mexico as of their own liues, if this war and mutenie had not ſoone bene qualified: foꝛ why? Cacama was valiant, ſtoute, and a good ſouldier, yea, and well furniſhed of men of warre: alſo the Citizens of Mexico, were deſirous of the ſame, foꝛ to redeem Mutezuma their Pꝛince, and to kill the Spaniards, oꝛ elſe to expulſe them out of the Citie.

But poꝛe Mutezuma remedied the matter, knowing oꝛ foꝛeſeeing, that warres would not pꝛeuaile, yea and beleeued, that in the end all ſhould fall vpon his backe. He dealt with certaine captaines and gentlemen that dwelt in Tezuco with Cacama, to appꝛehend him, and bꝛing him pꝛiſoner, conſidering that he was their king and yet aliue. But whether it were, that thoſe Captaines had ſerued Muzuma in the warres, oꝛ whether it were foꝛ gifts and rewards, they appꝛehended Cacama, being in counſell among them, treating of his warres pꝛetended, and embarked him in a boate armed foꝛ the purpoſe, and ſo bꝛought him to Mexico, without any further ſlaunder oꝛ ſtrife, and when he was comen to Mexico, they put him

Gg 3 on

The Conquest of

on a riche seate, as the kings of Tezcuco were wont to sitte vpon, being the greatest Prince in all that lande next vnto Mutezuma: and in this sort brought him before his vncle, who would not looke vpon him, but commaunded him to bee deliuered vnto Cortez, who incontinent clapped a paire of giues on his legges, and a paire of manacles on his hands, and put him into sure Guarde and custodie.

Cacama prisoner.

After that Cacama was in this order prisoner, with the consent of Mutezuma was elected Lorde and Prince of Tezcuco and Culhnacan, Cucuzca, Cacama his yonger brother, who was abiting in Mexico with his vncle, and fledde from his brother: Mutezuma did entitle him with ceremonies accustomed vnto Princes newly elected and chosen. So that forthwith he was obeyed in Tezcuco by Mutezuma his commaundement, for he was there better beloued then Cacama, who was somewhat of a crooked nature. In this sort was remedied all the former perill, but if there had bene many Cacamas, it would haue fallen out otherwise.

Here Cortes made kings, & commanded with as great authoritie as though he had obtained alreadie the whole Empire of Mexico: and certainly sithens his first entry into that countrey, he had an assured hope to win Mexico, and to be Lord ouer the whole state of Mutezuma.

The Oration that Mutezuma made vnto his Noble men, yeelding himselfe to the King of Castile.

After the imprisonment of Cacama, Mutezuma proclaimed a Parliament, vnto the which came all the Seniours Comarcans, and being all togither, hee made the Oration following vnto them.

My

the vvest India.

My kinsmen, friends and seruants, ye doe well know that eightéene yéeres I haue borne your king, as my fathers and Grandfathers were, and alwayes I haue béene vnto you a louing Prince, and ye vnto me good and obedient subiectes, and so I hope you will remaine all the dayes of my life. Ye ought to haue in remembrance, that either ye haue heard of your fathers, or else our aucuines haue instructed you, that wee are not naturalles of this Countrey, nor yet our kingdome is durable, because our forefathers came from a farre Countrey, and their King and captaine who brought them hither, returned againe to his naturall Countrey, saying that hee woulde sende such as shoulde rule and gouerne vs, if by chaunce hée himselfe returned not. Beléue ye assuredly, that the king which wée haue loked for so manie yeares, is hée that hath nowe sent these Spaniardes, which yée héere sée. Who doth certifie, that we are their kinsmen, and that they haue had notice of vs a long time: let vs therefore giue thankes vnto the Goddes, that nowe they are comen in our dayes, béeing a thing that wée so much desired. *A fonde beliefe.*

Ye shall nowe doe me seruice and pleasure, that yée yéelde your selues vnto this Captaine for vassals of the Emperoure King of Spaine, our soueraigne, I my selfe haue already yéelded me for his seruitor and friend, praying you that from hence forwardes yée obey him as yée haue obeyed mée. And that yée yéelde and pay vnto him the tributes, customes and seruice that ye were wont to pay vnto me, and in so doing, ye can doe me no greater pleasure. His heart then woulde not suffer him to speake anie more, with the sobbes, sighes, and teares, that fell from his eyes. All his subiects there present fell into a crie, wéeping and mourning, that for a good space they had no power to speake: they gaue shrikes, and *Poore Metuzuma.*

sighings,

sighings, vttering with their mouthes many dolefull, and sorrowfull spæches, yea that it pittied our owne men at the hearts. But in conclusion, they answered that they would obey his commaundement. Then Mutezuma and the Burgesses of Parliament in order yælded themselues for vassals of the king of Castile, promising loyaltie. This act was set downe by the Notarie, and with witnesses authorised. Then the Indians departed home to their houses with sorrowful hearts, God knoweth, as you may imagine. It was a straunge thing to sée Mutezuma wéep, with so many Noble men and Gentlemen, yea and with what grief they became subiects to an vnknowne Prince, but they could not otherwise do, séing that Mutezuma did commaund the same.

A true prophecie.

Also they had a certaine Prognostication and forewarning by their Priests of the comming from the East parties a straunge people, white of colour and bearded men, who should winne and rule that countrey. Likewise there was a secret talke among them, that in Mutezuma should ende and finishe, not alone the linage of Culhua, but also the Empire and kingdome: therefore some were of opinion, not to name him Mutezuma, which signifieth, agréed with misfortune. They say also that Mutezuma himselfe had many times answere of the Oracle of the Gods, that in him shoulde finishe the Mexican Emperours, and that no childe of his shoulde succéde in his kingdome, and that hee should lose his seate in the eight yeare of his raign: and for these causes he woulde neuer procure war to withstand the Spaniards, beléeuing that they should be his successours. Yet on the other side, he thought his opinion woulde take no place, for that he had raigned seuentéene yeares: But this should séeme to come from the prouidence of God, which giueth kingdoms and taketh them away.

Cortes

the weſt India.

Cortes gaue vnto Mutezuma moſte hartie thankes on the behalfe of the Emperour, and for himſelf, and comforted him, who was very ſad, promiſing alſo that alwaies he ſhould be king and Lord, and commaunde as heretofore he had done, and better, yea and alſo he ſhould be chiefe ruler of all the other landes and countreys, that he ſhoulde gette and bring to the ſeruice of the Emperour.

The Golde and Iewels that Mutezuma gaue vnto Cortez for tribute.

After certaine dayes that Mutezuma and his counſell had yælded their obedience, Cortes ſaide vnto him, how that the Emperour was at great coſtes and charges in his warres, wherefore it ſhould be neceſſary that his newe vaſſals ſhoulde begin to ſerue in ſome thing, and to pay their tribute, willing him to ſende throughout his dominion to ſee what coulde be gathered of Gold, and that he himſelfe ſhould beginne firſte to pay tribute to the crample of others. Mutezuma anſwered that he was contented ſo to doe, willing that ſome of his men ſhoulde goe vnto the houſe of foule for the ſame. There went many, and there ſawe golde in planches like bricke battes, Iewels, and péeces wrought in a hall and two chambers, which were opened vnto the. The Spaniards wondering at the ſight, would not touch any thing, without giuing firſte aduertiſement to Cortes, who incontinent went thither, and cauſed it all to be caried to his lodging: beſides this treaſure Mutezuma gaue vnto him rich clothes of cotten and feathers, maruelouſly woouen in figures & colours, it ſéemed without cōpariſon, for the Spaniardes had neuer ſéene the like: he gaue vnto him more, twelue ſhooting tronkes wherewith he himſelfe

was

The Conqueſt of

was wont to paſtime: ſome of them were painted with birdes, beaſts, floures & trees very perfite, a worke ſurely much to be commended: and ſome of them were engrauen very curiouſly, with their moulbes and pellets of golde.

He ſente alſo his ſeruants by two and two, and fiue and fiue, ech company with one Spaniarde, to the Lords of other prouinces, foureſcore, and a hundred leagues frō Mexico, to gather in golde for the accuſtomed tributes, and newe ſeruice to the Emperour. Euery Lorde and Seignior paide the quantitie appointed and taxed by Muteʒuma, in golde, plate, iewels, ſtones and pearles.

The meſſengers returned, although they had taried ſomwhat long on their iourney, of whom Cortes receiued all that they brought, and cauſed it to be molten, out of the whiche was had in fine golde. 600000. Caſtlins, of the value of ſeuen ſhillings and ſire pence the péce, and rather more, and alſo fiue hundred markes of plate, after ſire Ducates the marke.

This treaſure was deuided among the Souldiers, but not all: euery man was paide according to his office. The horſemen had twiſe as much as the fotemen. And Cortes was paide out of the ſtocke the money promiſed him in Vera Crux.

There came to the kings parte. 32000 Caſtlins and a hundred markes of plate, the which was wrought there in platters, ſaucers, cuppes, ewers and other péces, according to the Indian faſhion, to be ſét to the Emperour. Beſides this, the preſent that Cortes laide aſide, and take out of the ſtocke to ſend to the Emperour, was worth. 100000. Ducates, in pearles, precious ſtones, golde, and feathers, feathers and ſiluer, and many other iewels, as the gallant tronkes, whiche beſide their value were ſtraunge to behold, wrought with the brauery aforeſaide. This preſent appointed, was not ſent, for that and all the reſt was

after

the weſt India.

afterwarde loſt at the troubles in Mexico, as hereafter ſhall moreplainly appeare.

How Mutezuma required Cortes to depart from Mexico.

COrtes ſéing himſelfe rich and mightie, he occupied himſelfe in thrée things, the one was to ſende vnto Santo Domingo and other Ilands, newes of his procéedings and proſperitie, and alſo money to prouide menne, horſes and armour, for his owne company were too few for ſo greate a countrey. The other was, to take fully and and wholly the eſtate of Mutezuma, hauing him priſoner, and alſo at his commaundement Tlaxcallan, Coatelicamath, and Tuchintlec, knowing alſo that the Indians of Panuco, Tecoantepec, and Mechuacan, were mortall enemies to the Mexicans, who would aide and aſſiſt him hauing néede of their helpe, his thirde pretence was, to procure all the Indians to be Chriſtned, the which purpoſe he tooke firſt in hand, as a thing moſt needfull. On the other ſide, Mutezuma repented himſelfe, hauing newes that Pamphilo de Naruais was arriued, who came as enemie to Cortes, yea and after all this, he was at length driuen out of Mexico. Theſe notable things ſhalbe reherſed in their order. But now Mutezuma came, and deſired Cortes to depart out of his countrey, aduiſing him that otherwiſe bothe he and his menne were in peril of killing, ſaying alſo, that thrée eſpeciall cauſes moued him to this requeſte: the one was, the dayly ſute of his ſubictes, who enportuned him to come out of Captiuitie, and to murder the Spaniardes, ſaying, that it was a great ſhame for them to ſuffer their Prince to bée in priſon in the power of ſo fewe ſtraungers, whom they might vſe as a fotebal: hauing diſhonored the

Pp 2 and

and robbed them of their goods, gathering and heaping vp their golde for themselues, and for their king, who as séemed by their doings, was but a poore fellowe, and if he would not accept their offer and sute, that then of their owne authoritie they would take the thing in hande, for so much as hee refusing to be their king they woulde also refuse to be his vassals, giuing warning and aduice that hee should loke for no better rewarde at the Spaniardes hands, then Qualpopoca and Cacama his nephew had receiued, although they should flatter him neuer so much.

An other cause was, that the Diuell had appeared vnto him, and willed him to kill those Christians, or driue them out of the lande, threatning him that if he did not so, that then hee would goe from him and neuer talke any more with him, for (quoth he) with their gospels, baptisme and deuotion, they doe much displease mée. Mutezuma answered him, that there was no reason to kil them being his friendes and honest men, but he would entreate them to depart, (vnto this) the Diuell answered that he should do so, and therein he would receiue great pleasure, for either he woulde goe his way and leaue him, or else that Christian fellowes should depart, for they sowe here (quoth he) a Christian faith the which is much against our Religion, and cannot dwell both togither. Another cause was, that Mutezuma was not well pleased with the imprisonmét of Cacama, whom once he loued excéeding well: so in fine, secretly hee repented him of all that was past in the Spanyardes fauour, and chiefly by the perswasion of the Diuell, who saite that he coulde not doe vnto him a more acceptable seruice, and of greater pleasure to the Goddes, then to expell the Spaniardes and abolishe the name of Christians, and in so doing, the seate of kings should not finish in the linage of Culhua, but rather be enlarged, and his childrē shuld raign after him, wishing him not

the west India.

not to beléeue in prophesies, sithence the eight yeare was past, and was nowe in the eighteenth yeare of his raigne. For these causes, or possible for other which wee knowe not of, Mutezuma prepared an armie of a hundred thousand men so secretly, that Cortez knew not thereof, to the effect, that if the Spaniardes woulde not depart, beeing once more required, that then he meant not to leaue one of them aliue. With this determination, hee came foorth one day into the yard or Court, and had long conference and consultation with his Gentlemen about this matter. This done, he sent for Cortez, who liked not this newes, saying to himselfe, I pray God this message be of good purpose, and taking twelue of his men which were readiest at hand, went to knowe wherefore hée had sent for him. Mutezuma arose from the place where hée sate, and tooke Cortes by the hande, commaunding a stoole to be brought for him, and so sate them downe both togither, and beganne his talke as followeth. Sir, I beséech you to depart from this Citie and Countrey, for my Gods are sore offended with me, because I doo, and haue permitted you here so long: demaunde of mée what you please, and it shall be giuen you, because I loue you well: and thinke you not, that I giue you this warning in iest, but rather in good earnest, therefore it is conuenient, that you depart. It séemed strange vnto Cortez this talke. Also he saw by the countanance of Mutezuma, that some thing was a working, and before the interpreter of Mutezuma had made an end of his talke, Cortes willed one of his men to goe forthwith, and to aduise all his fellowes, saying, that the waight of their liues was in question. Then our men called to remembrance what was told thē in Tlaxcallon, considering that it was néedfull of courage & helpe from God to bring them out of that danger. When Mutezuma had ended his tale, I haue (quod Cortes) vnderstood

Hh 3   your

The Conquest of

your meaning and doe thanke you for the same: also I
would know when it is your pleasure that we should depart, and it shall be done. Euen when it please you (quoth
Mutezuma) take the time that you thinke meete, and a-
gainſt that time will I prepare an hundred waight of
gold for you, and fifty pound waight to each of your men.

  Cortez sayde, you knowe, that when I came into this
countrey, I commaunded all my ſhips to be sunke, so that
now I haue neede of time conuenient to build veſſels to
carry vs into our countrey: wherefore my requeſt is, that
you require some of your Carpenters to be called, to cut
downe timber for the purpose, for I haue men that can
make the veſſels. And this done, we wil depart, so that ye
giue vs the golde which you haue promised, and certifie
you the same to your Gods and vaſſals.

  Mutezuma receiued great pleasure at this anſwer, and
said, your requeſt ſhall be fulfilled: and incontinent he
sent for many Carpenters. Likewise Cortes prepared certaine of his marriners for Shipwrights. All the which
workmen went vnto great woods of Pinetrees, and there
cut downe the timber neceſſarie for the purpose. Mutezuma beeing a simple man, gaue credite to all Cortes his
talke: Cortes likewise aduertised his men of his proceedings, and said vnto them, Mutezuma would haue vs depart out of his Countrey, because his vaſſals and the Deuill hath entised him therevnto: wherefore it is needfull
that we build ſhipping, and therefore I pray you go with
these Indians, and procure to cut downe the beſt timber fit
for our purpose, and in the meane season God will prouide
for vs, whose affaires we haue now in hand, of remedie
and succour in such sort that wee lose not this fruitfull
countrey. It is also neceſſarie, that when you come vnto
the wood, that you make all the delay poſſible, giuing a
ſhew that you are busie occupied, and with great desire to
                                                        make

A subtill Fox.

the weſt India.

make an ende, that thoſe Indians may ſuſpect nothing of our pretence. Depart in Gods name, and aduiſe mee alwayes what doth paſſe in your affaires.

The feare that our men ſtood in to be ſacrificed.

Ight dayes after their departure toward the woods, arriued fifteene ſaile of Ships at the coaſt of Chalchicoeca. The Indians of that coaſt aduiſed Mutezuma thereof, who was not a little afraid with the newes, & called Cortes vnto him, who feared as much ſom vproze there, and when they ſhewed Cortes that Mutezuma was come forth into the yard, he ſuſpected that if Mutezuma pleaſed, they ſhould be all deſtroied. Wherfore he ſaid vnto his men, maſters & frinds, Mutezuma hath ſent me, conſidering what paſſed this other day, I hold it for no good token, I now goe to knowe his will: wherefore whatſoeuer happen, be you alwaies vigilant and ready, commending your ſelues to God. Remember alſo whom ye are, and who are theſe infidels, abhorred of God, and friends vnto the diuell, without weapon, & experience in war: if we chance to fight, the hands of each of vs ſhall ſhew by deeds with ſworde, the valor and courage of our hearts: yea, and although we all die, yet ſhall we remaine with victorie, for that we haue fulfilled the thing we toke in hand, and the ſeruice which we owe vnto God, as faithfull Chriſtians, with our dutie as true ſubiects to our prince. They all anſwered, ſaying, we will do all our poſſibilitie while life laſteth, without feare of perill or daunger, for we leſſe eſteeme death then honour. With this aunſwere Cortes went to Mutezuma, who ſaide vnto him, Senior Captaine, you ſhall vnderſtande that

that now you haue ships wherein you may depart, therefore now at your pleasure make you ready.

Cortes answered, not knowing of the shipping, saying, Mightie sir, when my ships are finished I will depart, nay (quoth Mutezuma) I meane not those ships, for there are ariued eleuen other shippes at the coast neare vnto Zempoallan, and shortly I shall be certified, whether the people that are come in them, are come ashore, and then shall we knowe what people, and how many are in number. Blessed is Iesu Christ (quoth Cortes) vnto whome I giue most heartie thanks for his great mercies shewed vnto mée, and to the Gentlemen of my companie. One of Cortes his men went to shewe the glad tidings to their followes, who then receyued double strength, praysing God, and embrasing one another with great pleasure and ioy. And Cortes with Mutezuma beeing in communication togither, came another post, who brought newes of fourescore horsemen that were landed, with eight hundred footemen, and twelue peéces of Ordinance, & shewed painted in a cloth the whole relation, both of men, horses, ships, and Ordinance.

At the time of néede prouideth God.

Mutezuma hearing the newes that this post had brought, arose from his seate, and toke Cortes in his armes, saying, now to I more loue you, then I haue done heretofore, and will this day dine with you. Cortes gaue him thankes for the one and the other, and in this sort went hande in hand to Cortes his Chamber, who willed his Spaniards not to make any extraordinarie ioy, or alteration, but that they should képe all togither with vigilant watch, and to giue heartie thankes vnto God for the comfortable newes. Mutezuma and Cortes dined togither with great content and pleasure, the one thinking to abide and to enioy the kings state and Countrey, the other thinking that then they would auoide the land.

But

the weſt India. 241

But notwithſtanding all theſe imaginations, a certaine Indian Captaine impoꝛtuned Mutezuma ſecretly to kill all Cortes his menne, being but few in number, and then ſhould he be the readier to diſpatch the others that were newly come, and not to permitte them to ioyne one with another: yea and againe, when the newe come menne ſhoulde know of the deathe of their countreymen, they would not preſume to abide in the lande.

With this counſell Mutezuma called many his friends and chiefe eſtates to counſell, propounding the caſe and iudgement of the Captaine, which being among them thoroughly heard, there were many of ſundꝛye opinions, but the concluſion was, to permitte the other Spaniardes to come, ſaying, the moꝛe enemies, the moꝛe gaine, and if we kill but thoſe whiche are here, then the others will returne to their ſhippes, and ſo ſhall we not make the ſolemne ſacrifice of them to the Gods, accoꝛding to our deſire. Mutezuma was occupied in this counſell with fiue hundꝛed noblemen and Gentlemen dayly, and accoꝛding to determination, they commaunded to cheriſh and ſerue Cortes and his company moꝛe then oꝛdinary, ſaying their ioy was at an ende.

How Iames Velaſques ſent Parnfilo de Naruais againſt Cortes.

Ames Velaſques being ſoꝛe agréeued, with deſire of reuenge againſt Cortes, not onely foꝛ his expences at the time of pꝛeparation of Cortes his fléete, whiche was but ſmall, but of méere hatred of the pꝛeſent honour and pꝛoſperitie of Cortes. Whereupon he inuéted great cauſes & quarrels againſt him, ſaying, and alleaging, that Cortes, hadde not giuen

I i accompt

account of his proceedings vnto him, being Gouernour of Cuba, and Cortes his deputie, but rather without his consent and knowledge, had sent to Spaine to the King, aduice of his discouery, as who would say, that was treason, or an euill fact: but chiefly his fury was, knowing howe Cortez had sent an honorable present, with the kings part or portion of treasure vnto Spaine, yea and whole relation of the discouery, with Francisco de Monteio, and Alounso Fernandez Portocarrero, the whiche proceedings Iames Velasques meant to disturbe, for that he had laide in ambush a couple of caruels, to haue taken Cortes his present, and messengers, the which his pretence and purpose tooke no place, so that with the prosperous newes of Cortes, his furie and madnesse the more encreased, imagining still his destruction.

And being occupied in these fonde imaginations, it happened that his Chaplin, one Benito Martine, brought letters from the Emperoure vnto him, with title and letters pattentes, of Generall and chiefe Gouernour of all that then was discouered, inhabited, and conquered in the land and coast of Yucatan. With this newes, Velasques began to triumph, not only so much for the honour, as also to driue Cortes from Mexico. Wherupon, he incontinent prepared his Fleete or Nauie of eleuen Shippes, and seuen Uergantines, with nine hundred men, and fourescore Horses, and appointed one Pamfilo de Naruaiz for Captaine Generall, and his Deputie, in the regiment of the Countrey: and for his more quicker dispatch, he himselfe wente with him throughout that Ilande, till they came to Guaniguanico, which is the Westermost harbor of the Ilande, and being there, Naruaes readie to depart for Mexico, and Velasques to returne to Cuba, came the Lisenciat Lucas Vasques de Aillon, a chief Iudge of Santo Domingo, in name of the whole Chancery, to require Velasques

the weſt India.

Iaſques vpon great penalties,that he ſhould not permit o₂ ſuffer Pamfilo de Naruaes to proceede on that voyage a‑gainſt Cortes, which woulde be cauſe of murther, ciuill warres, and other miſchiefes among the Spaniards, yea and that Mexico ſhould be in daunger of loſing, with all the reſt that was conquered, and in quiet to the Kings vſe, ſaying vnto him moreouer, that if there were any diſcord betweene them for goods,or poynts of honour, that then it did appertaine to the Emperour to iudge, and to determine the cauſe, and not that hee himſelfe ſhould be iudge in his owne cauſe,vſing force againſt the other par‑tie, praying them for the ſeruice of God & the King,that if they would goe to conquere, that then they ſhould ſeeke other Countryes, hauing ſo good an army and fleete, and Countries inough to ſeeke. This diligence, requeſt and authoritie of the Licenciate Aillon,to Velaſques and Nar‑uaez preuailed not: he ſeeing their obſtinacie and litle re‑gard to him being a chiefe Iudge, determined to go with Naruaez in his ſhippe, to let and diſturbe the great hurt that might followe, thinking there in the new Spaine to to perſwade Naruaes, better then in the preſence of Velaſ‑ques, yea and alſo if need ſhould be, to be a meane of quiet‑neſſe betwixt them. *A noble Iudge.*

Pamfilo de Naruaes,toke ſhipping in Guaniguanico,and ſailed till he came neer vnto Vera Crux,with al his fleete, and hauing intelligence that there were a hundreth and fiftie Spanyards of Cortes his band, he ſent vnto them a Prieſt, with one Iohn Ruiz de Gueuara, & Alonſo de Ver‑gara, to require them to receiue him for their Captaine and Gouernor.But the new Citizens would giue no eare to their talk,but rather apprehended them, and ſent them priſoners to Mexico to Cortes, to aduertiſe him of their embaſſage,wherupon Naruaes vnſhipped his men,horſes, armor,artillery, & went with them directly to Zempoallā.

The Conqueſt of

The Indian Comarcans being as well friends to Cortes, as vaſſals to Mutezuma, gaue vnto him golde, mantels, and victualles, thinking that they had bene Cortes his men.

The ſubſtance of a Letter that Cortez wrote vnto Mutezuma.

Before Cortes knew the effect of the comming of this new fléete, his head was ſore troubled, for, on the one ſide he was glad of the comming of his owne nation, on the other ſide, he lyked not ſo great an army. Likewiſe he imagined, that if they came to ſuccour him, hee helde the Countrey for conquered: alſo if that they were come againſt him, hee iudged the Countrey to bee loſt. He iudged alſo, that if they were come from Spaine, that then they had brought to him the thing loked for, but if they were come from Cuba, he feared ciuil warres. He alſo thought, that from Spaine could not come ſo many folke in ſo ſhort ſpace. Finally, he déemed, that his olde enemy Iames Velaſques was come perſonally, but when he knew the whole truth, then was hee much more penſiue, thinking that the thread of his proſperitie was cut aſunder, yea, and that they would bee a meane to ſtoppe the gappes of the whole diſcouery, both of the ſecretes of the land, mines, and treaſure, as alſo, in the knowledge of the friends or enemies of Mutezuma. It ſhould be alſo a let to inhabite the places which he had begunne, yea and alſo to Chriſten the Indians, which was the principall thing that he pretended, yea & a let or ſtop of many other things begun in the ſeruice of God and the prince, fearing alſo by flying from one inconuenience, to fall into many, and alſo if he ſhould permit Pamphilo de Naruaes to come vnto Mexico, it ſhould bee a meane of his perdition:

if

the vvest India.

if likewife he fhould encounter him, he feared fome rebel∣lion in the Citie, and the setting at libertie of Mutezuma, putting in perill his owne honour, life, and trauaile: and to auoyde all thefe daungers and inconueniences, he de∣termined remedie. Firſt, he difpatched two men, the one vnto Iohn Velafques de Leon, who was gone to inhabite at Coazacoalco, willing him at the fight of his letter to repaire vnto Mexico, giuing him aduife of the comming of Naruaez, and of the great néede that he ſtoode in, of him and his company. The other meſſenger he fent to Vera Crux, to bring full relation of the arriuall of Naruaes, and what was his pretence.

The letter fent to Iohn Velafques, came no fooner to his hande, but forthwith he obeyed and fulfilled the fame, con∣trary to the expectation of Naruaes, for hee was his bro∣ther in law, and kinfman vnto Iames Velafques. Cortes feeing his conſtancy, had him euer after that time in great eſtimation.

From the Vera Crux came twentie of the townes men with certificat what Naruaes had publifhed, and brought with them a prieſt, with Alonfo Gueuara, and Iohn Ruiz de Vergara, who had comen to Vera Crux to amotiue the towne, vnder colour that they had brought the commiſſi∣on from the king. Cortes on the other fide, fent vnto Nar∣uaes fignior Bartholome de Olmedo, with other two Spa∣niards, to offer vnto him his friendſhip, & otherwife to re∣quire & commaund him on the behalf of the king and of his own, as chiefe iuſtice of the land, and in the name of ye ru∣lers and Aldermen of the towne of Vera Crux, who were then in Mexico, and yt he fhould enter peaceably, without making any alteration vntil his authoritie and commiſſi∣on were féene and allowed, and to make no flaunter or vp∣rore to ye hindrance of the king his maiſters proceedings.

But all this diligence & letters of Cortes and the other

Ii 3   rulers

rulers preuailed not, he seeing this, set at libertie the priest that was brought prisoner, and sent him vnto Naruaez, with certaine rich collers of golde, and other Iewels with a letter, wherein he wrote, that he was more gladder of his comming in that fleete then any other, for the friendship and olde acquaintaunce that had bene betwixt them, desiring him that they mought talke and confer togither, alone, for to take order to prohibite wars, sedition, bloudshead and disquietnesse among them, being of one nation and brethren, requesting him to shew his commissiō from the king vnto him, or vnto the counsell of Vera Crux, and he would willingly obey it as reason did require: and if he had not brought any such commission, yet he would make some honest agréement with him. Pamfilo de Naruaes séeing himselfe strong and mightie, did little regard Cortes his letters, offers, nor requests, and chiefly because Iames Velasques was sore displeased with Cortes.

The talke of Narnaez to the Indians, and his answere to Cortes.

PAmphilo de Narnaez, declared to the Indians that they were deceiued with their opinion in Cortes, for that he alone was Captain Generall and chief Lord, and that Cortes was but a naughtie man, and so were all they of his company which are now in Mexico, who were all but his boyes, and that his present comming was to cut off Cortes his head, and to chasten the others, lykewise he meant to driue them all out of the countrey, and then to depart himselfe, and to leaue them in full libertie.

A foule brag.

The Indians gaue credite to his talke, séeing so many bearded men and horses, and thereupon began to attende and serue him, leauing their olde friendes in Vera Crux.

Also

the vveſt India.

Alſo Naruaes began to flatter Mutezuma, and ſent him worde that Cortes abode in that country againſt the will of his prince, and that he was a couetous rebell, who robbed his countrey, and that he pretended to kill Mutezuma and to make himſelfe king. Alſo that his comming was to ſet him at libertie, and to reſtore vnto him all that thoſe wicked fellowes had taken from him. And becauſe that others ſhould take example of their factes, he would commaund them all to be ſlaine, willing him to take no care, for in ſhort ſpace they would ſée each other. And that when he had ſet him at libertie with reſtitution of his goods, hée would incontinent depart his countrey. Theſe treatics were ſo foule and abominable, with the iniurious wordes which Pamfilo de Naruaes ſpake opely againſt Cortes and his men, yea they ſéemed odious vnto all his own hoſt and army, & ſome of his owne men checked him for the ſame, eſpecially Bernardine de Santa Clara, who ſéeing the countrey ſo peaceable, and ſo wel pleaſed with Cortes, he could not let but reprehend Naruaes in his wordes. Alſo the licenciat Aillon required him diuerſe times to ceaſe frō his ſlanderous talke, vpon paine of death, & loſſe of his goodes, and alſo not to proceed toward Mexico, for the great hurt that might enſue, with ſlander among the Indians, diſquietneſſe among the Spaniards, and offence to the Emperor his Maieſtie. Pamfilo de Naruaes being moued with his talke laide hand vpon Aillon, being a chiefe iudge for the king, and apprehended alſo his ſecretary, and an other officer, and forthwith ſhipped them, & ſent them to Iames Velaſques gouernour of Cuba. But when Aillon ſaw him ſelfe at ſea, and frée frō Naruaes, he began to threaten the Mariners, cōmanding them not to preſume to carrie him to Cuba to Velaſques his power, but only to Sāto Domingo, wher he was one of ỹ kings couſel in chācery: the mariners fearing the kings iuſtice, obeyed his cōmandment,

and

The Conquest of

and when he was aposted at Santo Domingo, he wholy enformed the Councell there, of Naruaes and his wicked dealing, whose testimonie and information did much blemish the credit of Velasques, & exalt the trauels of Cortes.

A cruell proclamation. After that Naruaes had shipped away Aillon, he proclaimed warre, with fire and sworde against Cortes, and promised certaine markes of Golde to him that shoulde apprehend or kill him, or Pedro de Aluarado, and Gonsalo de Sandoual, with other principall persons of his companie.

A mad reckoning. Also he made diuision of his goods among his men before they came to possesse it. Surely these three points were of a man without wisedome or discretion.

Many of Naruaes his companie did amotiue themselues, through the commaundement of the Licenciat Aillon, and through the fame and liberalitie of Cortes. Wherevpon incontinent one Pedro de Villalobos a Portingal, and sixe or seuen moe fled vnto Cortes, yea and others wrote vnto him, offering themselues to his seruice, if by chaunce they should encounter.

A good Captaine and wise. Cortes receiued the letters, but kept in silence from his companie the firmes of those which had written to him. Some do thinke that Cortes had suborned them with letters, faire promises, yea, and a horse loade of chaines and planches of golde, which he sent secretly to Naruaes his campe with a seruaunt of his, publishing likewise, that he had an army of two hundred Spaniards in Zempoallan, where he had none at all: these policies mought well be, for he was prudent, carefull and quicke in his businesse, and Painfilo de Naruaes was slouthfull and carelesse.

Naruaes made answer to Cortes his letter by seignior Bartholome de Olmedo, the substance of his message was, that forthwith hee shoulde repaire to the place where he was abiding, and there he should see the Emperors commission and order, wherin was authoritie giuen to him to take

the weſt India.

take and kéepe that countrey for Iames Velaſques, yea and that already he had made a towne of men onely, with all officers there vnto appertaining.

After this letter and meſſage ſente, he diſpatched likewiſe one Barnaldino de Queſada and Alonſo de Mata, to require Cortes to depart and leaue the countrey vpō pain of death, and to notifie vnto him theſe actes: by order of law. Cortes laide hande vpon Alonſo de Mata, becauſe he named himſelfe the kings Notary, and ſhewed no title or authoritie for the ſame.

The talke that Cortez had with his owne ſouldiers.

Ortes perceiuing the ſmall fruite that his letters (preſentes) and meſſengers, obtained at the handes of Naruaes, and that in no caſe, he would ſhewe his commiſſion whiche came from the king, he determined to goe vnto him, and according to the olde Prouerbe, face to face both get reſpect, and likewiſe if it were poſſible, to agrée vpon ſome good order and quietneſſe: wherupō he ſent Rodrigo Aluares his ſuruetor, with Iohn Velaſques, and Iohn del Rio, to treate with Naruaes of many matters, wherof thrée thyngs were the principaleſt. The firſt was, that they two might méete alone, or els ſo many, for ſo many, and that Naruaes ſhuld permit Cortes to abide in Mexico, and he withall his company ſhoulde cōquere Panuco or other kingdoms, alſo ÿ Cortes would pay the charges, and haue conſideration to gratifie his ſouldiers, or elſe that Naruaes ſhuld abide in Mexico, and deliuer vnto Cortez. 400. of his men, to the intent ÿ with them, and his owne men he might procéede to ſéeke other countreyes to conquere. Laſte of all, he required to ſée the

B k kings

kings commission, for that he would obey the same. Naruaes liked none of these offers, only he accepted that they should méete togither with ech of them ten Gentlemē for securitie, bound with solemne othe, and firmed this agréement with their names. But it tooke no effect, for Rodrigo Aluares aduised Cortes that Naruaes had made a snare to apprehend him, or to kill him at their méeting. Cortes vnderstoode the matter, or else he had some other intelligence by some that loued him wel. And this former agréement taking no place, Cortes determined to goe vnto him.

But before his departing, he declared vnto his companp, saying, I trust ye haue in remembrāce what & how much I haue done for you, since ý beginning of this enterprise, yea & also how louingly and friendly ye haue dealt for me? Ye shall now vnderstand that Iames Velasques, in stéed of thanks giuing vs, hath sent to murder vs, Pamfilo de Naruaes, who is a stubborn and an vnreasonable man, one readie to execute our good desertes done in the seruice of God and our Prince, with an euil reward. And ý cause is only, for doing our duetie in the sending of the kings parte and portiō to his Roiall person & not vnto him. Also this Naruaes hath already confiscated our goods, and giuen them to other men, and our bodies condemned to the Gallotres, yea and our fame and honour plaide at tables, with great iniuries and slanderous wordes proclaimed against vs, which things truly are not of a Christian, no nor yet we with Gods helpe will let the matter so to slippe: yea and though we ought to leaue the reuengment vnto God, yet we will not suffer them to enioy our trauails and paines, who are now comen white fingered to spoile the bloud of their neighbours, yea and like made men to striue against their owne nation, sowing slaunder among those Indians which serued vs as our frends, yea & procuring more cruel warres, then the ciuill war betwéene *Mario* & *Silla*, or of

Cesar

the weſt India.

Ceſar and Pompeio, who turned vpſidowne the Romaine Empire. Wherfore I do determine to meet him by ý way, and not to ſuffer him to come vnto *Mexico*, for it is better to ſay, God ſaue you, then they to come & ſay who is there? yea & though they are many, a good heart doth breake euil fortune, as it hath appered by vs, who haue paſſed through the pikes ſince our comming hither: moreouer, I doubt not but that many of Naruaez his company will come vnto vs. Therefore my deare friends do I giue you aduiſe of my pretence, to the entent that thoſe which will goe with me, may prepare themſelues, and thoſe that will not, let them remain to keep Mexico and Mutezuma, which is as much in effect. At the end of his talke he promiſed great rewards if that with victory hee returned. His men anſwered all with one voyce, that they were all at his commandement, and readie to fulfill his will, yet ſome feared the pride and blindneſſe of Panfilo de Naruaes: on the other ſide the Indians began to be luſtie, to ſee diſſention among the Spaniardes, and that the Indians of the coaſte were ioyned in league with the new come men.

The requeſts of Cortez to Mutezuma.

After all this talke and anſwere of his ſouldiers, hee went to viſit and to commune with Mutezuma for to depart on his iourney, with ſomewhat the leſſer care, and alſo to proue the mind and will of Mutezuma, vnto whom he vttered his mind as followeth. Sir, you know the loue that I haue, and deſire to ſerue you, and chiefly the truſt againe, that you will haue to my companions when I am gone from this Citie. Therefore I pray you, that it may pleaſe pleaſe you to remaine here in this lodging, and to haue regarde vnto theſe ſtraungers, which I leane with *Oh wiſe* you: alſo I commend vnto you, the golde and Iewelles *Cortes.* whiche is in their cuſtodie, and giuen vnto vs of your owne liberalitie. For I do now goe to ſignifie vnto thoſe

Kk 2 which

The Conquest of

which of late are comen in the new fléete, how your highnesse doth commaunde that I departe from this land, and that they doe not agrauate or molest your subiectes, nor yet presume to enter into your countrey, but that they remaine on your coast, vntill we bee readie to departe with them, accordyng to your will and pleasure. And if in the meane season, any of your subiects be so vnaduised, as to molest my men, which now remaine in your power and Guarde, that then it may please you to be their shielde, succour, and onely defence. *Mutezuma* promised to fulfil his request, wishing him moreouer, that if any in his iourney shoulde offende him, then immediatly to aduise him, and that he would send his men of war to chasten them, yea and also (if it pleased him,) he woulde giue vnto him guides to safe conduct him through his owne dominion to the Sea coast, who should prouide him of all necessaries by the way. Cortes kissed his handes for his curtesie, with moste hartie thankes for the same, and gaue vnto him certaine Spannishe apparell, and other glasen Iewels, and also other like treasure to his Noble men, which stoode by at all the talke. But in effect he tolde him not what he pretended to doe, nor yet the newes of *Pamfilo de Naruaes* his proceedings was not come to his eare, or else, it may be that *Mutezuma* dissimmuled the matter with inwarde pleasure, that one Christian should kill the other, thinking thereby to haue most sure his libertie, and the Goddes pleased.

The imprisonment of Pamfilo de Naruaez.

Cortez was so well beloued among his companie, that they offered willingly to goe with him, by reason whereof he chose 150. men fitte for his iourney, and other 200. in guard of *Mutezma* and the Citie, with

the weſt India.

with Pedro de Aluarado, for their Captaine. He left alſo with them the artillarie, and foure Foyſts ready made, to haue the lake in ſubiection, beſeeching them onely to haue ſpeciall regarde, that Mutezuma fled not from them to Naruaes, and not to permit him to goe out of their fort or ſtrong houſe.

With thoſe few Spaniards Cortes tooke his iourney with no more but eight or nine Horſemen, and certaine Indians for his ſeruice, and cariage.

Paſſing through Chololla and Tlaxcallon, he was honourably receiued and lodged, and about fifteene leagues from Zempoallan, where Naruaes was abiding, he mette with two Prieſts, and his olde eſpeciall friend Andres de Duero, who had lent him money for the ſetting forth of that voyage. Theſe three perſons came to require him to obey the Generall lately come as Lieutenant to the Gouernour Velaſques, and to deliuer vnto him the countrey, with all the fortes or Caſtels therein, aduiſing him, that if he would not accompliſh the ſame, that then he woulde proceede againſt him, euen as an enemie and Rebell, to the execution of death. Likewiſe, if he would fulfill the requeſt made vnto him, that then he ſhould haue libertie, and conuenient ſhipping to depart, both for him, and as many as would goe with him. Cortes anſwered, that hee would rather ſuffer death, then to leaue the Countrey, which hee had conquered and pacified with his handes and induſtrie, without anie commaundement from the Emperour: and (quoth he) if agaynſt all equitie and iuſtice, he will contend with me in warre, I will defend me as well as I may, and if I haue the victorie (as I truſt in God, and the right that I haue on my ſide,) I ſtand in neede of ſhipping, and if I be ſlaine, &c. Therefore I doe require him to ſhewe vp his commiſſion and authoritie had from the Emperour, for vntill

A ſtoute man.

The Conquest of

I doe both see and read the same, I will accept no a-
greement; and if (quoth he) that he refuse the same, that
then I dare warne, admonish, and require him to returne
to Cuba, the place from whence he came, and if he will not
obey my precept, I will then apprehend him, and sende
him prisoner in yrons to the Emperour: and with this
aunswere dispatched the three messengers, sending also a
Notarie of his owne, to commaund him to take his shipping, and to depart without making any alteration in
the countrey, or the ensuing of further murders and strife
and if not, that vpon Whitsunday, which was within
three dayes following, he meant to bee with him at supper. Pamfilo de Naruaes made a mockerie and ieast at
his commaundement, and tooke Prisoner the Notarie
which came from Cortes, with that order, holding Cortes
for madde, who made so many bragges with so small a
companie. And before Iohn Velasques de Leon, and Iohn
de Rio, Cortes his friends, he mustred his men, who were
in number fourescore hargabushers, a hundred and twentie Crossebowes, fiue hundred men with other weapon,

An vncertaine reckoning.

and fourescore horsemen, saying, how will Cortes defend
himselfe against vs, nay at length he will know his dutie: he promised money to him that should either kill, or
take Cortes prisoner. And the same offer made Cortes
against Pamfilo, who made a rounde of his footemen, and
skirmished with his Horsemen, shooting off his artillarie,
to put in feare the poore Indians.

Naruaes signified againe vnto *Mutezuma* with the
messengers, who caried all the triumph and muster painted, all his former dealings, but hearing that Cortes was
nere at hand, he sent out his light Horsemen to discry his
Campe.

All Naruaes his Horses were readie sadled and bride-
led, and his men armed. Cortes entred so close and secret
that

the west India.

that no man almost heard him, and the first worde hée spake, hauing all his men within with him, was, shut the gates, and strike, downe with him. There were at that time many shining wormes, which with their glistering séemed matches of Hargabush, so that if one péece at that time had béene discharged, they would haue béene in a great feare.

Naruaes, béeing about to put on his priuie coate, came one vnto him, saying: Sir, Cortes is néere your lodging, let him come in (quoth he) for he commeth to talke with me. Naruaes had his men in foure Towers of his lodging, and he himselfe was in the one, with a hundred Spaniards, and at his doore thirtéene péeces of Ordinance ready charged. Cortez commanded his chiefe Shiriffe, Gonsallo de Sandoual, with fortie or fiftie of his followes, to go vp into Naruaes his chamber, and he himselfe with other twentie men aboue at the doore to defende and kéepe that none might enter thereat, vntil he had finished his businesse. The residue of his men besieged the other Towers, so that they might not succour one another.

Naruaes hearing the noyse, would néedes fight, although hée was required to stay his handes, and comming out at his Chamber doore, they strake out one of his eyes with a pike, and then they laide hande vppon him, dragging and drawing him downe the stayres by the héeles, and when hée sawe himselfe brought before Cortes, he sayde, oh Senior Cortes, thanke your great fortune in hauing my person prisoner: who answered him as gaine, oh Naruaes, the hauing of thy body prisoner, is the least thing that I haue done, sithence I came into this land. Cortes commaunded forthwith to lay him in yrons, and to carrie him to the rich towne of Vera Crux, where he abode prisoner certaine yeares.

This combat endured but a while, for within one hour

A darke night for Naruaes.

Pamfila

The Conqueſt of

Pamfilo de Naruaes, and the chiefeſt of his companie were taken priſoners, and their weapons & armor taken from all the reſt. There were ſlaine of Naruaes his men ſixeténe, and of Cortes his ſide were killed only two perſons with a péece of Ordinance. They had no leyſure to giue fire to their Ordinance, with the great diligence and haſt of Cortez, ſauing vnto one péece that killed the two men. The touch holes were ſtopped with waxe, through the great raine that had fallen. By this meane thoſe that were ouercome, did take occaſion to imagine that Cortes had ſubor̄ned the maſter gunner, and others.

Cortes vſed great ſobrietie and diſcretion, for he would not permitte any of the priſoners to bee reuiled or miſuſed with any iniurious wordes, no nor yet Naruaes, who had ſpoken ſo much euill of him, although many of his men deſired reuengement. Pedro de Maiuenda ſeruant to Iames Velaſques, who was chiefe Stewarde to Naruaes, fledde to the Shippes with all the ſtuffe that hée coulde get, without any let of Cortez. Here may you ſée what difference and aduantage is betwixt man and man, what did each of theſe Captiues ſay, thinke, and doe, ſeldome time doth happen, that ſo it we of one nation doth ouercome ſo many of the ſame nation, eſpecially the greater number being freſh, luſtie, and in a ſtrong holde.

The Rebellion of Mexico againſt Cortez.

After that Cortes had obtained victorie againſt Naruaes, he knew very wel the moſt part of his company, vnto whom hée ſpake curteouſly, praying them to forget the things paſt, and ſo would he alſo. And alſo likewiſe, that it might
pleaſe

the weſtIndia.

pleaſe them to goe with him to Mexico, which was the richeſt Citie of all that India. He alſo reſtored to euery man his armour and weapons, which were taken from them in their ouerthrow. He alſo left very fewe of them priſoners with Naruaes. The Horſemen tooke the fielde with ſtomacke to fight, but after they had heard of his offer, they ſubmitted themſelues. In concluſion, all thoſe that were come, hoping of ſpoyle, were glad to accept his offer, and to goe with him with faithfull promiſe truly to ſerue him.

He receiued his power in Vera Crux, and brought thither the nauie of Naruaes. He alſo diſpatched two hundred Spaniards to the riuer of Garay, and ſent alſo Iohn Velaſques de Leon with other two hundred men, to inhabite of Coazacoalco. He diſpatched alſo a Spaniard by poſte to Mexico, with newes of the victorie, and he himſelfe followed towarde Mexico, with the great care that he had of thoſe whome hee had left there in guarde of Mutezuma and the Citie.

The Poſte that went on this iourney, in ſteede of thankes, was ſore wounded by the Indian Rebelles, but although he was ſo hurte, yet he returned to Cortes, with newes that Mexico was reuolted, and that they had burned the foure Forſtes, alſo aſſieged the Spaniſhe houſe, and throwne downe a wall, and myned another, yea and ſet fire vppon the munition, taken away their vittailes, and had broughte them to ſuche extremitie, to be either ſlaine, or remaine priſoners, ſauing that Mutezuma commaunded to ceaſſe the combatte, yea and for all that they woulde not leaue their armoure, nor depart from the ſiege, only they ſomewhat amayned their furie for their princes ſake.

Theſe newes were ſorrowfull to Cortes, for thereby his pleaſure was turned into care, the rather to make

Ll haſt

haſt to ſuccoure his friendes and fellowes, for if he hadde delayed his comming but a ſmall while, he had founde them eyther ſlaine, or elſe their bodies ready to ſacrifice: but his greateſt comforte was, that Mutezuma remained ſtill priſoner. He muſtered his men in Tlaxcallan, and founde of his Spaniſhe nation a thouſand fotemen, and néere a hundred Horſemen. He procéeded forwardes towarde Tezcuco, where he founde none of the Gentlemen of his acquintance, nor yet he there was receiued, as in time paſt he had bin, but rather he found a greate alteration, in the Countrey, and alſo may townes without people, or elſe rebelled. Tezcuco met with him a Spaniarde, whome Aluarada had ſente to deſire him to come vnto them, and to certifie him of all the premiſſes, ſaying moreouer, that with his comming their furye woulde be pacified.

With this meſſenger came another from Mutezuma, who declared vnto Cortes, that his Lorde was innecent of all that was done, praying him, that if he had conceiued any euill opinion againſte him, to putte away the ſame againe, and that it mighte pleaſe him to goe directly to his own houſe, where he aboue his comming, with the Spaniſhe guarde that he hadde lefte with him, who were aliue and in god healthe as he hadde lefte them.

With this meſſage, Cortes and his companye repoſed all that nighte, and the nexte day, beíng Midſommer daye, he entred into Mexico at dinner time, with his hundred Horſemen, and the thouſande footemen, with a greate companye of theyr friendes of Tlaxcallan, Huexecinco, and Chololla, but he ſaw but few folke in the ſtréets, and ſinal entertainment, with many bridges broken, and other euill tokens.

He came to his lodging, and all thoſe of his companie

the WeſtIndia.

nie whiche coulde not well be lodged there, hē ſent them to the great Temple. Mutezuma came forth into the yard to receiue him, full heauie and ſorrowfull, as it ſéemed, of that offence which his ſubiectes had done, excuſing himſelfe: and then euerye one entred into his lodging and Chamber: but the ioy and pleaſure of Pero de Aluarado was incomparable, ſaluting the one the other, with demaundes and queſtions howe they fared, yea and how much the one company declared of proſperitie and pleaſure, the other againe replied as much of ſorrow and trouble.

The cauſes of the Rebllion.

Ortes procured to knowe ỹ principal cauſe of the inſurrection of the *Mexican* Indians, and hauing a generall day of hearing, the charge being laide againſt them, ſome ſaid, that it was through the letters & perſwaſion of Naruaes: Others anſwered, their deſire and meaning was, to expell the ſtraungers, according to agréemente made, for in theyr ſkirmiſhes they cryed nothing but gette you hence, get you hence: Other ſayde, that they pretended the libertie of Mutezuma, for in their Combates they woulde ſaye, lette goe oure God and King, if you liſt not to be ſlaine. Others ſaide, that they were Théues, and hadde robbed theyr golde and plate from them, which was in baleue more then ſeauen hundred thouſande duckettes: Others cryed, hére ſhall you leaue the golde that you haue taken from vs. Others ſaide, that they coulde not abyde the ſighte of the Tlaxcaltecas, and other theyr mortall enemies. Manye beléued that the mutinye was for throwing downe theyr Goddes and Idolles:

Ll 2   Eache

The Conqueſt of

each of theſe cauſes were ſufficient to rebell, howe much moꝛe altogither.

But the chiefeſt and moſt pꝛincipall cauſe was, that after the departure of Cortes towarde Naruaes, happened a ſolemne holiday, which the Mexicans were wont to celebꝛate, and deſiring to obſerue the ſame, as they were wont to do, they came and beſought Captaine Aluarado to graunt them licence, and not to imagine that they were ioyned togither to kill the Spaniardes. Aluarado gaue them licence, with ſuch conditions, that in their ſacrifice ſhoulde no mans blond bee ſpilte, noꝛ yet to weare any weapon.

At this feaſt, ſire hundꝛeth Gentlemen and pꝛincipall perſons ioyned togither in the great Temple: ſome too ſay, that they were moꝛe then a thouſande perſons of greate eſtate, but that nighte they made a maruellous great noyſe, with coꝛnets, ſhels, clouen bones, where with they made a ſtraunge muſicke: they celebꝛated the feaſt, their naked bodies couered with tele, made and wꝛought with pꝛecious ſtones, collers, girdles, bꝛacelettes, and many other Iewels of golde, ſiluer, and aliofar, with gallant tuffes of feathers on their heades. They daunced a daunce called Mazenaliztli, which is to ſay, deſerte with paine, and ſo they call Mazauali a huſbandman. This daunce is like Netoriliztli, which is another daunce. The manner is, that they laie mattes in the Temple yarde, and with the ſounde of their Dꝛummes, called Atabals, they daunce a round, hande in hande, ſome ſinging, and others anſwere, which ſonges were in the honoꝛ and pꝛaiſe of the God oꝛ Sainte, whoſe feaſte it is, hoping foꝛ this ſeruice to haue raine, coꝛne, healthe, victoꝛie, peace, chilꝺꝛen, oꝛ anye other thing that they may wiſh foꝛ, oꝛ deſire.

Theſe

the vveſt India. 261

Theſe Indian Gentlemen being occupied in their daun=
ſing and ceremonies, it fortuned that Pedro de Aluarado
went to the Temple of Vitzilopuchtli to beholo their do=
ings, and whether his going was of his owne accorde, or
by the conſent of his companie I am not certaine, although
ſome ſay that he was aduiſed how the mutinie was ther
conſpired, as after did follow: others holde opinion, that
their onely going to the Temple was to beholde the mar=
uailous and ſtraunge daunce. And then ſeing them ſo
richly attired, they coueted their Gold and Iewels which
they ware, and beſieged the Temple with tenne Spani=
ardes at each dore, and the Captaine entred in with fiftie
men, and without any Chriſtian reſpect ſlewe and murde=
red them all, and tooke from them all their treaſure. Al=
though this fact ſeemed odious vnto Cortes, yet he diſſimu=
led the matter, for feare leaſt he ſhould hurt his owne pro=
cedings, as time did then require, not knowing what neede
he might haue of them, but eſpecially to auoide contention
among his company.

The thretnings of the Mexicans againſt the Spaniardes.

He cauſe of this rebellion, being well
knowen, Cortes demaunded how their e=
nimies fought, mary (quoth they) after
they had taken weapon againſt vs for
the ſpace of ten dayes arew, they neuer
ceaſed with great fury to aſſault and com=
bat our houſe, and we with feare leaſt Mutezuma ſhoulde
eſcape and flee vnto Naruais, durſt not goe out of dores
to fight in the ſtreete, but onely to defende the houſe with
eſpeciall care of Mutezuma, according to your charge gi=
ue vnto vs. Alſo we being but few, and the Indians many,
who

The Conquest of

who still refreshed their men, they did not only weary vs, but also put vs in great feare and cleane out of courage, yea, and if at the greatest brunt Mutezuma personally had not ascended to the toppe of the wall, commaunding them if euer they meant to see him aliue, to stay and ceale from their enterprise.

At the sight of Mutezuma they were all amazed, and incontinent ceased the combat and assault. They said also that with the newes of the victorie had agaynst Pamfilo de Naruaes, Mutezuma required his men to leaue off from their pretence: notwithstanding the Indians calling to remembrance, that Cortes was comming with a greater company, at whose returne they should haue the more so doe, began a fresh to assault the house, whereupon some doe thinke, that it was agaynst the will of Mutezuma. But it followed, that one day the Spaniards standing in great perill, charged their greatest péece of ordinance, & giuing fire, the péece discharged not: the Indians seeing the same, beganne a fresh with a maruellous terrible noise, vsing staues, bowes, launces, and stones, that came as thicke as haile, saying, nowe will we redéeme our king, sette our houses at libertie, and reuenge our iniuries. But in the middest of their furie the péece went off, without any more priming or touch, with a great and fearefull thundering, the péece béeing great and full of hayle shotte, with the maine pellotte, made a straunge spoyle among them, and with feare they retired. But yet they began to say, well, well, shortly shall your flesh be boyled, although we meane not to eat it, for truly it is very carraine, and good for nothing. But yet we will bestow the same vpon the Eagles, Lions, Tigers, and Snakes, who shal be the graues for your filthie carkases.

But forthwith if ye let not Mutezuma depart, and restore him to his libertie, ye shall quickely haue your reward

the vveft India.

ward for your prefumption and pride, who durft be so bold as to lay hand on Mutezuma being our God and Lord, that giueth vs our dayly foode. And yet yee with your filthy theeues handes presumed to touch him, oh why dooth not the earth open & swallow you, which taketh other mens goods? But marke the ende, for our Gods whose religion you did prophane, will rewarde you according to your desert: and if they do not shortly execute their wrath, then let vs alone, for we will out of hand make an ende of you. And as for those theeues and villaines of Tlaxcallan your slaues, shall not depart praysing their games, who nowe presume to take their maisters wiues, yea & to demaund tribute of them, vnto whome they themselues are tributors. These and such like wer the words of the Mexicans. But our men, although they were in a maruellous feare, yet they reprehended their folly as touching Mutezuma, saying that Mutezuma was no God, but a mortal man as they were, and no better, and that their Gods were vaine idols, and their religion most false and abhominable, and that onely our God was holy, iuft, true, and infinite.

The great extremitie and danger that our men were put in by the Mexicans.

Hearing the former talk in defence of the house, and prouiding of things neceffarie, the night paffed away. And in the morning to prooue the Mexicans intent, Cortes commanded the market to be vsed as in time paft. Aluarado wished Cortes to shew himselfe toward him as agreeued & not wel pleased, making as though he wold apprehed & correct him for the things paffed, thinking that Mutezuma & his men would

would haue entreated for him. Cortes passed not for that talke, saying that they were infidels, diuellish and wicked people, with whome suche complementes should not be vsed.

But he commaunded a certaine principal Gentleman of Mexico, who stoode there present, that out of hand he should commaund the market to be furnished as in times past. This Indian vnderstanding ȳ Cortes had spoken euil of them, made as though he went to fulfil his commaundement: but hee went to proclaime libertie, publishing the heinous & iniurious words which he had heard, so that in short space the matter began to waxe hotte, for some went and brake downe the bridges, others went to call all the Citizens, who ioyned themselues togither, and besieged the Spaniards house, with such straunge noyse that one could not heare another: the stones flew like haile, dartes and arrowes filled the Spaniards yarde, which troubled them much. Cortes seeing this broyle, he with certaine of his men went out at one doore, and an other Captain at another, with eache of them two hundreth men. They fought with the Indians, who slew foure Spaniards, and wounded many moe, and of them were slaine very fewe, with their succoure and defence at hande. If our men fought with them in the streetes, then would they stoppe their passage at the bridges: if they assaulted their houses, then they were beaten with stones from the toppe of their houses which were flat ruffed, and at their retire they persecuted them terribly.

They set fire vppon the Spaniards house in sundrie places, but chiefly in one place they coulde not aslake the fire a great while, vntill they threwe downe certaine chambers and walles, whereas they had entered at pleasure, had it not bene for the Artillerie, Crossebowes, and handgunnes, which were there in defence of that place.

This

the West India.

This combat endured all that day untill night, yea and in the night also they had their hands full: our men had litle leisure to sleepe, but rather spent the night in mending the walles & doores, and curing the wounded men who were moze then foure score, and likewise to set their men in order and readinesse for the fight of the next day following.

It was no sooner day, but the Indians began their assault a fresh, with moze courage and furie then the day before, so that our men were faine to trust to their artillery, the which the Indians feared not a whit: for if a shot carried ten, fifteene or twentie Indians at a clappe, they would close againe as though one man had not bene missing. Cortes came out with other two hundzeth men, and gate some bzidges, burned some houses, and slew many that defended them. But the Indians were so many in number, that no hurt appeared, yea and our men were so fewe in comparison of them, that although they fought all the day, yet had they much adoo to defend themselues, how much moze to offend. That day neuer a Spaniard was slaine outright, but thzee score of them were wounded and hurt, whereby they had inough to do to cure them for that night, and to procure remedie and defence against the hurts which they recciued from the house toppes. They inuented Engines A straunge of timber made vpon wheeles, and foure square, couered inuention. on the toppe, and with an Art to passe through the streets: there were placed on eache of them, twentie men with Pikes, Hargabush, Crossebowes, and one double Base. Behinde the Engines went men with shouels and Mattocks, to throw downe houses, bulwarkes, and to rule and gouerne the Engines.

M m   The

The death of Mutezuma.

All the while that the Engins were a making, our men came not out to fighte, being occupied in the worke, but onely to defend their lodging. The enemies thinking that they were all sore hurte and wounded, began their warres againe, reuiling them with many iniurious wordes, threatening them, that if they would not deliuer Mutezuma, that they would giue them the most cruellest death that euer man suffered, and came with great force to haue entred the house.

Cortes desired Mutezuma to goe vp into the Zotle, which is the toppe of the flatte roufe of the house, and to commaund his subiects to cease from their heate and fury. At Cortes his request hee went vp, and leaned ouer the wall to talke with them, who beginning to speake vnto them, they threw so many stones out of the streete, houses and windowes, that one happened to hit Mutezuma on the temples of his head, with which blow he fell downe to the ground: this was his ende, euen at the hands of his owne subiects and vassals against their willes: for the truth is, that a Spaniard helde a Target ouer his head, whereby they knew him not, nor yet would beléeue that hee was there, for all the signes and tokens which were made vnto them. Cortes forthwith published the hurt and daunger of life of Mutcuma: some gaue credite to his tale, and otherfome would not, but rather fought very stoutly. Three dayes Mutezuma remained in extréme paine, and at the ende departed his life.

And becaufe it should appeare that his death was of the stripe that they had giuen, and not by any hurt receiued at their hands, he caufed two Gentlemen of Mexico, who were prisoners, to carry him out vpon their backes,
who

the west India. 267

who certified the Citizens of the certeintie of his death, that at that presente time were giuing battery to the house. But yet for all this they woulde not leaue off the combat, nor yet the warres, as some of our men thought they woulde, but rather proceeded on their purpose, with greater courage and desire of reuenge. And when they retyred, they made a pitifull lamentation, with preparation to bury their king in Chapultepec. On this sort died Mutezuma, who was holden for a God among the Indians. Some say that hee desired to be Baptised at the Shrouetide before his death, and they prolonged the matter, thinking at Easter following to haue Christened him with honour and triumph. But as it happened, it had bene better to haue done it at that time according to his request. But with the comming of Pamfilo de Naruaes the thing was also delayed, and after he he was wounded it was likewise forgotten, with the troubles that they were in. It was credible enformed, that Mutezuma was neuer consenting to the death of any Spaniarde, nor yet in conspiracie against Cortes, but rather loued him entierly: yet some are of another opinion, and both giue good reasons to approue their arguments, but the truth could not well be knowen, for at that time our men vnderstoode not the language, and againe, Mutezuma after his death, lefte none to open that secrete.

The Indians affirme that he was of the greatest bloud of all his linage, and the greatest king in estate, that euer was in Mexico. It is also to be noted, that when the kingdoms do most florish, then are they niest to a change, or else to chaunge their Lord, as both appeare in this historie of Mutezuma. Our men lost more by ye death of Mutezuma then the natural Indians, if we consider the murder and destruction that incontinent did follow. Mutezuma was a man very moderate in his diet, and not so vitious

as

as other Indians, although he had many wiues. He was also liberall and frée harted: hee was estéemed for a verie wise man, in my iudgement he was either wise in letting things passe after that sort, or else a very fole, that did not vnderstand their doings: he was as deuout as warlike, for he had bene present in many battailes: and also other nine times victorie man for man in the field, he raigned seuentie yeares and certaine moneths.

The combat betweene the Spaniards and the Indians.

After the death of Mutezuma, Cortes sent vnto his Nenewes, and to the other Noble men who maintcined the warres, desiring them to come & speak with him, and they came, vnto whome Cortez spake from ye wall where Mutezuma was slaine, saying, that it were méte that they should cease from war, and to chose another king, and also to bury the dead, and that he would come to his buriall as his friend: likewise he signified vnto them, that for the loue he bare vnto Mutezuma who had intreated for them, hee had staied from the finall spoyle of the Cittie, and correction of them for their rebellion and obstinacie. But now that he had not vnto whome to haue respect, hee would both burne their houses, and chasten them, if that they submitted not themselues to his friendship.

They answered, that they woulde neyther leaue the wars, nor yet estéeme his friendship, vntil they saw themselues in their libertie, and their wrongs wholly reuenged, yea and that without his counsell they could elect the king vnto whom of right the kingdome did appertain.

And

the weſt India.

And ſithens the Gods hath taken our welbeloued Mutezuma, we will giue his body a Sepulchre, as vnto ſuch a King doth appertaine: yea and if he would goe and beare his friend Mutezuma company to the Gods, that then he ſhould come forth, and they would quickly diſpatch him: and as for the reſidue, they would haue rather war then peace, yea and that they were not menne that did yéelde with wordes. Alſo ſéeing their King was dead, for whoſe reſpecte they ceaſed to burne their houſes, roſt their bodies, and eate their fleſhe, but nowe (quoth they) if ye depart not, we will not dally long time with you.

Cortes finding them ſtout and ſtubborne, liked not the bargaine. Againe he knewe well that their meaning was, that if they hadde departed from the Citie, to haue ſpoyled and murdered them by the way. And ſéeing that their liues, rule and gouernment conſiſted in ſtrength of hand and good courage, he came forth in a morning with the thrée ingines, foure péeces of Ordinance, and fiue hundred Spaniards, and thrée thouſand Tlaxcaltecas to fight with the enemies, and to burne and ſpoyle their houſes. They broughte the engines néere vnto certaine greate houſes whiche ſtode néere vnto a bridge, caſting theyr ſcaling ladders on the walles, and ſo got vp to the toppe where manye people were, and there combatted a while, but ſhortly turned to their forte againe, without doing any greate hurte, with one Spaniarde ſlaine, and manye wounded, and alſo the engines broken and ſpoyled, yea the multitude of Indians were ſo thicke, and flewe vpon the Ordinance in ſuche ſorte, that they hat no leyſure to diſcharge them. The ſtones came alſo ſo thicke from the houſe toppes, that the encinies were ſone at an end. And the Citizens hauing houſed them againe in the forte and lodging, began to amende the hurt done in their houſes, and to recouer the ſtréetes that were loſt: alſo the greate

Temple,

Temple, in the Tower whereof, fiue hundreth principall men hadde fortified themselues with vittailes, stones, and long Launces, piked with iron and flint stone verie sharpe, but truly they did much hurt with stones. This Tower was high and strong, as I haue before declared, and stode néere vnto the Spaniardes fort, which from that Tower receyued much hurt. Although Cortes was somewhat sadde and heauie, yet he ceased not like a good Captaine to comfort and encourage his menne, and alwayes was the first man at anie brunt or assay, and his heart coulde not permit him to remaine penned vp in that fort, wherefore he toke thrée hundred Spaniardes, and went to assiege the high tower. Thrée or foure dayes he ceased not that enterprise, but coulde not come to the toppe, béeing so high a thing, and manie persons in defence of the same, well prouided, with fit munition for the purpose, so that our men came dayly tumbling downe the stayres, flying to their house with broken pates, so that our Spaniardes dismaied more and more, and many murmured at the matter: you may well iudge howe Cortes his heart was afflighted, for the Indians encreased still in courage, hauing the better hand, and dayly victorie from the high Tower. But nowe Cortes determined to leaue his house, and not to returne therevnto againe, vntill he had wonne the Tower. He bound his Target to his arme which had béene hurt before, and beséeged the Tower againe with many of his men, Tlaxcaltecas and other friends, and many times although they were beaten downe, rose againe succouring one another, till at length they got to the toppe, and there fought with the Indians, till some of them lept out of the Tower, and stood hanging vpon the liffs of the wall, which were thrée in number, the one higher then the other, and a fote broade. Some fell downe to the ground, who besides their falles, were

A valiant man.

the weſt India.

were receiued vpon the ſwordes point, and in this ſorte they left none aliue. Three houres they fought on the top of the Tower, becauſe ye multitude of Indians wer great. In concluſion, the whole fiue hundred men ther dyed very valiantly, and if their weapon and knowledge had ben equall, the victory had ben doubtfull. Cortez ſet fire on all the Chappels, and other three Chappels, where iofinit Idols were, yet thoſe ſilly Indians loſt no pointe of courage with the loſſe of their Temple and Gods, which touched them at the hearte, but rather began with more furie to aſſault the Spaniſh houſe.

Pow the Mexicans refuſed the offer of peace made by Cortez.

Ortes conſidering the great multitude of Indians his enimies, and alſo the greate courage, with deſire of reuengement: and waying alſo how his men were weak and wearied with fight, yet (I may ſay) with great deſire to goe from thence, if that the Citizens would haue ſuffered them: he began againe to require them with peace, and to deſire them of truce, ſaying vnto them alſo, that they ſhould conſider how, that many of their ſide were ſlaine, and yet they coulde kill none of them. They being more hard harted then before, aunſwered that they vtterly refuſed his offer, ſaying that they woulde neuer haue peace with thoſe who had ſlaine their men and burned their Goddes: yea (quoth they) and although ſome of vs are killed, yet we alſo doe both kill and hurt, for yee are mortal men, and not immortall, as we are: behold ye alſo the number of vs, vpõ Zoties, in windowes and ſtraetes: aſſure your ſelues there are three times as many within the houſes. So we ſhall ſooner make an end of you killing one and one, then you ſhall doe of vs by

killing

The Conquest of

killing a thousand by thousande, or ten thousand by ten thousand: for ending all these whome yee see, there will come so many moe, and after them so manie moe: but if ye were once killed, there would come no moe Spaniardes, yea, and when our weapons cannot throughly destroy you, that then wee will serue you to death with hunger and famine, yea, and though now you would depart, it is to late, because the bridges is throwne downe, and the cawseys broken, and succour by water you haue none. In these communications the day was spent, and night at hande, their heads occupied and hearts full heauie, for hunger alone had béene inough to finish their dayes, without any further warre. That night, the one halfe of the number of Spaniardes armed themselues, and late in the euening came forth into the Citie. The Indians now being not accustomed to fight at such hours, the Spaniardes burned aboue thrée hundred houses in one stréete, and in some of them found many Citizens, of whome they left not one aliue. They burned and spoyled thrée Zoties néere vnto their owne lodging, which hadde greatly annoyed them before. The residue of the Spaniardes which abode at home, amended the engins, and repaired their houses. As this iourney happened well vnto them, early in the morning they procéded out againe, and went to the bridge where their engins had béene broken, and although they found there great resistaunce, yet the matter imported their liues. They fought with noble courage, and got many Towers, houses and Zoties. They wan also foure of the eight bridges which were in the Citie, leauing gard in those places which were wonne, returning to their campe with many wounds, béing both wearie, and full of care and sorrow.

The next day they came forth againe, and wanne the other foure bridges, and dammed them vp with earth, in
such

the weſtIndia.

such sort, that the Horsemen that way followed the enemies to the firme lande. Cortes being occupied in damming vp the ditches, and making plaine way of the bridges, there came certaine messengers vnto him, saying, that neare at hand, abode many noble men and Captaines to treate of peace, requiring him to come vnto them, praying him to bring Tlamacazque his prisoner, who was one of the principalleſt of the Diuels Cleargie there, to heare the treatie of the matter.

Cortes went, and carried the Prieſt with him, whome he appointed to require them to ceaſſe from contention, and to remoue their siege, but hee came not backe with answere. All this was a fayned fetche, to see the ſtate of the Chriſtian Campe, or elſe to recouer their religious Tlamacazque. Cortez seeing their deceit, went his way to dinner, and was no sooner set at his meate, but certaine Tlaxcaltecas came running in with an open crie, saying, that their enemies hadde recouered againe the bridges, and wente armed vp and downe the ſtreetes, and hadde also ſlaine the moſte of the Spanyardes that were lefte in guarde of the bridges. Incontinent Cortez went out with the Horsemen, who were readieſt at that time, and made way through the troupe of enemies, following them euen vnto the firme lande, but at their returne, the footemen that were hurt and wearied in keeping of the ſtreete, could not ſuſteine the force and furie of the infinite number of Indians, which came vpon them, yea with much adoo they could escape home to their fort. The multitude was not so great of Indians in the ſtreete, but also by water in Canoas, so that ſtones flew on both ſides, and galled our men cruelly. Cortes was hurt in one of his knees very sore, whereupon it was blowne abroade through the Citie, that Cortes was ſlaine, which newes did greatly discourage our men, and much animate the

Indians.

The Conqueſt of

Indians. But yet Cortes for all his paine and hurt, ceaſed not to embolden and encourage his ſouldiers, who ſet a freſh vpon the enemies. At the fartheſt bridge fell two Horſes, which troubled much our men that followed. Cortes made ſuch way among the Indians, that the Horſemen had reaſonable paſſage, and being the hindmoſt man himſelfe, he was in great perill of taking. It was a maruell to ſee what a ſpring he gaue with his Horſe, and thereby eſcaped, but in concluſion, with ſtones they were forced to returne to their hold, being very late.

Aſſone as he had ended his ſupper, he ſent ſome of his men to guard the ſtreete and bridges, and to defende the ſame againſt the enemie. They were ſomewhat ioyfull of their proceedings and good ſucceſſe which they hadde the ſame day.

Howe Cortez fledde from Mexico.

But Cortes waying the ſubſtaunce of the matter, ſawe in effect that his ſide went to wracke, wherefore he requeſted his men to depart from thence, who were not a litle ioyfull to heare their Captain pronounce that ſaying, for fewe or none of them eſcaped vnhurt & wounded. They feared death, but yet wanted not ſtomacke and heart to die. The Indians were ſo many, that if the Chriſtians ſhould but only haue cut their throats without reſiſtance, yet they had bin to fewe for that purpoſe.

They were alſo in ſuch neceſſitie of bread, that pinched them ſore. Their powder and ſhotte was ſpent, and almoſte all other prouiſion. Their houſe was welnigh beaten

the weſtIndia.

beaten downe about their eares. All theſe cauſes were ſufficient to leaue Mexico, and to ſéeke to ſaue their liues: yet on the other ſide, they iudged it an euil caſe, to turne their backes to their enemies, for (quoth they) the very ſtones riſeth vp againſt him that flieth. They feared againe the paſſage of the arches where the bridges hadde bene, ſo that now they were full beſet with ſorrowe, care, and miſerie: but in fine, they all agreed to depart that night, for many dayes before, one of their companie called Botello, who preſumed to haue good ſkil in the Art of Nigromancie, did declare vnto them, that if they would depart from Mexico at a certaine houre appoynted, that then they ſhould eſcape, or elſe not: but whether they gaue credite to his ſayings or no, they fully determined to depart that night, and like vnto politicke and good Souldiers, they prepared a bridge of tymber to carrie with them, to paſſe ouer the arches where bridges had bene. This is moſt certaine, they were all priuie and agreed to the departure, and not as ſome report, that Cortez fled away, leauing aboue two hundreth Spanyardes in the houſe, who knewe nothing of his departure, and were afterwardes all ſlaine, ſacrificed, and eaten in Mexico, for out of the Cittie hee could not haue departed ſo ſecretely, but it ſhoulde haue come to their eares: howe muche more out of one houſe, where they were all togither.

Cortes called Iohn de Guzman his Chamberlain, commaunding him to open the Hall where the treaſure was, and called all the officers and others, to ſée the diſtribution of the ſame. Firſt the Kings portion was deducted, and hee gaue a Horſe of his owne, and men to carrie it: and for the remainder, he willed euery man to take what he liſted, for he gaue it franckly vnto them. The ſouldiers which had come with Naruaez, & now ſerued Cortes, were

ſome-

The Conqueſt of

Reward of a couetous minde.

ſomewhat hungry of treaſure, ſo that they tooke as much golde and other riches, ae they might poſſibly carry, but it coſt them deare, for at their going out of the Citie, with the waight of their heauie burthens, they could neither fight, nor yet make haſte on their way, vpon which occaſion, the Indians caught many of them, and drew them by the héeles to the ſlaughter-houſe of Sacrifice, where they were ſlaine and eaten: yet thoſe that eſcaped, had eache of them ſome profite, for that praie was well worth ſeuen hundreth thouſand Duckets: but being things wrought in great péeces, they were troubleſome to carrie, ſo that he which carried leaſt, eſcaped beſt. Yet ſome too thinke, that there remained in that houſe a great part of the treaſure, but it was not ſo, for after our men had taken what they would, then came in the Tlaxcaltecas, and made ſpoyle of all the reſt.

Cortes gaue charge to certaine of his men, to gard with much reſpect, a ſonne and two daughters of Mutezuma, Cacama, and his brother, and many other great Gentlemen his priſoners.

He alſo appointed other fortie men to carry the bridge of timber, and other Indians to carry the Ordinance, and a litle graine of Centli that remained.

The vantguard hee committed to Gonſalo de Sandoual, and Antonio de Quiniones: and the rerergarde hee committed to Pedro de Aluarado, and he himſelfe remained with a hundreth men, to vſe his diſcretion. In this order, and with good deliberation, at mignight he departed from Mexico in a darke myſt, and ſo quietly, that none of the Indians knew thereof, commending themſelues vnto GOD, beſéeching him in their prayers, to deliuer them from that preſent daunger, and then hee tooke the way of Tlacopan, being the ſame way that he came into the Citie.

The

the vvest India.

The first arche whereof the bridge was throwne down, they passed with the timber bridge which they caried with them at ease.

In this meane time the watche and espies which warded in the hieſt temples, had descried their flight, and began to sounde their instruments of warre with a marueilous crie, saying, they flie, they flie: And sodenly with this noyse, they hauing no armour to put on, nor other impedimēt, ioyned an infinit company of them togither, and followed with great celeritie, yea and with suche a heauie and terrible noise, that all the lake pronounced the Eccho, saying, let the cursed and wicked be slaine, who hath done vnto vs such great hurte.

But when Cortes came to plante his bridge vpon the second arche of the Citie, there mette him a greate company of Indians to defende the same, yet with much adoe he planted his bridge and passed therevpon with fiue horsemen and a hundred Spaniardes, and with them procéeded through the Calsey to the maine lande, passing many perilous places, wherein swamme both man and horse, for the bridge of timber was broken: this done, he lefte his fote menne on the firme lande, vnder the gouernment of Iohn Xemarillo, and returned back with the fiue horsmen for to succour and helpe the residue of his company which were behinde. But when he came vnto them, he found some fighting with great courage, but many slain. He lost also his golde and farduage, his ordinance and prisoners, yea in fine he found, a maruellous change and alteration of the estate he lefte them in, whereupon like a good Captaine he shewed his wisdome and valour, helping and recouering as many of his men, as he might, and brought them into safetie. He lefte also Captaine Aluarado to succour the rest.

But Aluarado with all his power and strength could not

The Conqueſt of

not reſiſt the furie of the enemies, wherefore with the Launce in his hande hee beganne to flie, ſeeing the great ſlaughter of his companie, ſo that hee was forced to paſſe ouer the dead carkaſes, yea, and vpon ſome that were not thoroughly dead, who made a lamentable, pitifull, and dolefull mone. And comming to the next arche, whoſe bridge was broken downe, of neceſſitie he tooke his lance, and therewith leaped ſuch a ſpace, that the Indians were amazed to ſee, for none of his fellowes coulde doe the like, although they approued the enterprise, and were drowned for their labour.

When Cortes ſawe this ſorrowfull ſight, he ſate him downe, not to take any reſt for his wearineſſe, but onely to bewaile the dead men, yea, and alſo them that were aliue and in great daunger, and alſo to ponder the vnſtedfaſtneſſe of the cruell fortune in the perdition of ſo manie his friends, ſuch great treaſure and lordſhippe, ſo great a Citie and Kingdome, but alſo to bewaile the ſorrowfull eſtate that hee himſelfe ſtoode in, ſeeing the moſt of his men wounded and hurt, and knowing not whither to go, for that he was not certaine of the helpe and frient ſhippe of Tlaxcallan. Yea and what hard heart, would not haue relented to behold the dead bodies, who a little before had entred that ſame way, with ſuch magnificall triumph, pompe and pleaſure. But yet hauing care of thoſe whom he had left on the firme lande, he made haſt to Tlacopan.

This ſorrowfull night, which was the tenth of July, in An. 1520. were ſlaine about 450. Spaniards, 4000. Indian friends, and 46. horſe, yea and (as I iudge) all the priſoners which were in his companie. If this miſhap had fortuned in the day time, poſſible ſo many and ſo great a number had not periſhed. But where it fortuned by night, the noiſe of the wounded was ſorrowfull, & of the victors horrible and feareful. The Indians cried victory, calling vpon

their

the vveſt India.

their diuelish and filthie Gods with ioy and pleaſure: our men being ouercome, curſed their vnfortunate lot, yea the hower, and he that brought them thither, others cried vnto God for ſuccour, others ſaid helpe, helpe, for I ſtande in daunger of drowning. I know not certainly whether mo periſhed in the water or the lande, hoping to ſaue themſelues by ſwimming and leaping ouer the ſluces and broken places, for they ſay that a Spaniarde was no ſooner in the water, but an Indian was vppon his barke. They haue great dexteritie and ſkill in ſwimming, ſo that catching any Spaniard in the water, they would take him by the one arm, and carry him whither they pleaſed, yea and wold vnpanch him in the water. If theſe Indians had not occupied themſelues in taking the ſpoyle of thoſe that were fallen and ſlaine, certainely one Chriſtian had not eſcaped that day. But in fine the greateſt number of Spaniards that were killed, were thoſe that went moſt laden with gold plate and other iewels, and thoſe which eſcapd were they that caried leaſt burdens, and the firſt that with noble courage made way to paſſe through the troupe of Indians.

Nowe wee may ſafely ſay, that the couetous deſire of gold, whereof they had plenty, was cauſe of their death, and they may annſwere that they died rich. After that thoſe which had eſcaped, were paſt the calſey, the Indians ſtaied, and followed them no further, either for that they contented themſelues with that which they had done, or elſe they durſt not fight in open field: But principally it is thought, that they abode to mourne and lament for the death of Mutezuma his children, not knowing till then their ſorrowfull ende. But now ſeing the thing preſent before their eyes, they wrang their hands, and made a pitiful dole and crie, and the rather becauſe they themſelues had ſlaine them againſt their wils.

The

The battell of Otumpan, a notable victorie.

He inhabitāts of Tlacopan, knew not how our men came spoiled, hurt, and ouerthrowen, and againe our men stood in a maze, & knew not what to doe, nor whither to go. Cortes came vnto them and comforted them, and placed them in order before him, requiring them to make hast, vntill they might come into the broad field, before such time as the men of Tlacopan should heare of the newes passed, & so to arm thēselues and ioine with fortie thousand Mexicans, who after the mourning for their friends, came marching after them. He placed in the vantgard the Indians his frends, & passed through certaine tilled ground, and continually fought as they went, vntill they came to a high hill, where was a tower, and a temple, which is called our Ladie church at this day. The Indians slue some of the Spaniards which came in the reregard, and many of their Indian friends, before they could get vp to the top of the hill. They lost much of the gold that had remained, and with great hazard escaped through the multitude of Indians with life: their horses which remained aliue, were foure and twentie, who were tired both with trauell and hunger, and the Spaniards their maisters, with the residue could scarcely stirre hand or foote with wearinesse of fighting, and penurie of hunger, for all that day and night they ceased not from fight, eating nothing at all.

A wearie iourney.

In this Temple were reasonable lodgings, where they fortified themselues as well as they might, and dranke one to another, but their supper was very slender. After their simple feast was ended, they went and beheld

an

the weſt India.

an infinite number of Indians, which had beſet them almoſt round about, making a maruellous ſhoute and crie, knowing that they were without victuals, whiche onely is a warre worſer then to fight with the enemie. They made many fiers with the woode of ſacrifice, rounde about the tower and temple, and with this policie, at midnight departed ſecretely. It happened that they had Tlax- *A painful man.* calteca to be their guide, who knew wel the way, aſſuring to bring them into the iuriſdictiō of Tlaxcallan: with this guide they began to iourney. Cortez placed his wounded men and fardage in the midteſt of his company, the souldiours that were whole and in health, he deuided into the vantgarde & regard: he could not paſſe ſo ſecretly, but that they were eſpied by the Indian ſcoute, whiche was néere at hand, who gaue aduiſe therof incontinent. Fiue horſmē which went before to diſcouer, fell among certaine cōpanies of Indians, which attended their cōming to robbe thē, and ſéeing the horſemen, they ſuſpected ye the whole army was at hand, wherupon they fled, but yet ſéeing them few in number, ſtoo & ioyned with the other Mexicans, that folowed & purſued our men thrée leagues, until they came to a hil where was another temple with a good tower and lodging, where they lodged that night without ſupper. They departed in the morning from thence, and wente through a cragged & naughtie way, to a great towne the enhabitantes whereof were fledde for feare, ſo that they abode there two daies to reſt thēſelues, to cure their men, and horſes: alſo they ſomwhat eaſed their hūgery ſtomaks and carried from thence prouiſion, although not much, for they had none to carrie it. And being departed frō thence, many enemies purſued thē & perſecuted them very ſore. Likewiſe ye guide erred out of his way, & at légth came to a little village of few houſes, where they repoſed ye night. In the morning they procéded vppon their way, and the

Do enemies

The Conqueſt of

enemies ſtill purſuing and troubled them ſore all the day.

Cortez wounded with a ſling.

Cortes was wouded with the ſtripe of a ſling, and therwith was in greate daunger of life, for his head ſo rancked, that of neceſſitie they were forced to take out certaine péeces of his ſkull, wherupon he was driuen to ſéeke a ſolitarie place in the wilderneſſe to cure him, and in going thitherwardes, the enimies wounded fiue Spaniardes and foure horſes, whereof one died, and that was eaten among them for a ſumptuous ſupper, and yet not ſufficient for them all, for there was none of them which were not vexed with hunger. I ſpeake not of their wountes and wearineſſe, thinges ſufficient to haue made an ende of life. But certainely the Spaniſhe nation can abide more hunger then any other, and eſpecially theſe with Cortes did ſhewe the proofe. The nexte day in the morning departing from a little Uillage, and fearing the multitude of enimies, Cortes commaunded ech horſeman to take a ſicke manne behinde him, and thoſe that were ſomewhat ſtronger, to holde by the horſe tailes and ſtirroppes: he likewiſe made churches for otherſome to eaſe them, and would not leaue one of his men behinde him to be a pray and ſupper for the Indian enimies. This aduiſe was very profitable as things fel out, yea alſo there were ſome of them that caried vpon their backe their fellowes, and thereby were ſaued. They had not iournied a full league into a plaine fielde, when there mette them an infinite number of Indians who compaſſed the round about, and aſſaulted our men in ſuch ſorte, that they verily beleued that day to ende generally their liues, for there were many Indians that durſt wraſtell with our men, man to man, yea and layd ſome of them in the duſte, and drewe them by the héeles, whether it were with the great courage which they had, or whether it were with the trauail, hunger and hurtes of our men I know not, but greate pitie.

Oh noble Cortez.

the weſt India. 283

ſie it was to ſée, how they were drawne by the Indian enimies, and what grieuous mone they made.
   Cortes that wente with vigilant care comforting his men, as muche as was poſſible to doe, and well peruſing the great daunger that they were in, commending himſelfe to God, ſette ſpurres to his horſe and made way thorow the greateſt troupe of Indians, and came vnto the captaine generall who bare the Royall ſtandart of *Mexico*, and paſſed him through with his Lance, whereof he incontinent died. But when the Indians ſawe the ſtandart fallen, they threw their aunciente on the grounde and fled, ſcattering them héere and there like men amazed, knowing not whither to fly, for ſuch is their cuſtome in warre, that when they ſée the generall ſlaine, they forthwith leaue the field. Then our weary ſoules began to recouer hart and ſtrength, and the horſemen followed the to their great annoyance and ſlaughter. It was credibly reported, that there were that day in field. 200000. Indians. And the field where this battaile was fought is called Otumpan: there was neuer a more notable facte done in India, nor greater victory ſince the firſt diſcouery of the ſame. And as manye Spaniardes as ſawe Hernando Cortes fight that day, did holde opinion, that neuer one man did more greater feates in armes, and that he only was the meane in his owne perſon to ſaue and deliuer them all.

Oh valiant Cortex.

100000. Indians.

The entertainment which the Spaniardes had in Tlaxcallan.

After this victory obtained, Cortes with his company went to lodge in a houſe planted alone, in a plaine grounde, from whence appeared the Mountaines of Tlaxcallan, whereof our mènne muche reioyced: yet

Do 2 on

on the other side they stoode in doubt whether they should
finde them their friendes in such a daungerous season, for
because the unfortunate man that flieth, findeth nothing
in his fauour, for all thing that he pretendeth, happeneth
cleane contrary. That night Cortes himselfe was scoute,
not because he was more whole then his fellowes, but
like a good Captaine, he deuided the trauaile and paines e-
qually, euen as their hurte and damage was come.

Being day, they iournied in plaine and straight way,
directly to the Mountaines and Prouince of Tlaxcallan,
they passed by a sweet fountain of water, where they well
refreshed themselues, and after they came to Huazilipan, a
towne of Tlaxcallan, of 4000. housholds, wher they were
louingly receiued, & abundantly prouided for three dayes,
which they abode there refreshing and curing their weary
bodies. Some of the townes men would giue them nothing
without payment, but the moste parte did vse them very
gently: Unto this Towne came *Maxixca*, Xicotencatlh,
Axotecalth, and many other principal persons of Tlaxcallan, and Huexozinco with. 50000. men of war, who were
going to Mexico to succour the Spaniardes, knowing of
their troubles, but not of their hurt and spoile, yet some
holde opinion that they hauing certaine knowledge of
all their mishappes and flight from Mexico, came only to
comforte them, and in the name of all their communaltie and state, to offer them their Towne, in conclusion,
they seemed sorowfull for their misfortunes, and a-
gaine ioyfull to see them there: Yea some of them with
anguishe of harte wepte, and sayde, we did aduise and
warne yee, that the Mexicans were Traytours and wicked persons, and yet ye woulde not beleeue vs: we do
pittie and bewaile your troubles, but if it please you,
lette vs goe thither to reuenge your iniuries, and the
death of your Christians, and our Citizens: and if now ye
will

50000. men.

Faithfull
friendes.

the weſt India.

will not, that then it may pleaſe you to goe with vs home to our houſes, for to recreate your perſons, and to cure your wounds.

Cortes did cordially reioyce, to heare and finde ſuch ſuccour and friendſhip, in ſuch good men of warre, whereof he ſtoode in doubt as he came thitherward. He gaue them moſt heartie thankes for their louing offer, curteſie, and good will. He gaue vnto them of ſuch Jewels as remayned, and ſaid vnto them, the time will come, that I ſhall deſire your helpe againſt the Mexicans, but now preſently it is needfull to cure my ſicke and wounded men.

The noble men that were there preſent, beſought him to giue them leaue to ſkirmiſh with the Indians of Culhua, for as yet many of them wandered thereabout. Cortes graunted their requeſt, and ſent with them ſome of his men, which were luſtie, and in good health, who proceeded forth all togither, and in that iourney ſlue many Indian enimies, ſo that after this time, the enemies appeared no more. Then with triumph, pleaſure, and victorie, they departed toward the Citie, and our men followed. It is credibly reported, that twentie thouſande men and women met them by the way with ſundry kinds of meates: I doe beleeue that the moſt of them came to ſee them, for the great loue which they bare vnto them, and likewiſe to enquire of their friendes which had gone with them to Mexico, of whō few returned. In Tlaxcallon they were honourably receiued, and well vſed. Maxixca gaue his houſe to Cortes, and the reſidue of his companie were hoſted at Gentlemens houſes, who cheriſhed them exceedingly, whereby they forgat the paynes, ſorrowes, and trauels paſt, for in fifteene dayes before, they lay on the bare ground.

Certainly the Spaniardes were much indebted to the Tlaxcaltecas, for their loialtie and faithfull friendſhip,

Oo 3　　　eſpecially

especially vnto that good and vertuous Gentleman Maxixca, who threwe Xicotencatl downe the stayres and
steps of the chiefe Temple, for giuing his counsell to kill
the Spaniardes, meaning to reconcile himselfe to the
Mexicans.

He also made two Orations, the one to the men, and
the other to the women, in the great fauour and praise
of the Spaniards, putting them in remembrance, howe
that they had not eaten salt, nor worne cloth of cotton wol
in many yeares before, vntil now that their friends were
come: and to this day these Indians doe much presume of
their fidelitie, and likewise of the resistaunce and battell
they made with Cortes in Teoacazinco, so that now when
they celebrate any great feast, or receiue any Christian
bizeking, there commeth of them out into the field sixtie
or seuentie thousand men, to skirmish and fight in the
same order as they did with Cortez.

The protestation and request of the Souldiers to Cortez.

When Cortes departed first from Tlaxcallon toward Mexico to visit Mutezuma, he left there twentie thousand
Castlins of gold and moe, besides the
kings portion which was sent with
Monteio and Portocarrere. He left
there also many other things if néede
should haue hapned in Mexico of mo-
ney, or other things to prouide his men in Vera Crux, and
this he left there also, to proue the fidelity of his friends in
Tlaxcallon. And after he had obteyned the victorie against
Naruaes, hée wrote vnto the Captaine that he should send
for the same, for reason required that in all things they
should haue their parts.

The

the weſt India.

The Captaine of Vera Crux ſent fiftie Spaniardes and ſix Horſmen for the ſame, who at their return, were ſlain and taken priſoners with all that treaſure, by the men of Culhua, who had rebelled through the comming of Pamfilo de Naruaez, robbing & ſpoiling ſundry dayes. But when Cortes vnderſtood this newes, his ioy was turned to ſorow, not onely for the gold and treaſure ſo much, as for the loſſe of his men, fearing alſo ſome other warre or vprore to haue bene in the rich towne of Vera Crux, whereupon he ſent a meſſenger thither, who returned in ſhort time certifying that all the inhabitauntes there were in good health, and alſo all the Comarcans quiet, and without any token of alteration. This newes and anſwere pleaſed Cortes and all his company, which deſired to go thither, but he would not permit them, wherefore they beganne to murmure and to exclaime, ſaying: what thinketh Cortes, what meaneth he to do with vs? why will he kæp vs here to die an euill death? what haue wee offended him, that he will not let vs goe? we are alreadie full of wearineſſe, our bodies are yet full of freſh woundes, we haue ſpent our bloud, and are now without ſtrength and apparell: we ſæ our ſelues in a ſtraunge Countrey, and full of miſery, enuironed with enemies, yea and without hope to come to that high place from whence we fell, yea then mighte we be accounted for worſe then madde men, to come into the perilles from whence wee eſcaped: wæ meane not now to ende our liues ſo deſperately, as he woulde haue vs, for with the inſatiable thirſte of honoure and glorie, hee eſtæmeth not his life, neyther ours. He doth not likewiſe conſider, that he wanteth men, horſes, artillerie, and armoure, things ſo neceſſarie for the warres, yea, hæ alſo wanteth victuall, which is a thing moſte principall of all: what ſhall wee ſay, but that he erreth, and is deceiued, in giuing credite to

theſe

The Conqueſt of

theſe Tlaxcaltecas, who are like vnto the other nations of India, which are light, chaungeable, and louers of new things, yea and rather, in effect of troth, they better loue the Culhuacans, then the Spaniſh Nation, yea & although they now diſſemble, yet when they ſhall ſee a great army of Mexicans come vpon them, they will then deliuer vs aliue, to be eaten, and ſacrificed, for it is an olde rule, that friendſhip doth not long endure betwixt them that are of ſundry religion, apparell, and ſpéech.

After all theſe complaints and murmurations among themſelues, they made a proteſtation and requeſt, in form as it were in the name of the King and all the companie, praying him incontinent to depart from thence, and to go with them to the Towne of Vera Crux, before the enemies might diſturbe their way and paſſage, and then they to remaine both bought and ſolde, and ſhut vp as it were in a priſon: alſo they declared, that in Vera Crux they ſhoulde haue better opportunitie to make themſelues ſtrong, if that he meant to returne againe vpon Mexico, or elſe to take ſhipping, if ſo it ſhould ſéeme conuenient.

Cortes hearing this requeſt, and determination of his Souldiers, was at his wittes ende, imagining that their pretence was, onely to procure him to goe from thence, and afterwardes to rule him at their pleaſures, and being a thing cleane contrary to his pretended purpoſe, he anſwered them as followeth.

The

the weſtIndia.

The Oration made by Cortez, in anſwere
to his Souldiers demaund.

Y maiſters,I would do and fulfil your
requeſt, if it were a thing meete and
conuenient for you,for there is not one
alone of you, howe much more all in
generall,for whome I ſhould not willingly aduenture my goods and life, if
he ſhould neede the ſame: for why? your
deeds haue bin ſuch,that I ſtand bound
neuer to forget them, or elſe to ſhew my ſelfe an ingrate-
full man. And thinke you not good friends,although I do
not fulfill the thing whiche you ſo earneſtly deſire, that
therfore I eſteem not your authoritie:but in not granting
to the ſame,I do exalt and eſteem you in greater reputation: for why? in our departing now from hence,our honor
is blotted and ſtained for euermore, and in abiding here,
we ſhall like valiant men preſerue the ſame. What nation is there, that had rule, dominion, and Empire in this
world,that hath not bin ouercome at ſome time? What famous Captain returned home to his houſe, for the loſſe of
one battaile? none truly,for he that doth not perſeuer,ſhal
neuer triumph with Lady victory:he that retireth,ſhew-
eth that he flieth, and remaineth a mocking ſtocke for all
men: but he that ſheweth nobly his face, doth vtter the
courage of his heart,yea & is both feared,and alſo beloued.

If we now ſhould depart from hence,theſe our friends
would accept and iudge vs for cowardes, and refuſe per-
petually our friendſhip. Likewiſe our enemies would
iudge the ſame, and neuer hereafter ſtand in feare of vs,
which ſhould bee a great ſhame vnto our eſtimation. Is
there any among vs,that would not hold himſelfe affren-
Pp ted,

The Conquest of

ted, if it shoulde be saide, that he turned his backe and fled, how much more would it be a dishonor for vs all to haue the same resport?

I doe muche maruell at the greatenesse of your inuincible heartes in battell : you were wont to be desirous of warres, and nowe that suche iust and laudable warre doth offer it selfe, you doe feare and refuse the same: sure it is a thing cleane contrary to our nature. What is hée that will prate of harnes, and neuer weare none? It was neuer yet séene in all this India and new world, that any of our nation retired with feare. And woulde you nowe that it should be said, that Cortes and his company fledde, being in securitie, and without perill or daunger? I beséech God not to permitte any suche thing. The warres doe muche consist in fame: why then? what better thing would you desire, than to be héere in Tlaxcallan in dispite of all youre enimies, yea proclaiming open warres against them, and they not dare to annoy vs? Therefore you may well consider, that héere you are more sure then if you were from hence, so that héere in Tlaxcallan you are honored with securitie and strength, and besides this, you haue al things necessarie for phisick and medicine, to cure youre woundes and obtaine youre health: yea, and I am bolde to saye, that if you were in youre owne naturall Countrey, you should not haue the like, nor yet be so much made off.

I do nowe meane to send for our men that are in Coazacoalco and Almeria, and so we shall haue a reasonable arme: yea and although they come not, wée are sufficient, for we were fewer in number when first we entred into this Countrey, hauing no friendes: and likewise you knowe well, it is not the number that doth fighte, but the couragious hearte and minde. I haue séene one of you discomfite a whole army, as Ionathas did, yea and many

among

the WeſtIndia.

among you haue had victory againſt a thouſand, yea ten thouſand Indians, as King Dauid had againſte the Philiſtines. I loke dayly for Horſes from the Ilandes, and other armoure and artillerie we ſhall haue from Vera Crux. And as for vittailes, take you no care, for I will prouide you abundantly, for they are things that alwaies followe the Conquerours: and as for theſe Citizens of Tlaxcallan, I binde my ſelfe that you ſhal finde them truſtie, loyall, and perpetuall friendes, for ſo they haue promiſed me vppon their ſolemne othes, yea, and if they had meante otherwiſe, what better opportunitie of time could they haue wiſhed, then theſe latter dayes, where as we lay ſicke in their owne beddes and houſes, yea ſome of vs lame, wounded, and in manner rotten, and they like louing frientes haue not only holpen you, but alſo ſerued you with diligence of ſeruantes, for they woulde rather chooſe to be your ſlaues, then ſubiectes to the Mexicans: theyr hatred is ſuche to them, and their loue ſo greate to you. And becauſe you ſhall ſee the troth, I wil now proue them and you, againſte theſe of Tepeacac, who ſlewe of late dayes twelue Spaniardes. And if this iourney happen euill, then will I follow your requeſt, and if it pleaſe God that it happen well, then will I entreate and pray you to follow my counſell.

The Souldiers hearing this comfortable ſpeeche, beganne to lay aſide their deſire to goe from thence to Vera Crux. They aunſwered generally, that they woulde obey his commaundemente, it ſhoulde ſeeme with the promiſe made, touching the ſucceſſe of the victory in Tepeacac, and lightly ſeldome it happeneth, that a Spaniard ſaith no, when he is required to goe on warfare, for it is holden for a diſhonor and ſhame.

The Conqueſt of

The warres of Tepeacac.

Cortes founde himſelfe at hearts eaſe with this anſwer, for it was a thing that had much trobled him: and vndoubtedly if he had followed his fellowes demaund, he ſhould neuer haue recouered Mexico againe, and they likewiſe had bene ſlain in the way towards Vera Crux, for they had many perillous places to paſſe. Ech one of them waxed whole of his wounds, ſauing ſome which died for want of loking to in time, leauing their woundes filthie & vnbound, as Surgions do affirme, with alſo their great trauel and weakneſſe. And likewiſe other ſome remained lame & halt, which was no ſmall grief and loſſe: but the moſt part recouered health, as I haue declared. After twentie dayes fully paſt, which they had aboue in Tlaxcallan, Cortes determined to make war with the Indians of Tepeacac, which is a great Towne, and not far from thence, for they had ſlaine twelue Spaniards, which came from Vera Crux, towards Mexico. Likewiſe they were of the league of Culhua, and therfore were holpen by the Mexicans, and did many times great hurt to the inhabitants of Tlaxcallan, as Xicotencatl did teſtifie. Cortez deſired his louing friend Maxixca, and diuers other Gentlemen, to goe with him, who forthwith entred into counſell with the ſtates & communaltie of the Citie, and there determined with generall conſent to giue vnto him fortie thouſand fighting men, beſides many Tamemoz, who are fote carriers, to beare the baggage, victuall, and other things. With this number of Tlaxcaltecas, his own men and horſes, he went to Tepeacac, requiring them in ſatiſfaction of the death of the twelue Chriſtians, that they ſhould now yéeld themſelues to ye obedience of the Emperor, and that hereafter neuer moreto receiue any Mexicā

into

the vveſt India.

into their towne or houſes, neither yet any of the Prouince of Culhua.

The Tepeacacs anſwered, that they had ſlaine the Spaniards for good and iuſt cauſe, which was, that being time of warre they preſumed to paſſe through their countrey by force, without their will and licence. And alſo that the Mexicans and Culhuacans were their frendes and Lords, whome alwayes they would friendly entertaine within their towne and houſes, refuſing vtterly their offer and requeſt, proteſting to giue no obedience to whom they knew not, wiſhing them therefore, to returne incontinent to Tlaxcallan, except they had deſire to ende their wearie dayes.

Cortes inuited them diuerſe times with peace, and ſeeing it preuailed not, he began his wars in earneſt. Their enimies likewiſe with the fauour of the Culhuacans were braue and luſty, and began to ſtoppe and defend their pretended entrance. And they being many in number, with diuerſe valiant men among them, began to ſkirmiſh ſundry times, but at the end they were ouerthrowne, and many ſlaine, without killing any Spaniard, although manie Tlaxcaltecas were killed that day.

The Lords and principall perſons of Tepeacac ſeeing their ouerthrow, and that their ſtrength could not preuaile, yeelded themſelues vnto Cortes for vaſſals of the Emperour, with condition to baniſh for euer their allyed friends of Culhua. And that he ſhould puniſh and correct at his will and pleaſure, all thoſe which were occaſion of the death of the twelue Spaniards. For which cauſes and obſtinacie, at the firſt Cortes iudged by his ſentence, that all the Townes which had bene priuie to the murder, ſhould for euer remaine captiues & ſlaues: others affirme, that he ouercame them without any condition, and corrected them for their diſobedience, being Sodomites,

Pp 3   idola-

The Conquest of

idolaters and eaters of mans flesh, and chiefly for example of all others. And in conclusion, they were condemned for slaues, and within twentie dayes that these wars lasted, he pacified all ý prouince, which is verie great: he draue from thence the Culhuacans: he threw down the idols, and the chiefest persons obeyed him. And for more assuraunce he built there a towne, naming it Segura de la Frontera: he appointed all officers for the purpose, being a towne situated in the high way frō Vera Crux to Mexico, wherby the Christians and straungers might passe without daunger. In these warres serued like faithfull friendes the Indians of Tlaxcallan, Huexozinco and Chololla, promissing the like seruice & succour against Mexico, yea, and rather better then worse. With this victorie the Spaniardes recouered great fame, for they were thought to haue béene slaine.

The great authoritie that Cortes had among the Indians.

After that these things were finished, Cortes cōmaunded and gaue licence to all the Indian friends, to returne home vnto their houses, except his assured frends of Tlaxcallan, whom he kept in his company for the wars of Mexico: he now dispatched a post to VeraCrux, commaunding that foure of the ships which Naruaes had brought, should be sent with al spéed to the Iland of Santo Domingo, for men, horses, armor, pouder and other mution, also for woollen cloth, linnen, shoes, and many other things: and wrote his letters for the same to the licenciat Rodrigo de Figueroa, & to the whole magistrates of Chancery, certifying them of all their procéedings in that country, beséeching them of helpe and succor, and

the vveſt India.

and that forthwith to be ſent vp by the meſſengers.

This done, he ſent twentie horſemen, two hundred Spaniards, and many Indians vnto Zacatami, & Xalaxinco, which were townes ſubiect to the Mexicans, and placed in the high way to Vera Crux, who had ſlaine certaine Spaniardes paſſing that way. This companie went thither, with their accuſtomed proteſtations, which preuailed not, whereupon followed fire and ſpoyle, many Gentlemen and other principall perſons came to yéelde themſelues to Cortes, more for feare than for good will, crauing pardon for their offence, promiſing alſo not to offend againe, nor yet at any time to take armour againſt the Spaniards. Cortes pardoned them, and then his armie returned, with determination to kéepe his Chriſtmaſſe in Tlaxcallan, which was within twelue dayes folowing. He left a Captaine with thrée ſcore Spaniards in the new towne of Segura, to kéepe that paſſage, and alſo to put in feare the Comercans that dwelled thereabout: he ſent before his whole armie, and hee himſelfe went with twentie horſemen from thence to Coliman, to lodge there that night, being a Citie of his allied friends, and there to ordaine and make by his authoritie, both Noble men and Captaines, in lue of them which died with the diſeaſe of ſmall pockes. He aboade there thrée dayes, in the which the newe Lordes were ordained, who afterwardes remained his eſpeciall friends. The next day hée came to Tlaxcallan, béeing ſixe leagues diſtant from thence, where he was triumphantly receiued. And truly at that time he made a iourney moſt worthy of renowne and glorie.

At this ſeaſon his deare friend Maxixca was departed this tranſitorie life, for whome he mourned cloathed in blacke, after the Spaniſh faſhion: he left behind him certaine ſonnes, of whom the eldeſt was xij. yeares of age,

whome

The Conqueſt of

whome Cortes named and appointed for Lord of his fathers eſtate, and the commons did certifie it to appertaine vnto him. This was no ſmall glorie for Cortes to giue eſtates, and alſo to take them away at his pleaſure, yea and that thoſe Indians ſhould haue him in ſuch feare and reſpect, that none durſt doe any thing in accepting the inheritaunce of their fathers without his good will and licence.

Now Cortes procured that euery man ſhould make his harneſſo, weapons and prouiſion ready and in good order: he made alſo great haſte in building Vergantines, for his timber was alreadie cutte and ſeaſoned: hee ſent vnto Vera Crux for ſayles, tackle, nayles, roapes and other neceſſarie things, whereof there was ſtore remaining of the furniture of the ſhips that were ſunke. And hauing want of pitch, for in that countrey the Indians knew not what it ment, he commaunded certaine of his mariners to make the ſame in the high mountains where was ſtore of Pine trees, and not farre from the Citie.

The Vergantines that Cortes commaunded to be built, and the Spaniards which he had ioined togither to beſiege Mexico.

He fame of proſperitie which Cortes enioyed, was wonderfully blowne abroade with the newes of the impriſonment of Mutezuma, and the victory againſt Pamfilo de Naruaez, whereupon there came many Spaniardes by twentie and twentie in a companie from Cuba, Santo Domingo, and other Ilands. Although that iourney coſt ſome their liues, for in the way they were murdered by thoſe of Tepeacac and Xalacinco, as is before declared, yet notwithſtanding there
came

the weſt India.

came many to Tlaxcallan, whereby his hoſte was much encreaſed, beſæching him to make haſte towarde the warres.

It was not poſſible for Cortes to haue eſpies in Mexico, for the Tlaxcaltecas were knowen by their lippes, eares, and other tokens, and alſo they had in *Mexico* garde and great enquirie for that purpoſe, by reaſon whereof he could not certainely knowe what paſſed in thoſe parties, according as he deſired, for to haue prouided himſelf of things néedefull: yet a Captaine whiche was taken priſoner in Huacacholla, certified ý Cuetlauac Lord of Iztacpalapan, Neuewe to Mutezuma, was elected Emperour after his Uncles death, who was a wiſe and baliant man, and hé it was that had driuē Cortes out of Mexico, who now had fortified Mexico with many bulwarkes and caues, and with many and ſundry ſortes of weapons, but chiefly very long Lances, yea and planted them in the grounde to reſiſte and moleſt the horſemen. He proclaimed pardon and fré libertie, without paying any tribute for the ſpace of one whole yéere, yea and further as long as the warres ſhould laſt, he promiſed alſo great rewardes to all them that ſhoulde kill any Chriſtian, or expulſe them from that Countrey. This was a policie whereby he gatte muche credit among his vaſſals, yea and gaue them greate courage to play the baliant men. All this newes was found to be true, ſauing onely Cuetlauac was dead. And that Quahutimocein, nenew alſo, as ſome do ſay, of Mutezuma, raygned at that time, who was a baliant man and a good warrier, as hereafter ſhalbe declared, who ſente his meſſengers throughout his Empire, proclaiming as greate rewardes as Cuetlauac had done before, declaring vnto them, that it was more reaſon to ſerue him then ſtraungers, and alſo to defende theyr olde auncient Religion, and not to credite ſuche Chriſtians as woulde make

Q q   them

themselues Lords of other mens goods, yea, & make them slaues and captiues as they had done in other places. Quahutimoc encouraged much his subiects, and kindled with his talke their wrath against the Spaniardes: yet there were some prouinces that gaue no eare to his information, but rather leaned to our side, or else medled with neyther side. Cortes seeing the effect of the matter, determined forthwith to begin the warres: he mustered his men on Saint Steuens day, and found fortie horsmen, and fiue hundreth and fortie footemen, whereof foure score were Hargabuthiers, and Crossebow men, nine peeces of Ordinance, and little powder: his horsemen bee diuided into foure squares, and his footemen into nine: he named and appoynted Captaines, and other officers for the hoste, vnto whom in generall he spake as followeth.

The exhortation of Cortez to his Souldiers.

My louing brethren, I giue most hartie thanks vnto Iesu Christ, to see you now whole of your woundes and free from diseases: likewise I much reioyce to see you in good order trimly armed, yea and with such desire to set againe vpon *Mexico*, to reuenge the death of our fellowes, and to winne that great Cittie, the which I trust in God shall bee brought to passe in short time, hauing the friendship of Tlaxcallan and other prouinces, who haue as great desire to see the ouerthrowe of the Mexicans, as we our selues, for therein they get both honor, libertie and safegard of life. Also it is to be considered, that if the victory should not be ours, they poore soules should be destroyed and remaine in perpetuall captiuitie. Also the Culhuacans do abhorre them worse then vs, for recei-

the weſt India.

receiuing vs into their houſes and countrey: therefore ſure I am that they will ſticke vnto vs vnfainedly. I muſte nedes confeſſe their vnfained friendſhip, for preſente workes doe teſtifie the ſame. They will not onely be a meane to bring others their neighbours to our ſeruice, but alſo haue now in readineſſe, 100000. men of war, to ſend with vs, beſides a great nūber of Tameme & or carriers to carrie al our prouiſion. Yee alſo, are now the ſame which alwaies heretofore ye haue bene, for I as witneſſe being your captaine, haue had the victory of many battails fighting with a. 100. yea and 200000. enimies: we got alſo by ſtrength of arm many ſtrong cities, yea and brought in ſubiection many prouinces, not being ſo many in number as we are nowe, for when we came firſte into this countrey we were not ſo many as now preſently we are. Againe in Mexico they feare our comming: it ſhould alſo be a blot vnto our honour that Quahutimoc ſhuld inherit the kingdome that coſt our fried Mutezuma his life. Likewiſe I eſtéeme al that we haue done is nothing, if we win not Mexico, our victories ſhoulde alſo be ſorowfull if we reuenge not the death of our deere fellowes. The chiefe and principal cauſe of our comming into this countrey, was to ſet forth the faith of Ieſu Chriſt, & therwithal doth follow honour and profit which ſeldome times do dwel togither. In thoſe fewe daies that we were in Mexico, we put downe the idols, we cauſed ſacrifice and eating of mans fleſhe to be layde aſide, and alſo in thoſe dayes wee beganne to conuert ſome to the faith. It is not therefore nowe reaſon to leaue of ſo laudable an enterpriſe, ſo well begunne. Let vs nowe goe whither holy faith doth call vs, and where the ſinnes of our enimies deſerueth ſo great a puniſhment, and if ye well remember, the Citizens of that citie were not content to murder ſuch an infinite number of men, women & children before the idols,

The Conquest of

in their filthie sacrifice, for honour of their Diuelishe Goddes, but also to eate their fleshe, a thing inhumaine, and much abhorred of God, and al good men doth procure, and especially Christians, to defende and punishe suche odious customes.

Besides all this, they committe that horrible sinne for the which the fiue cities with Sodom were burned by fire from heauen: Why then what greater occasion shoulde any man wishe for in earth, then to abolish such wickednesse, and to plant among these bloudie tirants the faith of Iesu Christ, publishing his holy gospel? Therfore now, with ioyfull hearts lette vs procéde to serue God, honour our nation, to inlarge our Princes dominions, and to enriche our selues with the goodly pray of Mexico, to morrow God willing we will beginne the same.

All his men answered with chéerefull countenaunce, that they were readie to depart when it pleased him, promising their faithful seruice vnto him. It should séeme the rather with the desire of that pleasure and great treasure which they had eight moneths enioyed before.

Cortes commaunded to proclaime throughout his army, certaine ordinaunces of warre for the good gouernement of his host, which he had written among others: and were these that followeth:

That none should blaspheme the holy name of Iesu.
That no Souldier should fight with his fellowe.
That none shoulde play at any game, his horse nor armour.
That none should force any woman.
That none should robbe or take any Indian captiue without his speciall licence and counsellers.
That none should wrong or iniurie any Indian their fréds: he also taxed vpon worke and apparell, for cause of the excessiue prices that they were there solde for.

The

the weſt India.

The exhortation made by Cortes to the Indians of Tlaxcallan.

THe next day following, Cortes called before him all the Lordes, Captaines, and principall perſons of Tlaxcallan, Huexocinco, Chololla, Chalco, and of other townes, who were there preſent at that time, ſaying as followeth. My lordes and friends, you know the iourney which I haue in hand, to morrow God willing I will depart to the war and ſiege of Mexico, and enter into the land of your enemies and mine: And the thing that now I doe require, and alſo pray, is, that you remaine faithful and conſtant in your promiſe made, as hereunto you haue done, and ſo I truſt you will continue. And becauſe I cannot bring ſo ſoone my purpoſe to paſſe according to your deſire and mine, without the Uergantines which are now a making, and to bee placed in the lake of Mexico, therefore I pray you to fauour theſe workmen which I leaue here, with ſuch loue and friendſhip, as heretofore ye haue done, and to giue them all things neceſſarie for their proviſion, and I doe faithfully promiſe to take away the yoke of bondage, which the inhabitants of Culhua haue laid vpon you, and alſo will obtaine of the Emperour great libertie and priuiledges for you.

All the Indians ſhewed countenance of obedience, and the chiefeſt Gentlemen auſwered in few wordes, ſaying, we will not onely fulfill your requeſt, but alſo when your veſſels are finiſhed, we will bring them to Mexico, and we all in generall will goe with you, and truly ſerue you in your warres.

302   The Conquest of

How Cortes tooke Tezcuco.

Ortes departed from Tlaxcallan with his fauiours in good order, which was a goodly sight to beholde, for at that time he had eightie thousand men in his hoste, and the most of them armed after their manner, which made a gallant shew: but Cortes for diuerse causes would not haue them al with him, vntill the Bergantines were finished, and Mexico beseeged, fearing want of vittaile for so great an army: yet notwithstanding he toke twenty thousand of them, besides the carriers, & that night came to Tezmoluca, which standeth fiue leagues from Tlaxcallan, and is a village apperteining to Huexocinco, where he was by the principall of the towne well receiued. The next day he iourneyed foure leagues, into the territorie of Mexico, and there was lodged on the side of an hill, where many had perished colde, had it not béene for the store of wodde which they found there. In the morning he ascended vpwards on this hill, and sent his scoute of foure fotemen, and foure horsmen to discouer, who found the way stopped with great trées newly cut downe, and placed crossewise in the way: but they thinking that yet forwardes it was not so, procéeded forth as well as they might, till at length the let with great hugie trées was such, that they could passe no further, and with this newes were forced to returne, certifying Cortes that the horsemen could not passe that way in any wise. Cortes demaunded of them, whether they had séene any people, they answered no, wherevpon he procéeded forward with all the horsemen, and a thousand fotemen, commaunding all the residue of his armie to follow him

with

the weſt India.

with as much ſpéede as might bee, ſo that with that companie which hée carried with him, hee made way, taking away the trées that were cutte downe to diſturbe his paſſage: and in this order, in ſhort time paſſed his hoſte, without any hurt or daunger, but with great paine and trauell, for certainly if the enemies had béene there to defend that paſſage, our men had not paſſed, for it was a verie euill way, and the enemies alſo thought the ſame to bee ſure with the trées which were croſſed the way, whereupon they were careleſſe of that place, and attended there comming in plaine ground: for from Tlaxcallan to Mexico are thrée wayes, of the which Cortes choſe the worſt, imagining the thing that afterwards fell out, or elſe ſome hadde aduiſed him how that way was cleare from the enemies. And being paſt this crooked paſſage, they eſpied the lake of Mexico, and gaue vnto God moſt heartie thankes for the ſame, and there made a ſolemne vowe and promiſe, not to returne, vntill they had wonne Mexico, or loſt their liues. They abode there and reſted themſelues, till all the whole armie were come togither, to diſcende downe into the plaine, for nowe they might deſcrie the fires and beacons of their enemies in ſundrie places, and all thoſe which hadde attended their comming by the other two wayes, were now gathered togither, thinking to ſette vppon them betwixt certaine Bridges, where a great companie aboade, expecting their comming: but Cortes ſent twentie Horſemen, who made way among them, and then followed the whole armie, who ſlue manie of them, without receyuing anie hurt. And in this order they came to Quahutipec, which is of the iuriſdiction of Tezcuco, where they aboade that night, and in that place founde neyther manne nor Woman: but not farre off was pitched the Campe of the Indians of Culhua,

which

The Conqueſt of

which might be néere a hundred thouſand men of warre, who were ſent by the ſeniors of Mexico, and Texcuco, to encounter our armie, in conſideration whereof, Cortes kept good watch with tenne Horſemen, and all his Souldiers were warned to be in a readineſſe at a call, if néede ſhould happen.

The next day in the morning he departed from thence toward Tezcuco, which ſtandeth thrée leagues diſtant, and procéeding on their iourney, foure principall perſons, inhabitants of Tezcuco, mette with them, bearing a rod of golde, with a little flagge, in token of peace, ſaying, that Coacuacoyozin their lord had ſent them to deſire him not to make any ſpoile in his countrey, and likewiſe, to offer his friendſhip, praying alſo, that it might pleaſe him with his whole armie to take his lodging in the Towne of Tezcuco, where he ſhould be well receiued. Cortes reioyced with this meſſage, although hee ſuſpected that it was a fained matter, but one of them hee knewe verie well, whome he ſaluted, ſaying: My comming is not to offend any, but rather to do you good. I will alſo receiue and hold your Lord for a friend, with condition, that hée doe make vnto mee reſtitution of the treaſure which hée toke from fiue and fortie Spaniards, and thrée hundreth Tlaxcaltecas, all which were by his commaundement alſo ſlaine of late dayes. They aunſwered that Mutezuma cauſed them to be murthered, who had likewiſe taken the ſpoile, and that the Citizens of Tezcuco were not culpable in that fact, and with this anſwer they returned.

Cortes went forward on his way, and came to Quahutichan, and Huaxuta, which are ſubiects of Tezcuco, where he and all his hoſt were plenteouſly prouided of al things neceſſarie, and threw downe the Idols. This done, hée entred into the citie, where his lodging was prepared in a great houſe, ſufficient for him and all the Spaniardes,

with

the weſt India.

with many other the Indian friends. And becauſe that at his firſt entry, he ſawe neither women nor childrē, hee ſuſpected ſome treaſon, and forthwith proclaimed, vppon paine of death, that none of his men ſhould go out. The Spaniardes began to triumph in their lodgings & chambers, placing euery thing in good order. In the euening they went vp into the Zoties and galleries, to beholde the Citie, which is as bigge as Mexico, and there they ſawe the greate number of Cittizens that fledde from thence with their ſtuffe, ſome towardes the mountaines, and others to the water ſide to take boate, a thing ſtraunge, to ſée the great haſte and ſtirre to prouide for themſelues, at the leaſt there were twentie thouſand like boates (called Conoas) occupied, in carrying houſhold ſtuffe and paſſengers. Cortez would faine haue remedied it, but that night was ſo nigh at hand, that hee could not. He would gladly alſo haue apprehended the Lord, but he was one of the firſt that fledde vnto Mexico. Cortes cauſed many of the Cittizens, to be called before him, and hauing in his company a yong gentleman of a noble houſe in that countrey, who was alſo laſt chriſtned, and had to name Hernando Cortez, being his godfather, who loued him well, ſaid vnto the citizens, that this new Chriſtian lord, Don Hernando, was ſon vnto Zezaualpincintli their louing Lord, wherefore he required them to make him their king, conſidering that Coacnacoyocin, was fled vnto the enemies, laying alſo before them his wicked fact in killing of Cacuza his owne brother, only to put him from his inheritance and kingdom, through the enticement of Quahutimoccin, a mortall enemy to the Spaniards. In this ſort was Don Hernando elected king, and the ſame therof being blowne abroade, many Cittizens repaired home againe to viſite their new Prince, ſo that in ſhort ſpace the Citie was as well repleniſhed with people, as it was before, and being

R r   alſo

The Conquest of

also well vsed at the Spaniards hands, they serued them diligently in all things that they were commaunded. And Don Hernando abode euer after a faithful friend vnto the Spaniards, and in short time learned the Spanish tong: and son after came the inhabitants of Quahutichan, Huaaxuta and Auntenco, to submit themselues, crauing pardon, if in any thing they had offended. Cortes pardoned them, and gaue them licence to depart home vnto their houses.

Quahutimoc, Coacnacoijo, and other magistrates of Culhua sent to rayle vpon those townes, for yeelding themselues to the Christians, but they laide holde vppon the messengers, and brought them vnto Cortez, of whome he enformed himselfe of the state of *Mexico*, and sent them backe againe, requiring their Lords of peace and friendship: but it preuailed not, for they were fully armed for the warre.

At this instant certaine friendes of Iames Velasques went vp and downe the Campe, procuring secretly a mutenie among the souldiers, to haue them to returne to Cuba, and vtterly to destroy Cortes his procedings. This thing was not so secretly wrought, but that Cortez had knowledge, whereupon he apprehended the doers therof, and by their confessions the matter did plainely appeare, whereupon he condemned to death one Antonio de Villafania, who was naturall of Samora, and forthwith executed the sentence, where with the punishment and mutinie was ended, and ceased.

. The

The Spaniards which were sacrificed in Tezcuco.

Daily encreased Cortes in strength and reputation, and many townes as well of the parts of Culhua as others, came vnto his friendship & obedience. Within two dayes that Don Hernando was made King, came certaine Gentlemen of Huaxuta and Quahutichan, to certifie vnto him, how all the power of the Mexicans was comming towards them, and to know if it were his pleasure, that they should carrie their wiues, children, and other goods into the Mountaines, or else to bring them where hee was, their feare was so great. Cortes made vnto them this answere, saying: be ye of good courage, and feare ye not. Also I pray you to commaunde your wiues and families to make no alteratiō, but rather quietly to abide in your houses. And concerning the enimies, I am glad of their comming, for ye shall see how I will deale with them. But the enimies wente not to Huaxuta, as it was thought: neuerthelesse Cortes hauing intelligence where they were, wente out to encounter them, with two pieces of Ordinaunce, twelue horsemen and two hundred Spaniards, with many Indians of Tlaxcallan. He fought with the enemie, and slew but few, for they fledde to the water. He burnt certaine townes where the Mexicans were wonte to succour themselues. The next day came the chiefest men of three townes to craue pardon, and to beseech him not to destroy them, promising neuer to harbour nor succour, any of Culhua. The

Rr 2

The Conquest of

The Mexicans hearing what these townes men pretended, with greate ire made a foule correction among them, as did appeare by many of them, which came vnto Cortes with broken heads, desiring reuengement.

The inhabitants of Chalco, sent also vnto him for succour, declaring that the Mexicans made great spoyle among them. But Cortes being ready to send for his Vergantines, could not relieue them all, and especially with Spaniards: wherefore he remitted them to the helpe of the Tlaxcaltecas, and vnto them of Huexocinco, Chololla, Huacacholla and other friends, promising that shortly he would come himselfe. But this answere pleased him not, yet for the present néede, they required his letters to bee written vnto those townes. And being in this communication, there came messengers frō Tlaxcallan, with newes, that the Vergantines were readie, and to know if he stood in néede of any succour, for of late, (quoth they) we haue séene many beacons, and fiers, which are greater tokens of warre, then heretofore hath bene séene.

There came at that time, a Spaniard also from Vera Crux, with certaine newes, that there had arriued a ship, which had brought thirtie Souldiers besides the Marriners of the shippe, with eight horses, great store of ponder, shotte, Crossebows, and Harquebushes. The pleasant newes reioyced much our men, whereupon Cortes sent forthwith to Tlaxcallan for the Vergantines, Gonzalo de Sandoual, with two hundreth Spaniardes, and fiftéene horsemen, and commaunded that in their way they should burne and destroy the towne where the fortie fiue Spaniards, and thrée hundreth Tlaxcaltecas were slaine, with fiue horses moe, when Mexico was last besieged: and that village is in the iurisdiction of Tezcuco, and bordereth vpon the territory of Tlaxcallan, yea, and for that purpose he would gladly haue corrected and punished the dwellers

of

the vveſt India.

of Tezcuco, but time then permitted not the ſame, although they had deſerued more puniſhmẽt then ye others. For why? in their towne they were ſacrificed and eaten, yea, and the wals painted with their blood, ſhewing moreouer perfit tokens, how it was Spaniards blood. They pluckt off alſo the horſes ſkinnes, and tanned them in the haire, and afterwards hung them vp, with the horſeſhoes in their great temple, and next vnto them the Spaniards garments, for a perpetuall memorie.

Sandoual went vnto that place with determinate intent to follow his commiſſion, and alſo before he came to the place, he found writtẽ in a houſe with a cole, theſe words: Here in this houſe was a priſoner the vnfortunat Iohn Iuſt who was a Gentleman, and one of the fiue horſemen that were taken. But the people of that town, being many, fled when they ſaw the Spaniardes approch néere vnto them. But Sandoual followed them, and ſlue manie of them: he tooke alſo priſoners many women and children, who yéelded themſelues vnto his mercy, and their bodies for ſlaues. He ſéeing ſo little reſiſtance, and beholding the pitifull mone of the wiues for their huſbandes, and the children for their fathers, had compaſſion on them, and would not deſtroy their towne, but rather cauſed the dwellers to come again, and pardoned them, with oath, that here after they ſhoulde ſerue them truely, and be vnto them loyall friends. In this ſort was the death of the Chriſtians reuenged, yet Sandoual aſked them howe they ſlue ſo manie Chriſtians without reſiſtaunce, marie (quoth they) we made an ambuſh in an euill and narrowe way, aſcending vp a hill, and there as they went vppe by one and one, we ſpoyled them, for there, neither horſes, nor other weapon could defend or helpe them, ſo that wee tooke them priſoners, & ſent them to Tezcuco, where, as is before declared, they were ſacrificed in the reuengement

Rr 3 of

The Conquest of

of the impzifonment of Calama.

How the Vergantines were brought from Tlaxcall to Tezcuco.

Owe when the enemies which murthered the Spaniards, were reduced and chaſtened, Sandoual proceded forward towarde Taxcallan, and at the border of that prouince, he met with the vergantines which were brought in péeces, as tables, planches, & nailes, with other furniture, the which eight thousand men carried vpon their backes.

There came alſo foz their ſafeconduct twentie thouſande men of warre, and a thouſand Tamemez, who were the carriers of vittailes, and ſeruaunts. Then the Spaniſh Carpenters ſayde vnto Sandouall, that foz as much as they were nowe come into the Countrey of enemies, it might pleaſe him to haue regard therevnto, foz dangers that might happen: he allowed well their iudgement.

Now Chichimecatetl, being a principal man, and a valiant alſo, was captaine of a thouſand men, and deſired to haue the vauntguard with the Tymber, and hauing had the ſame charge hitherto, it ſhould bee an affrent foz him, to bee put from it, and gaue manie reaſons in his behalfe. But notwithſtanding his requeſt, he was entreated to take the reregard. And that Tutipil and Teutecatl captaines, verie principall gentlemen, ſhould haue the vauntgart, with ten thouſande men. In the middeſt were placed the Tamemez, and thoſe that carried the ſoyſt, with all the apparell of the Uergantines. Before thoſe two captaines, went a hundred Spaniardes, and eight

the vveſt India. 311

eight horſemen, and behind and laſt, came Sandouall with all the reſidue, and ſeuen horſemen. But now although Chichimecatetl was offended, touching his firſt charge, nowe much more becauſe the Spaniardes were not in his companie, ſaying (quoth he) ye take mee not for valiant, or elſe not faithfull. That matter being pacified, and euery thing in good order, they tooke their way towarde Tezcuco, with a marnellous noyſe, crying, Chriſtians, Chriſtians, Tlaxcallan, Tlaxcallan, and Spaine.

On the fourth day they entred into Tezcuco, in verie good order, with the ſounde of drummes, ſnaile-ſhelles, and other like inſtrumentes of Muſicke, and agaynſt their entry into the Citie, they put on all their brauerie of cloathes, and buſhes of feathers, which truely was a gallant ſight: they were ſixe houres in entring into the towne, keeping their array.

Cortes came foth to receiue them, and gaue great thankes vnto the Gentlemen, and all the companie, and prouided them of good lodgings and entertainement.

Of the Docke or trench which was
made to lanch, the Ver-
ganties.

Any Prouinces of India, came to ſubmitte and offer theyr ſeruice vnto Cortes, ſome for feare of deſtruction, and others for the hatred which they bare to the Mexicans: So that nowe Cortez was ſtrong both with Spaniardes and Indians. Alſo the Spaniſhe Captaine of Segura, ſent a Letter to Cortes, the which letter he had receyued of
another

The Conqueſt of

another Spaniard, the effect therof was as followeth. Noble gentlemen, diuerſe times I haue wꝛitten vnto you, but as yet I neuer receiued anſwere, noꝛ yet now doe I thinke otherwiſe, notwithſtanding yͤ ſhall vnderſtand, that the Culhuacans haue done much hurte in this countrey, but we remaine with victoꝛy. This pꝛouince deſireth to ſée and know Captain Cortes, foꝛ to render themſelues vnto him, and nowe they ſtand in néede of our nation, wherefoꝛe it may pleaſe you to ſend vnto vs thirty Spaniardes.

Cortes, aunſwered the letter in ſuch ſoꝛt, that he then pꝛeſently coulde not ſende the thing deſired, foꝛ that he was readie to the ſiege of Mexico: notwithſtanding hée gaue them great thankes, with hope ſhoꝛtlie to ſée them. He that wꝛitte the foꝛmer letter, was one of the Spaniardes that Cortes hadde ſente to the pꝛouince of Chinanta, a yére paſſe, to enquire of the ſecretes of that place, and to ſéeke foꝛ gold and other commodities. And if it ſo happened, that the Loꝛde of that place made that Spaniarde a Captaine, againſte the Culhuacans theyꝛ enimies, foꝛ Mutezuma made them warre béing farre from Mexico, becauſe they had entertained the Spaniardes. But thꝛough the induſtrie of that Chꝛiſtian, the Loꝛde aboade alwaies with victoꝛye, and hauing vnderſtanding that ſome of his nation were in Tepeacac, he wꝛote ſo often as the letter declareth, but none of them came to their handes, but only this laſt letter: our men reioyced much to heare that the Spaniardes were aliue, and alſo the Loꝛde of Chinanta to be their friende: likewiſe they marneiled much howe they had eſcaped, foꝛ at the time that they fledde from Mexico, all other Spaniardes that were abiding in the Mines and other Loꝛdſhippes, were ſlaine by the Indians.

Cortes

the weſt India.

Cortes made his preparation for the ſiege of Mexico with all haſte, and furniſhed him with ſcalling ladders, and other neceſſaries, fitte for ſuch a purpoſe. His Vergantines being nayled, and throughly ended, he made a ſluce or trench of halfe a league of length, twelue foote broad and more, and two fadome in depth. This worke was fiftie dayes a doing, although there were foure hundred thouſand men dayly working, truly a famous worke and worthy of memory.

The Vergantines were calked with Towe and cotten woll, and for want of tallow and oyle, they were (as ſome reporte,) driuen to take mans greaſe, not that they ſlewe men for that effect, but of thoſe whiche were ſlaine in the warres. The Indians who were cruell and bloudy butchers, vſing ſacrifice, would in this ſort open the dead bodye, and take out the greaſe. The Vergantines being lanched, Cortez muſtered his men, and founde nine hundred Spaniardes, of the which were 86. Horſemen, and a hundred and eightéene with Croſſebowes and Hargabuſhes, and all the reſidue had ſundry weapons, as ſwordes, daggars, Targets, Lannces, and Halbertes. Alſo they had for armour, corſelets, coates of maile, and Jackes. They had moreouer thrée great péeces of caſt yron, fiftéene ſmall péeces of braſſe, and tenne hundred waighte of powder, with ſtore of ſhotte. All that ye haue heard, was the prouiſion that Cortes had for the ſiege of Mexico, the ſtrongeſt and greateſt Citie in all India and newe world. In eache Vergantine he placed a péece of braſſe. He proclaimed againe all the inſtitutions and ordinances of the warre, praying and commaunding that they might be well and faithfully obſerued, and ſaid, Brethren and my fellowes, now do you ſée our veſſels readie, yea and alſo you doe remember howe troubleſome a thing it hath beene to bring them hether with the coſt and ſweate

A ſtrange tallowe.

The Conqueſt of

of our friendes, and one of the chiefeſt hopes that I haue ſhortly to winne Mexico are theſe veſſels, for with them we will burne all their Canoas, or elſe we will ſo locke them vp, that they ſhall not help them, whereby we will annoy our enimie as much that way, as your army ſhall do by land. I haue alſo a hundred thouſand men of warre my friends to beſiege this Citie, who are (as you know) the valianteſt men in al theſe partes. You haue alſo your vittailes prouided abundantly, and that which now importeth, is, that you play the menne, as heeretofore you haue done, and moſt humbly to pray vnto God for victorie, for that this warre is his.

The order of the hoſt and army of Cortez for to beſeege Mexico.

THe next day following, Cortes ſent vnto the prouinces of Tlaxcallan, Huexocinco, Chololla, Chal, and other Townes, warning them within tenne dayes to come vnto Tezcuco, with their armour, weapon, and other neceſſaries, for the ſiege of Mexico. He certified them alſo, how the Hergantines were readie with all other furniture accordingly, and the Spaniardes were very deſirous to loſe no time, wherefore they meante not to delay their pretence, farther then the day appointed.

The Indian hearing this newes, and becauſe they would not come to late to the beginning of the aſſaulte, came incontinent, and entred into Tezcuco in good order of warre, aboue ſixtie thouſand men, gallantly trimmed after their vſe and cuſtome. Cortes friendly welcommed them, and prouided them lodgings accordingly.

On Witſonday, all the Spaniardes came into the fielde, whereas Cortes made three chiefe Captaines, among

the weſt India.

mong whome he deuided his whole army. Vnto Pedro de Aluarado the firſt Captaine, he appointed thirtie horſemen, and a hundred and ſeuentie footemen of the Spaniardes, two péeces of ordinance, and thirtie thouſande Indians, commaunding him to campe in Tlacopan. Vnto Criſtoual de Olid the ſeconde Captaine, he gaue thrée and thirtie horſemen, and a hundred and eightéene footemen of the mpaniſh nation, two péeces of ordinance, and thirtie thouſand Indians, and appointed him to pitch his camp in Culhuacan. To Gonſalo de Sadoual who was the third Captaine, he gaue thrée and fwentie Horſemen, and 160. footemen, two péeces of Ordinance, and 40000. Indians, with commiſſion to chooſe a place to pitch his Campe.

In euery Mergantine he planted a péece of ordinace, ſire hargabuſhes, or croſſebowes, and 13. Spaniards, men moſt fitteſt for that purpoſe. He appointed alſo Captaines for eache, and himſelfe for general, whereof ſome of the chiefeſt of his companie began to murmure that wente by lande, thinking that they had ben in greater daunger, wherefore they required him to goe with the maine battell, and not by water. Cortes little eſtéemed their words, for although it is more daunger in the water then in the land, yet it did more imporſe to haue greater care in the warres by water, then on the land, becauſe his men had béene in the one, and not in the other.

On the tenth of May, Aluarado, and Criſtoual de Olid departed, and went that night to a Towne called Acolman, where was betwéene them greate diſcorde touching their lodgings, yea and if Cortes had not ſente to take vp the matter, much miſchiefe had enſued. The nexte day they lodged in Xolotepec, which was not inhabited. The thirde daye they came vnto Tlacopan, which was alſo as all the Townes of the lake, without people, there they were lodged in the Lordes houſe of the Towne.

Sſ 2 The

The Conqueſt of

The Tlaxcaltecas began to view Mexico by the cauſey, and fought with their enimies, vntill the nighte made them to ceaſſe.

On the thirtéenth of May, Criſtoual de Olid came to Chapultepéc, and brake the conduites of ſwéete water, whervpõ Mexico was deſtitute of the ſame, being the cõduit ẏ did prouide all the Citie. Pedro de Aluarado with his company procured to amende all the broken places of the cauſey, that the horſemen might haue frée paſſage, and hauing muche to do in theſe affaires, he ſpente thrée dayes, and fighting with many enimies, ſome of his men were hurt, and many Indian friendes ſlaine. Aluarado aboue in Tlacopan with his army, and Criſtoual de Olid retired to Culhuacan with his mẽ, according to the inſtruction receiued from Cortez, and fortifies themſelues in the Lordes houſes of the Towne, and euery daye ſkirmiſhed with the enimies, and ſome went to the Townes néere at hande, and brought Centli, fruite, and other proniſion. In this buſineſſe they occupied théſelues a whole wéeke.

The Battaile and victory of the Vergantines againſt the Canoas.

He newe King Quahutimoc hauing intelligence how Cortes had launched his Vergatines and ſo mighty a power to beſége Mexico, entred into counſell with the chiefeſt péeres of his Realme. Some were of opinion, and did prouoke him to the wars, conſidering their great multitude of people, and fortitude of the Citie.

Others were of opinion, who tendred muche the common weale, that no Spaniarde that ſhoulde happen to be

the weſt India.

be taken priſoner ſhould be ſacrificed, but rather to be preſerued for concluſion of peace if néede ſhould ſo require. And finally ſome ſaid, that they ſhould demaund of their God, what was beſt to doe.

The King that inclined himſelfe more to peace than to warre, ſaide that he would remitte the matter to the iudgement of the idolles, and that he would aduiſe them what anſwere ſhould be made vnto him: but in heart hée deſired to come to ſome honeſt order and agreement with Cortes, fearing the thing that after did enſue. But ſéeing his Counſell and ſubiects ſo determined to war, he commaunded foure Spaniardes which he had priſoners in a Cage, to be ſacrificed vnto the Goddes of warre, with a great number more of Indians.

He ſpake to the Diuell in the image of Vitzilopuchtli, who aunſwered him, that he ſhould not feare the Spaniards béeing but fewe, nor yet thoſe which were comen to helpe them, for that they ſhould not long abide in the ſiege, commaunding him to goe forth and to encounter them without feare, for he would helpe them, and kil his enimies. With this anſwer of the diuil, Quahutimoc commaunded forthwith to breake downe the bridges, watch the Citie, make bulwarkes, and to arme fiue thouſande boates, and ſaide vnto the Spaniardes, that the Goddes would bée pleaſed with the ſacrifice of their bodies, the Snakes filled with their blod, and the Tigres relieued with their fleſh, they ſaide alſo to the Indians of Tlaxcallan, ah ye Cuckold knaues, ſlaues & traitors to your gods, and king, will you not repent the wickedneſſe which yée haue committed agaynſt your maiſters, therefore ſhall you nowe die an euill death, for either you ſhall die with hunger, or elſe vpon the knife: and then will we eat your fleſh, and make thereof a ſoleumne banquet, as the like hath heretofore neuer bén ſéene, and in token thereof, hold

A Diuelliſh ſentence.

Sſ 3 take

take these armes and legges which we throwe vnto you of your owne men, which we haue now sacrificed for the obtaining of victorie. And after these warres, wee will go vnto your Contrey, and spoile your towne, and leaue no memorie of your bloud or generation. The Tlaxcaltecas laughed at their madde talke, and sayd, that it should be better for them to yéelde, and submitte themselues to Cortes his mercy, and if not, yet it were more honorable to fight then to bragge, willing them to come out into the field. And bad them assuredly beléeue, that the ende of all their knauerie was at hand: it was a world to heare and sée the bragges and crakes on both sides. Cortes hearing of all these matters, sent Sandoual to take Iztacpalapan, and he embarked himselfe to méete him at that place.

Sandoual combatted the towne on the one side, and the townes men and people with feare fledde vnto Mexico, on the other side by water: he burned the towne. Cortes came at that time to a strong rocke like a tower, situated in the water, where many men of Culhua were, who séeing them approch with their Uergantines, set their beacens on fire, and threw downe vpon them stones and shot off their arrowes. Cortes went a shore with a hundreth and fiftie men, and combatted the Fort, till at length hée wanne the battlement, which was the Idians best defence, and with much adoe hée came to the top, and there fought vntill he had not left one aliue, sauing women and children. It was a fayre victorie, although fiue and twentie Spaniards were hurt and wounded, yet the fort was strong, and the ouerthrow a great discouraging of the enemie.

At this instant were so many beakons and other fires made rounde about the lake, and vpon the hilles, that all séemed a light fire. And also the Mexicans hearing that the Uergantines were comming, they came out in their boates,

the weſt India.

boates, with fiue hundreth Gentlemen which came to ſée ſuch newe kinde of Veſſelles, and to proue what they were, béeing a thing of ſo great a fame. Cortes embarked himſelfe with the ſpoile of the fort, and commaunded his men to abide all togither for the better reſiſtance, and becauſe the enemies ſhould thinke that they feared, wherevppon they might without any good order giue the onſet vpon the Chriſtians, and ſo to fal ſuddenly into the ſnare. But it followed, that when they came within ſhot of the Spaniards Ordinaunce, they ſtayed abiding more companie, but in ſhort ſpace there came ſo many Canoas, that it ſéemed a wonder to beholde: They made ſuch a terrible noiſe with their voices, drummes, Snaile ſhelles, and other like inſtruments of warre, that they could not heare one another, with ſuch great crakes and bragges, as they had done in time paſt.

And being both parties in a readineſſe to fight, there happened ſuch a poupe winde to the Vergantines which came from the ſhore, that it ſéemed maruellous. Cortes the prayſing God, commaunded all his captaines to giue the onſet altogithers, & not to ceaſſe vntil the enemies ſhould be driuen to retire into Mexico, for that it was the pleaſure of God to ſende vnto them that proſperous winde in token of victorie. This talke ended, they beganne to ſet vpon the enemie, who ſéeing the Vergantines come with ſuch luckie wind, yea & ſuch a ſight as the like vnto them had not béene ſéene, they beganne to flie with ſuch great haſte, that they ſpoiled, brake, and ſunke many of them, and ſuch as ſtode to defende themſelues were ſlaine, ſo that this battaile was ſone ended. They purſued them two leagues, vntill they hadde locked them vp in the water ſtréetes of Mexico, and toke many Lordes and Gentlemen priſoners. And the key of all theſe wars conſiſted in this victory, for our men remained for lords of

the

The Conquest of

the whole lake, and the enemie with great feare and losse: they had not béene so soone spoyled, but that there were so many of them, who disturbed one another. But when Aluarado, and Cristoual de Olid, saw the fortunat successe of Cortes by water, they entred the cawsey with their armie, and tooke certaine bridges and bulwarks, and draue the Indians from them, with all their force and strength. But with the helpe of the Bergantines which came to them, the Indians were driuen to runne a whole league vpon the cawsey, and where they found the cawsey broke, they procured to leape ouer, and so fell into the midst.

Cortes procéeded forwards, and finding no Canoas, hée landed vpō the cawsey that commeth from Iztacpalapan, with thirtie men, and combatted two towers of idolles which were walled with wall of lime and stone: it was the same place wher Mutezuma receiued Cortes. He wan those towers in short time, although they were defended with all possibilitie: he vnshipped thrée péeces of ordinance to scoure the cawsey, which was full of enemies: at the first shot, he did great hurt among them, & being the night at hande, they seased on both sides for that day. And although Cortes had determined otherwise with his Captaines, yet he aboade there that night, and sent to the campe of Gonsalo de Sandaual, for powder and fiftie men, with halfe the companie of Indians of Culhuacan.

How Cortes besieged Mexico.

He night of Cortes his abiding there, was perillous, for he had not aboue a hundreth men in his companie, and about midnight set vpon him many Mexicans, both by water and lande, although they accustomed not to fight in the night, but the Bergantines times made them soone to retire.

In the morning came vnto Cortez from Criftoual de Olid, eight horſmen, and foure ſcore foote men. The Mexicans combatted the Towers, where Cortes was lodged, who incontinent came forth and draue them alōg the calſey, vntil he had wonne another bridge & a bulwarke, and made a great ſpoile among them, with the ordinaunce and horſemē, purſuing them to the vtmoſt houſes of the Citie: and becauſe many of the Canoas which were on the other ſide of the Calſey galled Cortes and his menne, he brake downe ſo muche of the calſey, that he might well paſſe ſome of his Bergantines to the other ſide, the which with few encounters ſhutte vp the Canoas on that ſide, within the ſuccour of Mexico: and in this wiſe he remained Lord ouer bothe the lakes.

The next day Sandaual departed from Iztacpalapon toward Culhuacan, and in this way he tooke and ſpoiled a little Citie that ſtandeth in the lake, becauſe they came out to reſiſt him. Cortes ſente vnto him two Bergantines to paſſe his men where the calſey was broken. Sandoual left his company with Criſtoual de Olid, & went to Cortes with tenne horſemen, and when he came he found him in fight with the enemies, and he alighting from his horſe, an Indian perſed him through the foote with a dart. Many Spaniardes were hurte that day, but their griefe was well reuenged, for from that day forwarde the Indians courage was muche abated. With the paines, labour, and victory, alreadie obtained, Cortes might now at eaſe pitch his campe at his owne pleaſure where he would, and alſo prouide his army of victuals: ſire dayes he ceaſed not ſkirmiſhing, and the Bergantines likewiſe found out channels that they might goe rounde aboute the Citie, yea and wente ſpoiling and burning many houſes within the Suburbes.

E t   Mexico

The Conqueſt of

Mexico was beſieged in foure places, although at the firſt they determined but three. Cortes was placed betwixt the two Towers of the calſie: Pedro de Aluarado in Tlacopan: Criſtoual de Olid in Culhuacan: Gonſalo de Sandoual in Xaltoca: for they had aduice that the ſame way they would flie out of the Citie, ſeeing themſelues in any daunger. It would not haue grieued Cortes to haue left a paſſage for the enimie, but onely becauſe they ſhould not profit themſelues vpon the land, and prouide ỹ Citie that way of armour and victual, yea, he alſo thought to preuail againſt his enimies better vpon the lande then vpon the water. And againe accoꝛding to the olde prouerbe, When thine enimie flieth make him a bridge of ſiluer.

The firſt ſkirmiſh within the citie of Mexico.

Cortes pretended to enter the Citie, and to gette what he could, and alſo to ſee what ſtomacke the enimie had: he ſent to aduiſe his captaines, that eche of them ſhoulde doe the like, requiring them to ſend vnto him ſome of their horſemen and footemen. He gaue ſpeciall commaundemēt to Criſtoual de Olid to haue regard to the keeping of his calſey, and to forſee that the inhabitātſ of Xochmilco, Culhuacan, Iztacpalapan, Vitzilopuchth, Mexicalcinco, Cuetlauac, and other cities thereabouts come not that way behind them and vnwares. He commaunded that the Uergantines ſhould goe along the calſey on both the ſides, if any neede ſhould happen. Cortes early in the morning came out of his campe with 200 Spaniards, and 80000 Indian frends: they had gone but a ſmall ſpace, when they met with their enimies well armed, keping the gappe where the calſey was broke, which broken place mought be a ſpeares length, and as much in depth.

the weſt India.

depth. They fought with them, who for a great ſpace defended themſelues behinde a bulwarke, but in fine, he wanne the paſſage, and followed them vnto the entrance of the citie, where was a Tower, and at the foote thereof a bridge drawen, where a good ſtreame of water paſſed. This place was very ſtrong to combat, yea and fearefull to behold the paſſage where the draw bridge was. They ceaſed not ſhooting of arrowes and hurling of ſtones, ſo that our men coulde not come neere, vntill the Wergantines came, and by meanes of them they wanne that fort with leſſer paines then they imagined: for without the Wergantines it had not bene poſſible to haue entred the Citie.

The enimies being now fled from that holde, our men alanded there, with the Indian friendes, who incontinent dammed vp the broken place with ſtones and earth. The Spaniardes of the vantgarde, toke another bulwarke, whiche was planted in the largeſt and fayreſt ſtreete of the Citie, and purſued the enemy to another draw bridge, which remained, but with one poſte or beame, vppon the which many of the Indians paſſed ouer, and then toke the beame awaye and abode to defende the place: but when our men approached & ſawe how the matter went, Cortes commaunded two peeces of Ordinaunce to be broughte; with the which, and with their Harquebuſhes, they did great hurt among the Mexicans, who began to fainte, and loſe their courage, the which being vnderſtode, certaine Spaniarts ſwam ouer where the draw bridge was, with their weapons in their mouthes. But when the enemy ſawe them paſſe ouer, they began, as well from that place as from the houſe tops, roties and bulwarkes, which they had defended for the ſpace of two houres; to flie. Cortes and his whole army being paſſed ouer, he commaunded to damme vp that broken place of the drawe bridge,

Tt 2 with

The Conqueſt of

with earth, rubbiſh, and ſtones, and procéeding forwarde, they came to an other bridge which had no bulwarke, but was neare one of the chiefeſt places of the Cittie, and there placed a péece of Ordinaunce wherewith they did great hurt, and séeing them now paſt all the bridges, they determined to enter into the heart of the Cittie. When the Mexicans perceiued their determination, they began to prouide euery one for himſelfe, for ſome fled one way, and ſome another, but the moſt went to the great temple of Idols. The Spaniards and their friends purſued after them, and among the throng got into the Temple, where they ſlew many, and at length they went vp into the high Tower, and there threw downe the Idols, among whom they made a great ſpoyle.

Quahutimoc beganne to reprehend his men for their cowardie and flight, who gathered themſelues togither, and conſidering their ouerſight, and that there were no horſes, began a freſhe to ſette vppon the Spanyards, and with force and ſtrength draue them out of all the circuite of the Temple, and made them truſt to their féete. But when Cortes ſawe his men come flying, hée cauſed them to returne and to ſhewe face vnto the enemie, declaring vnto them how ſhamefull a thing it was to flie: But ſéeing the ſtrength and multitude of their enemies, they had no other remedie but onely to retire to the greate market place, yea & from thence alſo they were expelled, and loſt a péece of their Ordinance. But being now in this extremitie, there came thrée horſemen who played the valiant men, and made way through the troupe of enemies, who at the ſight of the horſes began to flie, and our men to follow with ſuch heart and courage, that in ſhort time they wanne the great Temple againe: then came other ſixe horſemen who ioyned with the other thrée, and lay in ambuſh, where they ſlew 30. Mexicans. The day being now

farre

the vvest India.

farre spent, and the night at hand, Cortez commanded his army to retire, and they obeying his commandement, had not so soone turned their backes, but an infinite number of enemies were at their héeles, who if it had not bene for the horsemen, had slaine many Spanyards, for they came vpon them like rauening dogs without any feare, yet with the succour of the horsemen, the enemie was put againe to flight, and our men burned many houses, to anoyd at their next comming the daunger of stones which were throwne from their toppes. The other Captaines, who were Sandoual and Aluarado, fought valiantly on the other side of the Citie.

The great hurt and damage in the houses of Mexico with fire.

IN this meane while, Don Hernando of Tezcuco, wente throughout his Lordship, to allure his vassall to the seruice and friendship of Cortes, according to his former promise: and whether it were séeing the Spaniards prosperitie in the siege of Mexico, or otherwise, he brought almost the whole prouince of Culhuacan, which is vnder the gouernment of Tezcuco, with six or seuen of his owne brethren, for more he could not, although he had more then a hundred brethren, as hereafter shalbe declared. One of them named Izclixuchilh, being a valiant yong man, of the age of four & twentie yeares, he appointed general Captain ouer fiftie thousand men of war, wel armed & trimmed according to their fashion. Cortes did frendly receiue & welcom them, giuing them great thanks for their aide and good wills. Of these new come men, he tooke into his own host thirty thousand,

Tt. 3 and

and diuided the residue equally among the other Captaines.

This was a sorrowfull newes to the *Mexicans*, to heare of the succour which Don Hernando hadde sent to serue Cortes, and with-holden the same from them, yea and also among them were come kinsmen, brethren, and fathers, to many of them which were in *Mexico*, in the seruice of Quahutimoc.

Two dayes after that these men were come, there came also men of Xochmilco, and certaine husbandmen of the Mountains, who spake the Othomitlh speech, beseeching *C*ortes to pardon their long tarrying, offering also both men and vittailes for the siege. Cortes was pleased with their comming and gentle offer, for they being his friends, he was assured of them of Culhuacan, and said vnto them, within these three daies (God willing) I will combate the citie, therefore against that time I pray you prepare your selues accordingly, and therin shall I know whether you be my friends or no: and with this answere they departed, promising to fulfill his request, as they did indeed. This done, he sent three Uergantines to Sandoual, and other three to Aluarado, for to disturbe any succour that might come from the land to the Citie, and likewise to defende and aide the Spaniardes at all times, when they would land vpon the cawsey, to combate the Citie, for he wel vnder stood how profitable those vessels would be neere vnto the bridges.

The captaines of the Uergantines ceased not night and day to runne the coast and Townes of the lake, where they toke many boates from the enemies, laden with men and vittaile, and permitted none to come into the Citie, nor yet any to come out.

The day appointed to the enemies for the combate, Cortes made his praiers vnto God, & then enformed each

Captaine

the vvest India. 327

Captaine what he should do, and came forth with twentie horsemen, three hundred Spaniards, and a great number of Indians, with their peeces of Ordinance, and where in three or foure dayes before they had not skirmished, time serued the Mexicans at wil to open al those places which were dammed vp before, and also to build better Bulwarkes then those which were throwne downe, attending with that horrible noise accustomed. But when they saw their Bergantines on each side, their ioy was turned into sorrow, and began to faint, the which our men vnderstoode well, and therewith alanded themselues vpon the cawsey, and wan the bulwarke and the bridge. Our army proceeding forward, set vppon the enemies, vntill they came to another bridge, the which was likewise wonne in short time, and this pursued from bridge to bridge, alwayes fighting, vntill they had driuen them from the cawsey and streetes.

Cortez for his part lost no time, for he with ten thousand Indians laboured to damme vp againe the sluces and broken places of the bridges, making the way plaine both for Horsemen and footemen: it was so much to doe, that all those ten thousand Indians were occupied therin from the morning vntill euening.

The other Spaniardes and Indian friends skirmished continually, and slue many of their enemies. Likewise the Horsemen so secured the streetes, that the enemies were forced to lock them vp in their houses and temples. It was a notable thing to see how our Indians played the men that day agaynst the Citizens: sometimes they would chalenge them the field: other times they would conuite them to supper, and shew vnto them legs, armes, and other peeces of mans flesh; saying, beholde your owne flesh which shal serue for our supper and breakfast, and to morrow we will come for more, therefore flie not,

you

you are valiant fellowes, yet it were better for you to die fighting then with hunger. And after all this speech, euery one of them called vpon the name of his owne Towne with a loude voyce, setting fire vpon their houses. The Mexicans were replenished with sorow, to see themselues so afflicted with Spaniards, but yet their sorrowe was so muche the greater, to heare their owne vassalles so raile against them, saying and crying at their own toties, victory, victory, Tlaxcallan, Chalcho, Xochmilco, and other Townes: the eating of their fleshe grieued them not, for they did the like.

Cortes seeing the Mexicans so stoute and hard harted, with full determination either to defence themselues or else to dye, thereupon he bethought himselfe vppon two things, the one was, that he should not obteine the treasure which he had seene in the time of Mutezuma: the other was, that they gaue him occasion totally to destroy the Citie. Both these things grieued him much, but especially the destruction of the Citie. He imagined with himselfe what hee might do, to bring them to acknowledge their error, and the hurt that might fall vpon them, and for these considerations hee pluckt downe their Towers, and brake their Idolles. He burned also the great house wherein hee was lodged before, and the house of foule which was néere at hand. There was not one Spanyard who had seene that magnificall building before, but lamented sore the sight: but to agréeue the Citizens, it was commaunded to be burned. There was neuer Mexican, that thought any humaine force, how much lesse so fewe Spanyards, should haue entred into *Mexico* in despite of them all, and to set fire vpon their principallest edifices within the citie. While this house was a burning, Cortes gathered his men, and retired to his Campe. The Mexicans would faine haue remedied the fire, but it was
too

the vveſt India.   329

too late, and ſeing our men retire, they folowed with their
noyſe accuſtomed, and ſlue ſome of our men, who were laden with the ſpoyle, and came behinde the reſt. The horſemen releeued our men, and cauſed the enemy to retire, in
ſuch wiſe, that before night all our men were in ſafetie
and the enemie was in their houſes, the one ſort full of ſorow,
and the others wearied with fight & trauell. The ſlaughter was great that day, but the burning and ſpoyle of houſes was greater, for beſides thoſe which we haue ſpoken
of, the Mergantines did the like where they went, and the
other Captaines alſo were not idle where they were appointed.

¶ Thinges that happened to Pedro de Aluarado,
through his bolde attempt.

Edro de Aluarado, would paſſe his army to the Market place of Tlatuluco,
for he tooke much paine, and was in
perill, in folowing the bridges which
he had gotten, beeing his firſt almoſt
a league from thence. And Aluarado, being a man of a haughtie courage,
thinking as well to get honor as his
Generall, and likewiſe being prouoked by his companie,
who ſaid, that it were a ſhame for them if Cortes ſhould
winne that Market place, being more nearer vnto them,
then vnto him: whereupon he determined to winne thoſe
bridges which as yet were vnwonne, and to place himſelf
in the Market place. He proceeded with all his army vntill they came to another broken bridge, which was ſirtie
paces of length, and two fadome deepe, the which with the
helpe of the Mergantines, he wanne in ſhort ſpace, and
gaue order to certaine of his hoſt to cullme it vp ſubſtan-
          T t   cially

cially, and hee himselfe pursued his enemies, with little Spaniards. But when the Citizens sawe so fewe in number, and all footmen, (for the horses could not passe the sluce so soone,) they came vppon them so sodeinly and fiercely, that they made our men to turne their backes, and trust to their legges, yea and our men fell into the water, they knew not which way. They slew many of our Indians, and foure Spaniards, who forthwith they sacrificed, and eate their flesh in the open sight of all the army.

Aluarado sawe his owne folly, in not beleeuing Cortez, who had alwaies forewarned him, not to proceede forward, or till he had made the way sure behinde him: but Aluarado his Counsellers paide their counsel with life, Cortes sorrowed for the same, for the like had happened vnto him, if he had giuen credite to their counsell. But as a prudent Captaine, he considered the matter better, for euery house was then an Iland, the calsey broken in many places, and the ioties or house toppes beset with stones, for these and such like places vsed Quahutimoc. Cortes went to see where Aluarado had pitched his Camp, and also to rebuke him for that which was past, and to aduise him what he should do: But when he came and found him so far within the libertie of the Cittie, and the daungerous places which had passed, he did highly commend his valiant and good seruice: he also communed with him of many things concerning the siege, and then returned to his owne camp.

Th

the vvest India. 331

The tryumph and sacrifice which the Mexicans made for their victorie.

Ortes delaied the time, to pitche his Campe in the Market place of Mexico, although daily his men entred and skirmished within the Cittie, for the causes before alleaged, and likewise to see if Quahutimoc would yéeld himself. And also the entrie could not bee but very daungerous, for the great multitude of enemies that filled vp the stréetes.

All his company Spaniards ioyntly, with the Kings Treasurer, séeing the determination of Cortes, and the hurt alreadie receiued, besought and also required him to passe his Campe vnto the Market place: who aunswered them, that they had spoken like valiaunt men, but as yet (quoth he) it is not time conuenient, and we ought to consider better of the matter: for why? the enemies are fully determined to ende their liues in defence of that place. But his menne replied so muche, that hee was compelled againe to graunt their request, and proclaimed the entrance for the next day following. He wrote also in his Letters to Gonsalo de Sandoual, and to Pedro de Aluarado, the instructions of the thinges that they shoulde doe, whiche was in effect, to Sandoual, that hee shoulde remoue his Campe with all his fardage, as though hee woulde retire and flie, and that vppon the calsey hee shoulde haue tenne horsemen in ambushe, behind certain houses, to the intent that when the Citizens should espie them flie, and would pursue after, then to passe betwixt them and home with the saide horsemen, and

Vv 2   after

The Conqueſt of

after the hurt done among them, in this ſort, that then he with all his army ſhould come where Pedro de Aluarado abode, with other tenne horſemen, a hundreth footemen, and the Nauie of Uergantines, and leauing with him his men, ſhould then take three of the Uergantines, and to procure to winne that broken bridge, where Aluarado of late receiued the foyle: and if he fortuned to winne that place, that then he ſhould damme it vp, and make it ſure, before he paſſed any further: and the like order he gaue vnto him for all other broken places that he ſhoulde paſſe.

Unto Aſunrado he gaue commiſſion, that he ſhould paſſe as farre into the Citie as he might poſſible, requiring him alſo to ſende vnto him eightie Spaniardes. He alſo appointed the other ſeauen Uergantines, to paſſe into both the lakes, with three thouſande Canoas. He deuided likewiſe all his army into three companies, he made they had three waies to enter into the Citie. By the name of theſe routes or ſtreets, [illegible] dittos, with ſeuentie Spaniardes, [illegible] Indians, [illegible] and many other looſe houſes; to [illegible] trouſes, and to [illegible] broken places, and to make the way plaine.

The ſeconde charge he commaunded to George de Aluarado and Andres de Tapia, with eight Spaniardes, ſeſshe thouſand Indians, [illegible] and eight horſemen. Cortes [illegible] a great number of [illegible] and a [illegible] Spaniardes footemen, of the which were [illegible] boweres and harquebuſes, and commaunded [illegible] with were eight horſemen, [illegible] not to [illegible] other, and at one time they aſſayled

ing

the vvest India.

ing the hearts of valiant men, greatly annoying the enemie, and wan many bridges, but when they came nere vnto the towne house called Tianquizcli, there gathered togither such a number of the Indian friends, who before their eyes, sealed, entred, and robbed their houses, that they thought assuredly, that the same day the citie had bin wonne. Cortez commaunded that they should proceede no further, saying, that they had done sufficiently for that day, for also he feared afterclappes. He likewise demaunded whether all the broken bridges were made sure, in the which (quoth he) consisteth the perill and victorie. But those that went with the Treasurer, following victorie and spoile, had left a bridge not well dammed vp, but verie hollowe and false, the which was of twelue paces broad, and two fadom in depth. Then Gortes was aduertised hereof, he went thither to remedie the same, but hée was in some roome, when he sawe his men flying, and leaping to the water, with feare of the cruell enemies, which followers who leapt after them into the water, to kill them. There came also along the causey manie Indian boates of enemies, who tooke many of the Indian friends and Spaniards aliue. Then Cortes and other fiftéen persons, which were with him, serued for no other purpose but to helpe out of the water those that were fallen, some sore wounded, and others halfe drowned, and without any other persones the multitude of enemies so beset Cortes and his companie that it was helping there men, and to escape with life, that he had no regard to those that were perished. Upon certain Mexicans laid hand vpon Cortes, he had truly the bene carried away if it had not bin for one Francisco de Olea his seruant, who cut off at one blow the armes of that that had hold of him, and he by the come ones that stood lykewyse, so that he escaped to saue his life also. The meane Antonio de Quinnonez

U b 3   Captaine

The Conqueſt of

captaine of the guard, who caught Cortes by the arme, and by force pluckt him out of the throng of enimies, with whom valiantly he fought. But then with the fame that Cortez was priſoner, came many Spaniards, amõg whom was one horſeman, to whõ made ſome roome, but in ſhorſe ſpace they thruſt him through the throte with a launce, and made him to retire. The fight ceaſed a little, and Cortez had a horſe brought vnto him, on the which he lightlye amounted, and gathering his men togither, came to the ſtréete of Tlacopan, which was large and faire. There died Guzman his Chamberlaine, giuing a horſe vnto his maiſter, whoſe death was much lamented amõg them all, for he was a man valiant, honeſte, and welbeloued. There fel alſo into the water two horſes, the one was ſaued, but the other was killed by the Indians. As the Treaſurer and his company were Combatting a bulwarke, the enimies threw out of a windowe three Spaniards heads vnto them, ſaying, the like they would doe with their heads, if they went not from thence the ſoner. They ſeing this ſight, and likewiſe conſidered the great hurte and ſpoile made among them, began to retire by little and little.

The Mexican Prieſts went vp into the Towers of Tlatelulco, and made their fiers in chafing diſhes, and put thereunto the ſwéete gum of Copalli in token of victorie, and forthwith ſtrippcd fiftie Spaniards captiues as naked as they were borne, and with their fine raſors opened them in the breaſtes, and pluckt out their hartes for an offering to the Idols, and ſprinckled their bloud in the ayre. Our men ſéing before their eies the dolefull ſight, would fain haue gone to reuenge the cruel cuſtome. But as time then required, they had inough to doe to put themſelues in ſafetie, through the greate troupe of Indians which came vpon them, who now feared neither

horſe

the vvest India.

horse nor sword. This day as ye haue heard, were fortie Spaniards sacrificed, and Cortes wounded in one of his legges, and thirtie moe of his men: they lost a péece of Ordinance, and foure horses. Also that day was slaine aboue two thousand Indian friends, and many Canoas lost, and the Bergantines in great daunger, and the captaine and maister of one of them were wounded. Whereof the captaine died within eight dayes, the same day were also slaine foure of Alvarado his men, that day was an vnfortunate or dismall day, and the night heauy, sorowfull, and replenished with lamentable griefe among the Spaniards and their friends. On the other side, the Mexicans triumphed with ioy, and made great bonefires, blewe their hornes, stroke vp their drummes, daunced, banqueted, and dranke themselues drunke: they also opened their strétes, and bridges, as they were before, and placed their scout and watch about the Citie. And as sone as it was day, the king Quehutimoc, sent two Christians heads, and two horse heads into all the comercanes there about, to signifie their victorie, and to require them to forsake the Christians friendship, promising in short space to make the like ende of all those that remained, and deliuer the countrey from war. These things encouraged some prouinces to take armour agaynst Cortes, being his allied friends, as Mahualco, and Cuixco. This newes was sone blowne abroate into many Prouinces, where vppon our men feared rebellion among their newe friends, yea and mutinie in their owne campe, but it pleased God that it fell out otherwise. The next day Cortes came out again e to fight, to shewe face to the enemies, but he turned again from the first bridge, without doing any great act.

The

The Conqueſt of

The determination of Cortez to deſtroy the Citie of Mexico.

Chichimecatl, a noble man of Tlaxcallan, (who had brought the Timber of the Brigantines from whence it was wrought, and was placed in the companie of Aluarado, at the beginning of the siege of Mexico,) ſeeing that the Spaniards fought not as they were wont to do, but alone with the men of his owne Countrey, went to try to compaſſe the Citie, being a thing which before hee had not attempted, came aſſault againſt thoſe which defended a certaine wall, and toke great paine to it, and marched his Citie and inne, and in ſhort ſpace wanne the lodge, where hee left foure hundreth Archers, and followed after the enemie, who of moduerie deede, thinking to take him at his returne, and at length the enemie retired wholly him, when they made a ſure retraite, for the time they tarryed. There were many hurt and ſlaine on both ſides, to that with the dead carkaſes they ſtopped at will. But they thought to ouerthrow him at the time, not knowing of the foure hundreth Archers which were there to defend Chichimecats returning. By meanes of which, hee paſſed at pleaſure, (to the great griefe of the Mexicans,) and eſcaped not a little amazed to ſee the valour and bolde attempt of the Tlaxcaltecas.

The Spaniards likewiſe highly commended the fact, to ſee where our men combated not as they were wont to do,

the

the weſt India.

the Mexicans imagined that the cauſe was cowardiʒe, infirmitie, or want of vittailes: whereupon one daye at the ſunne riſing, they ſet vpon Aluarado his Campe, which being eſpied by the watch, they began to crie, arme, arme, who came forth as well footemen as horſemen, and put them to flight, at which retire many of ye Mexicans were drowned, and others ſore hurt and wounded. Then ſaid the Mexicans, that they deſired to talke with Cortes, who came vnto a drawe bridge to knowe what they woulde haue, vnto whom ſomtime they ſaid, that peace was their requeſt, and other times they demaunded truce, but finally required that the Spaniards ſhoulde depart from that Countrey. All this policie was but to féele what ſtrength and courage our menne had, and to haue truce for a certaine time, for to prouide them of ſuch neceſſaries as they wanted, for their determinate purpoſe was, to die in the defence of their countrey and religion. Cortes anſwered, that truce was not conuenient for either partie, but peace was laudable at al times, the which for his part, although he hadde beſieged the Citie, ſhould not be denied: therefore he willed them to vſe his plentiful eſtate of vittails, and their owne néede and neceſſitie of the ſame. They being in this communication with their interpreters, appeared an aunctient olde man on the top of the bulwarke, who in the ſighte of them all, pluckt bread out of his ſatchell péece by péece, and began to eate, giuing them to vnderſtand, that they ſtoode in no néede of vittailes, and ſo made an ende of their talke.

The ſiege of this Citie ſéemed a long time to Cortes, for in néere fiftie dayes that he had begun the ſame, yet could not he bring his deſire to paſſe, yea and much marueiled, that the enimies could enture ſo lōg a ſeaſon with dayly ſkirmiſhing, and alſo how they refuſed peace and concord, knowing how many thouſands of them had ben

X r ſlaine,

The Conqueſt of

ſlaine, and ended their miſerable liues with hunger.

Yet once again he ſent this laſt meſſage vnto them, that if they would not yælde themſelues, then he hauing them enuironed by land and water, would ſlea them all, and not permit any kinde of victuall to come vnto them, ſo that their extremitie ſhould be ſo great, that they ſhould eate one another: their anſwere was, that firſt the Spaniards ſhould taſte of the ſame cup, ſo that threatning encreaſed their courages, and occupied themſelues in carying ſtones to the Market place, and many other ſtrætes, to ſtoppe the way againſt the Horſes and their maiſters.

Cortes, although it græned him to deſtroy totally ſo beautifull a Citie, yet he determined to bring all the houſes of the ſtrætes that he ſhould winne, to be equall with the ground, and to ſtop with them the Chanels of water. He communed the matter with his Captaines, who liked well of his intent, although it was a troubleſome thing. He alſo aduertiſed the Gentlemen Indians his friends of his determination, who highly commended his deuice.

Cortes ſæing the towardneſſe of all his army, he called and prepared all his labourers, with their pikeaxes and ſhouels, ſo that in theſe affaires, and in ſetting his men in good order, he ſpent foure dayes, and then he began to combat the ſtræte, which goeth directly to the Market place, then fainedly the Citizens deſired peace. Cortes ſtaied, and aſked for their King: they anſwered, that they had ſent for him, whereupon Cortes tarried an houre, and then they began to reuile him, and to throw ſtones, and ſhot at him. The Spaniards ſæing this, gaue the onſet, and wan a fort, and came into the chiefe place of the Citie. They cleanſed the ſtrætes of the ſtones which they had laide to diſturbe their paſſage, and ſtopped ſo vp the water ſtræte in that place, in ſuch wiſe, that neuer after it was opened againe, and forew downe all the houſes, making

the

the weſt India.

the entrance into the Citie an open plaine high way, and then retired to their Campe. Alſo ſixe dayes arow they did the like, without receiuing any hurt, ſauing the laſt day two horſes were hurt.

The next day Cortes laid an ambuſh with fiftie horſmen, and ſent before him the Uergantines, but he himſelf with thirtie horſemen, abode in certaine great houſes in the Market place. They fought that day in many places of the citie, and at the retire, one ſhot off a handgun, which was the token that thoſe which lay in ambuſh ſhuld come forth. The enemies followed our men, that ſeemed to flée with maruellous courage. But they were not ſo ſoone paſſed the ſnare, when Cortes came forth with his thirtie horſemen, ſaying, Upon them, vpon them: By this onely meane were ſlaine aboue fiue hundred Mexicans, beſides the priſoners.

Our Indian friends had a good ſupper that night with mans fleſh, which as yet they would not be perſwaded to leaue. Certaine Spaniards went vp into a Tower of Idols, and there opened a ſepulchre, where they found fiue hundreth Caſtlines in golde: With this ouerthrowe the Mexicans remained in ſuch feare, that all their threatenings and tryumphs were turned into mourning: and after when they ſawe our men retire, they would not follow them, fearing the like daunger, ſo that this was a meane, the ſoner to win Mexico.

The

The Conqueſt of

The hunger and infirmitie which the Mexicans ſuffered with great courage.

TWo poore ſoules who were vexed with hunger, came in the night ſeaſon out of the citie vnto Cortes his Camp, who certified, how the Citizens were in greate neceſſitie, and ſo many dead with hunger and ſickneſſe, that there were heapes of dead bodies in the houſes, only to keepe cloſe their extreame miſerie: and ſaid alſo, that in the night ſeaſon manie came out to fiſhe betweene the houſes with feare of the Vergantines, and others came out to ſeeke for woode, hearbes, and rootes to eate.

Cortes hearing theſe newes, determined to knowe the troth thereof, ſo that the nexte night he commaunded the Vergantines to goe round about the Citie, and he himſelf with fifteene Horſemen, a hundred footemen, and manye Indian friends, placed themſelues betwixt certaine houſes, with order of his eſpies, to aduertiſe him what they ſhoulde ſee. It was no ſooner tap, but manye poore folke came out to ſeeke for foode, and when Cortez had intelligence thereof, he made a greate ſlaughter among them, whereas at that time of vnarmed men, women, and children, were ſlaine to the number of eight hundred: and the Vergantines on their ſide made another ſpoile. The pittiful noiſe being heard into the Citie, the Citizenes were aſtoined, and knew not what to doe, fearing the like ambuſhe that they had ſeene and fealt the day before, and alſo wondered, that at ſuch an houre not accuſtomed, the Spaniardes were ſo nigh. The nert day following, being S. James his euen, Cortez entret againe into the Citie, accoding as he had done before, and wanne the ſtreete of Tlacopan, where he burned the riche and faire houſes

A cruell fact of Cortes.

of

the vveſt India.

of king Quahutimoc, which were motted rounde about: ſo that now of foure parts of the citie, three parts were won, and the Spaniardes might ſafely paſſe from Cortes his Campe, to the Campe of Aluarado, by reaſon that all the houſes were burned, and beaten downe plaine with the grounde.

But yet the poore Mexicans would ſay to the Indians of Tlaxcallan, goe to, goe to, make haſt, burne and deſtroy theſe houſes, for time will come that ye ſhall build them a‑ *A true pro‑*
gaine at your owne coſt. For if we haue victory, then ſhall *pheſie.*
ye build them for vs, and if we be ouercome, then ſhall ye build them for theſe ſtraungers.

Within foure dayes after, Cortes entred the Citie a‑ gain, and alſo Aluarado on his ſide, who to ſhew his haul‑ tie ſtomack, laboured all that was poſſible to get two To‑ wers of the Temple of Tlatelulco, the which at the length he wan, although he loſt three horſes in the combat.

The next day following, the horſemen walked vp and downe in the greate Market place at pleaſure, the poore Mexicans beholding that ſorrowful ſight from their houſes. And as the Spaniards went walking in the Citie, they founde heapes of dead bodies in the houſes, ſtreetes, and *An extreame*
in the water: they found alſo the barke of trees and rootes *penurie.*
gnawen by the hungrie creatures, and the men ſo leane and yellow, that it was a pitifull ſight to beholde. Cortes yet againe required them to yeelde, and they although they were ſo leane of bodie, were ſtrong in heart, and an‑ ſwered that he ſhould not ſpeake of any friendſhippe, nor yet hope of their ſpoyle, for when no fortune would fa‑ uoure them, then they woulde either burne their trea‑ ſure, or throwe it into the lake, where they ſhould neuer profite thereby, and that they would fight while one alone ſhould remaine aliue. At Cortes his next entry into the Citie, he founde the ſtreetes full of women, children, olde

folke,

folke, and many miserable sicke persons which were perishing for want of foode.

Cortes commanded that none of his army should doe any hurt vnto such miserable creatures. The principall folke who were whole and sound, they stoode in their Zoties or house tops, without weapon, and clothed in mantels. It was thought that they kept a certaine holy day, peace was againe offered, but they aunswered with dissimulation. The next day following Cortes required Aluarado on his side to combat a streete of 1000. houses that was not yet woon, and that he would do the like on the otherside: for a little space the Citizens defended theselues; but their defence endured not, but were driuen to flie, being not able to resist the force of their contraries. So that the Spanish armie wanne also that streete, and slue 12000. Citizens, the murther was so great because the Indian friends would shew no mercy or compassion vpon them, although they were required to the cōtrary. So that now the Mexicans hauing lost this streete also, the houses that were not beaten down could scarcely hold the people that were aliue, the streetes also being so full of dead carkasses and sicke bodies, that our men could not passe, but must neepes tread vpon them. Cortes desirous to see what remained of the Citie to win, went vp into a high tower, and hauing well vewed the Citie, he iudged that of eight parts one remained yet to win. And y next day following he assaulted the same, with speciall commandement giuen to his army, not to kill any but onely such as should resist.

The sorowfull Citizens bewailing their vnfortunate fate and destiny, besought the Spaniards to make an end, and to kill them all out of hande. Then certaine of the horsmen called *Cortes* in great hast, who went vnto them incontinent, hoping of some agreement of peace: and standing at the brimme of the water neere vnto a drawe bridge,

bridge, the Mexicans said, Oh Captaine Cortes, considering that thou art the child of the Sun, why doest thou not entreate the Sunne thy father, to make an ende of vs: oh thou Sunne that canst go round about the world in a day and a night, we pray thée make an end of vs, and take vs out of this miserable life, for we desire death to go and rest with our God Quetcauatlh who tarieth for vs. After these speaches they made a lamentable crie, calling vpon their Goddes with loude voyces. Cortes aunswered what hée thought good, but yet could not perswade them to yélde, truly it was a pitifull sight to behold. *A sorrowfull tale.*

The imprisonment of Quahutemoc.

Cortes séeing the great extremitie that those poore wretched people were in, thinking nowe that they woulde yélde vnto him, thereupon he spake to an Uncle of Don Hernando de Tezcuco, who was taken prisoner thrée dayes before, whom he desired to goe to the king, and treate of peace: this Gentleman refused the message, knowing the determinate will of Quahutimoc, but through much entreatie he granted to his request. So the next day following Cortes entered into the Citie, and sent that Gentleman, and certaine Spaniardes before him. The Indian guarde of that stréete receiued him with the honor which vnto such a noble man did appertaine. He procéeded forward toward the king, & being come where he was, he declared vnto him his embassage. When Quahutimoc had heard his tale, he was so moued with ire and choler, that forthwith he commanded him to be sacrificed, and gaue the Spaniards for their aunswere blowes with stones, staues and arrowes, saying also that they desired death, and no peace, and fought so stoutly that day, that they slue many of our men, and one horse. Likewise on their side many were slaine. *An euill reward.*

The next day Cortes entred the Citie againe, but hée fought not, hoping then that they would submitte themselues, but yet the Citizens had no such thought. He came néere vnto a certaine bulwarke on horsebacke, and spake vnto certaine Gentlemen with whome he was acquainted, saying, that now within a short space he could make an ende of their finall destruction, but yet of méere compassion he wished it not, for the loue which he bare vnto them, so that they woulde in time render themselues: whcrefore(quoth he)eutreat ye the king to doe the same, and in so doing ye shall be well vsed, and haue vittailes sufficient. The Gentlemen hearing these words, fell on wéeping, and answered, that now they knew well their errour, and felt their losse and destruction, notwithstanding they were bound to obey their king and Gods. But yet(quoth they)abide a while, and we wil certifie Quahutimoc what you haue said, & in short space they went and returned againe; saying that the next day without fayle their Lord would come and talke with him in the market place. With this answere Cortes returned to his campe, and thought at their méeting to conclude an honourable peace. So against the next day he caused a Canapie and chaire of estate to be set in the market place, according to the Mexican vse, and also a dinner to be prepared. The day following came Cortes at the houre appointed, with many of his men armed, but the king came not: neuerthelesse he sent fiue noble men to treate of the matter, excusing the king, saying he was not well at ease. Cortes welcomed those Gentlemen, and was glad of their comming, hoping thereby to conclude and make some good ende. And when they had dined and well refreshed their hungrie bodies, Cortes gaue them victuals, and desired them to returne againe to to the King, and to declare vnto him that without his presence the conclusion coulte not bee certaine.

certaine. They went and returned againe within two houres, and brought vnto Cortes certaine mantels made of cotten woll, very good & well wrought, with answere, that the king would not come in any wise, both for shame and feare. And the next day these messengers came again, saying that the king would come to the place appointed. But yet he came not, although Cortes attended his comming more then foure houres, who seeing the mockery, he forthwith sente Sandoual with his Mergantines one way, and he himselfe went another, combatting the houses & fortres that yet remained, where he founde small resistaunce, so that he might doe what he pleased. There was that day slaine and taken prisoners aboue 40000 persons, and their he retired to his campe. The lamentable crie and mourning of the women and children woulde haue made a stony hart relent, the stench also of the dead bodies was wonderfull noisome. That night Cortes purposed to make an end the next day of the wars, and Quahutimoc pretended to flie, and for that purpose had enbarqued himselfe in a Canoa of twelue ores. When the day appeared, Cortes with his men, and foure péeces of ordinance, came to the corner where those that yet remained were shut vp, as cattell in a pounde. He gaue order to Sandoual and Aluarado what they should do, which was, to be ready with their Mergantines, and to watche the cōming out of the Canoas which were hidden betwixt certaine houses, and especially to haue regard vnto the kings person, and not to hurte him, but to take him aliue. He commaunded the residue of his men to force the Mexican boates to goe out, and he himselfe went vp into a Tower, enquiring for the King, and there founde Xihuacoa, gouernour and Captaine generall of the Citie, who woulde in no wise yéelde himselfe. Then came out of the Citie a greate multitude of olde folkes, men, women and childrē, to take boate. The throng was

was so great with hast to enter the Canoas, that many by that meanes were drowned in the lake. Cortes required his men not to kill those miserable creatures: But yet he could not stay the Indians his friends, who slue & sacrificed aboue fiftéene thousand. After this, there was a great rumor among the common people, that the king would flie, making a piteous mone, and saying that they sorrowfull creatures knew not whither to go: But yet procuring to go into the Canoas, which were so full that there was no roume for them, by reason thereof many were drowned.

The men of warre stood in the house toppes and ioties beholding their perdition. All the nobilitie of Mexico were embarked with the King. Then Cortes gaue signe with the shot of a handgun, that his Captaines should be in a readinesse, so that in short space they wanne fully and wholy the great citie of Mexico. The Bergantines likewise brake in among the fléete of boates, without any resistance, and euery one sought where he might best succour himselfe, the Royall Standart was beaten downe. Garcia Holguin, who was Captaine of a Bergantine, had espied a great Canoa of twentie ores déepe, laden with men. And one of his prisoners saide vnto him, that the king went in that great Canoa. Holguin being glad of the newes, gaue chase to that Canoa and ouertooke him. In his foreship he had thrée Crossebowe men. And when Quahutimoc who stood on the puppe of the Canoa readie to fight, sawe those bowes ready bent, and many drawen swordes, he yéelded himselfe, declaring that he was the king. Garcia Holguin being a glad man of his prisoner, tooke and carried him vnto Cortes, who receiued him reuerently. When Quahutimoc came neare vnto him, he laide his hand vpon Cortes his dagger, saying, I haue done all my possibilitie to defend me and mine, according to my dutie, hoping not to haue come to this estate & place where now I stand: And considering

the vvest India.

considering that you may do with me what you please, I beséech you to kill me, and that is my only request. Cortes comforted him with faire words, giuing him hope of life and seniory, and tooke him vp into a iotie, requiring him to commaund his subiects to yéeld and render themselues: he obeyed his request. At that time there was about thrée score and ten thousand persons, who in séeing their Prince, threw downe their weapons, and submitted themselues.

The taking of Mexico.

IN the order before declared, wanne Hernando Cortez the famous Citie of Mexico, on Tuesday being the thirtéene of August, An. 1521. in remembrance whereof, and of the great victory, euery yeare on that day they make a sumptuous feast and solemne procession, wherein is carried the Standart royall, with the which the Cittie was wonne. The siege endured thrée moneths, and had therein 200000. Indians, 900. Spaniards, 80. horses, 17. péeces of Ordinance, 13. Vergantines, and 6000. Canaos. In this siege were slaine fiftie Spaniards and sire horses, and no great number of the Indians their friendes. There was slaine on the contrary side a hundreth thousand, and some affirme many moe: but I speak not of them that died with hunger and pestilence.

At the defence of the citie were all the nobilitie, by reason whereof many were slaine. The multitude of people was great, who eate litle, dranke sault water, and slept among the dead bodies, where was a horrible stenche: for these causes the disease of pestilence fell among them, and thereof died an infinite number. Wherevpon is to be considered, their stedfast determination, for although they were afflicted with such hunger, that they were driuen to eate boughes, ryndes of trées, and to drinke salt

Py 2 water,

water, yet would they not yeelde themselues. But at the laste they woulde haue submitted them, and then their king Quahutimoc woulde not, because at the beginning they refused his will and counsell, and also with their generall deaths, should appeare no cowardise, for they kept the dead bodies in their houses to keepe that secrete from theyr enimies. Here also is to be noted, that although the Mexicans eate mans fleshe, yet they eate none of their owne Citie or friendes, as some doe thinke: for if they had, there woulde not so many haue died with hunger. The Mexican woman were highly commended, not only because they aboade with their husbandes and Fathers, but also for the greate paines they tooke with the sicke and wounded persons, yea and also they laboured in making slings, cutting stones fitte for the same, and throwing stones from the iotties, for therein they did as much hurte as their men. The Citie was yeelded to the spoile, and the Spaniardes tooke the Golde, Plate and Feathers, the Indian friends had all the rest of cloth and other stuffe.

Cortes commaunded great bonfiers to be made in token of victory, and also to mortifie the horrible stenche of the dead bodies, whome he likewise commaunded to be buried, and some of the prisoners menne and women he caused to be marked in the face, for the Kings slaues, and pardoned all the residue. He commaunded the Uergantines to be brought a shore, and appointed one Villa Fuerte, with 30. men to guard them, fearing least the Mexicans should by fire or otherwise destroy them. In this businesse he occupied himselfe foure dales, & then remoued his camp to Culhuacan, where he rendred hartie thankes to all the Gentlemen his friendes, promising to gratifie their good and faithfull seruice, desiring them to departe home to their houses, considering the warre was at an ende, whereupon

the vvest India.

whervpon they departed almost all in generall, both rich and iocond with the spoile of Mexico, and also to remaine in the fauour and grace of Cortez.

Maruellous signes and tokens of the destruction of Mexico.

Ot long before Hernãdo Cortes came vnto the new Spaine, did many nights after the midnight appeare in the air, and in the same port and place where Cortes entered into that land, great lightning of fire, which amounted vpward, and sodenly vaded away. The Mexicans at that time sawe flames of fire toward the Orient, where now Vera Crux standeth, with a great and thicke smoke, that seemed to touch the heauen and earth: this sight was fearefull vnto them.

They also saw the figures of armed men fight in the air one with another, a new and strange sight for them, and a thing that filled their heads with imaginations: for when there was a prophecie spoken of among them, howe that white men with beards should come and rule their kingdom in the time of Mutezuma, the Lords of Tezcuco and Tlacopan were much amazed, saying, that ye sword which Mutezuma had, was the armes of those folke, whose figures they had seene in the aire, with their apparell and attyre. Mutezuma had much ado to pacifie them, faining that the weapon and apparell was of his forefathers, and because they should see the troth thereof, he gaue them the sword, and willed them to breake it if they could, and they prouing to breake the same, and could not, they maruelled thereat, and also were resolued of their opinions.

It shoulde seeme that a little before these things happened

pened, some of *Mutezuma* his subiects found a Chest of apparell, and a sword in it on the Sea coast, which came floting out of some shippe that had wracked there about, and brought it to their prince. Others affirme, that the cause of alteration among the Noble men, was, when they saw the sword and apparell that *Cortes* had sent vnto Mutezuma by Teudilli, seeing it a thing so like the attire of the figures which they had séene in the ayre, but howsoeuer it was, they beléeued with those new tokens, that their kingdome should haue an end, when they sawe those strangers come into their countrey.

The same yeare that *Cortes* came into Mexico, appeared a vision vnto a certaine *Malli*, which is to say, a slaue taken in the warres to be sacrificed, who at the time of his death and sacrifice, bewailed his sorrowfull end, calling vpon the God of heauen, who at that instant saw in spirit a vision, and heard a voyce, bidding him not to feare that death, for the God whom hee called vpon would haue mercie vpon him, willing him also to say vnto the priests and ministers of the Idolles, that their wicked sacrifice and bloudshedding was néere at an ende, and that there was a people at hand, that should take away all that wicked and abhominable religion.

This Malli was sacrificed in the middest of the market place of Tlatelulco, where at this day is the place of execution.

They remembred, & noted well the words of the Malli, and the vision which they called a breath from heauen.

The earth also brake opon, out of the which issued a maruellous great streame of water, with manie great fishes, which they vsed and helde for a strange prognostication.

The Mexicans did report, that when on a time *Mute-zuma* came triumphantly with victorie of Xochnuxco,

said

the vvest India.

said vnto the Lord of Culhuacan: Now (quoth he) Mexico is strong & inuincible, for I haue in subiection Xochnuxco, and other prouinces, so that now I am without feare of any enemie. The Lord of Culhuacan answered, saying, trust not good king too much, for one force forceth another, with the which answer, Mutezumas was not a little offended. But when Cortes had taken them both prisoners, then he called to remembrance the former talke, and held that saying for a prophesie.

The building vp againe of Mexico.

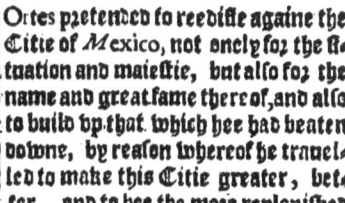

Ortes pretended to reedifie againe the Citie of Mexico, not onely for the situation and maiestie, but also for the name and great fame thereof, and also to build vp that which hee had beaten downe, by reason whereof he trauelled to make this Citie greater, better, and to bee the more replenished with people. He named and appoynted Iudges, Aldermen, Attourneys, Towne clearke, Notaries, Scauengers, and Sergeants, with all other officers, necessarie for the common weale of a Citie. Hee diuided the Citie among the Conquerors, hauing first taken out places for Churches, market places, Towne house, and other necessarie plottes to build houses, profitable for the common weale. He also separated the dwellings of the Spaniardes from the Indians, so that the water passeth and maketh diuision betwixt them. He procured many Indians to come to the building of the Citie, for auoyding charges, although therein he had somewhat to do, by reason that many kinsmen of Quahatimoc were not as yet come vnder obedience.

He

He made Lord of Tezcuco, Don Carolus Iztlixuchitl, by
the consent of the citie, in place of Don Hernando his brother, who was deceased, and commaunded manie of his
vassals to labour in the workes, because they were Carpenters, masons, and builders of houses. He promised also to them that were naturals of the Citie of Mexico,
plottes to build vpon, inheritance, freedome, and other liberties, and the like vnto all those that would come and
inhabite there, which was a meane to allure manie thither. He set also at libertie Xihuaco the generall Captaine, and made him chiefe ouer the Indians in the Citie,
vnto whome he gaue a whole streete. He gaue likewise
another streete to Don Pedro Mutezuma, who was son to
Mutezuma the king. All this was done to winne the fauour of the people. He made other Gentlemen Seniors
of little Ilands, and streetes to build vpon, and so inhabite, and in this order the whole situation was reparted, and the worke began with great ioy and diligence:
But when the same was blowne abroade, that Mexico
should be built againe, it was a wonder to see the people
that resorted thither, hearing of libertie and freedome, the
number was so great, that in a whole league compasse
was nothing but people both men and women. They laboured sore, and eate little, by reason whereof, many sickned, and pestilence followed, whereof dyed an infinite
number. Their paines was great, for they bare on their
backes, and drew after them, stones, earth, timber, lime,
bricke, and all other things necessarie in this sort, and by
little and little, Mexico was built againe with a hundred
thousand houses, more stronger and better then the olde
building was. The Spaniardes also built their houses
after the Spanish fashion. Cortes built his house vpon the
plotte where Mutezuma his house stode, which renteth
now yearely foure thousand duckets a yeare. Pamfilo de
Naruaez

the weſt India.

Naruaez accuſed him for the ſame, ſaying, that he hadde ſpoyled the woddes and mountaines, and ſpente ſeauen thouſand beames of Ceder trées in the worke of his own houſe. The number ſéemeth more hére then there, for where all the Mountaines are repleniſhed with Ceder trées, it is a ſmall matter. There are Gardines in Tezcuco, that haue a thouſand Ceder trées for walles and circuite, yea and there are Ceder trées of a hundred & twenty foote long, and twelue foote in compaſſe from ende to ende. They built faire dockes couered ouer with arches for the Vergantines, whereas (for a perpetuall memorie) all the thirtéene Vergantines do remaine vntill this day. They damned vp the ſtrétes of water, where now faire houſes ſtand, ſo that Mexico is not as it was wont to be, yea and ſince the yéro of 1524. the lake decreaſeth, and ſometime caſteth out a vapour of ſtench, but otherwiſe it is a wholſome and temperate dwelling, by reaſon of the Mountaines that ſtandeth round about it, and well prouided through the fertillitie of the Countrey, and commoditie of ý lake, ſo that now is Mexico one of the greateſt Cities in the world, and the moſt noble in all India, as well in armes as policie. There are at the leaſt two thouſande Citizens, that haue each of them his horſe in his ſtable, with riche furniture for them. There is alſo great contractation, and all ſortes of occupations. Alſo a money houſe, where money is daily coyned: a fayre ſchole, which the Viizeroy Don Antonio de Mendoſa cauſed to be made. There is a greate difference betwixte an inhabitant of Mexico, and a Conqueror, for a Conqueror is a name of honor, and hath landes and rentes, and the inhabitaunt or onely dweller, payeth rente for his houſe. When this Citie was a building, and not thoughly furniſhed, Cortes came from Culhuacan to dwell there. The fame of Cortes, and maieſtie of Mexico, was blowen

abroade

The Conqueſt of

abroad into farre prouinces, by meanes whereof, it is now ſo repleniſhed, as I haue before declared, yea and hath ſo many Spaniards, who haue conquered aboue 400. leagues of land, being all gouerned by the princely ſeat of Mexico.

How the Emperour ſent to take account of Cortes of his gouernment in the new Spaine.

IN theſe daies Cortes was the man of the greateſt name of all the Spaniſh nation, although many had defamed him, & eſpecially Pamfilo de Naruaes, who was in the Court of Spaine accuſing him. And where of long time the Councell of India had receiued no letters from him, they ſuſpected, yea and beleeued, what ſoeuer euill was ſpoken of him. Whervpon they prouided the Admirall Don Diego Colon, for gouernour of Mexico, who at that time went to lawe with the king, pretending the ſaid office and many others, with condition to carrie at his owne coſt a thouſand men to apprehend Cortes. They prouided alſo for Gouernor of Panuco, one Nonio de Guſman, and Simon de Alcaraua portingall, for gouernour of Honduras. To kindle more this miſchiefe, and to ſet this buſines forward, one Iohn de Ribera, the Attourney of Cortes, was a fitte and an earneſt inſtrument againſt his maiſter, and the cauſe was, for falling out with Martin Cortes, father vnto Hernando Cortes, about foure thouſand Duckets which Cortez had ſent by him to his father, which money the ſaid Ribera his Attourney kept to his owne vſe, and therefore raiſed many ſlanders againſt his maiſter, yea and credit was giuen to his tales, but on a night he had a morſell of bacon giuen him vpon a ſkaffolde, wherewith hee was choked in the

The reward of a knaue.

the weſt India.

the chiefe time of his buſineſſe. Theſe newe officers, and their proviſions, were not ſo ſecretly obteyned, but the matter was ſo ſecretly talked in the Court, which at that time was abiding in the Citie of Toledo, and the proceedings ſeeme not iuſt vnto the frends of Cortes. The Commendator Pedro de Pina, opened the matter to the Licenciat Nouez, and vnto father Melgareto, whervpon they reclaimed of the Councels determination, beſeeching them to ſtay for a ſeaſon, to ſee what newes ſhould come from Mexico. Alſo the Duke of Beiar tendred the cauſe of Hernando Cortes, for that Cortes by promiſe of faith and troth was aſſured in mariage to his brothers daughter, named the Ladie Iane de Zuniga, who appeaſed the Emperour his anger, and the ſaid Duke became ſuretie to anſwere in all cauſes for him.

The matter ſtanding in this eſtate, there arriued in Spaine, Diego de Zoto, with a whole Coluerin made of ſiluer, & 70000. caſtlins in gold, the newes whereof was blowne ouer all Spaine. And to ſay the troth, this preſent was the cauſe that Cortes was not put out of his office, but a Iudge of reſidence was ſent thither to take an account of him. Now a wiſe and a learned man was ſought for that purpoſe, yea ſuch a one as could rule the matter, for ſome ſouldiers are oftentimes vnmanerly: wherevpon they thought the Licenciat, Lewes Ponce de Leon, a fitte man, who had bin Lieutenant to Don Martin de Cordoua, Earle of Alcaudete, and chiefe gouernor of the Citie of Toledo. This Licenciat with power ſufficient, was ſent vnto the new Spaine, who carried in his company as aſſiſtant, the batchler Marcus de Aguilar, who had ruled in time paſt, in a worſhipfull office of Iuſtice in the Iland of Santo Domingo.

With proſperous weather they departed from Spaine, and in ſhorte time arriued at Vera Crux,

The Conqueſt of

Cortez hauing newes of their arriuall by foote poſtes within two dayes. And vppon Midſommer day came letters to Cortes from the Licenciate Ponce, with another letter from the Emperour, whereby he vnderſtood ẏ cauſe of their comming. He returned backe incontinent an aunſwere, and deſired to know which way he would come to Mexico, either by ẏ way inhabited, or elſe the other way which is néerer. The Licenciate replyed, that he woulde for a while abide in Vera Crux, to refreſh himſelfe, béeing ſeaſicke, and a man ẏ had not héeretofore at any time paſſed the ſeas, thinking that Cortes meante to haue done iuſtice on certain offenders, yea & alſo to haue taken him by the way: wherefore he ſuſpected, that Cortes had ſent, becauſe he woulde knowe which way he meant to come, wherevpon he ſecretely tooke poſt horſe, with certaine Gentlemen, and other religious perſons that came in his company,& paſſed through the Townes, although it was the farther way, and made ſuche haſt, that in fiue dayes he came to Iztacpallapan, refuſing the entertainment and proviſion of meate and lodging that Cortez had prepared by his Gentlemen, that wēt both the waies to méete him.

In Iztacpallapā they receiued him with great feaſt and maieſtie, but after dinner, the Licenciate fell a vomiting, and the moſt of his companye, and after the vomite, they fell into a fixe. They thoughte that certaine hearbes was the cauſe thereof, which were in a diſhe of curdes. The Licenciate was ſomewhat gréedie of the curdes, and tooke the diſhe, and offered it to father Thomas Ortiz, no (quoth the ſtewarde) his reuerence ſhall haue another diſhe, no (quoth father Ortez) I will none of theſe, nor yet of anye other, of whiche wordes there were afterwardes Uerſes made, ſuſpecting ſomething of the curdes : but truely there was no hurte, or anye euill thing putte in them, (as héereafter

ſhall

the vveſt India.

ſhall be declared) for the Comendador, Procano, who was then chiefe Sheriffe, did eate of all thoſe diſhes, yea in the ſame diſh that the Licenciat eate of, who neither vomited nor yet receiued any hurt or alteration. But I think, that they comming hote, weary and hungry, did eate to much, and dranke alſo colde water, whereby their ſtomackes reuolted, and thereof followed the flixe with vomit. On the behalfe of Cortes, there was preſented to the Licenciat a rich preſent, but he refuſed it.

Cortes with all the flower of Gentlemen in Mexico, came to receiue him, and giuing him the right hand, they went togither vntill they came to Saint Frances Abbey, where after their praiers made, Cortes demaunded to ſée the Kings proviſions, who anſwered, that the next day he would ſhew them vnto him: then they accompanied him to his houſe, where he was well lodged.

The nexte day following, all the magiſtrates of the Citie met the Licenciat in the Cathedrall Church, and by acte, before the Notary, he preſented his authoritie from the Emperour. He toke the Mares of Juſtice from the Judges and Sargeants, and incontinent reſtored them againe, and ſaide with gentle ſpéech, this rodde of the Senior Gouernour, I will haue for my ſelfe. Cortes with all the other Magiſtrates, kiſſed the Emperours letters, and put them vpon the crown of their heads, in token of great obedience, ſaying, that they woulde obſerue and obey all that was therein conteined, as the commaundement of their King and Lord, requiring the ſame to be ſet downe by act and teſtimony.

After theſe things done, they proclaymed the reſidence and account of iuſtice, of Hernando Cortez, to the intent that all perſons who coulde accuſe him of any vnrightfull dealing, ſhould come & make their complaint, and to haue remedy for the ſame. There ſhould you then ſée the ſtirre

and

The Conquest of

and talke among them, euery officer fearing his owne cause, with desire to see the ende of their businesse.

The death of the Licenciat Luys Ponce.

A madde daunce.

THe Liceciat comming one day from Saint Frances abbay from seruice, fell into an extréeme burning feuer, and lay him downe in his bedde, where he remained the space of thrée dayes, as a man out of his wittes, and the feuer stil encreasing, so that on the seuenth day he yéelded vp the ghost. In the time of his sickenesse he receiued the communion, and made his last will & testament. He left for substitute in his office, the bacheler Marcus de Aguilar. Cortes made as great sorrow for his death, as if he had bene his owne father, his funeralles were celebrated with great pompe.

The enimies of Cortes published, that he died of poison. But the Licenciat Pero Lopez, and Doctor Hoieda, who were his Phisitions, swore that he died of a burning feuer, and shewed a further cosequence, that the euening before he deceased, he desired them to play the measures vpon a lute, and as he lay in his bedde, shewed with stirring his féete the compasses and pointes of the daunce. It was a thing which diuers persons saw, and forthwith he lost his spéeche, and that night toward the dawning of the day he yéelded vp his spirite. I thinke that fewe men do die dausing, as this Lawier did. The number of a hundred persons came out of Spaine with the Licenciat, whereof the moste parte died by sea and on the lande. It was suspected to be a pestilence, for one of them infected another. There were in his company many Gentlemen, and ech of thé had an office. There was a Frier who was

a

a very slaunderous fellow, & reported that Cortes had poisoned the Licenciat, and also that the Licenciat had an expresse order from the Emperour to cut of Cortes his head, assoone as he had take the Mare of Justice from him. The subtle Frier, had thought to haue gotten mony of the one, and thankes of the other, and at the ende had nothing.

How Cortez came into Spaine.

Here one Alonso de Estrada gouerned the state of Mexico, as substitute of Marcus de Aguillar, according to the Emperours commaundement, Cortes considered with himselfe that it was not possible for him to haue againe his office, except he wente personally to the Emperours court, where he had many aduersaries and fewe friendes, so that he was afflicted on every side: yet he in fine, determined to goe into Spaine, as well for businesse of importaunce of his owne, as also matters touching the Emperor and his new kingdomes, whereof I will rehearse particularly some.

As touching his owne causes, first he being a man of good yeeres, went to marry, hoping to haue children, vnto whom he might leaue the profite of his labour and paine: also to appeare before the King his maister face to face, and to enforme his Maiestie what Landes and Kingdomes hee had wonne and brought vnto his royall crowne: To signifie likewise vnto him, of the dissention among the Spanyardes his subiectes in *Mexico*, and to answere for himselfe, to any false reportes which has bene made against him: And finally, to receiue a condigne rewarde for his worthie and faithfull seruice. Cortez being in these imaginations, there was brought

The Conquest of

brought a letter vnto him, from the reuerend father Garcia de Loaisa, ghostly father vnto the Emperor, and afterwarde was ordeyned Cardinall, in the which letter hee counited him earnestly to come vnto Spaine, to the entent that the Emperours Maiestie might both see & know him, assuring him of his friendship. After the receit of this letter, he made all the haste possible to depart vppon his iourney, ceasing from his voyage which he had in hand, for to inhabite the Riuer De las Palmas. Before his departure, he dispatched two hundreth Spaniards, and three score and tenne Horsemen, with many Mexicans, for the countrey of Chichimea, to inhabite there, finding the land riche of siluer Mines, as it was reported, giuing vnto those men expresse order, that if the people of that Prouince did not entertaine them with friendship, that then they shuld accept them as enemies, and forthwith to make warre, and to take them for slaues, for that they are a barbarous people: He wrote his letter to Vera Crux, to prepare with all spéede two good shippes, and for that purpose he sent Pero Ruiz de Esquiuel, who was a Gentleman of Siuill: But hee went not on the iourney, for a moneth after, they founde him buried in a little Ilande of the lake, with one hande out of the graue, which was eaten with dogges and foule: hee was buried in his doublet and his hose: he had one onely wound in his forehead: And a Negro, his slaue, who went in his company, was neuer heard of, nor yet the Canoa and Indians that went with him, so that the truth of his death was neuer knowne.

Cortes made an Inuentary of his moueable goodes, which was valued at two hundreth thousande Castlins of golde: he left for gouernour of his owne estate, the Licenciat Altamirano his kinsman, with other two friends: hee furnished two shippes, and proclaymed frée passage and victuals vnto all those that would go in his company:

he

the vvest India.

he shipped for his owne account a thousand fiue hundred markes of siluer, twentie thousand Castlins of good gold, and ten thousand Castlins of bace golde. He toke in his company Gonsalo de Sadoual, Andres de Tapia, and other of the chiefest of the conquerours. He brought with him a Sonne of Mutezuma, & another Sonne of Maxixca, who was become a Christiã, & named Don Lorenso, with many other Indian Gentlemen of Mexico, Tlaxcallan, and other cities: eight players with a cudgell, twelue tenis players, with certaine men and women of that Countrey who were white of colour, and other dwarfes and defor̄med persons. He brought also wild beasts, as Tigres and other strange beasts called Aiotocheli, and one Tlaquaci. Moreouer he brought a great number of mantels made of feathers and Conny heare, Targets, bushes or tuffes of galant feathers, and looking glasses of stone. In fine, he came like a great Lord, and arriued in Spaine, in the end of the yeere 1528. the Courte being then in Tolledo. The newes of his arriuall was blowne through out al Spaine, and euery one desirous to see him.

The honour which the Emperour shewed vnto Hernando Cortes, with rewarde.

THe Emperour receiued Cortes magnificially, and to giue him the greater honour, he went and visited him at his owne lodging.

The Emperour being in a readines to passe into Italie, to be ther crowned with the Emperiall crowne, Cortes went in his maiesties company vnto the Citie of Saragoza, whereas his Maiestie calling to remembrance his worthie seruice, and valour of his person, made him Marques del Valle de Huaracac, according

The Conqueſt of

cording to his deſire, on the .vi. of July, An. 1528. and Captaine generall of the newe Spaine, with all the prouinces and coaſt of the ſouth ſea, chiefe diſcouerer and inhabiter of the ſame coaſte and Ilandes, with the twelfth parte of all that after that time ſhoulde be diſcouered, for a ſure inhabitance to him and his diſcentrntes: he offered vnto him alſo the habite of the order of Knighthoode of Saint Iames, the which offer Cortes refuſed, becauſe there was no rent giuen with the habite, but he beſought his Maieſtie to graunt vnto him the gouernment of Mexico, the which requeſt the Emperour denied, becauſe that no Conquerour ſhould thinke that the office of gouernment and iuſtice is due vnto him, for the like demaund was deſired of the king Don Fernando, by Criſtoual Colon, who firſt diſcouered the Indian, and alſo the great Captaine Gonſalo Hernandoz de Cordoua, who conquered Naples. Cortes deſerued much, and alſo the Emperour gaue him much, to honour him as a moſt bountifull and gratefull King, who neuer taketh away that which once he giueth. He likewiſe gaue vnto Cortez all the kingdome of Michuacan, but he had rather haue had diuers other townes which he demaunded, many other great fauours and rewards he receiued at the Emperours hands, but the principall are thoſe before declared.

The Mariage of Cortez.

Hen it was knowen in Spaine, that the lady Katherin Xuares, wife vnto Cortes, was deceaſed in India, by interceſſeurs he was aſſured vnto the Duke of Beiar, his brothers daughter, who was named the lady Iane of Zuniga: her fathers name was Dō Carolus de Arrellano, earl of Aguilar. This lady was

the vvest India.

a bewtifull Dame, and her brethren noble personages, who were highly in fauour with the Emperour. And Cortes to match with so honorable an house and linage he iudged himselfe fortunate and well married.

Among many Iewels which Cortes broughte with him, were fiue moste riche and fine Emeraldes, whiche were valued at a hundreth thousande Duckets: the one was wrought like vnto a Rose, another like a Cornet, an other like a fishe with the eies of Golde, which was a maruellous péece of worke, being wrought among Indians: an other péece was wrought like vnto a bell, with a great and riche pearle for the clapper, garnished with golde, ingrauen about with letters, which saide, Blessed is he that created thée. The fifth was made like a cuppe with the fote of gold, and had foure little chaines of gold, that were ioyned all at the top togither, in a great pearle, and the brimme of this cuppe was of gold, with this verse ingrauen round about, Inter natos mulierum non surrexis maior. For this onely péece the Marchantes of Geneua did offer fourtie thousand Duccates, for to sel the same again to the great Turke. But at that time Cortes would not giue it for any money, although afterwarde he lost them all in the warres of Argel, being there with the Emperor. It was told Cortes that the Empresse desired to haue those péeces, meaning to demaunde them of him, and that the Emperour shoulde pay for the same, for which cause he sent them to the Lady his newe wife, with many other Iewelles before he came at the Courte, and there, when he was enquired for them, he answered, and excused him selfe, for then certainely he gaue such Iewels vnto his Espouse, that the like neuer Lady had in Spaine. And after he was maried to the Lady Iane of Zuniga, he departed with her to the newe Spaine, with title of Marques.

The riche Emeraldes.

The Conquest of

How the Chancerie was first placed in Mexico, and certaine diuelish pretences wrought against Cortes.

Efore Cortes his cōming into Spaine, Pamfilo de Naruaez his old enemie, went vp and downe in the Court, procuring the conquest of the riuer De Palmas and Florida, where at the last he died, and alwaies when he saw time cōuenient, he made complaints against Cortez, yea and to the Emperours owne handes he deliuered a scrole of many articles, among the which was one, wherein he affirmed that Cortez had as many barres of golde and siluer, as in Biscay were barres of yron, and offered to proue the same: but although it was not true, yet it was suspicious. He also earnestly procured that he should be punished, saying that he had plucked out one of his eyes, and killed with poisō the Licenciat Luys ponce de Leon, and Francisco Garay. Through his many and importunat petitions, it was determined to send to Mexico, Don Pedro de la Cueua, who was both fierce and seuere, and Lord Steward of the Emperour his house, and afterwarde made generall of the ordinance, and chiefe Comendador of the order and knighthood of Alcantara, who finding the accusation true, should cut off Cortez his head.

But as God woulde, in the meane season came the testimoniall from the Doctor Hoieda, & the Dicenciat Pero Lopez phisitiōs, who had cured the persons that were reported to haue bene poisoned, wherupon that commission ceased. And when Cortez came into Spaine, Don Pedro de la Cueua would many times laugh and iest with him, saying, From farre places long lies.

The Emperour and his councell of India, prouided a
Court

the vveſt India.

Court of Chancerie in Mexico, as chiefe place, where as all controuerſies and matters of right throughout the new Spaine, might there bee determined, and alſo to correct the mutinies, and partes taken among the Spaniardes: likewiſe to take reſidence and account of Cortes, and to bee ſatiſfied both of his ſeruice and offences. Moreouer that they ſhould viſite the officers, and royall Treaſorie there. Nunio de Guſman was appointed preſident and gouernour, with other foure Licenciates for Iudges to accompanie him. He departed toward Mexico, Anno. 1529. and at his comming, he began to vnderſtand in his regiment and office, with the Licenciate Iohn Ortiz, for the other thrée Iudges died by the way. Cortez being nowe abſent, and vppon his iourney towarde Spaine, this newe Iudge made a terrible reſidence and condemnation againſt him, and commaunded all his goodes to be ſolde by out-thrappe, for a great deale leſſe then his goodes were worth, and in his abſence they called him by Proclamation: but if he had béene there preſent, his life had béene in danger, although face to face ſome reſpect is had, and it is an ordinarie rule that the Iudge ſheweth rigour againſt him that is abſent. This hatred was not only againſt Cortes, but alſo againſt his friendes, for hée apprehended Pedro de Aluerado, who was newly come from Spaine, becauſe he ſpake in the fauour of Cortes, laying to his charge the rebellion of Mexico, when Naruaes was there. He alſo apprehended Alonſo de Eſtrada, and many others, doing manifeſt wrongs vnto them.

In ſhort ſpace the Emperour had more complaintes againſt Nunio de Guſman, and the other Iudge, then had béene heretofore againſt any other, whereupon hee was put out of office in the yeare 1530. His wrongful dealing in iuſtice was not onely proued in Mexico, but alſo in the Court of Spaine, with many perſons that were come

Before the Iudges came, Cortez was gone to Spain.

from

from thence, so that the next President and Judges that went thither, did pronounce Nunio de Gusman and his fellow for partiall Judges, and enemies vnto Cortes, and condemned him to pay all his goodes whiche were euill sold. But when Nunio de Gusman vnderstood that he was put out of office, he then was afraid, and toke his iourney against the Teuchichimecas, seeking after the Towne of Culluacan, from whence the Mexicans descended. He caried in his companie fiue hundred Spaniardes, whereof the most were horsemen, and many of them went as prisoners, and against their willes.

In Mechuacan he toke prisoner the king Caconcin, who was a great friend vnto Cortes, a seruitor vnto the Spaniardes, and vassall to the Emperour, and as the same goeth, he toke from him ten thousand markes of plate, and much golde, and afterward burned him, and many other Gentlemen, and principall persons of that kingtome, because they should not complaine, saying, that a dead dogge biteth not. He toke from thence sixe thousand Indians for the seruice of his armie, and with them conquered Xalixco, which is now called the newe Gallizia. He aboue there, vntill the Vizeroy Don Antonio de Mondoza, and Chancerie of Mexico, caused him to be apprehended, who sent him prisoner into Spain, to giue account of his office. If Nunio de Gusman had béene so good a gouernour and Judge, as he was in bloud a Gentleman, he had then entoyed the best plot of all the West India, but he behaued himselfe euill, both with the Indians and Spaniardes.

The same yeare that he came from Mexico, went thither for president Sebastian Ramirez, who was a Bishop, and had in time past béene president in Santo Domingo, and the Licenciates Iohn de Salmeron, Gasco Quiroga, Francisco Ceynes, and Alonso Maldonado, for Judges to accompanie him.

These

the vveſt India.

Theſe Judges gouerned well the land, and cauſed the Citie of Angels to be inhabited, which the Indians called Cuetlaxcoapan, that is to ſay, a Snake in water. The reaſon was, becauſe they haue two fountaines, the one of euil water, and the other of good. This Citie ſtandeth twentie leagues from Mexico, in the high way to Vera Crux. The Biſhop ſet the Indians at libertie, and therefore many Spaniards departed from thence, who had inhabited there before, and went to ſeeke their liuing at Calixco, Hunduras, Quahutemallan, and other places where warre was.

The returne of Cortes to Mexico.

AT this ſeaſon arriued Cortes at the rich Towne of Vera Crux, and when his comming was publiſhed, how he came with tite of Marques, and had brought his wife with him, an infinite number of Indians came to viſite him, and almoſt all the Spaniards of Mexico, ſo that in fewe dayes there came a thouſande perſons of his owne nation, who made their complaintes vnto him, how they were vndone, and that the Judges which had bene there, had deſtroyed both him & them, and aſked his iudgement whether that nowe they might kill both them and theirs. Cortes hearing their odious requeſt, reprehended them, and alſo gaue them hope ſhortly to releeue their neceſſitie with newe diſcoueries, and in this order fearing ſome mutinie, he held them in pleaſure and paſtime.

When the Preſident heard how Cortes was viſited of the Spanyardes, they commaunded forthwith euery one of them ſhould immediately returne to Mexido, or elſe where their dwelling places were vpon pain of death, yea, and they were about to apprehende Cortes for a ſtirrer of

The Conquest of

of by2ore, and to sende him backe againe prisoner into Spaine. But when he sawe how some these Judges were moued, he commaunded to proclaime himselfe openly in Vera Crux, Capteine Generall of all the dominions of the new Spaine, and there caused the Emperours letters pattents to bee read, which thing being knowen to the Mexican Judges, it caused thē to wring their noses. After this diligence ended, he departed toward Mexico with a great company of Spaniards and Indians, among whom were a good company of horsemen: but when he came to Tezcuco, the President sent to commaund him not to enter into Mexico, vpon paine of losse of his goods, and his bodie to be at the kings pleasure.

Hee obeyed the commaundement with great wisedome, being a thing conuenient to the seruice of the Emperour, and profite of the land, which he had wonne with great toile and labour: but yet he abode in Tezcuco with a greater maiestie and Court, then the President in Mexico, and wrote vnto him, that he should consider his good will and whole intent, and not to giue occasion to the Indians to rebell, and for the Spaniardes hee might assure himselfe.

The Indians vnderstanding the discord betwixt the president and Cortes, flue as many Spaniards as they coulde get at aduauntage, so that in sewe dayes there wanted aboue two hundred of the Spanish nation, being slaine as well in Townes, as in the high wayes, yea and also they had communed among themselues to rebell in deede. But when the Bishop and the Judges heard this newes, they began to feare the matter, and considering that they had no better remedy, nor other sure defence, but only ȳ name valor, person and authoritie of Cortes, they sent to desire him to come vnto Mexico, whereupon hee obserued their commandement and request, and went toward the Citie,

well

the weſt India.

well accompanied with men of warre, ſo that he ſhewed himſelfe in eſtate a generall Captaine. All the Citizens came out to receiue him and the lady Marques his wife: his entrie into the Citie was a day of great pleaſure among them. Then the Preſident and Iudges entred into counſell for to remedie the great hurt which had bin done by the Indians. Cortes toke the matter in hand, and apprehended many Indians, of whome ſome bee burned, others were torne with dogs, he did ſuch correction, that in ſhort time all the Country was quiet, and the high waies without daunger, a thing worthie of great thankes.

The Letters that the Indians vſed in Mexico.

THere hath not bene founde Letters at any time in the Weſt India, onely in the new Spaine were vſed certaine figures which ſerued for Letters, with the which they kepte in memorie, and preſerued their antiquities. The figures that the Mexicans vſed for Letters are great, by reaſon whereof they occupie great volumes: they engraue them in ſtone or timber, and painte them vpon walles, and alſo vpon a paper made of cotten wooll, and leaues of the trée Metl. Their bookes are great and folden vp like vnto our broade cloathes, and written vpon both ſides. There are ſome bookes rolled vp like a péece of flannell. They pronounce not b, g, e, f. Therefore they vſe much p, e, l, r. This is the Otical ſpéech, and Nahual, which is the beſt, plaineſt, and the moſt eloquent, in all new Spaine. There are ſome in Mexico that do vnderſtand each other by whiſtling, which is ordinarily vſed among louers, and théeues, a ſpéech truly to wonder at, and none of our men could come to the knowledge thereof.

Bbb   The

The Conquest of

The order how to recken.

Ce	One
Ome	Two
Ei	Thrée
Naui	Foure
Macuil	Fiue
Chicoace	Sixe
Chicome	Seuen
Chicuei	Eight
Chiconaui	Nine
Matlac	Tenne
Matlactlioce	Eleuen
Matlactliome	Twelue
Matlactlomei	Thirténe
Matlactlinaui	Fourténe
Matlactlinacui	Fifténe
Matlactlichicoace	Sixténe
Matlactlichicome	Seuenténe
Matlactlichicuei	Eighténe
Matlactlichiconaui	Nineténe
Cempoalli	Twentie

Euery number is simple vntill you come to sixe, and then they count, sixe and one, sixe and two, sixe and thrée. Ten is a number by himselfe, then you must count tenne and one, tenne and two, tenne and thrée, tenne and foure, tenne and fiue.

Then you count, tenne, fiue, and one, tenne, fiue, and two, tenne, fiue, and thrée. Twentie goeth by himself, and all the greater numbers.

The

The Mexican yeare.

THe Mexicans yeare is thrée hundreth sixtie dayes, for they haue in their yeare eightéene moneths, and euery moneth contéineth twentie dayes. They haue other fiue odde dayes, which goeth by themselues, in the which they vsed to celebrate great feastes of cruell and bloudy sacrifice, with much deuotion. And reckoning after this sort, they could not chose but erre, for they could not make equall the punctuall course of the Sunne. Yea the Christian yeare is not perfit, although we haue learned Astronomers. But yet these simple Indians went néer the marke.

The names of the moneths.

Tlacaxipeualiztli.
Tozcutzli.
Huei Tozeuztli.
Toxcalt.
Ecalcoaliztli.
Tocuilhuicintli.
Hueitecuilhuitl
Miccailhuicintli.
Veymiccailhuitl.
Vchpaniztli.
Pachtli.
Huei Pachtli.
Quecholli.
Panquecaliztli.
Hatemuztli.
Titielh.
Izcalli.
Coa vitleuac

The Conquest of
The names of Dayes.

Cipactli	A Spade
Hecatl	Aire or Windes
Calli	A House
Cuez Pali	A Lizart
Coualt	A Snake
Mizquintli	Death
Macatl	A wilde Hart
Tochtli	A Conny
Atl	Water
Izcuyntli	A Dogge
Ocumatli	An Ape
Malinalli	A Brome
Acatlh	A Cane
Ocelotl	A Tigre
Coautli	An Egle
Cozcaquahutl	A Bussard
Olin	A Temple
Tepatlh	A Knife
Quiauitl	Raine
Xuchitl	A Rose.

Although these twentie names serue for the whole yeare, and are but the daies of euery moneth, yet therfore euery moneth beginneth not with Cipactli, which is the first name, but as they followe in order, and the fiue odde dayes is the cause thereof. And also because their wéeke is of thirtéene dayes, which changeth the names, as by example, Cecipactli can go no further then vnto Matlactlomeiacatl, which is thirtéene, and then beginneth an other wéeke: and we do not say Matlactlinaui Ocelotl, which is the fourténth day, but we say Ceocelotl, which is one, and then recken the other sir names, vnto twentie.

And

the vvest India.

And when all the twentie dayes are ended, begin againe to recken from the first name of the twentie, but not from one, but from eight. And because ye may better vnderstand the matter, here is the example.

    Cecipactli.
    Omehecatl.
    Ei Calli.
    Naui Cuezpali.
    Macuilcouatl.
    Chicoacen Mizquinth.
    Chicome Macatl.
    Chicuei Tochtli.
    Chiconauiatl.
    Matlaciz Cuintli.
    Mailactlioce Ocumatl.
    Matlactliome Malinialli.
    Matlactlomei Acatlh.

The next weeke following doth begin his dayes from one. And that one is the fourteenth name of the moneth and of the dayes, and saith:

    Ceotelotl.   Macuil Tecpatl.
    Omecoautli.   Chicoacen Quiauitl.
    Eicozcaquahutli.   Chicome Xuchitl.
    Naui Olui.   Chicoei Cipactli.

In this second weeke, Cipactli came to fall on the eight day, being in the first weeke the first day.

    Cemacatl.
    Ometochtli.
    Eiatl.
    Naui izcuintli.
    Macuil Ocumatli.

The Conquest of

And so procéede on to the thirde wéeke, in the which this name *Cipactli* entreth not, but Macael, which was the seuenth day in the first wéeke, and had no place in the second, and is the first in the third. This reckoning is no darker then ours, which we haue in a.b.c.d.e.f.g. For they also change with time, and run in such sort, that a. which was the first letter of this moneth, commeth to bee the fift day of the next moneth, and the thirde moneth be counteth to be the third day, and so orderly doeth the other fire letters.

The accounting of yeares.

These Mexicans had another order to recken their yeares, which excéeded not aboue foure in number, as one, two, thrée, foure, wherewith they account a hundred, fiue hundred, a thousand, and as many moe as they list. Those foure figures or names are, Tochtli, Acatlh, Tecpatlh, Calli, and do signifie a Conny, a Caue, a Knife, and a House, saying.

Ce Tochtli	One yeare
Ome Acatlh	Two yeares
Ei Tecpatlh	Thrée yeares
Naui Calli	Foure yeares
Macuil Tochtli	Fiue yeares
Chioacen Acatlh	Sixe yeares
Cicome Tecpatlh	Seuen yeares
Chicuei Calh	Eight yeares
Chiconaui Tochtli	Nine yeares
Matlactli Acatlh	Ten yeares
Matlactlioce Tecpatlh	Eleuen yeares
Matlactliome Calli	Twelue yeares
Matlactliomei Tochtli	Thirténe yeares

the vvest India.

So that the reckoning passeth not aboue thirtéene, which is one Wéeke of the yeare, and endeth where he began.

Another Weeke.

Ce Acatlh	One yeare
Ome Tlepatlh	Two yeares
Ei Calli	Thrée yeares
Naui Tochtli	Foure yeares
Macuil Acatlh	Fiue yeares
Chioacen Tecpatlh	Sire yeares
Chicome Calli	Seuen yeares
Chicuei Tochtli	Eight yeares
Chiconaui Acatlh	Nine yeares
Matlactli Tecpatlh	Ten yeares
Matlactlioce Calli	Eleuen yeares
Matlactliome Tochtli	Twelue yeares
Matlactliomei Acatlh	Thirtéene yeares

The third week of yeares.

Ce Tecpatlh	One yeare
Ome Calli	Two yeares
Ei Tochtli	Thre yeares
Naui Acatlh	Foure yeares
Macuil Tecpatlh	Fiue yeares
Chioacan Calli	Sire yeares
Chicome Tochtli	Seuen yeares
Chicuei Acatlh	Eight yeares
Chiconaui Tecpatlh	Nine yeares
Matlactli Calli	Ten yeares
Matlactliome Tochtli	Eleuen yeares

Twelue

The Conquest of

Matlactliome Acatlh — Twelue yeares
Matlactliomei Tecpatlh — Thirteene yeares

The fourth Weeke.

Ce Calli	One yeare
Ome Tochtli	Two yeares
Ei Acatlh	Three yeares
Naui Tecpatlh	Foure yeares
Macuil Calli	Fiue yeares
Chioacen Tochtli	Sixe yeares
Chicome Acatlh	Seuen yeares
Chieuei Tecpatlh	Eight yeares
Chiconaui Calli	Nine yeares
Matlactli Tochtli	Ten yeares
Matlactlioce Acatlh	Eleuen yeares
Matlactliome Tecpatlh	Twelue yeares
Matlactliomei Calli	Thirteene yeares

Each of these weekes, which our men cal Indition, doth containe thirteene yeares, so that all the foure weekes make two and fiftie yeares, which is a perfite number in the reckoning, and is called the yeare of grace, for from fiftie two yeares, to fiftie two yeares, they vsed to make solemne feasts, with straunge Ceremonies, as hereafter shall be declared. And when fiftie two yeares are entred, then they begin againe, by the same order before declared, vntill they come to as many mo, beginning at Ce Tochtli, and so forward. But alwayes they begin at the Conny-figure. So that in the forme of reckoning they keepe and haue in memorie, things of 850. yeares, and by this Cronicle they know in what yeare euery thing hapned, and how long euery king reigned: howe many children they had, and all things else that importeth to the estate of the gouernment of the land.

The

the vvest India.

The Indians beleeued that fiue ages were past, which they called Sunnes.

THe Indians of Culhua did beléeue that the Gods had made the world, but they knew not how, yet they beléued that since the creation of the world foure Sunnes were past, and that the fift and last is the Sunne that now giueth light to the world.

They helde opinion that the first Sunne perished by water, and at the same time all liuing creatures perished likewise.

The second Sunne (say they) fell from the heauēs, with whose fall all liuing creatures were slaine, and then (said they) were manye Giantes in that Countrey, and certaine monstrous bones, which our men found in opening of graues, by proportion whereof, some should séeme to be men of twenty spannes high.

The third Sunne was consumed by fire, which burned day and night, so that then all liuing creatures were burned.

The fourth Sunne finished by tempest of ayre or winde, which blew downe houses, trées, yea and ye mountaines and Rockes were blowen asunder, but the linage of mankinde perished not, sauing that they were conuerted into Apes. And touching the fift Sunne, which now raigneth, they know not how it shall consume. But they say, that when the fourth Sunne perished, all the world fell into darkenesse, and so remained for the space of fiue and twenty yeares continually, and at the fifteenth yeare of that fearefull darkenesse, the Gods did forme one man and woman, who brought forth children, and at the end of the other tenne yeares, appeared the Sunne, whiche was newly borne vppon the figure of the Conny day, and

Ccc there-

The Conqueſt of

therefore they begin their account of yeares at that day, and reckoning from the yeare of our Lord 1552. their age or Sunne is 858. ſo that it appeareth that they haue vſed many yeares their writing in figures: and they had not onely this vſe from Cetochli, which is the beginning of their yeare, moneth, and day, of their fifth Sunne, but alſo they had the ſame order and vſe in the other four Sunnes which were paſt: but they let many things ſlip out of memorie, ſaying, that with the new Sunne, all other things ſhould be likewiſe new. They held alſo opinion, that three dayes after this laſt Sunne appeared, all the Goddes did die, and that in proceſſe of time the Gods which now they haue, and worſhip, were borne. And though theſe falſe opinions, our Diuines did ſoone conuert them to the knowledge of the true lawes of God.

The nation of the Indians called Chichimecas.

IN the land now called new Spaine, are diuers & ſundry generations of people: but they holde opinion, that the ſtock of moſt antiquitie, is the people now called Chichimecas, which proceeded out of the houſe of Aculhuacan, which ſtandeth beyonde Xalixco, about the yeare of our Lords, 720. Many of this Generation did inhabite aboute the lake of Tenuchtitlan, but their name endedby mixture in marriage with other people. At that time they had no King, nor yet did builde either houſe or towne. Their only dwellings was in caues in the mountaines. They went naked, they ſowed no kind of graine, nor vſed bread of any ſort. They did maintaine themſelues with rootes, hearbes, and ſiluester frutes: and being a people cunning in ſhooting with the bowe, they killed

the vvest India.

led Deare, Hares, Connies, and other beastes and foule, which they eate also, not sodden or rosted, but rawe, and dryed in the Sunne. They eate also Snakes, Lizards, and other filthy beasts, yea, and at this day there are some of this generation that vse the same diet. But although they liued such a bestiall life, and being a people so barbarous, yet in their diuellish religion they were verie deuout. They worshipped the Sunne, vnto whom they vsed to offer Snakes, Lizards, and such other beastes. They likewise offered vnto their God all kinde of foule, from the degree of an Eagle, to a little Butterflie. They vsed not sacrifice of manslaughter, nor had any Idolles, no not so much as of the Sunne, whom they held for the sole and onely God. They married but with one women, and in no degree of kinred. They were a stoute & a warlike people, by reason whereof they were Lords of the land.

The coronation of the kings of Mexico.

ALthough one brother was heyre to an other among the *Mexicans*, and after their deceasse, did inherite the Sonne of the eldest Brother, yet they tooke no possession of the state or name of king, vntil they were annointed and crowned openly.

As soone as any king of Mexico deceassed, and his funeralls ended, then were called to Parliament the Lord of Tezcuco, and the lord of Tlacopan, who were the chiefest estates, and then in order all other noble men, who owed any seruice to the Mexican Empire. And being come together, if any doubt of the inheritance of the Crowne happened, then the matter was decided with all haste: then the newe king being knowne, he was stripped starke naked, except a cloath to couer his priuie parts, and in this sorte was carried among them, to the great Temple

The Conquest of

of Vitzilopuchtli with great silence, and without any ioy or pleasure: Two Gentlemen of the Citie whose office it was, leade him vppe the staires of the Temple by the armes, and before him wente the Princes of Tezcuco and Tlacopan, who that day did weare their robes of Coronation, whereupon was painted their armes and title. Merie fewe of the Laitie wente vp into the Chappels, but onely those that were appointed to attire the newe king, and to serue in other Ceremonies, for all the residue stoode vpon the steppes and belowe, to beholde the Coronation. These Magistrates being aboue in the Chappell, came with great humillitie and reuerence, knéeling downe vpō their knées before the Idoll of Vitzilopuchtli, and touched the earth with one finger and then kissed the same. Then came the high priest cloathed in his pontificall vestmentes, with many others in his company, who did weare surplifces: and without speaking any worde, they painted or couloured the Kings person, with ynke made for the purpose, as blacke as any cole. After this Ceremonye done, they blessed the annointed King, and sprinckled him foure times with a certaine holly water, that was made at the time of consecration of the God, made of dowe or paste, with a sprinckle made of boughes of Cane leaues, Ceder, and willow leaues. Then they put vpon his head, a cloth painted with the bones and skulles of dead men, and next they clothed him with a black garment, and vpon that another blew, and both were painted with ye figures of dead mens skulles & bones. Then they put about his neck certaine laces, whereat did hang the armes of ye Crowne. And behind his backe they did hang certaine little bottels ful of powders, by vertue whereof he was deliuered from pestilence and diseases, according to their opinion: yea & therby witches, nor witchcrafts could not hurt him, nor yet euill mēnne deceyue him. In fine, with

The ointment.

the vvest India.

with those relickes he was sure from all perill and daunger. Upon his left arme they bound a little bagge of incense, and then brought vnto him a chaffing dish of timbers made of the barke of an Oke tree. Then the king arose, and with his owne hande threw of the same incense into the chaffing dish, and with great reuerence brought the same to the God Vitzilopucheli, and after he had smoked him therewith, he satte him downe, then came the high Priest and toke his oath to maintaine the religion of the Goddes, to kepe also all the lawes and customes of his predecessours, to maintaine iustice, and not to agrauiate any of his vassals or subiects, and that he should be valiant in the warres, that he should cause the Sunne to giue his light, the clowdes to yelde raine, the riuers to runne, and the earth to bring forth all kinde of graine, fruites, and other nedefull hearbs and trees. These and many other impossible things the newe king did sweare to performe: and then he gaue thankes to the high priest, and commended himselfe to the Goddes, and to the lokers on, and they who brought him vp in the same order, carieth him downe againe. Then all the people cried, the Goddes preserue the new king, and that he may raigne many yeares in health with al his people. But then some began to dance, other to play on their instruments, shewing outwardly their inward ioyes of heart. And before the king came to the fote of the steppes, all the noble men came to yelde their obedience, and in token of louing and faithfull subiectes, they presented vnto him feathers, strings of snaile shelles, Collers, and other Iewelles of golde and siluer, also mantels painted with death, & bare him company vnto a great hall within the compasse of the temple, and there left him. The king sitteth downe vnder his cloth of estate, called Tlacatecco, and in four daies departeth not out of the circuite of the temple, the which

The Conquest of

he spendes in prayers, sacrifice and penaunce, he eates then but once a day, and euery day he bathes himselfe, and againe in the night in a greate ponde of water, and then lettes himselfe bloud in his eares, and senseth there with the god of Water, called Tlaloc: he likewise senseth the other gods, vnto whome he offereth bread, flowers, Papers, and little Canes, tied in the bloud of his owne tongue, nose, handes, and other partes of his body. After the foure dayes expired, then come all the Noble men to beare him company to his pallaice, with greate triumph and pleasure of all the Citie, but after his consecration fewe or none dare looke him in the face.

And now with the declaring of the actes and Ceremonies that the Mexican kings are crowned, I shall not neede to rehearse of other kings, for generally they all do vse the same order, sauing that other Princes goe not vp to the toppe of the Temple, but abide at the foote of the steppes to be crowned, and after their Coronation they come to Mexico for their confirmation, and then at their returne to their countrey, they made many drunke feasts and banquets.

The opinion of the Mexicans concerning the Soule.

He Mexicans did beleue that the Soule was immortal, and that they receiued either ioy or paine according to their desertes & liuing in this world, vnto which opinion al their religion did attaine, and chiefly appeare at their burials. They helde for an assured faith, that there were nine places appointed for soules, & the chiefest place of glory to be neere vnto the Sunne, where the soules of those which were

god

the vvest India.   383

good men slaine in the warres, and those which were sacrificed were placed, so that all other sortes of euill persons their soules abode on ye earth, and were deuided after this sorte, children that were dead borne went to one place, those which died of age or other disease went to another, those which died of sudden death to another, those which died of woundes or contagious diseases went to an other place, those which were drowned went to another, those which were put to death for offence by order of Justice, as for robbery and adultery to another: Those which slewe their fathers, mothers, wiues or children, to another place by themselues, also those who slew their maisters or any religious person went to another place. The common sorte of people were buried, but Lordes and rich men had their bodies burned & their ashes buried. In their shrowts they had a great difference, for many deade bodies were buried better apparrelled then when they were on liue. Women were shrowed after another sort. And he that suffered death for adultery, was shrewded like vnto the God of lechery, called Tlazoulteutl, he that was drowned like vnto the God of water named Tlacoc, and he that died with drunkennesse was shrewded like vnto the God of wine called Ometochtli. But the souldier had an honorable shrewde like vnto the attyre of Vitzilopuchtli, and the like order in all other sortes of deathes.

The buriall of Kings in Mexico.

When any King of Mexico happened to fall sicke, they vsed forthwith to put a visor vppon the face of Tezcatlipuca, or Vitzilopuchtli, or some other Idoll, whiche visor was not taken awaye, vntill

The Conquest of

vntill they sawe whether the king did amend, or else die: But if he chaunced to die, then word was sent throughout all his dominions to bewaile his death, and also other postes were sent to call the noble men that were his nighest kinsmen, and to warne them within foure dayes to come vnto his buriall.

The dead bodie was laid vpon a faire matte, and was watched foure nights, with great lamentation and mourning: then the bodie was washed, and a locke of haire cut from the crowne of his head, which was preserued as a great relicke, saying that therein remained the remembrance of his soule. This done, a fine Emerald was put in his mouth, and his bodie shrowded in seuenteene riche mantles, of colours, both rich and costly wrought. Upon the vpper mantle was sette the deuise or armes of Vitzilopuchtli or Tezcalipuca, or some other Idoll, in whome the King had great confidence in his life time, and in his temple should the body be buried. Upon his face they put a visor, paynted with foule and Diuellish iestures, besette with many Iewelles, precious stones, and pearles. Then they killed his slaue, whose office was to light the Lampes, and make fire vnto the Goddes of his Pallaice. These things done, they carried the dead bodie vnto the Temple: some followed him with dolefull tune, others sung the death of the King by note, for so was the custome.

The Noble men and Gentlemen of his houshold carried Targets, Arrowes, Mases, and Ensignes to throwe into the fire where the body should be buried in the Temple. The high Priest and all the Clergie receiued him at the Temple gate, with a sorrowfull song, and after hee had saide certaine words, the bodie was throwne into a great fire made for the purpose, with all the Iewels that hee had about him, and all the other things which was

brought

the weſt India.

brought to honour the buriall: alſo a dogge newly ſtrangled with an Arrowe, which was to guide him his way. In the meane while that the king and dogge were burning, the Prieſts ſacrificed two hundred perſons, howbeit in this Ceremonie there was no ordinary taxe, for ſometimes they ſacrificed many moe: they were opened with a raſour of flinte in the breaſtes, and their hearts taken out and throwne into the fire where the kings bodie was. Theſe miſerable perſons being ſacrificed, and their bodies throwne into a hole, they beleeued aſſuredly that thoſe ſhoulde ſerue for his ſlaues in another worlde: ſome of them were Dwarffes, monſtrous and deformed perſons, with ſome women. They placed about the dead bodie of the king before his buriall, Roſes, Floures, and ſundry diſhes of meate and drinke, and no creature durſt touch the ſame, but onely the Prieſts, for it ſeemed to be an offering.

The next day following, all the aſhes were gathered togither, and the teeth with the Emerald that was in his mouth, the which things were put into a cheſt, poynted on the inſide with horrible figures of diuels, and the locke of haire which was cut from his crowne, and another locke of haire which was preſerued from the time of his birth. Then the cheſt was lockt, an an image of wood made and cloathed like vnto the kings perſon, which was ſet on the toppe of the cheſt. The obſequies endured foure dayes, in the which the wiues and daughters of the king offered great offerings at the place where his bodie was buried, and before the cheſt and his image.

On the fourth day after the buriall, fifteene ſlaues were ſacrificed for his ſoule, and on the twentith day, other fiue perſons were alſo ſacrificed, likewiſe on the ſixtie three, and foureſcore, which was lyke vnto the yeares minde.

Ddd   The

The order of buriall of the Kings of Michuacan.

The kingdome of Michuacan is almoste as great as the Empire of Mexico, and when any king of that countrey happened to be visited with sicknesse, and brought to such extremitie, ý hope of life were past, according to the opinion of Phisitions, thē would he name and appoint which of his Sonnes shoulde inherite the estate, and being knowen, the new king or heire, incontinent sent for all the gouernours, Captaines, and valiant souldiours, who had any office or charge to come vnto the buriall of his Father, and he that came not, from thenceforth was helde for a Traytour and so punished. When the death of the olde King was certaine, then came al degrées of Estates and brought presents to the newe king, for the approbation of his kingdome, but if the King were not throughly dead, but at the point of death, then the gates were shut in, and none permitted to enter, and when his life was departed, then beganne a generall crie and mourning, and they were permitted to come where their dead king lay, and to touche him with their handes: this being done, the carkasse was washed with swéete waters, and then a fine shirte put vpon him, and a paire of shoes made of a Déere skinne put on his féete, and aboute his ancles were tied certaine belles of golde, about his wristes of his handes were put Manyllios of Turkies, and other bracelets of golde, likewise aboute his necke they hung other collers of precious stones and golde, and rings in his eares, with a greate Turkise in his neather lippe. Then his body was laide vpon a large beare, whereon was placed a good beede vnder him: on his one side lay a bowe with a quyuer of arrowes, and on his

the weſt India.

his other ſide lay an image made of fine mantels of his owne ſtature or highneſſe, with a greate tuffe of fine feathers, ſhoes vpon his féete, with bracelets, and a coller of gold. While his worke was a doing; others were buſied in waſhing the men and women whiche ſhoulde be ſlaine for to accompany him into hell: theſe wretched folke that ſhould be ſlaine were banqueted & filled with drinke, becauſe they ſhoulde receiue their death with leſſe paine. The newe king did appoint thoſe who ſhoulde die for to ſerue the king his father, but yet many of them had rather haue bene without his ſeruice, notwithſtanding ſome ſimple ſoules eſtéemed that odious death for a thing of immortall glory. Firſt, ſeuen Gentlewomen of noble parentage were appointed to die, the one to haue the office of kéeper of his iewels which he was wont to weare, another for the office of cup-bearer, another to giue him water with a baſon and ewer, another to giue him alwaies the vrinall, another to be his Coke, and another to ſerue for laundreſſe. They ſlewe alſo many woman ſlaues, and frée maydens, for to attend vpon the Gentle women, and moreouer, one of euery occupation within the citie. When all theſe that were appointed to die were waſhed & theyr bellies full with meate & drinke, then they painted their faces yellow, and put garlandes of ſwéete flowers vpon each of their heads. Then they went in order of proceſſion before the beare wheron the dead king was carried, ſome wente playing on inſtrumentes made of ſnaile ſhelles, others played vpon bones and ſhelles of ſeaturtils, others went whiſtling, and the moſt part wéeping: the ſonnes of the dead king & other noble men carried vpō their ſhoulders the beare where ỹ corſe lay, & procéeded with an eaſie pace towarde the Temple of the God Cúricaueri: his kinſmen went round about ỹ beare, ſinging a ſorrowfull ſong. The officers and houſhold ſeruants of the Court w other

Magistrates and rulers of iustice bare the Standarts and diuers other armes.

About midnight they departed in the order aforesaide, out of the kings pallace, with great light of fire brandes, and with a heauie noyse of trumpets and drummes. The Citizens which dwelt where the coarse passed, attended to make cleane the streete. And when they were come to the temple, they went foure times rounde about a great fire made of the wood of Pine trée, which was prepared to burn the dead bodie: then the beare was laide vppon the fire, and in the meane while that the bodie was burning, they mawled with a clubbe those which had the garlandes, and afterward buried them by foure and foure, as they were apparelled behinde the temple.

The next day in the morning, the ashes, bones and Iewels, was gathered & laide vpon a rich mantle, the which was carried to the temple gate, where the priests attended to blesse those diuellish relickes, wherof they make a dowe or paste, and thereof an image which was apparelled lyke a man, with a visor on his face, and all other sorts of Iewels that the dead king was wont to weare, so that it séemed a gallant idoll. At the foote of the temple staires, they opened a graue ready made, which was square, large, and two fadom déep, it was also hanged with new mats round about, and a faire bed therin, in the which a religious man placed the idoll made of ashes, with his eyes towarde the East part, and hung round about the walles, Targets of gold and siluer, with bow and arrowes, and many gallant tuffes of feathers, with earthen vessels, as pottes, dishes, and platters, so that the graue was filled vp with housholde stuffe, chests couered with leather, apparell, iewels, meate, drinke, and armor. This done, the graue was shut vp, and made sure with beames, boords, and flored with earth on the toppe.

All

the vveſt India. 389

All thoſe Gentlemen which had ſerued or touched any thing in the buriall, waſhed themſelues, and went to dinner in the Court or yard of the Kings houſe without any table, and hauing dined, they wiped their hands vpon certaine lockes of Cotten wooll, hanging downe their heads, and not ſpeaking any worde, except it were to aſke for drinke. This Ceremonie endured fiue dayes, and in all that time no fire was permitted to be kindled in the City, except in the kings houſe and temples, nor yet any corne was ground, or market kept, nor none durſt go out of their houſes, ſhewing all the ſorow that might be poſsible for the death of their king.

The order of Matrimony among the Indians.

IN Tlaxcallan and many other cities, was vſed a principall ceremonie and token of mariage, that ẏ Bridegrome and his Bride, agaynſt the day of mariage, had their heades polled, which was to ſignifie, that from that day forwarde, all childiſh orders ſhoulde be laide aſide, and from that time newe haire might grow, to declare another kinde of life. The chife knot of marriage vſed in *Michuacan*, was, that the Bride doe looke directly vpon her ſpouſe, for otherwiſe the matrimonie was not perfite, nor auailable.

In Mixteoapan which is a great prouince, they vſe to carrie the Bridegrome to be married vpon their backes, which is to be vnderſtoode, that he goeth againſt his will, but yet they take handes, in token that the one ſhall helpe the other, and then they knit both their mantels togither with a great knot, ſignifying that they ought continually, while life laſteth, to dwell togither.

Ddd 3 The

The Conquest of

The Indians called Macatecas, consume not their Matrimonie in twentie dayes after their mariage, but abide in fasting and prayer all that while, sacrificing their bodies, and annointing the mouthes of the Idols with their owne proper bloud.

In Panuco the husbandes buy their wiues for a bow, two arrowes, and a nette, and afterward the father in lawe speaketh not one worde to his sonne in lawe for the space of a whole yeare. And when the husband happeneth to haue any childe, he lieth not any more with his wife in two yeares after, for feare least she might be with childe againe before the former childe were out of daunger, although some doe sucke vntill twelue yeares of age, and for this consideration they haue many wiues. Likewise there is an order among them, that no woman may touch or dresse any thing being with their menstruall ordinarie.

Diuorcement was not permitted without a iust cause and authoritie of Iustice, among those who were openly married, but the other sort might be as easily forsaken as taken.

In Mechuacan was not permitted any diuorcement, except the partie made a solemne oath, that they loked not the one on the other stedfastly and directly at the time of their marriage. But in Mexico they must proue how the wife is barren, foule, and of a naughtie condition: but if they put away their wiues without order and commaundement of the Iudge, then the haire of the offenders head is burned in the market place, as a shame or punishment of a man without reason or wit.

The paine of adulterie was death, as well for the man as the woman: but if the adulterer were a Gentleman, his head was decked with feathers after that he was hanged, and his bodie burned, and for this offence was no pardon,

the vveſt India.

pardon, eyther for man or woman, but for the auoiding of adulterie, they doe permit other common women, but no ordinarie ſtewes.

Of the Iudges and order of Iuſtice.

IN Mexico were twelue Iudges, who were all noble men, graue, and well learned in the Mexican lawes. Theſe men liued onely by the rents that properly appertaine to the maintenaunce of Iuſtice, and in anie cauſe iudged by them, it was lawfull for the parties to appeale vnto other ſwelue Iudges, who were of the princes bloud, and alwayes abode in the Court, and were maintained at the Kings owne coſt and charges. The inferiour Iudges came ordinarily once euery moneth to conſult with the higher. And in euery fourescore dayes came the Iudges of euery Prouince within the Mexican Empire, to conſult with the Iudges of *Mexico*, but all doubtfull cauſes were reſerued to the King, onely to paſſe by his order and determination. The Painters ſerued for notaries, to paint all the caſes which were to be reſolued, but no ſute paſſed aboue fourescore dayes without finall end and determination. There were in that citie twelue Sergeants, whoſe office was to arreſt, and to call parties before the Iudges. Their garments were painted mantels, wherby they were knowne a farre off. The priſons were vnder ground, moyſt and darke, the cauſe whereof, was to put the people in feare to offend. If any witneſſe were called to take an oath, the order was, that he ſhoulde touch the ground with one of his fingers, and then to touch his tongue with the ſame, which ſignified that hee had ſworne and promiſed to ſpeake the troth with his tong, taking witnes therof, of ye earth which did maintain him. But ſome do interprete the oath, yt if the partie ſware

not

The Conquest of

not true, that then he might come to such extremitie, as to eate earth. Sometime they name and call vpon the God of the crime, whose cause the matter touched.

The Iudge that taketh bribes or gifts, is forthwith put out of his office, which was accounted a most vile and shamefull reproch. The Indians did affirme that Necaualpincintli did hang a Iudge in Tezcuco, for giuing an vniust sentence, he himselfe knowing the contrarie. The murther is executed without exception.

The woman with childe that wilfully casteth her creature, suffereth death for the same, because many women did voluntarily vse that fact, knowing their children could not inherite. The punishment of adulterie was death.

The Theefe for the first offence, was made a slaue, and hanged for the second. The traitor to the king and common weale, was put to death with extreme torments.

The woman taken in mans apparell died for the same, and likewise the man taken in womans attire. Euery one that chalengeth another to fight, except in the wars, was condemned to die. In Tezcuco the sinne of Zodomie was punished with death, and that law was instituted by Necaualpincintli, and Necaualcoio, who were Iudges, which abhorred that filthy sin, and therefore they deserued great praise, for in other prouinces that abhominable sinne was not punished, although they haue in those places common stewes, as in Panuco.

The order of cruell Sacrifice vsed among the Indians.

AT the ende of euery twentie dayes, is celebrated a festiuall feast called Tonalli, which falleth continually ỹ last day of euery month, but the chiefest feast in ỹ yere, when most men are sacrificed & eaté, is at the

the vveſt India.

the ende of euery fiftie two yeares. But the Tlaxcaltecas and other common weales, do celebrate this feaſt euerye fourth yeare.

The laſt day of the firſt moneth is called Tlacaxipe-ualiztli, on the whiche day were ſlaine a hundred ſlaues, which were taken in the warres, and after the ſacrifice, their fleſh was eaten in this order. All the Citizens, gathered themſelues togither in the high Temple, and then the Miniſters or Prieſtes came and vſed certaine ceremonies, the which being ended, they toke thoſe which were to be ſacrifiſed, by one and one, and laid them vppon their backes vppon a large ſtone, and then the ſlaue being on liue, they opened him in the breaſt, with a knife made of flinte ſtone, and toke out his heart, which they threw immediately at the fote of the Aulter, as an offering, and anointed with the freſh bloude, the face of the God Vitzilopuchtli, or any other Idoll. This done, they pluckt off the ſkinnes of a certaine number of them, the which ſkinnes ſo many aunctient perſons put incontinent vppon their naked bodies, all freſhe & bloudy, as they were fleane from the deade carkaſſes. And being open in the backe part and ſhoulders, they vſed to lace them, in ſuch ſortz that they came fitte vppon the bodies of thoſe that ware them, and being in this order attired, they came to daunce among many others. In Mexico the king him ſelfe did put on one of theſe ſkinnes, being of a principall captiue, and daunced among the other diſguiſed perſons, to exalte and honor the feaſt, and an infinite number followed him to behold his terrible ieſſure, although ſome hold opinion that they followed him to contemplate his greate deuotion. After the ſacrifice ended, the owner of the ſlaues did carry their bodies home to their houſes, to make of their fleſhe a ſolemne feaſte to all their friendes, leauing their heades and hartes to the Priests, as their dutie and offering. And the skinnes were filled with cotten wooll, or strawe, to be hung in the temple, and kings pallaice, for a memorie.

The slaues when they went to their sacrifice, were apparelled in the habite or deuise of the Idol vnto whom eachof them did commend himselfe: and moreouer they decked them with feathers, garlandes and floures. Many of these sort of people, do goe to the slaughter with ioyfull countenaunce, dauncing, demaunding almes through the Citie for their sacrifice, all the which almes is due vnto the priestes. When the gréene corne was a foote aboue the ground, they vsed to go vnto a certain hil which was appointed for such deuotion, and there sacrifised two children, a boy, and a girle of thrée yéeres of age, to the honor of Tlaloc god of water, beséeching him therefore deuoutlye, to haue alwaies a care to prouide them water: these children were frée borne, and therfore theyr hartes were not taken out of their bodies, but after that their throts were cut, their bodies were wrapped in a new mantel, and then buried in a graue of stone.

The feaste of Tozoztli was, when the fieldes of Maiz were growen two foote high, then a certaine summe of merchandise was gathered among the dwellers in the Towne, wherewith were bought foure little slaues betwixt the age of fiue and seuen, and they were likewise sacrificed to the god Tlaloc, for continuall shoures of rayne. And those dead bodies were shut vp in a caue appointed for the same purpose. The beginning of this sacrifice of foure children was, at the time when in foure yeares space it rained not, in the which season the springs were dried vp, and all gréne things perished: wherefore they were forced to leaue the countrey, and went to inhabite at Nicaragua. In the moneth and feast of Hueitozotli, when the corne fieldes of Maiz waxed ripe, then euery

the vvest India.

uery one in generall gathered his handfull of Maiz, and brought it vnto the temple for an offering, with a certaine drinke called Atuli, whiche is made of the same Maiz. They brought also the sweete gum Copalli to sense the gods which do cause the corne to growe: and also that night they ceased not dauncing without drunkennesse. At the beginning of summer they celebrate an other feast called Tlaxuchimcaco, with all kinde of Roses and sweete floures that might be gotten, and thereof they vsed to make garlandes to set vpon the Idols heades, and so spente all that day in dauncing. And to celebrate the feast called Tecuilhuitli, al the gentlemen, and principall persons of ech prouince, do come vnto the Citie, on the euening of the feast, and then they apparell a woman with the atire of the Gods of salt, who daunced among a great company of her neighboures. But on the nexte day she was sacrificed with all the Ceremonies and solemnitie accustomed, and all that day was spent in great deuotion, burning of incense in the fire pannes of the temple.

The merchants who had a temple by themselues dedicated to the god of gaines, made their feast vppon the day called Miccailhuitl, wherein they slewe many slaues in sacrifice, which they had bought, and banqueted that feast with mans flesh, dauncing all the day. The feast of Vchpaniztli they sacrificed a woman, and afterwarde her bodye was flaine, and her skinne put vppon an Indians backe, who daunced two dayes a row with al the townsmen, which were apparelled in their best attire to celebrate ye feaste. The day of Hatamutzeli the feast is kept in Mexico, where they enter into ye lake wt a greate nüber of Canoas, & there they drown a boy & a girle in a little boat, which they cause to be sunke, in suche sorte, that neuer after that boat appeareth again: & they hold opinion that

Eee 2   those

The Conquest of

those children were in company with the Goddes of the lake. So that, that daye was spente in feasting in the temples, and annointing the Idols cheekes, with gum called Vli. There were some Images that had their faces two inches thicke with that gum.

The order of certaine religious women.

On the backe side of euerye greate Temple, in euerye Cittie was made a greate Hall or lodging, standing alone, where as many women did eate, drincke, lodge, and leade their liues. And although such houses had no orders, they abode there sure inough. These woman which lay in the houses of the Gods, were of sundry intentions. But none of them came to abide there al their life time, although among them were some olde women. Some entered into those religious houses being sicke and diseased, hoping there to recouer theyr health: others came thither through pure neede, and necessitie, to be there relieued: other some came thither to be good and vertuous: and some entered into the religion, hoping that the Goddes woulde giue vnto them riches, and long life. But generallye their comming thither was, to haue good husbandes, and manye children: eche one of them vowed the time that shee would or ment to abide in that order, and after that time expired they married.

The first thing that they did comming into the religion, was to polle their heads, to be knowen from others.

Their

the vvest India.

Their offices were to spinne cotten wooll and feathers, and to weaue cloth, for to apparell the Goddes and themselues, to sweep the parte and lodgings in the temple (for the stayres and high chappels, the ministers themselues did make cleane) they vsed also to let them blood in certaine partes of the body, to offer to the Diuellish Idols. On euery festiual day they went on procession with the priestes, but it was not lawfull for them to presume to go vppe the staires of the temple, nor yet to sing. They liued on almes, for their kinsfolke being rich, did maintaine them with almes as a charitable seruice done vnto the Goddes: their foode was boyled flesh, and hote bread, to the intent that they should offer thereof to the Goddes, that they might tast of the smoke of that victual: they vsed to eate in communitie, and lay altogither in one dormitorye, as a flocke of sheepe: they lay alwaies in theyr clothes, for honestie sake, and also to be the sooner ready in the morning to serue the Gods, & to go to their worke. And yet I know not why they should put off their clothes, for they went almost naked. On the holy dayes they vsed to daunce before the Gods, and she that either talked or laughed with any religious or secular person, was reprehended for the same. And if any of them committed whoredome, then both the man and the womā were slain, yea they beléeued that all suche offenders fleshe woulde rotte and consume away, and especially those which had lost their Virginitie in the time of their religion. So that with feare of punishmente and infamie, they were good women all the while that they aboade there.

How

How the Diuell appeared to the Indians.

He Diuell did many times talke with the Priestes and with other rulers and perticular persons, but not with all sorts of men. And vnto him to whome the Diuel had appeared, was offered and presented great gifts. The wicked spirit appeared vnto them in a thousand shapes, and fashions, and finally hee was conuersant and familiar among them verie often. And the fooles thought it a great woonder, that Gods would be so familiar with mortall men. Yea they not knowing that they were Diuels, and hearing of them many thinges before they had happened, gaue great credite and beleefe to their illusions and deceits. And because hee commaunded them, they sacrificed such an infinite number of creatures. Likewise, hee vnto whom hee had appeared, carried about him painted, the likenesse wherein he shewed himselfe the first time. And they painted his image vppon their dores, benches, and euerie corner of the house. And as he appeared in sundrie figures and shapes, euen so they painted him, of infinite fashions, yea and some foule, grieslie and fearefull to beholde, but yet vnto them, it seemed a thing delectable. So this ignoraunt people giuing credite to the condemned spirite, were growne euen to the highest hill of crueltie, vnder the color of denout and religious persons, yea they had such a custome, that before they would eate or drinke, they would take a little quantitie, and offer it vnto the Sunne and to the earth. And if they gather corne, fruite, or roses, they would take a leafe before they would smell it, and offer the same, and he that did not obserue these and such other ceremonies, was iudged one that had

not

the vvest India.

not God in his heart, yea, and (as they say) a man out of Gods fauour.

The Viceroyes of Mexico.

He greatnesse of the newe Spaine, the Maiestie of Mexico, and the qualitie of the conquerours, required a man of notable bloud to gouerne, whereupon the Emperour sent thither Don Antonio de Mendosa, brother vnto the Marques de Moniar, for Viceroy, at whose arriuall there returned from thence Sebastian Camires, who had gouerned that countrey with great discretion, and worthy commendation. In recompence whereof the Emperour made him President of the Chancerie of Vallodolid, and Bishop of Culuca. Don Antonio de Mendosa, was appointed viceroy in the yeare. 1534. who carried with him many artificers verie expert in their sciences, likewise through his intercession, a money house was erected in Mexico: he also caused silke to be made and wrought in that countrey, and planted many Mulberie trees for the same, Although the Indians little care for such things through their slouthfulnes and great liberty. This viceroy Don Antonio, called all the Bishops, Cleargie, and learned men togither, to consult vpon ecclesiasticall matters, which tended to the doctrine of the Indians. At that instant was decreed, that the Indians shoulde bee instructed onely in the Latin tong, which they learned very wel, and also the Spanish tong. They learned the Musicke with good will, especially the flaute: their voyces are not good for the pricke song. At that season was also decreed, that no Indian should take order of Priesthood.

The

The viceroy Don Antonio, built certaine townes with Romaine pillers, in honor of the Emperour, and caused his name to be grauen in Marble. He also began the key or wharfe in the porte of Medellin, a costly and necessarie worke: he also reduced the Chichimecas to ciuell liuing: he spente much mony in the entraunce of Sibola, without any profit, and also thereby remained an enimie to Cortes. He likewise discouered much land on the south coast nere Xalixco: he sent also shippes to Molluca, for spices, which were lost: he behaued himselfe very prudently, in the rebellion time of the Indians of Piru.

The Emperour commaunded him afterwarde to goe vnto the Piru for viceroy, considering the Licenciat Gasca, who gouerned there, was returned into Spaine, and likewise hauing vnderstood his good gouernement in the new Spaine, although some complaintes were made of him. It grieued Don Antonio de Mendosa, to depart from the newe Spaine, where he found himselfe well beloued among the Indians, who had cured him of sundry diseases with bathes of Hearbes, where before he was starke lame, and also possessed of lands, Cattle, and other riche things, which he was loth to leaue. Likewise he desired not to haue to deale with other newe men, whose conditions he knew not, although he knewe that the Piruleros were stubborne and vnruly fellowes. But of necessitie he was compelled to take that iourney by lande from Mexico to Panama, which standeth fiue hundred leagues distant, in the yeare a 1551. And that yere came Don Luys de Valasco for viceroy to Mexico, who was a Gentleman wise and discreet in his gouernement. The office of viceroy in the newe Spaine, is a charge of great honor and profit.

The

the west India.

The conuersion of the Indians.

OH how greately are those Indians bound to praise God, who being seruants of Satan, and lost sheepe, yet it pleased the goodnesse of the almightie to haue compassion of them, who hath giuen them light to come of darkenesse, and brought them to the knowledge of their cruell and abhominable life, and hath now giuen vnto them the holy Ghost in baptisme: oh most happie Cortez, thy paines was well imploied, oh valiant Conquerors, your names shall liue for euer. I am now bolde to say, that all that lande which is conquered in the newe Spaine, the people therof are generally conuerted vnto the faith of Jesus Christe: oh what a great felicitie is it vnto those blessed kings who were the beginners thereof.

Some doe saye, that in the newe Spaine onely are conuerted Christians fiue Millions. Others hold opinion of eight Millions. And other some doe assuredly affirme, that aboue ten Millions are Christened. But in conclusion, I am assured, that within the limittes of foure hundred leagues, there are none vnchristened.

The conuersion began with the Conquest, but with the diligence in prosecuting the warres, little good was done, vntill the yeare 1524. and then the matter went forward effectually, by reason that certaine learned menne wente thither for the same purpose.

At the beginning it was a troublesome thing to teach them, for wante of vnderstanding the one of the other, wherefore they procured to teache the children of Gentlemen which were most aptest, the Spanishe tong,

Fff and

The Conqueſt of

and they likewiſe learned the Mexican ſpæche, in the which language they daily preached. It was at the firſt a painfull thing to make them leaue thoſe Idols in whome they had euer beléeued, yea and the diuell gaue them cruell warres in ſpirite, and many times, in appearing in diuers formes vnto them, threatening, that if they did call vpon the name of Ieſus Chriſt, it ſhould not raine, and that all their delight and pleaſure ſhould bee taken from them, prouoking them ſtill to rebellion againſt the Chriſtians, but his wicked counſell would not preuaile.

Through great puniſhment they haue left off the horrible ſinne of Sodomie, although it was a great griefe to put away their number of wiues.

There are now in the new Spaine eight Biſhoprickes, whereof one is an Archbiſhoprickе.

The death of Hernando Cortes.

Here was a great contention betwéene Hernando Cortes, and Don Antonio de Mendoſa, the Wizeroy, as concerning the prouince of Sibola, for each of them pretended a title vnto the ſame through the Emperors gift, the one by meanes of his office of Wizeroy, and the other by his office of Captaine Generall, vppon the which matter they grewe into ſuch hatred, that perfect friendſhippe coulde neuer after take place betwéene them, although at the beginning they were familiar and louing friendes : but mallice grew to ſuche extremitie, that each of them wrote vndecently againſt other, to the Emperour their maiſter, the which their doings, blemiſhed both their credits.

Cortes

the west India.

Cortes went to lawe with the Licenciat Villa Lobos, the kings Atturrney, about certaine of his vassalls, and also the Vizeroy assisted againste him as muche as hée might. Upon consideration whereof, he was enforced to come into Spaine in Anno. 1540. and brought Don Martin his sonne and heire, being a childe of eight yeares of age, and his sonne Don Luys, to serue the prince: he came very rich, but not so rich as the first time. He entred into great friendship with the Cardinall Loaisa, and the Secretarie Cobos, but it preuailed not, for the Emperor was gone into Flaunders about matters of Gant.

In the yeare 1541. the Emperour personally went to the siege of Argel, with a mightie army, and Cortes with his two sonnes went also thither to serue him, with a good company of men and horses, but it pleased God to raise vp such a tempest, wherewith the most part of the fléete perished. Cortes then being in the Galley of Don Henrike Enrikes, called the Esperanca, and fearing to lose his rich Emraldes and other Iewels, at the time that the Galley was driuen by violence of weather vppon the shore, he then bound about him the said fiue rich Emraldes, estéemed th a hundreth thousande Duckates, yet notwithstanding through the throng of people, and haste to escape out of oese and mire, the Iewels fell from him, who could neuer heare more of them, so that the present warres cost him more then any other, except the Emperours maiestie, although Andrea de Oria lost eleuen Galleys.

But the losse of treasure gréeued him not so much, as the excluding him out of the Councell of the warres, whereas other yong Gentlemen of lesse knowledge and abilitie were accepted, which was a cause of great murmuring among the hoste. And where in the Councell of warre it was determined to leaue the siege and to depart, it gréeued many, whereupon Cortes made an open offer,

Fff 2   that

that he alone with the Spanish nation would presume to take Argell, hauing but the one halfe of the Tudescos and Italians, if it woulde please the Emperour to graunt vnto him the enterprise. The Souldiers on the land did highly commende his courage, but the Seamen woulde giue no care vnto him, so that it is thought that the offer came not to the Emperoures knowledge. Cortes went vp and downe in the Courte a long season, being sore afflicted, in a certaine sute about his vassals, and also the processe and allegations of Nunio de Guzman, laide vnto his charge in his residence. The whole processe was seene in the counsell of Indias, but the iudgemente was neuer pronounced which was a greate hartes ease for Cortes. And then he departed from the Courte toward Siuill, with determinate will to passe vnto the newe Spaine, and to ende his life in Mexico, and also to receiue the Lady Marie, Cortes his daughter, who was come from India, and promised in mariage vnto Don Aluar Perez Osorio, with a hundred thousand Ducketes in dowry, and her apparel, but the marriage toke no effecte, through the faulte of Don Aluar and his father.

He then fell sicke of a flixe and indisgestion, which endured long, so that on his iourney towarde the Citie of Siuill, he departed this trensitorie life, in a little Village called Castilleia de La Cuesta, which standeth a mile from the citie of Siuill, on the second of December, Anno 1547. being three score and three yeares of age.

His body was deposited with the dukes of *Medina Sidonia*.

He left a sonne and three daughters begotten of the Lady Iane de Zuniga, his wife, his sonne was called Don Martin Cortes, who did inherit his fathers estate, and was married vnto the lady Ana de Arellano, his cousin, daughter to the Couutie, De Aguilar, by order of his father.

The

the vvest India.

The daughters vnto Cortes were named as followeth, the Ladie Donea Maria, Donea Catelina, and Donea Iuana who was the yongest. He had another sonne by an Indian woman, and he was called Don Martin Cortez. He had also another base sonne by a Spanish woman, who was named Don Luis Cortes, & three daughters by three seuerall Indian women.

Cortes built an Hospital in Mexico, and gaue order for a Colledge to be also erected there. He built also a Temple in Coioacan, where he willed in his Testament that bones should be buried at the charges of his Sonne and heyre. He situated foure thousand Duckets of rent, which yeeldeth yearely his houses in Mexico for the purpose aforesaid, of the which foure thousande Duckets, two thousand should be to maintaine the Students in the Colledge.

FINIS.

A Table expreſsing the
Chapters which are conteyned in this Hiſtorie.

The birth and linage of Hernando Cortez. Fol. 1
The age of Cortez when he paſſed into India. 2
The time that Cortez abode in Santo Domingo 5
Things that happened to Cortez in the land of Cuba. 6
The diſcouerie of new Spaine. 10
Inuentorie of treaſure that Grijalua brought 12
The determination of Cortez to prepare a fleete for diſ-
couerie. 16
The Nauie and men that Cortez carryed to the Con-
queſt. 20
Oration made my Cortez to his ſouldiers 24
The entrance of Cortez into the Iland of Acuſamil. 25
The Indians of Acuſamil gaue newes of bearded men. 29
A miraculous chaunce how Aguilar came to Cortez. 31
The Iland of Acuſamil 35
Religion of the people of Acuſamil. 40
Battell of Potoncan. 41
Battell of Cintla. 43
The Lord Tauaſco yeeldeth to the Chriſtians. 46
Queſtions demaunded by Cortez of the Cacike Ta-
uaſco. 48
Howe the Indians of Potonchan brake downe their I-
dols. 50
The good entertainment that Cortes had in Saint Iohn de
Vlhua. 51

The

The Table.

The talke of Cortez with Teudilli.	55
The prefent by Mutezuma vnto Cortez.	58
How Cortez knew of difcord in the Countrey.	61
How Cortez went to furuey the countrey with foure hundred men.	64
How Cortes rendred vp his office by policie.	67
How the fouldiours chofe Cortes for their Captaine generall.	69
The receiuing of Cortes into Zempoallan.	72
The talke of the Lord of Zempoallan with Cortes.	76
Things that happened vnto Cortez in Chiauitzlan.	80
The meffage fent by Cortez to Mutezuma.	83
Rebellron done by the induftrie of Cortez.	85
The foundation of the rich towne of Vera Crux.	88
The taking of Tizapanfinca.	90
The prefent that Cortez fent to the Emperor Charles for his fifth part.	92
Letters ingenerall from the Magiftrates of Vera Crux to the Emperour.	97
An vprore among the Souldiers againft Cortez, & the correction for the fame.	100
Cortez caufed all his fhips to be funke, a worthie fact.	102
How the inhabitants of Zempoallan brake downe their Idols.	104
How Olintlec exalted the mightie power of Mutezu.	107
The firft encounter that Cortez had with the men of Tlaxcallon.	112
How their ioyned a hundred and fiftie thoufande men againft Cortez.	116
The threatnings of the Indians campe agaynft the Spaniardes.	120
How Cortes cut off the handes of fiftie efpies.	124
The Embaffage that Mutezuma fent vnto Cortes.	126
How Cortez wan the Citie of Zimpanzinco.	129

The

The Table.

The defire that fome of the Spaniardes had to leaue the warres. 132
The oration made by Cortes to his Souldiers. 133
Howe Xicotencatl came for Embaſſadour to Cortes his campe. 136
The receiuing of Cortes into Tlaxcallan. 136
Defcription of Tlaxcallan. 141
Anſwere of the Tlaxcaltecas touching the leauing of their Idols. 145
Difcorde betweene the Mexicans and the Tlaxcaltecas. 147
Solemne receyuing of the Spaniards into Chololla. 148
The confpiracie of the Cholollans agaynſt the Spaniards. 152
Puniſhment for confpiracie. 155
Sanctuarie among the Indians was Chololla. 158
The hill called Popocatepec. 160
The confultation of Mutezuma concerning the comming of Cortes into Mexico. 162
Things that happened to Cortes in his iourney towarde Mexico. 164
The folemne pompe wherewith Cortes was receiued into Mexico. 169
The oration of Mutezuma to the Spaniards. 172
The maieſtie and order wherewith Mutezuma was ferued at his table. 175
Foote plaiers that plaied before Mutezuma. 178
The tennis play in Mexico. 179
The number of wiues that Mutezuma had. 180
A houſe of foule which were onely preferued for the feathers. 183
A houſe of foule for hawking. 184
The armorie of Mutezuma. 186
The gadens of Mutezuma. 187

The

The Table.

The court and guard of Mutezuma.	188
The great subiection of the people to their king.	189
The situation of Mexico.	192
The market place of Mexico.	196
The great temple of Mexico.	201
The Idols of Mexico.	204
The charnell house of Mexico.	206
How Cortez tooke Mutezuma prisoner.	207
The recreation of hunting which Mutezuma vsed.	212
How Cortes began to pluck down the Idols of Mexico.	214
The exhortation made by Cortes to Mutezuma and the citizens for the abolishing of Idols.	215
The burning of the Lord Qualpopoca & other Gent.	219
The cause of the burning of Qualpopoca.	220
How Cortes put a pair of Giues on Mutezuma his legs.	221
How Cortes sent to seeke for the mines of golde in diuerse places.	223
The imprisonment of Cacama king of Tezcuco.	227
The sorrowfull oration that Mutezuma made vnto his noble men, to yeeld them to the Emperour.	230
The gold and Iewels that Mutezuma gaue vnto Cortes for his first tribute.	233
How Mutezuma required Cortes to depart from Mex.	235
The feare that our men stand in to be sacrificed.	239
How Iames Velasques sent Pamfilo de Naruaes agaynst Cortez.	241
The substance of a letter that Cortes wrote to Naruaes.	244
The talke of Naruaes to the Indians, and his aunswere to Cortes.	246
The talke that Cortes had with his owne Souldiers.	249
The requests of Cortes to Mutezuma.	251
The imprisonment of Pamfilo de Naruaes.	252
The rebellion of Mexico.	256
The cause of the rebellion.	259

Ggg   The

The Table.

The threatnings of the Mexicãs againſt the Spaniards. 261
Great danger that our men were put in by the ſtrãgers. 263
The death of Mutezuma. 266
The combate betwene the Spaniards and the Indians. 268
How the Mexicans refuſed the offer of peace & amity. 271
How Cortez fled from *Mexico*. 274
Battell of Otumpan. 280
The entertainment of the Spaniardes at their returne to Tlaxcallan. 283
Proteſtation and requeſt of the ſouldiers to Cortes. 286
An Oration made by Cortez in anſwer to his ſouldiers demaund. 289
Warres of Teptacac. 292
The great authority that Cortes had amõg the Indians. 294
The vergantines that Cortes cauſed to be built, & the Spaniards which he had to beſiege Mexico. 296
Exhortation of Cortez to his ſouldiers. 298
Exhortation made to the Indians of Tlaxcallan. 301
How Cortez tooke Tezcuco. 302
Spaniards which were ſacrificed in Tezcuco. 307
Howe the Vergartines were brought from Tlaxcallan to Tezcuco. 310
Of the docke or trench which was made to launch the vergantines. 311
Order of the hoſt and army to beſiege Mexico. 314
Battell and victorie of the Vergantines againſt the Canoas. 316
How Cortes beſieged Mexico. 320
The firſt skirmiſh within the citie of Mexico. 322
Great hurt and damage in the houſe of *Mexico* by fire. 327
Things that happened to Pedro de Aluarado through his bold attempt. 329
Triumph and ſacrifice which the *Mexicans* made for victorie. 331

Deter-

The Table.

Determination of Cortes to deſtroy *Mexico*.	336
Hunger and infirmitie which the *Mexicans* ſuffered with great courage.	340
Impriſonment of Quahutimoc.	343
The taking of *Mexico*.	347
Maruellous ſignes & tokẽs of the deſtruction of *Mex*.	349
Building vp againe of the citie of *Mexico*.	351
Howe the Emperour ſent to take account of Cortez his gouernment.	354
The death of the Licenciat Luis Ponce.	358
How Cortez came into Spaine.	359
The honor which the Emperor ſhewed vnto Cortes with reward.	361
The Marriage of Cortez.	362
How the Chancerie was firſt placed in *Mexico*.	364
The returne of Cortes to Mexico.	367
The letters which the Indians vſed in Mexico.	369
The Mexican yeare.	371
The Indians beleeued that fiue ages were paſt, &c.	377
The nation of the Indians called Chichimecas.	378
The coronation of the kings of Mexico.	379
The opinion of the *Mexicans* concerning the ſoule.	382
The buriall of kings in Mexico.	383
The order of the buriall of the kings of *Michuacan*.	386
The order of matrimonie among the Indians.	389
Of the iudges and order of Iuſtice.	391
The order of cruel ſacrifice vſed among the Indians.	392
The order of certaine religious women.	396
How the diuel appeared to the indiãs in a ſtrãge form.	398
The Viceroys of *Mexico*.	399
The conuerſion of the Indians.	401
The death of Hernando Cortes.	402

FINIS.

www.ingramcontent.com/pod-product-compliance
Lightning Source LLC
Chambersburg PA
CBHW022108290426
44112CB00008B/596